ALFRED HUGENBERG

(Courtesy Bundesarchiv Koblenz.)

ALFRED HUGENBERG

The Radical Nationalist Campaign against the Weimar Republic

John A. Leopold

New Haven and London, Yale University Press

Originally published with assistance from Phi
Alpha Theta.

Designed by John O. C. McCrillis
and set in Baskerville type by
Computacomp (UK) Ltd., Fort William, Scotland.
Printed in the United States of America by
The Vail-Ballou Press, Inc., Binghamton, N.Y.

Published in Great Britain, Europe, Africa, and
Asia (except Japan) by Yale University Press,
Ltd., London. Distributed in Australia and New
Zealand by Book & Film Services, Artarmon,
N.S.W., Australia; and in Japan by Harper &
Row, Publishers, Tokyo Office.

Library of Congress Cataloging in Publication Data

Leopold, John A   1937-
    Alfred Hugenberg: the radical nationalist campaign
against the Weimar Republic.

    Includes bibliographical references and index.
    1. Hugenberg, Alfred, 1865-1951. 2. Statesmen–
Germany–Biography. 3. Deutschnationale Volkspartei–
History. 4. Germany–Politics and government–1918-1933.
DD231.H8L46   943.085'092'4 [B]   77-4026
ISBN 0-300-02068-6

To Maureen Welsh Leopold

Contents

Illustrations

Preface

Virtually every book dealing with Germany in the first third of this century mentions Alfred Hugenberg. As chairman of the board of directors at Krupp's, as director of a huge propaganda syndicate, and as chairman of the German National People's Party, he played a key role in the campaign against democracy in Germany. His elitist nationalism, rooted in the social Darwinism of the late nineteenth century, expedited the ultimate ascendancy of the Hitler party. Examining this process, I have concentrated my research on the latter stages of Hugenberg's career and have analyzed his earlier activities only as a context for understanding the genesis of his power and strategy.

In my view, the career of Hugenberg demonstrates the pluralistic bases of historic development. Nevertheless, I am sure that my treatment of certain phenomena lends support to some Marxist interpretations of these events. Since this is not a philosophic treatise nor a psychological analysis, I have attempted to analyze the past *wie es eigentlich gewesen*. Despite this attempt, I am sure that the study mirrors my personal prejudices, which include an ardent dislike of rabid nationalism and social Darwinism.

Fortunately the Hugenberg family, in granting me free access to the *Nachlass* at Rohbraken, imposed no conditions whatsoever on my use of these papers. I am deeply indebted to them for their kindness and openness. The same must be said of Dr. Friedrich Freiherr Hiller von Gaertringen, who permitted me full use of the extensive Westarp Papers. Neither family, I am sure, will fully agree with my interpretations. I trust, however, that the documention cited will support my thesis and will encourage scholarly debate.

In researching and writing this book, numerous people and institutions have assisted me in a variety of ways. I am particularly indebted to a host of librarians and archivists who are mentioned specifically in the bibliographical essay. Dr. Friedrich

Engel-Janosi, currently of the University of Vienna, inspired my earliest research in German history. Dr. John K. Zeender, my mentor from The Catholic University of America, has given me continued encouragement. Professor Henry A. Turner of Yale University has been a kind friend and tireless adviser. The late Dr. George W. F. Hallgarten carefully read the manuscript and offered many insightful comments. Many others including Professor Hans Mommsen of Bochum University, Dr. Fritz Klein of the German Academy of Science in East Berlin, Dr. Dirk Stegmann, Dr. Larry Jones, and Dr. Alfred Vagts have been most helpful. To all of these scholars, I am deeply indebted. In the end, however, I alone am responsible for any shortcomings in this study.

Research for this work would not have been possible without grants from the *Deutscher Akademischer Austauschdienst* and the National Endowment for the Humanities. The generosity of these agencies and the personal interest of their administrators, especially Dr. Martin Mruk and Dr. Franz Eschbach, made my research in Germany extremely pleasant as well as intellectually rewarding.

Phi Alpha Theta, the International History Honor Society, awarded this work its annual manuscript award in 1975. I am particularly grateful to Dr. Donald Hoffman, International Secretary-Treasurer of the society, and Dr. Lynn Turner, chairman of the manuscript awards committee, for their help and encouragement.

Abbreviations Used in the Text and Notes

AA	*Auswärtiges Amt*—Foreign Office Archives of the Federal Republic of Germany
ADI	*Arbeitsausschuss Deutschnationaler Industrieller*, Working Committee of German National Industrialists
ADV	*Alldeutscher Verband*, Pan-German League
AH	*Archiv Hugenberg*, Hugenberg Family Archives at Rohbraken
BA	*Bundesarchiv*, Archives of the Federal Republic of Germany in Bonn and Freiburg
BbV	*Bergbaulicher Verein (Verein für die bergbaulichen Interessen)*, (Employer's) Mining Association (Association for the Mining Interests)
CVDI	*Centralverband Deutscher Industrieller*, Central Association of German Industrialists
DHV	*Deutschnationaler Handlungsgehilfenverband*, German Nationalist White Collar Workers' Association
DII	*Deutsches Industrie-Institut*, German Industrial Institute in Cologne
DNF	*Deutschnationaler Front*, German National Front
DNVP	*Deutschnationale Volkspartei*, German National People's Party
DVP	*Deutsche Volkspartei*, German People's Party
DVV	*Deutscher Verlags-Verein*, German Press Association
DZA	*Deutsches Zentral-Archiv*, German Central Archives in Potsdam
GA	*Verhandlungsbericht* *Verhandlungsbericht über die Sitzung des Gesschäftsführenden-Ausschusses des Alldeutschen Verbandes*, Records of the Meeting of the Executive Committee of the Pan-German League

GHH, HA   *Gutehoffnungshütte*, *Historisches Archiv*, Historical
              Archives of the *Gutehoffnungshütte A.G.* in
              Oberhausen

GSA   *Geheimer Staatsarchiv*, Secret State Archives in
              Berlin-Dahlem

HSA   *Hauptstaats-Archiv*, Principal State Archives of
              Rheinland-Westphalia in Düsseldorf

ISH   Institute for Social History in Amsterdam

KPD   *Kommunistische Partei Deutschlands*, Communist Party
              of Germany

LA   *Landesarchiv*, State Archives (of Schleswig-Holstein)

NSDAP   *Nationalsozialistische Deutsche Arbeiterpartei,* National
              Socialist German Workers' Party, the Nazis

NSSA   *Niedersächsisches Staatsarchiv*, State Archives of
              Lower Saxony

RDI   *Reichsverband der Deutschen Industrie*, Reich Associa-
              tion of German Industry

SA   *Stadtarchiv*, City Archives (of Düsseldorf)

SPD   *Sozialdemokratische Partei Deutschlands*, Social
              Democratic Party of Germany

WA   *Werksarchiv*, Factory Archives, depending on the
              name following—either the Factory Archives of
              the *Farbenfabriken Bayer A.G.* in Leverkusen or
              the Factory Archives of the *August-Thyssen Hütte*
              A.G. in Duisburg-Hamborn.

WP   Westarp Papers in Gaertringen

ZV   *Zechenverband*, (Employers') Mining Association

Introduction

In the last decades of the imperial era, radical nationalists agitated for a more aggressive policy both domestically and internationally. This national opposition confronted the emperor with demands for rabid antisocialist, antidemocratic, and proimperialist policies. Alfred Hugenberg, the self-made man who had risen to prominence in this era, identified himself with this aggressive stance. As a student of political economy and a founder of the Pan-German League, he advocated autarky and territorial expansion for Germany. As a leader among Ruhr industrialists, he picked up the challenge of the retired chairman of the Central Association of German Industrialists, Henri Axel Bueck, and demanded an end to the "yellow, red, and black internationals" that, he charged, were undermining Germany.[1]

Opposed to any compromise which would tolerate either democracy or socialism, Hugenberg demanded the total elimination of these movements. Only a patriarchal approach that viewed the corporation and the state as extended families could prosper the nation. In industry, the entrepreneur as lord of his house had to have ultimate authority; he provided a living for his workers and could tolerate only those company unions that sponsored loyalty to the firm. In government, the kaiser had to be a strong and determined leader who would decree the best for his subjects and rule with an iron hand. Controlled by aggressive elitists, German society would encourage rugged individualism within the state but would not disturb established corporations. Men of talent and property would be favored, but new men could fight their way to the top and win acceptance. Hugenberg, who had observed these rules and had acquired wealth and influence, found it easy to condemn as subversive all those who disagreed.

Because this patriarchal policy hardly aroused mass support, Hugenberg and some nationalist industrialists preferred manipulation and exploitation as the means of securing their goal. A political economist, Hugenberg was clearly aware of the realities of agricultural, industrial, and international economics. Expounding on the importance of laissez-faire for domestic economic development, he had clearly argued that reactionary Junkers hindered progress in agriculture, that the traditional middle class frustrated modern technological and corporate advancement, and that capitalism could not be condemned as Jewish exploitation.[2] Nevertheless, after 1909 Hugenberg deliberately determined that the best way to win votes and influence the imperial regime was to cooperate with the very reactionaries and racists whose existence he had proclaimed an obstacle to national development. Apparently the challenges of democracy and socialism so alarmed Hugenberg that manipulation of the masses became more important than proper education of the electorate. Convinced that political and economic democracy would ruin Germany, he was prepared to use any means to frustrate its acceptance.

Just prior to World War I, this mentality produced the political "cartel of the producing classes" (Kartell der schaffenden Stände). The goal was to rally artisans, farmers, shopkeepers, civil servants, and other petit bourgeois nationalists behind reactionary industrialists, radical Junkers, and Pan-German ideologues in a united bloc. This simplistic division of the nation into an arbitrary dichotomy of producers and parasites, creative and destructive forces, nationalist and antinationalist elements, propagandized a dual alternative for Germany—prosperity and development with the cartel or poverty and destruction with socialism and democracy. Sammlung, the unification of all nationalist forces, was the political ideal of these bourgeois nationalists.[3] Deeply committed to this tactic, Hugenberg and his allies sought to exploit this concept of nationalist unity in order to gain control of the state. Convinced that the end justified the means, he patronized the radical masses with the hope of using them to control society. The national opposition which ultimately triumphed in 1933 was the tragic result of such tactics.

1 The Beginning of Hugenberg's Career

Born in 1865, the only son of a National Liberal civil servant in Hanover, Hugenberg matured in a Germany bathed in the sentiment of nationalism. The moderate hardships that his mother suffered after the early death of her husband apparently influenced young Hugenberg in his determination that he and his heirs would never endure economic deprivation. Intellectually talented, the young man chose to follow his father's steps as a specialist in law and political economy. Deliberately suppressing his flare for literary expression and channeling his entire energy into his administrative career, Hugenberg found little time for friends and leisure activity.[1]

Though he sought to remain a private individual pursuing his personal fortune, Hugenberg never lost sight of governmental impact on economic life. His dissertation, completed under the guidance of Professor G. F. Knapp at the University of Strasbourg in 1891, clearly demonstrated this relationship. In *Internal Colonization in Northwest Germany,* the young doctoral candidate analyzed in detail the role of the state in fostering economic growth. This volume depicted three themes which always undergird Hugenberg's political views. First, the state would have to assist the farmer and totally abandon a laissez-faire approach to agriculture; second, the farmer would have to act as an entrepreneur and form a capitalist bulwark against Marxism; and third, Germany would have to expand its empire. Economic prosperity, he argued, demanded imperialism. In a world where Russia and the Anglo-Saxon powers had expanded their domains, Germany could only save the "power and significance" of the German "race" by doing the same.[2]

As a civil servant in several small towns and as a member of the Prussian Settlement Commission in Posen from 1894 to 1899, Hugenberg sought to implement these three principles. Critical of the government for its "inadequate" policy in dealing with the Poles, he left the bureaucracy and established a complex of

1

cooperative associations which strengthened the position of Germans in Posen. When he returned to civil service in 1904, he became a special adviser on the economic development of the East.[3] His experience led to the publication of his second book, *Bank und Kreditwirtschaft des deutschen Mittelstandes.* The work was essentially a paean to the capitalist spirit, which Hugenberg viewed as the basis of German economic strength and development. His response to the problems of modern society required neither massive state intervention nor a return to an idealized past but bureaucratic assistance in fostering agrarian individualism and capital accumulation through the use of cooperatives. The state had to encourage competition within its borders and not protect antiquated forms of economic activity.[4] With this as the desideratum, Hugenberg advocated legislation which would confiscate all large, nonproductive estates in the East and resettle them with small farmers. Confronted with strong opposition from Junkers and others opposed to this proposal, state officials hesitated in their advocacy of this legislation.[5] Hugenberg scorned their "pedantic political conscience" and again left the civil service.[6] He opened a whole new phase of his career by leaving the agrarian East and accepting a position on the board of directors of the *Berg- und Metallbank* in Frankfurt am Main.[7]

His success with the Jewish banking firm of the Mertons proved to be merely a stepping-stone to a still more influential position. In the spring of 1909, Gustav Krupp von Bohlen und Halbach, who had been "in search for a man of really superior intelligence," made him chairman of the ten-man board of directors of the Krupp firm in Essen.[8] Hugenberg worked in close collaboration with the owner of the firm, and in addition to presiding over general administration, he directed his own department, dealing with finances and economic policy.[9] Under his aegis the firm was reorganized and expanded; dividends went from 8 percent in 1908 to 14 percent in 1913.[10]

Though everyone was impressed with his "extraordinary" intelligence and obvious ability, there is no indication that Hugenberg, during his ten-year stay at Krupp's, ever developed anything more than a formal relationship with his employer.[11] The patrician aloofness of the securely established Krupps contrasted sharply with the dogged determination to succeed which characterized Hugenberg.[12] Indeed, Hugenberg seemed typical of that class of general directors which Georg Bernhard described as "being driven by an inferiority complex" because they know they are "dependent" and in the final analysis are as dispensable as any other employee. Lack of security made such a director "continually harder and more uncompromising than the owner himself."[13] Possibly as a psychological compensation, Hugenberg in these years emphasized the "inflexibility," "stubbornness," and "self-righteousness" which would later characterize his political career.[14]

Undoubtedly this attitude influenced his approach to the workers at Krupp's. His persistent aversion to socialism and democracy found fertile ground for further development. Concerned with the development of workers' quarters, he planned to make the "Kruppianer" into petit bourgeois who would own their homes and would even become junior share holders in the firm.[15] Enlightened as these ideas were, they nevertheless brought Hugenberg into direct conflict with socialist and Catholic unions. Disdaining the group, the chairman of the board preferred to deal with the individual and thus became a patron of the "yellow unions"—those company unions opposed to strikes. Hugenberg depicted employer and employee not as antithetical classes, but as the common producers of shared wealth; he championed the idea of the *Werksgemeinschaft,* the concept of an industrial community guided by patriarchal entrepreneurs.[16] Most workers did not look at theories but at results, and working and living conditions did not change much during Hugenberg's tenure.[17]

The social Darwinistic philosophy so prevalent in industrial circles during this era readily justified discrepancies in sharing the fruits of production. At the celebration of Krupp's centenary in 1912, Hugenberg was awarded the Red Order of the Eagle (Third Class with Bow) by the kaiser himself. At the ceremonies, the chairman of the board delivered a "masterful" speech criticizing the attempt to use universal manhood suffrage as a means of imposing class rule on the Reich. He insisted that neither voting nor legislation would advance the workers, but only a "very much richer, very much greater, and very much more powerful" Germany would be able to insure continued benefits for the industrial proletariat.[18]

A similar loyalty to the firm characterized Hugenberg's service in the Kornwalzer affair —a clear case of industrial espionage exposed by the Social Democratic deputy, Karl Liebknecht. The chairman of the board argued in the public press that an attack against Krupp constituted an attack against the military preparedness of Germany by international pacifists and socialists. Despite the fact that the courts had found certain members of the firm guilty of corrupt practices, the case was never pushed to its logical conclusion—neither Krupp nor Hugenberg was ever subjected to a criminal indictment.[19] This scandal was one of the rare times that Hugenberg moved into the limelight. Most of his influence was exercised through various pressure groups organized by, or in conjunction with, other firms in heavy industry.

Shortly after his appointment to Krupp's, Hugenberg became a member of the board of directors of the *Verein für die bergbaulichen Interessen in Oberbergamtsbezirk Dortmund* (*Bergbaulicher Verein,* BbV). This was a general association of coal mine owners in the Ruhr who cooperated to increase their political power and to share their technical expertise. Hugenberg, however, was never a *Bergmann,* a man directly involved with mining; he was much more concerned with the social and political ramifications of the industry. Thus his position in the *Zechenverband* (ZV), the more politically significant mining association which concentrated on employer-employee relations, was extremely important to him. At the end of 1912, he was chosen chairman of both organizations.[20] In 1910 Hugenberg also became vice-president and in 1913, president of the united chamber of commerce of Essen, Mühlheim, and Oberhausen.[21] He also assumed a leading role in the elitist directory of the Central Association of German Industrialists in the spring of 1911.[22]

Through these organizations Hugenberg nurtured contacts with colleagues who frequently shared his views and became his associates for life. Such certainly was the case with Emil Kirdorf of the *Gelsenkirchener Bergwerks A.G.,* the man who organized the Rhenish-Westphalian Coaling Syndicate, with Hugo Stinnes of the *Deutsch-Luxemburgische Bergwerks- und Hütten A.G.,* and with Albert Vögler, a Stinnes protégé. Freiherr Hans von und zu Loewenstein, the business manager of both the BbV and the ZV, also became an intimate of Hugenberg. Similarly, Wilhelm Beumer, an executive of the Essen chamber of commerce, served

Hugenberg not only in the Ruhr, but also as a member of the Prussian Landtag and as general emissary in political affairs.[23] With the support of these men and other magnates in heavy industry, Hugenberg concentrated the financial resources of the Ruhr and made his office a central clearinghouse for the distribution of political funds. Many industrialists fearful of democratic and socialistic movements had logically concluded that sporadic attempts to influence the electorate only during election years and then to manipulate parliamentary groups through select representatives had been inefficient and ineffective.

To rally the masses behind their goals, heavy industrialists had already begun infiltrating the media, but it was Hugenberg who emphasized the coordinated attempt to influence public opinion through the press.[24] After the impressive gains of the Social Democratic Party in the 1912 elections, reactionaries sought to rally nationalists behind a "cartel of the producing classes."[25] Since workers were reading more, Ruhr magnates hoped that proper headlines could foster industrial peace and political security. The goal was not the education but the manipulation of the voter. Shrewdly, Hugenberg realized the power of propaganda in mobilizing the masses. Not a propagandist himself, the chairman of the ZV merely created the channels for influencing men's minds. [26] In March 1914, the formation of the *Ausland G.m.b.H.* as a holding company for the coordination of industrial investments in the media marked the beginning of the Hugenberg concern.[27] A month later the first subsidiary of this corporation, the *Ausland-Anzeigen G.m.b.H.* was established to study foreign publications and to coordinate the advertising of heavy industrial firms interested in exports. Despite its purported international orientation, the new corporation received a pledge from key firms in heavy industry, promising to use it for all their ads "in the domestic and foreign press." They also agreed to pay a minimal contribution of two marks for each worker they employed so that the company could place ads for the "protection of the economic and national political interests of industry."[28] Whether the "cartel of the producing classes" could have formed a strong rightist bloc in peace time must remain hypothetical. In the summer of 1914, the assassination of Archduke Franz Ferdinand unleashed the terrible struggle for supremacy in Europe.

HUGENBERG AND WAR-TIME PROPAGANDA

The outbreak of the war allowed Hugenberg to renew an old alliance with the Pan-German League (*Alldeutscher Verband,* ADV). As he pursued his career, Hugenberg had deliberately de-emphasized his earlier connections with this aggressive organization because too many businessmen viewed it as an ultraradical association.[29] Hugenberg himself had the greatest sympathy for the ADV; indeed, he was one of its founders in 1890.[30] During its early years, he had helped to shape its policies and had specifically formulated plans for naval and colonial expansion.[31] In Posen, he had collaborated with league members in the formation of the *Ostmarkenverein.*[32] As a business leader, he favored Pan-German advocacy of the *Reichsverband gegen die Sozialdemokratie* and the ideal of the *Werksgemeinschaft.*[33] The onset of the war provided an excellent opportunity for Hugenberg to align himself openly with the league and to use Pan-German idealism to inspire war aims. With all his power in the Ruhr, Hugenberg intimately collaborated with Heinrich Class, chairman of the ADV, in propagandizing specific, expansionist goals.

In September 1914, the two men prepared an extensive memorandum detailing concrete war aims for Germany within Europe and the world. The Pan-Germans claimed that the ultimate goal of their program was the security of the German people—security from future attacks and security for internal development. According to them, Germany needed a colonial empire to supply her with raw materials, a market for surplus products, and also a war indemnity to subsidize a system of rural colonization and urban improvement. Specifically, Belgium would have to remain under German control by right of conquest; France would have to cede valuable territory from the Swiss border to the channel coast; British sea power would have to be broken; and Russia would have to be confined to the boundaries existing at the time of Peter the Great. Finally, in addition to expanding its African colonies, Germany would have to unite central Europe (including Scandinavia, Finland, Rumania, and Bulgaria) into a single economic unit.[34]

Cognizant of international pressures and aware of domestic opposition, the imperial government refused public ratification of such a patently aggressive program.[35] Despite the tepidity of the regime and even of his own superior, Krupp von Bohlen,

Hugenberg attempted to muster support by organizing industrial leaders who agreed with him and by cooperating with various pressure groups to arouse the public.[36]

At a meeting in the Prussian house of delegates on 7 November 1914, Hugenberg brought together representatives from the Central Association of German Industrialists, the Union of Industrialists, and the League of German Farmers, in order to give Class an opportunity to explain his and Hugenberg's plans for a victorious peace settlement. These groups essentially agreed with the demands but asked that Hugenberg, Class, and Hirsch rework some themes and bring back a revised proposal at a later date.[37] When, at the turn of the year, Chancellor Theobald von Bethmann Hollweg frustrated Class's attempts to propagandize Pan-German goals, Hugenberg continued working with other industrialists, particularly Stinnes, to promulgate these aims. In the name of the united chamber of commerce of Essen, Mühlheim, and Oberhausen, he calculatedly declared his repudiation of Bethmann's policy in a telegram congratulating Class for inspiring the entire nation. With deliberate boldness, he suggested that only the intervention of the kaiser and the military could prevent the acceptance of a humiliating treaty—a treaty which would result in the demise of the monarchy.[38] The economic pressure groups, which he mobilized, considered the clear presentation of war aims so important that they petitioned both the Reichstag and the chancellor for permission to discuss objectives openly. These men hoped that the public expression of goals for the "political, military, maritime, and economic" expansion of the nation would arouse a greater commitment on the part of the masses for a victorious settlement.[39]

The regime's refusal to advocate an expansionist peace encouraged heavy industrialists to begin their own policy of propaganda. As chairman of the mining companies' key associations, Hugenberg had already centralized funds for political investments. Now he became the pivotal figure in the decision to use the *Zechenverband's* organization as a channel for pooling war profits and investing them in the media. Spokesmen for the four largest companies, Hugenberg (Krupp), Stinnes (*Deutsch-Luxemburgische Bergwerks- und Hütten A.G.*), Kirdorf (*Gelsenkirchener Bergwerks A.G.*), and Wilhelm Beukenberg (*Phoenix A.G. für Bergbau und Hüttenbetriebe*), formed the *Wirtschaftliche Gesellschaft* as a private association to adminster a trust fund derived from the monies made available to them and other industrialists from their firm's discretionary accounts.[40] Stated in general terms, the purpose of this collaborative effort was "effectively to countermand threatening dangers in the economic and social fields."[41]

Through the use of diverse bank accounts and holding companies administered by additional trustees, Hugenberg and these industrial leaders masked their control. The *Ausland,* established in 1914, became one of their key corporations. The *Wirtschafts-dienst G.m.b.H.,* incorporated in May 1916, concealed investments made for "the improvement of economic news service and the management of press corporations."[42] A third firm, the *Deutsche Gewerbehaus A.G.,* established in February 1917, officially managed funds for the erection of business offices for the varied associations of German industry. Its larger purpose, however, was to participate "in various businesses and measures which appeared suitable to the corporation for the advancement of general German industrial and national interests."[43] Through these organizations, Hugenberg and his associates invested almost twenty-nine million marks during the war years. About seventy percent of this came from the corporations represented by the four major figures behind the *Wirtschaftliche Gesellschaft;* the remainder, from the firms originally involved in the formation of the *Ausland.*[44]

A significant portion of these funds went into the purchase and development of a major publishing house in Berlin, the *August Scherl G.m.b.H.* An innovative newspaper man, August Scherl was the German counterpart of America's William Randolph Hearst and of England's Lord Northcliffe. His firm published two major dailies. *Der Tag* with a circulation of 18,000–20,000 was aimed at intellectual circles in the Greater Berlin area; the *Berliner Lokal-Anzeiger* with a circulation of about a quarter of a million was a popular newspaper with a large advertising section for small buyers. In addition, Scherl published various weekly papers, periodicals such as the popular *Gartenlaube,* and address books for at least seven major cities. In 1912 the firm had a total sales income of M 25,900,000 which permitted a ten percent dividend.[45] Since the founders of the other two major publishing houses in Berlin, Rudolf Mosse and the Ullstein brothers, were Jewish and because the policy of their papers was too democratic for conservative circles, the importance of Scherl for articulating right-wing views was apparent. Neither government nor industry wanted to see the Scherl publications take a more liberal stance.[46] When the firm encountered financial difficulties in 1914, a loose association of businessmen, united in the *Deutscher Verlagsverein,* complied with a governmental request to assist Scherl.[47] Within two years, however, additional funding was needed. Hugenberg and the mining interests were prepared to act.

Negotiations with the government and careful examination of Scherl's accounts began in the secrecy which would characterize Hugenberg's involvement in the press until the middle years of the Weimar era. The firm needed not only seven million marks to cover its debts, but an additional two million for development.[48] Krupp's director agreed to undertake the challenge of making the firm solvent only if he and his allies could have complete control. Members of the *Deutscher Verlagsverein* agreed. Senator Johann Neumann of Lübeck, a reliable member of the Pan-German League and a trustee far removed from the Ruhr, became the head of a newly organized holding company, the *Hanseatische Truehand G.m.b.H.,* which purchased 1.6 million marks of stock. Either the Prussian government or Hugenberg's associates in Posen provided another million. The names of Beukenberg and Hirsch, as well as Hugenberg's crony, Leo Wegener, appeared on the list of investors. Baron Salomon von Oppenheim, one of the key men in the *Deutscher Verlagsverein,* maintained shares totaling M 1,390,000 but apparently held these in trusteeship for the *Zechenverband.*[49] Despite the fact that he would gain control of the firm, Hugenberg totally concealed his involvement.[50]

The intentions of the new owners were clear. In July 1916 at one of the first meetings including the new shareholders, Friedrich Swart, one of Hugenberg's intimates from Posen, clearly stated the determination to have the Scherl newspapers adopt a stronger position on the issue of war aims. Eugen Zimmermann, the general director of the firm, succeeded in preventing an immediate change in the editorial policy which had supported the chancellor.[51] The Hugenberg group, however, could not be easily put off; at a later meeting the new shareholders and their trustees emphatically pursued their demand for a more aggressive policy. Hugenberg's friend, Wegener, reported:

> Neumann delivered an excellent speech. The gentlemen should not believe that we were involved to have a good investment, we knew that nothing would come out of this and wanted to have political influence for our money. Hirsch was just as clear when he developed this further: the *Lokal-Anzeiger,* whether it wants to or not, must show its colors. Democratization threatens not only from below, but also from above.[52]

The purpose of heavy industry's investments in the press were rarely more baldly stated.[53]

In pursuit of his goal, Hugenberg developed a coherent plan which involved him in all areas of the newspaper industry. Influence over international news led him to invest in the *Deutscher Überseedienst G.m.b.H.* and in the *Telegraphen-Union;*[54] support for the nationalist press fostered the expansion of his advertising agency in the domestic field and ultimately produced the *ALA Allgemeine Anzeigen G.m.b.H.* in July 1917;[55] concern for the provincial press resulted in the formation of the *Vera Verlagsanstalt G.m.b.H.* which in 1917 began assisting select nationalist newspapers throughout Germany.[56]

Not surprisingly, Hugenberg's policy led him to support Field Marshal Paul von Hindenburg and General Erich Ludendorff rather than moderates such as General Wilhelm Groener.[57] Hugenberg also espoused the ideal of the Fatherland Party as a suprapartisan effort to rally the masses for an expansive peace.[58] To bolster his expansionist goals, he created more than propagandistic channels for the fulfillment of war aims. With men such as Stinnes, Kirdorf, and Beukenberg, he established three companies which would help Germany exploit Belgian resources: the *Industriegesellschaft 1916 m.b.H.* the *Bodengesellschaft 1916 m.b.H.,* and the *Verkehrsgesellschaft 1916 m.b.H.*[59] Similarly at the end of 1917, he formed the *Landgesellschaft Westmark m.b.H.* to develop the postwar settlement of French territory which he expected the Reich to annex. Much more elaborate plans were formulated for the colonization of the East through the *Landgesellschaft Kurland m.b.H.* and the *Neuland A.G.,* which were incorporated in 1918 after the Russian defeat.[60] Through these firms, over 37 million marks were invested in establishing cooperative funds for the settlement of independent farmers.[61]

The loss of the war in 1918 convinced Hugenberg not that his ideals were wrong, but merely that the internal opposition of democrats and socialists had betrayed Germany. He was convinced that the nation would ultimately rise phoenixlike from the ruins and claim its proper place in the world. The weakness of Germany after the Thirty Years War and the subsequent rise of Prussia, the defeat of Prussia by Napoleon followed by the triumphant "War of Liberation," and finally Bismarck's dramatic struggle to create a new empire—these were the historic parallels that nurtured his hopes. The strong emphasis on will and determination that had characterized the social Darwinistic and Nietzschean philosophies of the late nineteenth century reinforced his commitment. Unwavering conviction and self-righteousness sustained him.[62] Political necessity profoundly affected his tactics. Though he maintained his preference for working in the background, Hugenberg gravitated toward more active involvement in politics. His metamorphosis into a full-blown political leader was not rapid, but two important changes did take place. First, he left Krupp's and concentrated on the extension of his press syndicate so that it could reach millions of voters.[63] Second, he stepped from behind the wings and appeared on the political stage as a representative in the Reichstag. Realizing the necessity for popular support, Hugenberg sought to coordinate both activities in an attempt to develop the "national opposition," a radical *Sammlung* which would be capable of imposing his ideals on the structure of German society.

POSTWAR EXPANSION OF THE HUGENBERG CONCERN

Frustrated by the loss of the war, Hugenberg and the most reactionary segments of heavy industry did not abdicate their political role in the early years of the republic—rather they consolidated and refined it. Hugenberg remained chairman of the two influential organizations uniting the Ruhr's coaling community, the *Bergbaulicher Verein* and the *Zechenverband*.[64] As a key leader of heavy industry, he played a significant role in the formation of the Reich Association of German Industry (*Reichsverband der Deutschen Industrie,* RDI). In this new structure which united the major organizations of prewar German industry,

Hugenberg presided over the coaling division, the *Fachgruppe Bergbau,* which was one of the largest segments of the nation's industry. In the RDI, he became a member not merely of the executive committee, but also of the elite thirteen-man presidium.[65] Despite this, Hugenberg was no longer the director of any specific firm in heavy industry, and therefore, he involved himself more and more in the social and political aspects of industrial and economic development. His office was not only a center for coordinating the business interests of the coaling industry, but also a center for assessing and subsidizing a broad range of right-wing activities.[66] Political influence was what the men of the Ruhr wanted, and Hugenberg provided funds for a vast number of counterrevolutionary organizations.[67]

Most significant for the coordination of subsidies from the coaling community was the *Wirtschaftsvereinigung zur Förderung der geistigen Wiederaufbaukräfte,* established by Hugenberg in 1919. With this, the four-man trusteeship of the *Wirtschaftliche Gesellschaft* was extended to twelve; six leaders were to come from industry itself and six from other areas of society. The chief purpose of the organization remained similar—"the raising and distributing of loans from participating economic and political circles to suitable undertakings."[68] Under Hugenberg's aegis, this nonjuridical association enabled western coaling magnates to conceal the vast trust fund that had accumulated during the war years and at the same time invest this money in the pursuit of reactionary endeavors. As the linchpin in the total structure, Hugenberg engineered the entire system of investments and presided over the maze of ever-shifting corporations which concealed the involvement of heavy industry and exploited the structure of corporate law to avoid taxes. In this endeavor, numerous political, economic, and legal experts served Hugenberg, but he hired a retired naval captain, Johann Bernhard Mann, to be his most intimate collaborator.[69] In the investment of the funds at their disposal, Hugenberg and his associates once more turned to the press as a means of securing tangible assets which could influence public opinion.

German newspapers had always been clearly political in their approach; rightist, leftist, liberal, and Catholic publications followed evident partisan lines. This tendency continued after 1918 and facilitated the extension of counterrevolutionary propaganda into the media. Radical nationalists rejected the new political structure and maintained a loyalty to some transcendent concept of the state embodying their ideological ideals; they appealed to a higher justice which went beyond the materialistic and partisan interests attributed to Weimar's supporters. This psychology evoked strongly emotional rhetoric and fostered the creation of shibboleths such as the "war-guilt lie," the "stab in the back," and the "November criminals." Those who unqualifiedly endorsed these slogans became the "experts" who spoke for the true Germany; those who demurred were dilettantish, partisan politicians.[70] Right-wing propagandists embroidered these stereotyped notions into fanciful and malicious patterns. The Hugenberg press alone could not have created such provocative jargon, but his syndicate did encourage it and prosper with it. The clearer and stronger the distinction between right and left, the more Hugenberg and his reactionary associates could expect to rally ardent nationalists in a *Sammlung,* a unified bloc, which could destroy the republic.

Given this propensity for a simple dichotomy, many Ruhr magnates would have preferred one large right-wing party. Partisan tradition made this impossible; nationalists differed greatly from one another. In the winter of 1918–1919 with the threat of a real socialist revolution, Hugenberg felt forced to collaborate with any bourgeois group—even the newly established German Democratic Party.[71] As the revolutionary danger subsided, he became more and more exclusive in the distribution of his share of industry's largess. Rightist unity remained the goal, and the two major right-wing parties, the German National People's Party (*Deutschnationale Volkspartei,* DNVP) and the German People's Party (*Deutsche Volkspartei,* DVP), became the major beneficiaries of the Ruhr's subsidies. To assist them, two press organizations similar to the *Vera* were organized in October 1922—the *Alterum Kredit A.G.* for the DVP and the *Mutuum Darlehns A.G.* for the DNVP. Both corporations performed banking services permitting interested parties the opportunity to remain anonymous while de facto purchasing shares in a particular newspaper.[72] Through these and other means, Hugenberg ultimately gained control of approximately fourteen regional newspapers.[73]

In the 1920s, however, there were over 3,000 newspapers circulating in Germany. Control over fourteen would hardly maintain and/or produce the political climate that reactionary industrialists desired.[74] The *Wolff Telegraphen Büro* remained the only significant nationwide news agency in Germany. Since this news service was a semiofficial agency of the government, right-wing interests judged it to be unreliable.[75] Because industry as a whole was unable to agree on any united effort to deal with news circulation,[76] Hugenberg sought some way to extend the *Telegraphen-Union.* [77] In 1921 he deviously gained control of the *Dammert Verlag G.m.b.H.,* which skillfully edited the news and dispatched it to subscribing newspapers throughout Germany. Later the same year, the establishment of two agencies for business news, the *Deutscher Handelsdient* in Berlin and the *Westdeutscher Handelsdienst* in Essen, further extended the base of the *Telegraphen-Union.*[78] Hugenberg had not only succeeded in breaking the monopoly of the Wolff Telegraph Bureau, but had also established a basis for presenting a rightist slant on the news to papers throughout the nation.[79] In its full development, the *TU* employed over 250 correspondents and controlled thirty branch offices in Germany and the world. Through its services it circulated various specialized reports not only on economic and political life, but also on topics of lesser import such as sports, gardening, and the weather.[80] Over 1,600 papers subscribed to its news services. In its dispatches, the *TU* fostered a "nonpartisan" rightist approach by giving swift attention to developments favoring the nationalist parties, by carefully shortening communications of political opponents, and by just being silent on foreign developments which could aid the policy of the republic.[81]

While the political orientation of the *Telegraphen-Union* manifested itself in a more or less indirect fashion, Hugenberg created yet another company to influence the provincial press. Incorporated in September 1922, the *Wirtschaftsstelle für die Provinzpresse (Wipro)* combined assests of *Vera* and *Mutuum* with those of the *TU.* This new firm introduced local editors to the most modern printing methods and at the same time provided a subscription service which supplied regional papers with full stories that only had to be copied.[82] The *Matern* sent out by the central office were used as molds to form printing plates which could be used immediately.[83] In addition to serial novels, fashion news, holiday reports, etc., the subscription service included a news service on the events of the day. The *Wipro* reportedly supplied two variations in this last and politically most important dispatch—one for the "nonpartisan" papers and another for the nationalist, right-wing press.[84] Some 230 to 300 newspapers subscribed to this service.[85] Hugenberg's supporters could consequently boast that this syndicated news service exercised "a significant influence on that which is called 'the public opinion' in the country."[86]

At the same time that he extended his influence over the regional press, Hugenberg perfected his control over the Scherl *Verlag*.[87] With a free hand to reorganize the firm, he named Ludwig Klitzsch as the new general director to begin in January 1920.[88] Hugenberg developed unlimited confidence in the judgment of his new associate. Together they added a new daily newspaper to the firm's publications, the *Berliner Illustrierte Nachtausgabe*. This cheap tabloid appealed to the man in the street and by 1929 had reached a circulation of 216,600.[89] Scherl also increased its assets by exploiting its connections with industry in order to win publishing contracts for printing trade material such as industrial and commercial address books.[90] Under the direction of Hugenberg and Klitzsch, the firm not only weathered the difficulties of the inflationary period, but emerged as a strong, profitable enterprise. At the end of 1926, Scherl employed 6,530 men and women including 133 editors; it had become the cornerstone of Hugenberg's entire press syndicate.[91]

This very visible success of the Scherl concern led to the charge that Hugenberg was a war profiteer and an unscrupulous manipulator of the postwar inflation. This was undoubtedly true. During the period from 1914 through 1924 Hugenberg had securely established the basis of his entire syndicate. His business transactions were filled with: plans to buy and sell shares of different companies, the creation of new corporations as holding concerns to take over various firms, contracts with confidants acting as middlemen, and ever-present schemes to avoid taxes. Hugenberg exploited the corporate law, which he knew so well, and utilized his own financial acumen, which he had so finely developed, to secure his empire. He knew the rules of the game and manipulated them to full advantage.

Funding for the development of the Hugenberg syndicate came from key interests in the *Zechenverband* via the *Wirtschaftsvereinigung*, but not all of it came directly from the

Ruhr. The settlement associations, *Kurland* and *Neuland,* had amassed considerable investments from heavy industry. With no conquered land to colonize in the East, Hugenberg first planned to establish a national bank which would link agrarian Prussia with the industrial West.[92] Diverse agricultural and industrial interests frustrated this grandoise plan.[93] Lack of fluid capital in the East and, presumably, the dearth of funds for continued investment in the press gradually led Hugenberg to use eastern investments as a means of expanding his holdings in the media.[94] He later boasted that his agrarian ventures had permitted him to conceal the development of his press holdings from the Prussian government. The major holding company for his operations was the *Ostpreussische Privatbank (Opriba),* in which these eastern firms had been the original investors.[95] Changes in emphasis indicate that the development of Hugenberg's syndicate, like the unification of the Bismarckian Reich, might not have been the result of some grand plan, but the fortuitous result of maximizing advantages.

Until the period after inflation, it would seem that Hugenberg had been acting primarily as the champion of heavy industry, the coaling industry in particular. It seems equally true, however, that he had a strong personal motive—the strengthening of his own power base. His conflict with the Haniel family and the *Gutehoffnungshütte (GHH)* in Oberhausen clearly demonstrated this. In 1920, Karl Haniel had received through Stinnes three million marks from the *Zechenverband* in order to gain control of the *Münchener Neueste Nachrichten.*[96] Five years later, Hugenberg demanded that the stocks represented by this investment be turned over to his *Opriba,* the holding company for the *Wirtschaftsvereinigung* and, ultimately, the *Zechenverband.*[97] Hugenberg claimed that he alone had the right to control the mining association's investments in the newspaper industry. Stinnes was dead; Haniel refused to comply.[98] Challenging one of the most important families in the Ruhr and thus their general director of the GHH, Paul Reusch, indicated Hugenberg's confidence in his position.

Two years of bitter debate ensued. Haniel challenged Hugenberg's entire modus operandi and threatened to bring him to court for alleged illegal action in dealing with the *Deutscher Verlags-Verein* (DVV). Though most of the original investors in that association had sold their shares, Haniel maintained his. Hugenberg, who controlled the remainder of the DVV as well as Scherl, arranged for his holding company's purchase of the associations' remaining shares at 50 percent of face value. Haniel claimed that his sale undervalued the stocks by 150 percent. He charged that not only was he being defrauded financially, but that Hugenberg had acted illegally by not informing the DVV of this action and, also, that the proposal to dissolve the association in 1926 had been based on false grounds.[99] These were powerful charges and if ever aired in court would have become a potent weapon in the hands of heavy industry's political opponents. Some of the most important men of the Ruhr, Vögler, Thyssen, Winkhaus, von Loewenstein, and Brandi, tried to hush up the matter and reach an amicable settlement.[100]

Hugenberg remained adamant in his demands, and Vögler confessed to Reusch that Hugenberg was not an "easy" man to deal with.[101] He not only demanded control of *Knorr und Hirth G.m.b.H.,* the firm that published Haniel's south German papers, but he countered the charges of improper and illegal conduct. At the shareholders' meeting of the DVV in July 1927, Hugenberg's attorney, Dr. Günther Donner, announced that in 1924 the *Opriba* had received only the option to purchase the association's shares in Scherl; the actual purchase was not completed until after approval by the DVV stockholders' meeting in 1926. He also claimed that the reasons given for the dissolution of the DVV were valid. Donner thus rejected the case of the GHH against the *Opriba.* Hugenberg then announced the specific plan for dissolution. A new corporation, the *Zollernhof A.G.,* would provide the association's shareholders with stocks or bonds valued at 200 percent of their investment in the DVV.[102] Hugenberg thereby legally protected himself, but he still could not prevail against the GHH. Reusch brought so much pressure to bear on the *Zechenverband* that the coaling association supposedly threatened to break with Hugenberg unless he agreed to a settlement with Haniel. He did. Haniel maintained control of his south German publications.[103]

The conflict provides an insight into Hugenberg's strength and into the respect he commanded, while it exemplifies the hostilities which could divide the magnates of the Ruhr. A major factor in the confrontation was Haniel's assertion that Hugenberg's extreme rightist policy would alienate the readers of his papers.[104] In the end result, the dispute delimited Hugenberg's role as a spokesman for industry. He remained the most important manager of the *Zechenverband's* investments, but he would not be the sole spokesman for heavy industry.[105]

Though reactionary coaling barons continued to support Hugenberg, involvement in the media drew him further and further away from his original power base in the Ruhr. The basis for industrial support of Hugenberg's ventures lay in the statement, "the foundation of the structure to which our work is dedicated should be informed by two ideas: the concept of nationalism and the permeation of the principle of personality in cultural and economic life once more."[106] Just as socialism and democracy had been the prime enemies when the *Ausland* was formed in 1914, so they remained the foe throughout the Weimar era. The precise tactics to be used in combatting the enemy varied. The *Wirtschaftsvereinigung zur Förderung der geistigen Wiederaufbaukräfte* opted for the most reactionary policy. The smug title, the Economic Association for the Promotion of Intellectual Forces of Reconstruction, reflected the stilted and narrow-minded approach of the men who championed this kind of counterrevolution. In 1928 this association included: Hugenberg himself as chairman; his confidant, Mann; his trustee, Mayor Neumann of Lübeck; his closest friend, Wegener; his old Pan-German associate, the retired industrialist Kirdorf; his close collaborator, von Loewenstein; and the economist, Professor Ludwig Bernhard. In addition there were Vögler, general director of the *Vereinigte Stahlwerke;* Fritz Winkhaus, general director of the *Köln-Neuessener Bergwerksverein* (the Hoesch concern); Eugen Wiskott, deputy chairman of the *Bergbaulicher Verein;* Franz Witthoeft of the board of overseers of the *Commerz- und Privatbank;* and Johann Becker, a former minister of economics.[107]

These men administered a trust fund and foreswore profit from it, but the enterprises they sponsored were not unprofitable. Their private investments or the investments of their firms in any of the several Hugenberg corporations could and did return rich dividends. Moreover, the group was concerned not merely with the press, as such, but also with "propagandistic enterprises" and various "auxiliary undertakings."[108] In 1922, a contract detailing their community of interests was signed, and the *Werbegemeinschaft* was created. The purpose of this organization was to assist groups that were "very effective politically, but not commercially profitable."[109] Hugenberg was, of course, the chairman of this *Werbegemeinschaft*. When profits in the firms administered by the *Wirtschaftsvereinigung* were high, he had over M 600,000 at his disposal, and even in relatively bad years, as much as a quarter of a million marks could be used for political purposes.[110] Hugenberg had consequently created a very strong position for himself not only with regard to the media, but also in the politics of the state.

His power and independence were enhanced by yet another factor. While majority control of the several corporations of his concern remained the property of diverse corporate interests, he and his friends from Posen also owned shares in these enterprises. The value of these investments increased, and profits were frequently reinvested so that the personal wealth and the personal interest of Hugenberg and his private circle of associates grew significantly.[111] In his later life, Hugenberg was most proud of the creation of his "concern." He had apparently fulfilled his youthful ambition to gain power and prestige.[112] His baronial estate at Rohbraken endowed him with the image of the successful Wilhelminian entrepreneur who had strong roots in the land.[113]

So shrewd was Hugenberg's management of the funds at his disposal that friends and foes overestimated his power and financial ability. In his study of the Hugenberg concern, Bernhard alleged that Hugenberg secured control of the nation's largest film corporation, the *Universum Film A.G. (Ufa)*, without assistance from heavy industry. This exaggeration flattered Hugenberg and shielded the industrialists who continued to support him despite, or because of, his reactionary tactics.[114] The political advantage of controlling such a powerful medium as the film was not lost on heavy industry. Any cinematic presentation could be transformed into propaganda. An innocuous, escapist film could lure troubled minds into a world of material wonders, subtly advertising the products of German industry which could be attained by luck or hard work.[115] Yet the cost of producing a successful film would place definite limitations on propagandizing potential; a major film corporation could hardly become a political tool. Despite this, the corporation presented Hugenberg

and his allies with an excellent opportunity to extend their
sphere of influence. At the very least, conservative-nationalist
control of the *Ufa* would prevent republicans, Jews, and internationalists from monopolizing this medium. After extensive
negotiations, new stock was issued, and Hugenberg secured control of the corporation in 1927.[116]

Undoubtedly Hugenberg was a very powerful man. Though
he did not own the numerous enterprises called the "Hugenberg
concern," he effectively controlled them. No longer a leader in
heavy industry, he was not exactly the "Lord of Press and Film"
either—too many newspapers remained outside of his control,
and Germany's weak film industry could not be destroyed by
turning the *Ufa* into a propaganda mill. Nevertheless, Hugenberg's entrepreneurial success encouraged his adherents to
believe that he had the ability to solve Germany's economic
problems. His solutions, however, necessitated the acquisition of
political power.

POLITICAL ACTION AND THE DVNP

From the very beginning of the republican era, divergent interests prevented the Reich Association of German Industry
from supporting any particular party. Anxious to secure the
influence of heavy industry on the political process, Hugenberg
had encouraged the creation of a strong campaign fund under
the aegis of the Commission for the Collection, Administration,
and Disbursement of Industrial Campaign Funds.[117] He and
some of his associates were vexed when Carl Friedrich von Siemens of the electrical industry organized the Board for the
Reconstruction of German Economic Life and agreed to subsidize even the newly created German Democratic Party (*Deutsche
Demokratische Partei,* DDP),[118] but industrial opinion on the best
tactics to fight socialism varied greatly. Even ardent rightists
failed to attain unity. Gustav Stresemann refused to sanction the
dissolution of the old National Liberal Party and maintained a
core group in his new German People's Party. Unwilling to alienate this bourgeois faction, Albert Vögler, Hugenberg's close
associate, became the DVP's first treasurer and a prime mover in
the attempt to shape its policies.[119] Hugenberg himself favored
the more radically based DNVP.[120] Both men collaborated on
tactics and strategy and hoped that their parties were marching
separately toward the same goal.[121]

Hugenberg did not enjoy collaborating with political parties; he found them divisive and confining. He realized, however, that the goal of *Sammlung,* nationalist unity, had to have a political base, for he was convinced that in the "sick and crazy" climate of Weimar "the one thing that can really help is power and the use of power."[122] Without mass support, no rightist could gain control of the state. Since the DNVP was the most ardent counter-revolutionary party, Hugenberg hoped that it would become the core of the "national opposition."[123] Its avid nationalism and firm opposition to socialism united industrialists and Junkers as well as Lutheran pastors and military leaders, workers, civil servants, members of the middle classes, and newly enfranchised mothers, behind the party banner. Unfortunately for its founders, the DNVP emerged as a federation of interest groups rather than as a unified bloc. Only opposition united it; it was impossible to rally radical racists, Pan-Germans, Christian Socialists, responsible parliamentarians and rabid radicals behind a specific, positive program.[124]

Within the party, Hugenberg represented the most intransigent wing. Elected to the Weimar Assembly from the district of Posen,[125] he rose to denounce governmental intervention in the economy as a veiled form of communism.[126] He labeled Matthias Erzberger, the republic's minister of finance, a "traitor" for attempting to bind the nation to a system of "international economic slavery."[127] Clearly favoring crisis politics, Hugenberg publicly declared that the occupation of the Ruhr would be the result of the cabinet's policies and that it would be better if the regime allowed it to happen without the humiliation of attempted compliance.[128] Because so many Germans disagreed with him, Hugenberg concluded that the nation had not yet reached the nadir of its fortunes and consequently could not begin to rise. In the struggle for survival, Germany had been wounded, but it would take a greater blow to arouse the *furor teutonicus* and to inaugurate a nationalist revival culminating in a "third Reich."[129] In the meantime, the DNVP had to constitute a party of radical reform just as the Socialists had done before the war. The party had to reject any cooperation with democracy.[130] For Hugenberg, the imperial government had failed; there could be no going back. The task was to develop a powerful elite capable of dogmatic leadership. Such leadership would have to be accepted no matter what its origin. Despite his party affiliation,

Hugenberg continually identified himself as a rightist rather than as a partisan politician. In a somewhat prophetic statement, he argued that whoever would save the nation would have to "attract the masses behind him like the Pied Piper of Hamelin." He believed that "only a few will and can do this. We, the entire spectrum of nonsocialists, can do no more than prepare the way for these few. Hopefully we will find that which we desire."[131]

While he believed that one could "not be radical enough" when public interests were threatened, Hugenberg was disinclined to resort to violent or illegal opposition.[132] Eschewing exhibitionism, he shunned displays of power. After his initial speeches in the Weimar Assembly, he did not approach the speaker's podium for ten years.[133] In the Reich Association of German Industry, his name never appeared on the lists of speakers of the main meetings. Even in the more elitist presidium of that organization, he rarely voiced an opinion.[134] Still, his ability to marshal millions of marks for political contributions guaranteed him attention.[135]

Opposed to the Kapp putsch of 1920 and in favor of the expulsion of rabid racists from the DNVP in 1922, Hugenberg was convinced that the overriding issue was neither personality nor race and probably not even legality and nonviolence, but rather the most effective opposition to the republic.[136] His press syndicate fostered the amalgamation of a broad-based counterrevolutionary bloc. His friend, Gottfried Traub summarized this policy in Hugenberg's *München-Augsburger Abendzeitung:*

> Anti-Semitism can become no refuge for political narrowness and political unsuitability.... With merely shouting, "The Jew is guilty, kill him!" nothing has yet been accomplished. To govern a state, which should maintain its independence from all alien influences, a higher sense of political responsibility and a slow, determined education of the nation is necessary.[137]

Hugenberg considered anti-Semitism a tool which could be exploited and discarded; he himself measured a man by his loyalty to the nation rather than by the purity of his racial pedigree.[138]

According to the Hugenberg press, Adolf Hitler and his fellow putschists of November 1923 were misguided men seeking admirable goals with improper tactics. Hitler was an "exceptionally popular speaker" and an "organizer of unaccustomed talent" who was able to liberate "innumerable workers from the bond of international socialism" and convert them to the nationalist cause.[139] Nazi extremists, however, could promote anarchy. The fundamental rule had to be, "You must gather together and not scatter! You must bind together and not tear apart!"[140] There was no enemy on the right; there were only undisciplined idealists.[141] Only when a rightist collaborated in saving the Weimar regime was he liable to censure.

The inflationary trauma of 1923 had so crippled the economy that the state was tottering. The communist danger mounted; rightists propagandized the masses; separatists threatened to destroy the Reich. Leading German Nationals asserted that only a dictatorship could preserve the unity of the state.[141] Admiral Tirpitz encouraged Hugenberg to come to the fore because there was no other "personality in Germany who would be so suited to bring the 'expeditious' understanding necessary for the salvation of our country and so suitable in the situation...."[143] Hugenberg, however, did not have the political base for such decisive action. Not rightist counterrevolution, but rightist collaboration saved the Reich. Stresemann accepted the chancellorship and thereafter worked within the framework of Weimar to improve Germany's position both domestically and internationally. Hugenberg condemned such an approach and scorned Stresemann's action.[144] Enmity between the two men undoubtedly had a personal tone—but more important—Stresemann's heroic action broke the back of rightist resistance to the republic and gravely threatened the ideological solution favored by Hugenberg and other counterrevolutionaries.

The DVP and the DNVP no longer seemed to be marching separately toward the same goal. Participation in the republican regime provided a viable alternative to negativism. The inflation was ended; state unity was preserved; extremism on the right and left was suppressed. Pragmatic industrial leaders could appreciate such positive achievements; the counterrevolutionary impulse of many was diverted. Hugenberg hated Stresemann for this. He believed that instead of using the inflation as the catastrophe which could lead to the rebirth of Germany, the chairman of the DVP had settled for temporary and partial victories. Hugenberg, however, could not stem the tide. Compromise for the sake of order and prosperity set the tone for the following years. Even the DNVP would be affected.

During the Reichstag campaign in the spring of 1924, revision of reparations payments as envisaged by the Dawes Plan emerged as the central issue. With its counterrevolutionary ideology, the DNVP condemned this financial arrangement as an "enslaving plan of fulfillment."[145] Industry and agriculture did not fully concur. Both wanted a sound fiscal policy for the state; neither supported the DNVP exclusively. German National leaders could not countenance a purely negative program. The party demanded support for industry, agriculture, and the middle classes, i.e., the productive classes (schaffende Stände).[146] Enhanced appeal increased the party's representation from sixty-five to ninety-six seats. Including ten allied delegates from the National Farmers' Union (Reichslandbund), the DNVP became one of the strongest parties in the Reichstag.[147] Then the real debate on the Dawes Plan began. German National radicals remained adamant against every aspect of fulfullment. Acceptance was equated with sanction of the entire Versailles settlement. They argued that the state would lose its sovereignty by surrendering control over its railroads and by further enmeshing itself in the net of international capital. Pragmatists countered that the scale of reparations would be lowered and vital investment capital from American banks would bolster German industry and agriculture.[148] Uncompromising as ever, Hugenberg castigated the conciliatory stance of most major industrialists. Defiantly, he admonished, a "nationalist who has inwardly become a parliamentarian is nothing but a German democrat."[149]

When the majority of leaders in the Reich Association of German Industry favored acceptance of the Dawes Plan, only Hugenberg and three other members of the exclusive presidium reportedly voted against it.[150] From this point on, Hugenberg became less and less a spokesman for the majority of Ruhr industrialists. Involvement in his press syndicate drew him ever further away from the pressing business interests of heavy industry. In February 1925, he resigned from his chairmanships of the Bergbaulicher Verein and the Zechenverband, but he remained a member of the executive committees of these groups and continued to serve as chairman of the coaling division in the RDI.[151] As he forsook the pragmatism of most industrial leaders and yet maintained a symbolic stance as a spokesman for the Ruhr, Hugenberg emerged as the champion of German National radicalism.

Industrial and agricultural pressure to accept the Dawes Plan severely threatened the counterrevolutionary image of the DNVP. Acceptance of the proposal demanded constitutional revision, which required a two-thirds vote in the Reichstag. The parliamentary strength of the German Nationals made them the pivotal factor in all political calculations. As party chairman, Oskar Hergt tried to appease both radicals and compromisers within the party. His demands that the newly-elected Reichstag delegate, Admiral Tirpitz, become chancellor and that stringent conditions for the acceptance of the plan be accepted by the allies, failed.[152] Rejection of the plan seemed the only honorable alternative for the party. Outside of parliament, rightist radicals rallying behind the United Fatherland Associations and the German Industrial Union denounced the plan. In the Reichstag, thirty-three radical DNVP delegates united with racist colleagues in splinter factions to repudiate the Dawes proposal.[153] Still, "credit hungry" industrialist and agricultural organizations continued to lobby for acceptance.

With intimate associates on both sides, Hugenberg avoided taking a public stand. No one doubted his opposition to the plan, but in 1924 he did not yet enjoy a securely independent position which would allow him either to repudiate the compromisers or to sway the party behind his radicalism. For the sake of unity, he remained in the background. A doctor's note claiming that he had suffered a mild heart attack excused him from the Reichstag session which voted on the pivotal legislation. In a letter to Hergt, he privately explained that he had frequently avoided party caucuses because he disagreed with the leadership and yet did not wish to join the grumblers. Acceptance, he posited, implied that "two-thirds of the German people including those behind the German National People's Party are internally prepared to let the freedom, honor, and future of their land be sold in the expectation of a few pieces of silver."[154]

Party leaders such as Hergt and Westarp supported Hugenberg's ideological rejection of the Dawes Plan as did the party executive committee, but representatives affected more readily by pressures from organized industry, farming associations, and right-wing unions, opted for compromise. On Wednesday, 27 August 1924, shortly before the final reading of the bill on the controversial railway legislation, German National delegates in caucus voted 49 to 48 for acceptance. After the overwhelming denunciation of the plan by party councils, Hergt claimed to be "completely surprised" and concluded that the imposition of parliamentary discipline under such circumstances would be catastrophic.[155] German National delegates were left free to vote according to their consciences. The constitutional revision necessary for the implementation of the Dawes Plan was passed with the assistance of the DNVP.[156] Dissension within the party and within the entire right was paraded before the public. The Hugenberg press published the official explanation of the party claiming that there was no disagreement on principles, only a divergence in judging the particular situation.[157] But neither tactical maneuvering nor slanted reporting could paper over the deep cleft that had developed in the ranks of the DNVP. From then on the party was divided into the "Yea-Sayers" and the "No-Sayers"—those who voted for and those who voted against the Dawes Plan.[158]

Undoubtedly angry and frustrated by the acceptance of this legislation, Hugenberg still worked against a division in the German National party. Hugenberg's confidant, Captain Mann, revealed the strategy espoused by his chief when he explained to Admiral Tirpitz that the DNVP had to be preserved as the basis for "the desired Bourgeois Bloc." In this view, the party was nothing but the bureaucratic structure that could produce rightist unity. If the left wing of the party were to secede, nationalist forces would be fragmented. Most signigicantly for Hugenberg's tactics in this period, Mann noted that such a session would drive the right wing of the German Nationals into union with the German Racists (Deutschvölkische) and such an alliance would be "a danger to the Bourgeois Bloc."[159] Continued compromise by the German Nationals produced a radical change in Hugenberg's tactics in the following years.

2 The Politics of Polarization

Once Stresemann had demonstrated the viability of conservative collaboration in the Weimar regime, many rightist groups in industry and agriculture realized the fruitlessness of negativism. The counterrevolutionary consensus of 1919 was destroyed. Lobbyists from industry and agriculture, as well as nationalist unions, scrambled to gain maximum advantage for their constituents. The neoconservatism which developed among these groups frustrated radical nationalists, who demanded revolution and not evolution. In this rightist struggle, Hugenberg, the champion of the traditional radicals, emerged as chairman of the German National party.

The Struggle over the Nature of the DNVP

In the second Reichstag elections of 1924, the DVP and the DNVP continued their negative collaboration; they attacked not one another, but the Democrats and the Socialists. The goal was still the formation of a united bourgeois front, a *Bürgerblock*.[1] Hugenberg himself hoped that the DNVP would succeed in the *völkisch* task of uniting all classes and becoming the "decisive party" (*ausschlaggebende Partei*).[2] Results indicated that despite a German National gain of five seats, a rightist coalition would have to include not only the DNVP and the Stresemann Party, but also the Catholic Center and the DDP. The only other alternative was a great coalition including all parties from the DVP to the SPD. Fearful that participation of the Socialists in the cabinet would destroy rightist chances to influence social and economic legislation, organized interest groups pressured the DNVP to join with Stresemann. Moderate German Nationals interpreted the electoral results to mean that the masses accepted the party's support for the Dawes Plan and wanted a positive voice in government.[3] The ultimate result was the formation of the nonpartisan (rightist) cabinet of Chancellor Hans Luther. Technically, the regime was not a coalition supported by the parties of the right; it only had members of parties who acted in liaison with their delegations.[4]

The Hugenberg press assumed an ambivalent approach to the new government. The leading editorialist in *Der Tag*, argued:

> In accordance with its nonpartisan (*überparteilich*), rightist orientation, *Der Tag* would have every reason to greet the nonpartisan regime of Dr. Luther joyously, if we were of the opinion that it really was a nonpartisan cabinet with a decidedly rightist character. But we do not praise without reason and reason for praise is not at hand . . . .[5]

A more negative attitude was expressed by Traub's sharp condemnation of the politics of compromise in his editorial for the syndicate's *München-Augsburger Abendzeitung*.[6] Nevertheless, the lack of radical appeal in the last elections, the willingness of the *Reichslandbund* to have one of its leaders accept a cabinet post, and the emergence of Carl Duisberg, a leader of the chemical industry, as the replacement for heavy industry's Kurt Sorge as chairman of the Reich Association of German Industry—all indicated that the mood of the country was changing.

For the time being, Hugenberg kept his misgivings to himself; but two years later he published a series of essays which, he said , had been written in February and March of 1925.[7] He hissed, "It stinks in the German Reich," and the "false leaders" of the state belong in "asylums" and not in leading positions.[8] His worship of individualism and his condemnation of socialism and internationalism remained absolute. Compromises which permitted the latter doctrines to influence the state weakened vital forces.[9] A healthy economy had to permit agriculture and native industry to develop. The farmer remained the ideal individualist, but he had to have the opportunity to industrialize. At the same time, workers had to have the opportunity to become capitalists and, therefore, should be able to purchase their own homes so that they could get out of "rented barracks" (*Mietkasernen*), which fostered a hostile spirit of class strife. Similarly, employees should have the opportunity to buy stocks in their firms so that they could be imbued with the entrepreneurial spirit.[10] Socialistic and democratic ideologies frustrated real improvement in the economy and prolonged the "illness of this poor Germany."[11] A clear and direct formulation of national policy, according to

Hugenberg, had to recognize that only one thing was essential: the state had to permit the German "to live as man and as a member of the race, to perpetuate and increase the race, and also secure vital necessities for his progeny."[12]

A similar approach characterized Hugenberg's attitude toward the presidential election of 1925. When a right-wing coalition nominated Karl Jarres, Hugenberg editorialists were severely critical. According to *Der Tag,* "The national right has entered into business with democracy and the result is that its own position is made more difficult."[13] Despite reservations, however, the Hugenberg syndicate supported Jarres.[14] In the bi-election, German Nationals encouraged Field Marshal von Hindenburg to accept nomination for office.[15] Obviously, they hoped that a strong rightist president would use his constitutional powers to favor nationalist causes and ultimately prepare the way for monarchical restoration.[16] Hugenberg personally opposed the election of Hindenburg because it would add prestige to the republic and strengthen the commitment of the masses to Weimar. Nevertheless, his press supported the election of the field marshal.[17]

Pragmatically, Hugenberg sought to gain maximum advantage from collaboration,[18] but privately he made no secret of his distaste for compromise. For example, his party had agreed to accept the Accident Insurance Law, but Hugenberg vehemently opposed it on the basis of fiscal responsibility. In a printed version of an undelivered speech, he bemoaned the fact that the "No-Sayers" were "in a miserable minority" and complained:

> What help is it to our vanishing Fatherland, if in parliamentary debates on the German soul, the poisonous principle and theme of Socialism, to give the nation opium instead of bread, is, out of a sense of balance, accepted by a nonsocialist coalition—with the exception that the containers are smaller.[19]

The evolution of Stresemann's foreign policy confirmed Hugenberg's antipathy for collaboration. Throughout the spring and summer, the discrepancies between the foreign minister's tactics and the ideological position of the DNVP became more and more apparent. Stresemann began negotiations for the Locarno treaties without informing the German

Nationals. The surrender of Alsace-Lorraine, the acceptance of a mutual security pact with France and England, and the entrance of Germany into the League of Nations directly contradicted DNVP propaganda. Party leaders were in a quandry. Anxious to preserve the power they possessed over the formulation of fiscal policy, DNVP ministers and some members of the Reichstag delegation sought to delay any decisive vote on the maintenance of the current government. Radical forces had to press their case and opposition within the local party organizations had to threaten to secede before the Reichstag delegation finally abandoned its support for the cabinet at the end of October 1925.[20]

Division within the ranks of the right wing was once more very evident. The German National Reichstag delegate and spokesman for heavy industry, Walther Rademacher, understood the validity of Stresemann's approach. Former opponents of the Dawes Plan such as Paul Reusch, chairman of the *Langnam Verein* and of the Iron Producing Group in the RDI, realized that if the DNVP should leave the coalition, the SPD would gain a vital voice in the formulation of economic policy. Reusch and Haniel issued an open statement opposing the negative stance of the DNVP; they argued that the state needed "a strong bourgeois government" which would be able to conduct a peaceful and constructive foreign policy.[21] Leaders of the RDI—in particular Ludwig Kastl, the executive secretary, and, apparently, Duisberg, the chairman of this industrial association—would have preferred to see the total destruction of the German National party rather than accept a Socialist coalition.[22] Party leaders, however, avoided such a division by uniting the Reichstag delegation in opposition to the Locarno treaties.[23]

That the DNVP remained united during this period was of rather moot value for the country. A secession before the trauma of the depression might have permitted closer collaboration with Stresemann and the formation of a large, moderate rightist party. In this event, radicals such as Hugenberg would have been forced to leave the political arena or join the racist fringe. The German National party ultimately began to evolve a kind of tory-conservative approach, but some of its leaders, who preferred to unite Pan-German radicals and moderate nationalists only, realized the dangers of radicalism too late. Count Kuno

Westarp, elected chairman of the DNVP in March 1926, was one of the major bridge builders who struggled to maintain party unity during this period.[24]

Both Hugenberg and Westarp wanted a strong movement on the right. Hugenberg's frustration with and alienation from the parliamentary system, however, was much greater than Westarp's. Personally the count was a more benign and humane personality. Totally committed to a conservative, nationalist frame of reference, he could objectively evaluate arguments presented by his opponents. Years of parliamentary experience had tempered his ideology and had trained him in the necessity of political maneuvering.[25] Hugenberg had a very different personality. He has been described as "not a man, but a wall."[26] Listening to the arguments of others, he could remain totally passive, as though he did not even hear their rationale. Then when his discussant had completed his presentation, Hugenberg would rapidly and logically seize the essential weaknesses of the man's proposal.[27] Convinced of his own righteousness, Hugenberg expressed his disgust for "the spirit of talking, of pointless tacking (which is called *Realpolitik*), of tactical party maneuvering, of superficiality and lack of principle, and of the egocentric view of things."[28] He favored not bridge building, but a radical alternative.

Frustration with parliamentary government and the policy of Stresemann sparked Hugenberg's friends in the Pan-German League into action. That the ADV favored a *völkisch* dictatorship was no secret.[29] In January 1926, Class and his associates began organizing an "emergency community" and actually planned a rightist putsch.[30] Apparently, the chairman of the ADV was conspiring to have Hindenburg appoint a cabinet of personalities unacceptable to the Reichstag.[31] Once the new cabinet had assumed power, the president would, in this plan, dissolve the Reichstag. Before the new elections, Hindenburg would resign, and the chancellor would constitutionally assume his duties. The way would then be open for the issuance of an emergency decree suspending the present constitution and transforming the chancellor-president into a Reich Regent (*Reichsverweser*) with power to appoint regents for the several states. Various right-wing paramilitary units would then be used by the new regime to

counteract democratic and socialist oppositon.[32] Class's scheme
seemed preposterous but so did all the ideas in his "Kaiser Book."

Class envisioned Hugenberg as the strong personality who, as
minister of finance, would guide the new chancellor, Mayor
Neumann of Lübeck. Hugenberg's friend, Dr. Wegener would
take over the Ministry of the Interior, and Baron Hermann von
Lüninck of the Union of German Peasants' Associations would be
the new minister of agriculture.[33] There is no concrete evidence
that any of these men had agreed to assume these positions and
to participate in the conspiracy. Informed of the supposed
putsch before any revolutionary action had been taken,[34] the
Prussian Ministry of Interior acted so precipitately that rightists
claimed unconstitutional means were used to defend the constitution.[35] None of the supposed conspirators was ever brought
to trial except Class himself, and he was released "not *because of
proven innocence,* but because of *lack of sufficient evidence.*"[36]

The Hugenberg press denounced the entire police action as an
example of the SPD's arbitrariness in dispensing justice. Hugenberg repudiated rumors that he had fled the country and rejected the idea that he had agreed to accept a cabinet post in the
new government or in any government.[37] The rightist press
made much of the fact that a list of industrial leaders in the Ruhr
had been found at Class's home, and the Socialist government
had immediately ordered that the searches be extended to include the homes of such prominent men as: Vögler, general
director of United Steel combine; Winkhaus, chairman of the
Bergbaulicher Verein and the *Zechenverband;* Wiskott, deputy chairman, and Freiherr von Loewenstein, executive secretary, of these
mining interests.[38] The list was not necessarily a registry of those
willing to support the Class putsch but of the twelve men (including Captain Mann, Professor Bernhard, Kirdorf, Witthoefft, etc.)
who formed the *Wirtschaftsvereinigung zur Förderung der geistigen
Wiederaufbaukräfte.* Consequently, an important side effect of the
entire episode was the emergence of a clearer picture of the
Hugenberg concern than had previously been available.

The syndicate's spokesman, Ludwig Bernhard, published a
brilliant, propagandistic tract aimed at exalting Hugenberg's
financial ability and dedication to national service. He argued
that Hugenberg was not a scheming capitalist deriving personal
profit from the nationalist cause, but rather a champion of the

Raiffeisen cooperative movement who had saved the German press from the alien influence of the Jewish firms of Mosse and Ullstein. This double thesis was at once true and false. Bernhard stressed Hugenberg's role as chairman of a twelve-man committee presiding over a national trust that was administered for idealistic purposes. While the description of the firm was amazingly accurate, Bernhard totally obfuscated the fact that heavy industry provided this fund. In stressing the self-sacrifice of these men and Hugenberg in particular, he did not mention that salaries, dividends, and stipends from the several companies presided over by this *Wirtschaftsvereinigung* could enrich investors. The fact that profits from these investments might be used for subsidizing various right-wing groups and thus save mine owners from the need of assessing the treasuries of their firms was never directly stated. Moreover, in appealing for rightist sympathy, the Bernhard book made Hugenberg much more altruistic and uncompromising than he was and the syndicate much more monolithic and idealistic than it actually was.[39]

The frustrated putsch and the publicity given to his concern forced Hugenberg himself much more to the fore of German politics. His supporters did not see this as a bad thing. Indeed, the man very much behind this move to promote Hugenberg as a nationalist leader was his good friend, Leo Wegener.[40] Hard of hearing and suffering from a weak heart as well as other maladies, Wegener had retired to the Upper Bavarian village of Kreuth. Nevertheless, he played a key role in the Hugenberg concern and maintained an active correspondence with leaders in conservative nationalist circles. He and Hugenberg corresponded regularly and visited frequently.[41] More than any one, except perhaps Hugenberg's wife, Wegener had a tremendous influence on his friend.[42] While Hugenberg was taciturn and thought in highly technical and legal terms, Wegener was a vibrant personality who literally "bubbled with ideas"—many of which Hugenberg later accepted and reinterpreted in corporate and legislative language.[43]

Wegener idolized his friend and argued with Class that the different facets of Hugenberg's career uniquely qualified him for the leading economic position in the government.[44] In such a post, Hugenberg would either be the power behind the chancellor or, if necessary, assume the office himself.[45] Nevertheless, his own silent, methodical, introverted personality, coupled with lack of oratorical ability, warned Hugenberg that he did not have the personal qualifications to inspire confidence and thus fulfill an essential criterion for political leadership.[46] Hugenberg never seems to have pushed himself forward for such a post, yet he believed that factual work and not charisma was the key to good government. Convinced of his own ability, Hugenberg never stopped Wegener from touting his virtues and urging others to accept his political leadership. It was Wegener's idea to stamp the Hugenberg concern and the entire nationalist press with the term *Hugenberg press*. As he and Klitzsch agreed, "Hugenberg, wholly on his own, will then gradually be the embodiment of a healthy national movement." They concurred that an identification of Hugenberg with the nationalist right would "mean very much for the personal plans."[47] A "phalanx" would have to be built around Hugenberg to protect him and help move him forward.[48]

Despite the return of the DNVP to the opposition in May 1926, the discrepancy between the ideal goal and the compromising policy of interest groups increasingly disturbed Hugenberg.[49] Sharp reaction to the tactics of some industrial and agricultural leaders totally alienated him from moderates in these associations.[50] At the same time, however, Hugenberg believed that "dissociated from the economy, the national movement would very easily fall into the hand of demagogues [*Exaltados*] who lack a free view over the reality of things."[51] Disenchanted as he was, Hugenberg still hesitated to take the lead in publicly denouncing the new conservatism. Only further compromise by German National leaders would galvanize him into action.

At the end of January 1927, the DNVP entered the coalition government of Chancellor Marx. As the price for power, the German Nationals agreed to accept the membership of Germany in the League of Nations and the entire Locarno system as the basis of the country's foreign policy.[52] Later, the majority of the Reichstag delegates agreed to an extension of the Law for the Protection of the Republic, which contained a paragraph prohibiting the return of the kaiser to Germany. This monarchical principle helped to crystallize the conflict among conservative nationalist factions.[53] Challenging Westarp's leadership, Hugenberg found himself in the company of a minority of racists like Freytagh-Loringhoven, Pan-Germans like Gok, monarchists like

von Dommes, and reactionaries like Tirpitz.[54] He had opposed
negotiations for the coalition and then had warned Westarp that
the party could not support the principles of ideological opposition and at the same time compromise with republican policies.
Any attempt to sit on both chairs would mean that the party
would fall between the two.[55] Hugenberg expressed his oppostion to the Law for the Protection of the Republic by simply stay-
ing away from the Reichstag on the date that the majority of
German Nationals voted for it.[56]

The dilemma evoked by the party's compromise was clearly
articulated by Gottfried Traub. He wrote that, despite Westarp's
reasons for acceptance, this legislation involved a matter of principle more important than any tactical considerations. The party
was either monarchical or republican, and it should say which.
The easiest thing to do, according to Traub, would be to leave
the party—but he had to confess that there was no alternative
faction which he could support.[57] The Pan-German League had
anticipated the question that Traub raised and concluded that
establishing a new party would demand building up a whole new
organization and necessitate reliance on radical fringe-groups
such as the Hitler movement. This, Pan-Germans agreed, would
be like leading an "army without troops." The only viable alternative they saw was to capture control of the DNVP and force it
to change its course. Class had apparently discussed this alternative with Hugenberg, who fully agreed with the strategy.[58]

THE BASIS FOR HUGENBERG'S POWER IN THE DNVP

In the campaign to radicalize the DNVP, Hugenberg and the
Pan-Germans had several assets. Their first weapon was the exploitation of ideals. If interests could not unify the party, then
ideology might. The technique was to emphasize principles and
then to identify Hugenberg with them. Their second weapon was
the weakness of the German National party structure. The independence of regional party associations and the sociological
structure of these associations left ample room for Pan-Germans
to exert coordinated pressure. Hugenberg's influence over the
nationalist press was another asset for the radical nationalists.
Finally the power of the purse, which Hugenberg held, added
another valuable weapon to their arsenal.

In the beginning of 1927, Scherl published Hugenberg's
Streiflichter aus Vergangenheit und Gegenwart. The image projected by

this collection of speeches, letters, and essays was that of ideological consistency in the face of any and all opposition. The selections calculatedly sought to demonstrate Hugenberg's wisdom and the predictive validity of his policy before and during the war. Clearly the intent was to elicit greater credence in his criticism of contemporary political life. Hugenberg did not conceal his opinions about intraparty quarrels. He published his earlier letter to Hergt stating his opposition to the RDI's support of the Dawes Plan and clearly labeled himself as one of the "No-Sayers." Similarly, he included several undated essays criticizing the policy which moderates in his own party supported. Hugenberg's basic principles were the same as those he had espoused before the war. He simply demanded that the "survival of the fittest" once more become the "life principle of development."[59]

Such a position highlighted differences within the party. The unequivocal expression of these ideals and the bases of his support placed Hugenberg in direct opposition to the new conservatism that was developing on the left wing of the DNVP. Men such as Walther Lambach and Gustav Hülser, Gottfried Treviranus and Hans Schlange-Schöningen, were no less nationalist and no less hostile to Marxist socialism than was Hugenberg. But their ideals of national unity based on mutual cooperation and joint responsibility did not conform to Hugenberg's social Darwinism.[60] As these two flanks of the party approached an irreconcilable bipolarity, Westarp groped for means of uniting them. Hugenberg, however, sought to neutralize the count's conciliatory tactics by championing issues, such as constitutional revision, which were at once popular and radical.[61]

Finally on 27 September 1927, Hugenberg wrote to Westarp clearly articulating his antiparliamentary approach. He argued that participation in government impeded the party from attacking fundamental issues and that compromise would mean the loss of young people to the party. He counseled that the DNVP should have no compunction about using the power of propaganda to produce a new state system. To facilitate this, he requested that local German National organizations be allowed to criticize the parliamentary delegation—thus forming the conscience of the DNVP—and eventually "free the forces for a solution of the real task of the party." This would provide impetus to mold Germany's "leading classes" into a unified phalanx.

Moreover, on a purely tactical basis, Hugenberg asserted that this change would enable the party effectively to attack the government and capture the masses.[62]

Only later did Hugenberg send the chairman of the party a list of the twenty party leaders to whom he had sent the same letter. He had "inadvertently" omitted informing Westarp of his correspondence with these men. Among the names were key figures who favored Hugenberg's radicalism—General von Dommes, spokesman for the exiled kaiser; Theodore Duesterberg, the second leader of the Stahlhelm; Gottfried Gok, a leader of the Pan-German League; Erich Vagts, the head of the DNVP local organization in Bremen; and Grand Admiral Tirpitz, the honorary chairman of the party.[63] Westarp, no mean tactician himself, replied to Hugenberg that he too desired discussion of basic principles. He affirmed that there had to be and already was a mutual interaction within the DNVP, but he also asserted that publicizing regional criticism of the party's actions on the national level was inconsistent with disciplined party order.[64]

Checking the publication of dissident opinion within the party could not, however, stop the Pan-German attempt to infiltrate regional party organizations. The federal structure of the party allowed local bodies full control of their own affairs and freedom to select their own leaders, who ultimately chose the party leader.[65] The grass roots organization of the DNVP was never strong. Experts estimated that only about 15 percent of German National voters were card-carrying, dues-paying members.[66] Both the party central office and the local party organizations were dominated by members of the old aristocracy and the Wilhelminian bureaucracy as well as by representatives of professional lobbyists from agricultural and industrial organizations, right-wing unions, and various Lutheran organizations. The financial base of local party organizations was so weak that they could not support themselves and never met their obligations to support the central office.[67] Regional associations closer to the electorate tended to accept hard-line propaganda literally, but interest groups which filled the party coffers insisted on coalition and compromise. Parliamentary leaders schooled in rationalizing varied principles followed the dictates of lobbyists in the Reichstag but then reverted to an ideological approach when on the stump. The result was entrapment. Radicals expoited the

divergence of principle and practice. Had party leaders instructed their electorate in the realities of politics, the DNVP
might have evolved into the dynamic conservative party that
some Reichstag delegates belatedly envisioned.

Party disunity was reflected in the media. The DNVP controlled no daily paper; publications stressing a strong nationalist
position reflected the conglomerate nature of the party itself.[68]
Since Hugenberg managed the strongest nationalist press in the
country, he could and did exercise a great influence on attitude
toward the DNVP. He never submitted to party pressure and at
times allowed his press to criticize the government more severely
than the party itself did.[69] Scherl publications never took a
harshly negative attitude toward the German National party,[70]
but Hugenberg refused to check his journalists when they em-
barrassed German National leaders. As far as partisan politics
were concerned, the only obligation which he would assume was
that his publications would,

> on the basis of maintaining their independence, form an in-
> strument of definitely bourgeois, national policy which
> affirms the concept of private property and the foundations
> of an individual economy and preserves the great bases of
> tradition.[71]

In effect, Scherl journalists reported everything favorable to the
right, but editorialists bolstered Hugenberg's hard line.[72] During
these years, the circulation of Hugenberg's choice political
newspaper, *Der Tag,* ranged from 74,720 in 1926 to 71,270 in
1928; the *Berliner Lokal-Anzeiger,* which appeared twice a day, produced an average of 197,597 issues in 1926 and 215,502 in 1928; at
the same time, the *Berliner Nachtausgabe* grew in circulation form
59,631 to 151,000.[73] Undoubtedly the influence of Scherl on conservative circles in the capital and on subscribers throughout the
country was significant. However, because most people knew
what they were buying and because the circulation figures for
the more liberal Mosse and Ullstein presses were very comparable, the importance of Scherl has been overestimated.

Since most Germans generally subscribed to local papers
rather than to the more cosmopolitan press of the capital,
Hugenberg's involvement in regional newspapers was ex-

tremely important for the DNVP. Party officials estimated that five hundred to six hundred newspapers either supported the German Nationals or were favorable to them. Through the *Wipro,* the *TU,* and his other corporations, Hugenberg had considerable influence.[74] The fourteen or so papers that he directly controlled followed a line similar to that of the Scherl press.[75] His assertion that he rarely wrote for these publications and did not involve himself in their day-to-day affairs was true, but this does not disprove his direct influence on their policy.[76] Through representatives in the editorial offices, the Hugenberg strategy was relayed—particular actions and policies of the party were criticized while the DNVP as an organization was championed as the core of the national movement, the heart of a *Sammlung.*[77] Given the nature of the German press, Hugenberg's policies were important—especially for the DNVP—but they could hardly be responsible for the radicalization of the entire electorate.

Though the party did not possess its own daily, it did have direct contact with the press through its offical press releases. At the end of 1927, however, financial limitations necessitated uniting this service with Hugenberg's *Deutscher Schnelldienst.* Similarly, the *Täglicher Dienst für Nationale Zeitungen* and the *Amtliche Mitteilung der DNVP* also came under the control of the Hugenberg concern at the same time.[78] The party still maintained its own publications office, the *Deutschnationale Schriftenvertriebsstelle,* but its publication of the biweekly journal, *Unsere Partei,* and its production of various pamphlets and propagandistic literature depended on the availability of funds from the party's central office.[79] Here again, Hugenberg's influence was considerable since his contacts with the coaling magnates of the Ruhr could bring vital contributions to the party coffers. In looking back on 1927, Albrecht Philipp, one of the party leaders from Dresden, argued that Hugenberg's opposition to party policy froze vital contributions coming from industry and consequently forced Count Westarp, as party chairman, to seek out new funds.[80]

Some Ruhr businessmen—most specifically, Kirdorf, Thyssen, and Vögler—were dissatisfied with the economic policy of the DNVP. After they had returned to the cabinet in 1927, the German Nationals were involved in negotiations for a bill dealing with wages and hours, the *Arbeitszeitgesetz.* The intent of this bill

was to return to the eight-hour day with time-and-a-quarter pay
for overtime. Kirdorf argued that such a law would cut profits
and eventually hurt the worker himself. If the party persisted
with a policy of collaboration, Kirdorf warned, he and his friends
would draw the necessary conclusions for themselves and the circle they represented.[81] Hugenberg, of course, expressed his full
agreement with this criticism.[82] Westarp pointed out the danger
of industry's relying solely on one party: 75 percent of the German electorate were workers, and if they, too, supported only
one party, they would always have a majortiy. The count wanted
to discuss such problems with Kirdorf, Thyssen, Vögler, and
others.[83] Apparently he did meet with Thyssen[84] but was only
partly successful, for Thyssen later notified Westarp that as
"responsible leaders of the economy, we simply cannot tolerate
the continued disregard of our warnings."[85] Both Thyssen and
Kirdorf preferred a more radical approach, which ultimately led
them to support the NSDAP.[86] Precisely what this meant in terms
of financial subsidies remains disputed.

Hugenberg and the coaling industry had relatively high sums
which could freely be used to patronize rightist movements of all
kinds. Scherl records alone indicate that from an account totally
at his disposal, Hugenberg received M 1,050,000 in 1924, M
1,000,000 in 1925, M 529,200 in 1926, M 710,000 in 1927, and M
700,000 in 1928. In addition, a separate electoral fund at Scherl
dispensed M 200,000 both in 1924 and in 1928. The firm also
turned over M 300,000 in 1925 and, thereafter, M 325,000 for
each year through 1928 to the *Werbegemeinschaft,* a subsidiary
established by the *Wirtschaftsvereinigung zur Förderung der geistigen
Wiederaufbaukräfte* to support varied rightist undertakings.[87]
When to all this is added the power which Hugenberg had exercised over electoral funds directly contributed by businessmen,
there could be no wonder that politicians respected his power
and that less radical magnates from the Ruhr, such as Reusch
and possibly Krupp, sought to end his influence on heavy industry's political contributions.[88]

Hugenberg, however, was in a strong position. Having concentrated his energies on the development of his control over the
media, he had moved further and further away from industrial
circles which had originally supported him. Still a member of the
powerful presidium of the Reich Association of German Indus-

try, he opposed the tactical maneuvering of its leaders and disdained their attempts to collaborate with the regime. His nationalist insistence on autarchy and his diametrical opposition to all forms of unionism represented not the attitude of most businessmen, but the ideology of the Pan-German League. No longer concerned with the profits and losses of any industry other than the media, Hugenberg was free to criticize the immediate demands of industrialists for practical solutions, and he reverted to the simplistic solutions espoused by Pan-Germans since the prewar period.[89] Some Ruhr magnates such as Thyssen and the still influential, but retired, Kirdorf, undoubtedly favored his militancy. Others such as Vögler, Brandi, and Springorum, were ambivalent. Reusch, Duisberg, von Siemens, and others were undoubtedly opposed. Hugenberg, however, had the propagandistic advantage. Industrialists who opposed socialism and feared democracy had great difficulty in disassociating themselves from simplistic Pan-German ideology.

Hugenberg exploited this advantage to the full when his opponents challenged him. He refused to renegotiate the postwar arrangement which had been established by industry to channel political funds to the DNVP.[90] Confronted with this refusal, Count Westarp sought to circumvent Hugenberg by directly appealing to leaders in heavy industry. With the assistance of Reichert, business manager of the Association of German Iron and Steel Industrialists, the chairman of the DNVP with Reusch, Springorum, and Baron Thilo Wilmowsky, Krupp's brother-in-law, ultimately established a "Joint Committee of the German National People's Party and the People's Party.[91] Despite the appeal of the chairman of the *Bergbaulicher Verein* (Brandi), Reusch refused to include Hugenberg as a member of the committee. (In fact, he had originally made his cooperation dependent on the exclusion of Hugenberg.) The general director of the GHH laconically informed Brandi that the committee was already established and that his request to include another "parliamentarian" might best be directed to Westarp.[92] It was the conciliatory count who ultimately invited Hugenberg to participate in this joint endeavor.[93]

The new committee in no way reconciled Hugenberg to the policy of moderation and compromise. His *Streiflichter* had set the tone, and in a speech before the Committee of German National

Industrialists on 7 February 1928, he reiterated his position. With regard to the appeasing approach of colleagues in the DNVP and associates in the RDI, Hugenberg simply said:

> there is no longer any purpose in exchanging opinions over these matters. I will only state on this that my personal opinion has gone so far as to conclude that any government of the present state would not be in the position—as conditions now exist—to resolve difficulties.[94]

Cooperation was thus totally rejected. Any one who attempted it was in danger of being labeled an opportunist. Hugenberg was convinced that radical action was necessary, and he indicated his strategy when he commented:

> I was and am of the opinion that we have to come out of this war of position, in which German politics have come to a standstill in the last years, and return to a mobile warfare and that it is a matter of opening up this war of motion from where it is possible, to attract and have pushed to us other armies, if I can use that expression, which do not belong to our own.[95]

Thus while Pan-Germans like Kirdorf joined the Nazis, Hugenberg remained within the German National organization but sought to develop an opening to the radical right.

As Hugenberg had begun championing this approach, the party once more left the government and returned to the opposition in the beginning of 1928. Reasons for leaving included none of the fundamental objections raised by Hugenberg or other radicals within the organization. It was simply that the party leaders could not agree with the DVP and the Center on the nature of a school law.[96] Opponents of the German Nationals indicated that the party wanted to return to the oppositon so that it could maximize its propaganda during the forthcoming elections. This is, of course, exactly what the party could do most vociferously. More than ever before, however, the DNVP had a problem. When Hugenberg said that the time was ripe for a change from a policy of stability to one of movement, he placed his finger on a very grave issue.

The party structure that had been molded during and after the revolution of November 1918 did not meet the real needs of

society. Ideological approaches had forced some voters into uncomfortable categories. However, socioeconomic demands of
different groups emphasized interconnections among factions.
For instance, industrialist representatives in the DNVP, the DVP,
the Center, and the DDP could work together but had to heed
the general principles of their parties. At the same time, right-
wing unions had representatives in the DNVP and the DVP, but
frequently they had more in common with union leaders in the
Center and even the SPD than they had with the representatives
of industry in their own party. Such cross-connections were extremely important for the development of coalition government. However, when a particular group felt that a party did not
adequately defend its interests, its representatives could bolt the
party. So it was with *völkisch* radicals who left the DNVP, and with
agricultural representatives who joined the *Christlich-und Nationale
Bauernpartei,* and with the petite bourgeoisie who joined the
Wirtschaftspartei.

Those close to the political pulse of the country realized that
new forms of political organization would emerge. Some analysts
thought that union leaders and agricultural organizers might
unite the "little people" into a large party of the middle.
Westarp and industrialists such as Reusch apparently hoped that
the collaboration of the DVP and DNVP might produce a strong
bourgeois party to the right of the Center.[97] In contrast, Hugenberg emphasized the counterrevolutionary image of the German
National party as the focal point of a large national movement
and encouraged radicals who dreamed of uniting extremists
from the Stahlhelm, the ADV, the NSDAP, and various fatherland organizations into a single superright-wing party.[98] In effect,
he reverted to the themes of counterrevolution and crisis politics
that he had encouraged in the earliest days of the republic.

Despite these differences in approach, German National electoral propaganda sought to satisfy everyone. Westarp set the
tone when he described the party as "the bearer of national
idealism."[99] Behind the scenes, however, the determination of
candidates for election to the new Reichstag provided an opportunity for testing the strengths of different factions. As the advocate of radicalism, Hugenberg did not fare well in this contest.
Through Springorum of the *Ruhrlade,* the elite organization of
key leaders in the Ruhr, funds for the election of the major in-

dustrial candidates such as Reichert, Hasslacher, and
Rademacher came directly to Westarp.[100] Since these men did not
support his radicalism, Hugenberg was more concerned with
securing safe placement for his ally, Reinhold Quaatz, and for
Paul Bang, the economic expert of the ADV.[101] Industrial candidates paid from M 50,000 to M 100,000 for a secure position on
an electoral list.[102] Since the total budget of the party central
office for the election was M 403,970, these contributions from
industry were extremely important.[103] Because of the financial
resources   made   available   to   him   through   the
Wirtschaftsvereinigung—the coaling interests—Hugenberg played
an important role in financing partisan interests.[104] His refusal or
his delay in forwarding funds to the party treasurer was a potent
threat, and he used it readily. On the eve of the election when all
other possible funds had been exhausted, Westarp was so frustrated that he wrote Hugenberg:

> Evidently I must, if you persist in the point of view of your
> writing, immediately resign as party chairman and an-
> nounce the bankruptcy of the party.[105]

Apparently this ultimatum led to some settlement of the
problem. After all, Hugenberg did not want to destroy the
DNVP, but to redirect it.

In his personal campaign for reelection, Hugenberg was
mightily challenged by members of the *Jungdo,* Mahraun's
paramilitary organization. Fortunately for him, their inaccurate
and sometimes very personal charges allowed him the opportunity to sharpen his electoral image. Hugenberg followed the
Bernhard defense by emphasizing that he was not a plutocrat,
but a champion of the cooperative movement. He was not the
agent of heavy industry in the press, but the new Hermann who
saved the national press from the incursions of mobile capital
and international Jewry. Repeatedly, Hugenberg stressed *his independence* of industrial pressure groups and emphasized the need
for agricultural programs.[106] These themes, coupled with his demands for constitutional reforms, combined to present the total
image of the man indebted to no one and concerned only for the
nation. Hugenberg's electoral campaign was important not only
for his election to the Reichstag, but for his position in the national movement as a whole.

When the ballots of 20 May 1928 were finally counted, the DNVP—despite the favorable propaganda of the Hugenberg press—had lost almost two million voters. Its parliamentary representation in the Reichstag sunk from 111 seats to 78. The DVP, the Center, the DDP, and the BVP had all lost seats. On the left, the SPD gained one and a quarter million voters and the KPD, a half million. The Hugenberg syndicate headlined the results as a "sudden move (*Ruck*)" to the left.[107] Undoubtedly, German National losses were largely due to fragmented voting for small splinter parties representing particular interest groups, especially the traditional middle classes.[108] Party leaders would have to reevaluate their positon and seek ways of recouping these losses. Essentially, the DNVP would have to determine whether the decline was due to its failure to live up to its counterrevolutionary rhetoric or its refusal to cooperate more fully with moderate parties.

The battle took shape at a meeting of the Reichstag delegates on 12 June. Positing that a party with the strength of the DNVP had to accept responsibility, Count Westarp defended his leadership. He pinpointed the basic problem as the unwillingness of economic interests to compromise. In his view, only a policy emphasizing ideological questions could strengthen the party. Hugenberg immediately attacked the count and charged that cooperation and compromise had weakened the party. When other party leaders spoke of conciliating rightists in the DVP, with an eye toward the election of new Reichstag officers, Hugenberg deliberately shocked the group by proposing that they elect a communist. He insisted, "We absolutely have to reject the concept of positive cooperation." When Westarp argued that even opposition had to have its limits, Hugenberg retorted that the party should only enter the government when "a change in the system can be expected."[109]

THE ELECTION OF HUGENBERG AS PARTY CHAIRMAN

Three weeks after the election, an article by the German National Reichstag delegate, Walther Lambach, so intensified factionalism that a split in the DNVP seemed imminent. In the *Politische Wochenschrift,* Lambach theorized that for the general populace the esteem shown President von Hindenburg overshadowed that of the deposed monarchy. He argued that the popularity of the Socialist referendum on the confiscation of royal property and the contrasting electoral losses of the DNVP reflected this same decline of monarchical sympathy. He concluded that if the party were to develop a popular form of conservatism (*Volkskonservatismus*) and attract youth, it would have to accept nationalist republicans as well as monarchists into its ranks.[110]

Every German National knew the party platform and knew that restoration was not an immediate problem. Young conservatives might well have raised this issue purely as a means of attacking party reactionaries. The journal in which Lambach had published favored a dynamic conservatism. Its editor, Walther Ullmann, and other German National contributors promoted a cooperative conservatism that would enable the party to work within the state.[111] These DNVP leaders along with other intellectuals such as Wilhelm Stapel, the editor of *Deutsches Volkstum,* and Georg Quabbe, the author of *Tar a Ri,* fostered the development of a dynamic conservatism which, through a process of evolution, would produce important changes in German society.[112] Such young conservatives viewed Hugenberg as a reactionary who wished to restore the social conditions of the Wilhelmine era, whereas they projected a new type of society based on the organic relationship of mutually responsible classes. These men were not liberals or democrats in any traditional western sense,[113] but their ideas conflicted sharply with the social Darwinism propounded by Bang and the ADV. Despite its dislike of unions, the Reich Association of German Industry hesitated to challenge nationalist unions like Lambach's DHV. Hugenberg, however, was firmly convinced that the "characteristic of our bourgeois world today is the fear of laying hold of the true problems and relations of the moment."[114] It was not monarchism, but more fundamental issues that divided German Nationals.[115]

Industrial delegates in the DNVP Reichstag delegation feared that the entire Ruhr would be linked with Hugenberg's position and that his strong opposition to unions would create practical difficulties for industry. They complained that he was making it "wholly impossible" for them to cooperate with him.[116] Springorum, treasurer of the *Ruhrlade,* conferred with Hugenberg and bluntly confirmed that the iron industry would no longer work through him in the distribution of its electoral funds to the party central office. Hugenberg was "very concerned" (*sehr betroffen*) and agreed with Springorum that he and the other industrial delegates in the DNVP should collaborate.[117] The Ruhr, however, was not united in its political policy. The very fact that Springorum specified that the iron interests would no longer use Hugenberg as their political contact indicated that he did not speak for the coaling community. Obviously, the more radical attitude of a patriarch such as Kirdorf would have a great impact on the *Wirtschaftsvereinigung,* which Hugenberg firmly controlled.[118] Hugenberg calculated that if he could hold out against his opponents and force the DNVP to accept a more radical approach, industry would be compelled to accept his policy. From his experience in distributing political funds, Hugenberg knew that in the final analysis unscrupulous politicians could manipulate even the steel arm of the Ruhr.

Debate on party policy intensified with the discussion of the Lambach case in the German National Reichstag delegation. The majority of deputies avoided a substantive decision on the union leader's attitude and did not question his right to debate a basic principle of the party. They did, however, censure the public and negative manner in which he had approached the problem.[119] Hugenberg and his allies were not satisfied. At the meeting of the full party leadership on 8 and 9 July, Count Westarp argued that "positive cooperation" was not synonymous with surrender of principle and pleaded that a party which had lost one-third of its votes had to maintain unity above all else.[120] But under the leadership of General von Dommes, fifteen of the forty-five regional associations challenged Westarp's leadership and supported Hugenberg's radicalism.[121] They opposed the submission of the Lambach case to the party court and instead demanded his immediate expulsion from the DNVP. A full-day recess failed to produce a satisfactory compromise. While the majority of the regional associations endorsed Westarp's advocacy of judicial proceedings, the recalcitrant group abstained from voting.[122]

The day after the party meeting, the local chairman of the Potsdam party association (*Landesverband Potsdam* II), Steinhoff, announced that his group had expelled Lambach from the party. The regional executive committee determined that he had violated party canons and had brought the honor of the DNVP into question. Fundamentally, the rationale for expulsion represented the attitude of the Hugenberg faction.[123] Because the essential issue dealt with social and political policy, some of Lambach's friends encouraged him not to appeal the decision to the party's higher court. This alienation in the ranks of the right-wing workers' movement was precisely what major industrialists feared. Parliamentary collaboration of small farmers from the *Christlicher Nationaler Bauernbund* and white-collar employees might have resulted in the formation of a new party, which would have increased the pressure on the large landholders and heavy industry.[124] The conciliatory policy of Westarp and moderate leaders in the DNVP prevented such a development, and ultimately Lambach did appeal his case.

The day before the party court rendered its verdict, Hugenberg published his position.[125] The faith of a confused nation could rest only in men who combined ideas with action, he argued, not with parliamentarians and tacticians. The DNVP had to be viewed, "not as a parliamentary party in the proper spirit of the word, but as a grand group of men—as a community of opinion, not as a community of interests...." In the last years, under the influence of men who had catered to pressure groups, the party had suffered defeat. "Only an ideological party which is led and which leads can save the soul and the economy of the German people!" Arguing more specifically against Lambach, Hugenberg charged that the union leader had attacked a core principle and then demanded that anyone who would destroy German National principles would have to work outside the DNVP. In his view, the party that would save the nation was not a conglomeration of ideologically diverse bourgeois elements—such a "mishmash" (*Brei*), Hugenberg claimed, could not save or lead Germany. What was needed was a strong force of like-minded leaders who would use their common faith in the nation to rally a political bloc and mold it into a block of stone.[126]

The party court did not agree with Hugenberg and his allies. While the judges rejected the article on monarchism because of its form and content, they determined that Lambach did not mean to contravene party principle, but had only intended to aid the party by introducing the problem for discussion. The court declared that Lambach's personal devotion to the monarchy and his respect for it were beyond reproach.[127] Hugenberg had lost that battle, but the basic struggle among German Nationals transcended the Lambach case and focused on control of the party. A party congress, which could elect a new party leader later in the year, would ultimately decide the question. In his drive to reorient the party, the newspaper magnate had two important resources. The first was the unified determination of the fifteen party associatons that had opposed Westarp in July, and the second was a widely circulated report on the reform of the party structure.

Shortly after the decision was announced, the fifteen dissident organizations met in Berlin to discuss further action. Under the chairmanship of General von Dommes, they formally petitioned Westarp to summon a party congress for the end of October. The Lambach controversy would be the first topic on the agenda. These associations wanted the party to redesign its total economic policy, to introduce changes in the organization of the party, and to promote a plebiscite on constitutional issues. Through the altered course, which would underline the party's anti-Marxism, they expected to attract new voters—especially from the ranks of youth.[128]

The second tool exploited by Hugenberg dealt exclusively with the problem of party organization. In June, before the Lambach essay had engendered a full-blown controversy, the party leadership delegated Quaatz and Steinhoff to examine the party apparatus and to make recommendations for improvement.[129] They concluded that a general discontent existed within the DNVP and recommended a general overhaul of the party executive committee, the party bureaucracy, and the party leadership.[130] Before discussing their proposals with Westarp, they sent hundreds of copies of their report to party members throughout the country—a tactic that Wegener had strongly recommended.[131]

Apparently influenced by the Pan-German view that radical party members should determine DNVP policy, Quaatz and Steinhoff argued that Reichstag delegates should not interpret party principles. The two evaluators also claimed that the system of maintaining one party chairman and two deputies was inefficient and divisive. They advised that the offices of party chairman and chairman of the Reichstag delegation should not be united, as they were in the person of Westarp, for this involved the total party in tactical parliamentary measures. They proposed a three-man leadership for the party.[132] Precisely how such a triumvirate would control the party was not spelled out.[133] Westarp opposed this tripartite arrangement and asserted that any attempt to regulate the function of the Reichstag delegation would be an infeasible infringement of the constitutional responsibility of the delegates.[134]

Hugenberg and his Pan-German allies campaigned vigorously among the local party associatons.[135] His friends were glad that their leader was in an "excellent fighting mood."[136] Through Wegener, Hugenberg made contacts with the Stahlhelm in order to discuss the development of a rightist bloc.[137] Radicals propagandized that the conflict in the party was essentially a determination on "whether the large right which is perhaps being formed will stand under ideological-conservative or liberal-democratic leadership."[138] Such dramatic dichotomization had always characterized DNVP propaganda; now the radical faction used it against the party itself.

On 8 October 1928, Hugenberg met with the provincial organizations that supported him. After von Dommes had proposed that they nominate Hugenberg for the position of party leader, the newspaper magnate expressed his thanks and then pointed out that he would find it difficult to devote himself entirely to the party. He clearly stated that he could not cut himself off from his life's work, the administration of his press concern. He endorsed the idea of a triumvirate as a means of preserving the unity of the party, but not if it meant the sacrifice of principle. If he were to fulfill their expectations of party leadership, they would have to leave him full power to do as he thought best. No one raised any objections to Hugenberg's reservations, and the group unanimously endorsed von Dommes's resolution.[139] On the same day, representatives of the sixteen local party associations that supported Westarp met in Berlin. Moderates had agreed that the current structure of the party was inadequate for articulating party policy, but no agreement on the future direction of the party was reached. As the conference day approached, the party was split. Both sides negotiated, but neither intended to surrender its position.

The party congress opened on 20 October. Westarp's introductory remarks emphasized the seriousness of the crisis. The count predicted that what would happen in that hall could "become a turning point in the history of the entire German people." He accentuated the fact that the party's leadership problem was not solely a problem of personalities, but of basic political philosophy. In his estimation the delegates had to find a modus operandi that would enable the majority and the minority within the party to work together.[140]

While Westarp was speaking, Hugenberg's supporters passed out printed explanations of their candidate's positon.[141] This propaganda tactic fanned antagonisms. In the sharp debate that ensued, the former Reich minister of the interior, von Keudell, delivered a passionate repudiation of Hugenberg and virtually accused the newspaper magnate of buying votes. He charged that Hugenberg's personality did not make him a suitable party leader, that he would never be able to attract youth, and that the party's image would be severely weakened if the delegates elected as party chairman a man so intimately associated with industry. These charges interjected a strong note of emotionalism into the proceedings and probably alienated many of the undecided delegates at the meeting.[142] Hugenberg appealed to Count Westarp himself to defend this challenge to his probity, and Westarp felt forced to reject Keudell's personal attack.[143] Thus the imprudence of his adversaries worked to Hugenberg's tactical advantage. Hugenberg himself carefully exploited this in his own speech.[144]

That the newspaper magnate attempted to, or actually did buy votes is highly improbable. Certainly Hugenberg's proponents recognized his financial and organizational power, but Hugenberg was also an ideologue who upheld a definite political philosophy, which these men favored. For many delegates, Hugenberg was an idealist who could help finances and provide publicity for the party. After the electoral losses of May, all party leaders agreed on these necessities: the party had to inspire confidence in its ideals, solve its financial problems, and secure favorable publicity.[145] Hugenberg could satisfy these needs.

Debate over the election of a party chairman dragged on; moderates tried to win support for Hergt or even for some collegial group that would include moderate influence. Compromise seemed possible. Finally in a secret test vote, a bare ma-

jority agreed to accept Hugenberg as sole party chairman.
General von Dommes then moved that an official written ballot
be taken. No candidate formally opposed Hugenberg.[146] The
three men who counted the votes were sworn to secrecy and the
statistical results were not announced. Hugenberg had received a
majority.[147] The DNVP now had a new chairman and a new
course to follow.[148]

In a speech that he gave on the next day, Hugenberg delineated the general policy that the party would follow. He argued
that he did not intend to criticize individuals or the party, but
general trends in Germany. He clearly articulated his determination to guide the party according to long-range nationalist principles rather than short-range tactical advantage. In regard to
methodology, Hugenberg argued that the party had to be a
movement and the bearer of principle which would attract
splinter groups and other nationalistic organizations; he wished
to form a solid front that would eventually replace the Weimar
government with the dynamic leadership of a nationalist elite.[149]

Reaction to Hugenberg's election recognized that radicalism
had triumphed in the DNVP. The Centrist paper, *Germania,* predicted that the German Nationals would follow a sharply
different course with world-wide significance.[150] The *Vossische
Zeitung* claimed that the party under Hugenberg would rely on
reactionary industrial leaders and the paramilitary groups that
they supported; one of its staff writers insightfully predicted that
the DNVP would become the tool of Pan-German power politicians.[151] There can be no doubt that radicalism was triumphant
in the DNVP. The chairman of the ADV prided himself on the
victory and congratulated the leaders associated with the league
for preparing Hugenberg's election with "so much skill and
tact" and for presenting a "most unpleasant surprise" to their
opponents.[152] Similarly, Hugenberg's adherents rejoiced that "a
very strong combination of press and party organization is
formed, such as had never before been available to any party."[153]
The Scherl press and its regional publications clearly indicated
that the DNVP had taken a new course.[154]

The very source of Hugenberg's radical support and strength,
however, presented obstacles to the development of the party.
Even his nationalist critics charged that the head of the great
press syndicate was a plutocrat, that his publications, especially

the evening tabloid *Nachtausgabe,* were blatantly tolerant of immorality, that his movie houses showed antinational films, and most important of all, that his entire syndicate stood at the disposal of industry in its antiunion attitude.[155] If Hugenberg were to mold the DNVP and other rightist forces into a solid bloc, he had to overcome this image and rally powerful leaders to his side.[156] When the factual opposition of most industrialists and agrarians to Hugenberg's radicalism was added to this negative view, the liabilities of his leadership far outweighed the assets which he brought to the party.

For the managerial mind of Hugenberg, securing control of the DNVP apparatus was much easier than projecting a new image or extending his power base. He exploited the reform plan of Quaatz and Steinhoff and demanded extensive reorganization of the party. At the December meeting of local party delegates, Hugenberg cleverly concentrated power in a group of loyal supporters.[157] As Class later explained to the leaders of the ADV, the wide range of powers that Hugenberg had in organizing the party executive committee and in making party appointments made Hugenberg the virtual dictator of party policy. Class also pointed out that the real stronghold of dissidence within the party was the Reichstag delegation.[158]

Before introducing party statutes that would curtail the freedom of the German National delegation, Hugenberg hoped to gain wider popular support for his position. The proposed revision of the Dawes Plan provided an opportune vehicle for his propagandistic appeal. With the aura of a man respected as an economic expert, Hugenberg blamed the plight of the farmer and the economic difficulties of the middle classes on reparations payments. The hand of the reparations collector thus touched the two most dissatisfied groups in the German economy. The reparations issue also enabled him to mobilize popular concern with war-guilt and the Versailles settlement.[159] Hugenberg also pushed the DNVP further to the right as he began to emphasize his social program. He criticized welfare payments and union dues charging that such contributions prevented individual saving and self-help.[160] His press organization expanded this argument by publishing Gustav Hartz's *Irrwege der Sozialpolitik,* a book that attacked the entire welfare system and proposed replacing it by a system of compulsory saving.[161] At the same time, party policy cited the need for constitutional reform and presented proposals for sweeping changes in the structure of the state.[162] As it explicitly began to reshape the party, Hugenberg's heavy hand was felt in every area of policy.

Illness, in March 1929, prevented the new party leader from taking a direct part in discussion of constitutional reform,[163] but in April the DNVP executive committee adopted his plans. Apparently the threat of the dissidents, during this period of his illness, galvanized his determination to gain full statutory control over the Reichstag delegation.[164] At the meeting of the executive committee on 9 April, Hugenberg had Friedrich von Winterfeld introduce a resolution that would have given the party chairman the sole right to determine whether the party would participate in the government. The leader of the Reichstag, Count Westarp, had not been previously informed of this resolution and vociferously opposed it. Despite general subservience to Hugenberg, the committee was still unprepared to alienate a significant portion of the party's elected delegates without at least hearing their position. The resolution was tabled until the next meeting.[165]

In a stormy confrontation on 2 May the parliamentary delegation took up the von Winterfeld motion. The proposal evoked deep-seated suspicions and discontent. Old wounds were opened between those who had voted for the Dawes Plan and those who had voted against it, those who favored participation in the government and those who opposed it at all costs, those who supported Hugenberg and those who did not. The new party chairman rejected Hergt's attempt to assuage the combatants and simply remarked, "I want the debate to continue." The defeat of the resolution by a vote of 34–29 evidenced the opposition to Hugenberg in the Reichstag delegation.[166] Still Hugenberg was determined to control the DNVP parliamentarians. At the next meeting of the party executive committee, the members, including Westarp, agreed to a slightly modified version of the von Winterfeld proposal.[167] Hugenberg had full control of the party. His goals, however, demanded a Sammlung much larger than the DNVP provided.

3 The Attempt to Build a Radical Nationalist Bloc

In his desire to mold a united national bloc, Hugenberg pursued a policy of polarization. Rejecting attempts to establish a moderate, conservative consensus, Hugenberg debated political issues in terms of a simplistic, philosophic disjunction—a man was either for the nation or he was against it. Careful engineering of a political dichotomy would, he believed, force moderates to either end of the political spectrum and ultimately allow radical nationalists to seize control of the state. This simplistic, Pan-German tactic accounts not only for Hugenberg's direct appeal to the masses outside the traditional party structure, but also for his repudiation of the conservative cabinet of Chancellor Heinrich Brüning. Hugenberg's crisis politics exacerbated the discontent produced by the world economic crisis of 1929 and facilitated the ready acceptance of a radical national position by millions of voters. The discontented electorate, however, did not rally behind Hugenberg, but behind Adolf Hitler.

THE REICH COMMITTEE AGAINST THE YOUNG PLAN

To achieve his goal of *Sammlung*, nationalist unity, Hugenberg had a grand design to rally dissidents on the right. Just as his administrative skill and stubborn determination had secured him a firm position in the business world before the war and in the communication media after the war, so Hugenberg anticipated that these same qualities would reward his efforts in politics. He believed that "fate is only for the weak and the sick. The strong, the healthy man molds his fate and that of his nation (*Volk*) with his own will."[1] In the war of motion, which he intended to initiate on the political front, Hugenberg planned to cooperate with the Pan-German League in forming a general staff which would enlist radicals not only from the DNVP and the league, but also from dissident organizations such as the United Fatherland Associations, under Count Rudiger von der Goltz. He anticipated that an assemblage of "black-white-red" forces revitalizing the counterrevolutionary propaganda of the immediate postwar era could summon the six million nonvoters to the polls and initiate a swing to the radical right.[2]

Hugenberg's plan rested on sound political analysis. The political fermentation of 1928–1929 indicated that the party structure established after the war did not aptly represent the changing ideological, social, and economic scene of the coming decade.[3] While politicians like Stresemann dreamed of a new liberal organization and neoconservatives like Quabbe theorized about a different political movement, Hugenberg demanded a more radical alternative. In this, he relied heavily upon the collaboration of the Stahlhelm, the Union of Soldiers from the Front, organized by Franz Seldte and Theodor Duesterberg. Since the promulgation of their "Fürstenwald Hate Message," denouncing Weimar and all it represented, this veterans' organization had embarked on a clearly antiparliamentary course.[4] Even before his election to the chairmanship of the DNVP, Hugenberg had been in contact with Seldte and Duesterberg and was privy to their plans to initiate a plebiscite demanding changes in the constitutional order.[5] He capitalized on this momentum and sought to redirect it in line with his own plans.

In the spring of 1929, debate on the reparations issue once more surfaced as a highly emotional problem. Industrialists, agrarians, and politicians debated the meaning and significance of the nascent Young Plan. Hugenberg and radical propagandists immediately seized the issue as a golden opportunity for rallying the masses much more effectively than had the relatively abstract concepts of constitutional reform. A campaign against reparations could transcend party lines and entice millions of nonvoters to unite in condemnation of the republic. At a meeting of the DNVP executive committee on 15 June 1929, members agreed to the possibility of introducing a plebiscite against "tribute" and "slavery" for their "children's children" or a plebiscite against the "war-guilt lie." Party leaders determined that in this matter, the DNVP would not act as a party, but as a "member and strongest parliamentary representative of the nationalist movement."[6] Hugenberg then boasted that he had not become a party leader to sponsor ineffectual discussions in the Reichstag, but to free the national movement from the frozen and lifeless hands of the parliamentary system.[7] In a similar vein, his editorials continually emphasized the theme that the national front was finding itself and growing together by dint of an ineluctable drive.[8]

From the very beginning, however, Hugenberg's grand strategy was a serious gamble. Despite widespread condemnation of the policy of fulfillment and of international socialism, dissidence and discord continually characterized the German right. Certainly most of the leading industrialists did not favor the radicalism that Hugenberg advocated. When Albert Vögler, an intimate of the Hugenberg concern, dramatically resigned his post as an independent expert at the Paris negotiations and repudiated the Young Plan on 17 May 1929, he became a hero in the eyes of many of his colleagues in the Ruhr.[9] Nevertheless, his successor, Ludwig Kastl, executive secretary of the Reich Association of German Industry, accepted the settlement reached at Paris.[10] Diplomatically, the presidium and executive board of the RDI agreed with Kastl that the plan was a political resolution of the reparations crisis and, at the same time, conceded to Vögler the idea that the new financial burden would tax Germany beyond its limits. A decisive acceptance or rejection of the plan was avoided.[11] Similarly, the *Langnam Verein*, the Association for the Protection of Common Economic Interests in Rhineland and Westphalia, refused to endorse Thyssen's demands for unambiguous opposition to the plan. His strident tone was apparently modulated in the official position assumed by the chairman of the group, Paul Reusch, director of the *Gutehoffnungshütte A.G.*[12] The resolution of the *Langnam Verein* in effect agreed with the main thrust of the position assumed by the RDI. It simply read:

> The Young Plan represents a political and not an economic resolution of the reparations question. The Rhenish and Westphalian economic groups united in the *Langnam Verein* therefore refuse the responsibility for the possibility of fulfilling the plan.[13]

Disunity characterized the businessmen's approach to the Young Plan not merely because of divergent interests in international trade, but also because of conflicting attitudes toward the Weimar regime. Men such as Kastl spoke for moderates who still expected to work within the republic. In terms of foreign policy, such industrialists did not like fulfillment but would accept it as the only responsible tactic for ultimately terminating the system of reparations.[14] Domestically, these men rejected the radicalism of the German National right wing. Clearly antisocialist, these entrepreneurs preferred the development of a strong, right-of-center, laissez-faire party or coalition. On the other hand, a minority of disenchanted business leaders, such as Vögler, espoused a more radical approach. Fearful that the Young Plan would increase foreign investments in key German industries and undermine the national independence of the state,[15] they determined to support crisis politics. Radical industrialists knew that rejection of the Young Plan could terminate foreign credits and foster an assault on German currency in international markets.[16] Nevertheless, they preferred such economic disruption to acceptance of the plan. In this view, a national catastrophe was inevitable, and the more definitively Weimar could be labeled as the cause of the crisis, the more rapidly a national rebirth could take place. Hugenberg's elitist radicalism flourished among men like Kirdorf, who enthusiastically supported crisis politics, and he exploited the situation to win support for a national referendum. Fearing the failure of such a demagogic tactic, industrial leaders of the Ruhr, such as Fritz Springorum, treasurer of the *Ruhrlade*, were wary of a plebiscite. Nevertheless, the director of the Hoesch coal-and-steel combine and his allies were prepared to support a broad-based drive against the new reparations agreement if a nonpartisan (*überparteilich*) movement could be formed.[17] This notion was compatible with Hugenberg's view of the DNVP as the general staff of the national opposition.

Precisely how Hugenberg secured the collaboration of Adolf Hitler and the Nazis remains unclear. Though he had assisted in expelling racists from the party in 1923, the German National leader now needed them. Radical, nationalist opposition to Weimar would remain fragmented without the NSDAP. In establishing friendly personal contacts with Hitler, the intervention of Traub from the *München-Augsburger Abendzeitung*,[18] Otto Dietrich, a rightist newspaper editor from Essen, and Paul Bang, the Pan-German racist, could help smooth the way.[19] Certainly, Hugenberg and his colleagues in the *Wirtschaftsvereinigung*, i.e., the coaling magnates, had adequate funds at their disposal to establish an attractive subsidy for cooperation. In addition,

Scherl and the Hugenberg syndicate could provide valuable services for the Nazi press.[20] At the same time, exclusion from a united nationalist bloc might be interpreted as opposition. Hugenberg claimed that he had to "convince" Hitler to join the committee and apparently had to concede that the NSDAP could maintain its full independence.[21] Actually, the role of the Stahlhelm in a united rightist front was much more important to Hugenberg than that of the National Socialists. Stahlhelm membership extended from the center of the political spectrum to the extreme right, and the veterans' strong regional organization would be a valuable weapon for coordinating opposition to the regime.

In dealing with each group on the right, Hugenberg apparently emphasized the development of a united national front against reparations and against Marxism; he glossed over obstacles to a concrete and united platform. He was convinced that he could orchestrate the maintenance of national harmony and guide the development of a resounding crescendo that would end the cacophony of the republic. Aware of the vagueness of their program and refusing to surrender their autonomy, over four hundred representatives of dissident nationalist groups met in the former Prussian house of lords on 9 July 1929. The Hugenberg papers called it the birth of the united national front. Officially, the group called itself the Reich Committee for the German Initiative—precisely what the initiative would be was not spelled out.[22]

Hugenberg and Seldte were hailed as the leaders of this national committee. Hitler was there, but, in the papers directly controlled by Hugenberg, he did not merit banner headlines.[23] The *Reichslandbund*, an association of powerful landholders under the former minister Martin Schiele, the Christian National Farmers' Party (*Christlichnationale Bauernpartei*) under Albrecht Wendhausen, and Fritz Thyssen of the United Steel trust received as much or more publicity than the National Socialist leader.[24] Emphasis was on the establishment of a united front[25] with Hugenberg's DNVP the largest parliamentary force in the group. Even though he did not support the party system, it would be folly to proclaim that the German National chairman had organized the committee in order to bring Hitler to power. To argue that the Hugenberg press made Hitler *salonfähig* in this era is to distort the facts. The acceptance of Hitler by the German bourgeoisie is too complex a development to be explained in Cinderella fashion by the magic touch of Hugenberg's headlines. The collaboration of Ludendorff with Hitler in 1923 and the favorable coverage given the putsch trial in 1924 had made the Nazi leader a national figure. The attention that Kirdof and Thyssen bestowed on Hitler before the summer of 1929 made him known to industrial circles in the Ruhr and in Berlin. The flamboyance and shallowness which characterized the journalistic debate on fundamental issues had prepared the public for a demagogue such as Hitler well before 1929. In this evolutionary process, the entire German right, not solely Hugenberg and his press syndicate, were the overseers.[26] The inclusion of Hitler on the Reich Committee did not intentionally prepare the way for a Nazi dictatorship. Indeed, it seems that Hugenberg had intended to circumscribe Hitler's maneuverability and curb his radicalism by including the Nazis on this committee.

Hugenberg favored neither the social nor the economic policies of the Nazis. Just as the DNVP chairman did not want the Stahlhelm to assume an independent political position by organizing its own referendum, so he did not want the Nazis to extend their own particular power base. Just as Hugenberg did not want the Stahlhelm to deal with Springorum, for fear that a less radical consensus might affect the ideology of the committee,[27] so he wanted to assure the absorption of the more radical Nazis into a unified rightist bloc. While the public image of the committee was radical enough to satisfy the Nazis, an elitist Pan-German core would dominate its demagoguery. Though each organization on the committee controlled its own membership, the simple inclusion of the National Socialists would presumably mean that they would have to accept the joint decisions of the Reich Committee.

In effect, Hugenberg had carefully prepared his approach. Industry as well as the Nazis, the Stahlhelm as well as the DNVP would be maneuvered into positions where they would have to support the committee and the plan it presented. Since his newspapers were propagandizing this tenuous alliance as the establishment of the national front, any repudiation would appear to sabotage national interests and imply acquiescence to the "Paris tribute plan." Hugenberg intended the wide circulation of his press among nationalist readers to fuel this drive for a unified nationalist right. The tactic of organizing pressure groups and inciting popular passions was a standard attack used by the Pan-German League in Wilhelminian Germany.[28] Under a more democratic regime, Hugenberg's unified front simply carried this tactic forward by attempting to establish more tangible and visible control of rightist groups that were not easily manipulated by traditional elitists.[29] As chief of such a general staff, Hugenberg would play the key role.[30]

Confident that "above and beyond the party (DNVP) and classes a front has arisen that knows only one goal: how the revolution can be overcome and a nation of free men can again be made from the Germans,"[31] Hugenberg devoted his full attention to the Reich Committee. He communicated closely with Class of the Pan-German League and with the leaders of the Stahlhelm trying to influence all of the members of the presidium so that they would act "in the right way."[32] His greatest fear was that moderates in the national camp would weaken his drive to unite the radicals and would create a ground swell of compromisers in the nationalist opposition.[33]

The entire Reich Committee was structured to achieve this goal. Retaining as much power in his own hands as possible, Hugenberg not only sought to influence the membership of the controlling body of the Reich Committee, the presidium, but also of the specialized subcommittees.[34] Loyal representatives of his party and officials from his newspaper syndicate had key posts on the important subcommittees for finance and propaganda.[35] He sought to make himself the essential link between the committee and its industrial supporters. He even requested the treasurer of the DNVP to advance the Reich Committee M 22,000, before regular contributions began flowing into a central treasury.[36] Later he brought his own corporation more directly into play by allowing representatives of the *Ala* to offer the full assistance of its advertising facilities and by permitting the *Ufa* to plan propaganda films.[37] Hugenberg marshalled every resource he had. Scherl's accounts indicate that in addition to M 551,000 turned over to Hugenberg's discretionary account, M 400,000 were paid out "for special purposes."[38]

Because it would be the first direct and concrete statement expressing the unity of the national opposition, the exact formulation of a plebiscite proposal constituted Hugenberg's greatest challenge. On this problem, he worked closely with the Pan-German League and its legal consultants.[39] Constitutional and juridical technicalities in the precise articulation of a dissenting manifesto were extremely important. Hugenberg, Class, and their associates planned to have the proposal and its accompanying justification fully prepared so that they could present it to the Reich Committee in a cogently finalized form.[40] At Bad Kissingen during August, Hugenberg maintainted close contact with the leaders of the committee and the "Law Against the Enslavement of the German People" began to emerge.[41] The proposal demanded that the government call for an end to the occupation, reject the war-guilt clause of the Treaty of Versailles, refuse to accept additional financial burdens, and, finally, grant greater recognition to the old flag of the empire. The chancellor, ministers, and plenipotentiaries of the Reich who violated this law were to be punished with penal servitude.[42]

Stahlhelm moderates believed that the reckless stance of the National Socialists was compelling Hugenberg to advance a stronger bill than his own party would have permitted.[43] The newspaper magnate dismissed these veterans as saboteurs of his efforts. He conceded that the word "penitentiary" (Zuchthaus) might be dropped from the proposal so that "sensitive" Germans would not be offended. He did not object to the term himself and had no intention of dropping the penal clause in its entirety, since he believed the offenders would be guilty of high treason.[44] It is not clear whether the infamous penal paragraph originated with Hugenberg and the ADV or with the Nazis. Undoubtedly, however, Pan-German radicalism and Nazism found common ground in the condemnation of moderate politicians. Whatever the origins of the penal clause, once it was presented, the Nazis remained adamant in demanding its continued inclusion.

On 28 August the presidium of the Reich Committee met at Nuremberg. All of the leaders of the various groups were present except the representatives of the Reichslandbund and the Christian National Farmers' Party. Everything went as Hugenberg had calculated. After only minor revisions, the leadership endorsed the draft of the law presented by Hugenberg. The nexus between the "war-guilt lie" and the Young Plan remained intact. The issue of the flag was dropped, but, most important for subsequent developments, the presidium accepted the penal clause. The Reich Committee determined to initiate its proposal outside of the Reichstag before that body met in the fall.[45]

Hugenberg had successfully engineered his proposal through the committee without disrupting the unity of the newly allied bloc. The approval of leaders, to say nothing of the absence of the agrarian representatives, could not guarantee full support from their followers. The nationalistic right had continually cherished the cult of the individual personality and emphasized the free and creative role of individuals. Men who felt themselves powerful personalities in their own right—whether in industry, agriculture, or politics—could not be readily manipulated.[46] Many nationalists shied away from the Reich Committee. For them, the bloc that Hugenberg was seeking to create was too radical, too far to the right. They preferred a nationalist, antisocialist coalition closer to the center of the political spectrum. It was precisely this group that Hugenberg challenged. In his view, they would either have to join with him or sink into the mishmash of the middle and collaborate with socialism.

The profound split in the ranks of industry was obvious at the biennial meeting of the general assembly of the Reich Association of German Industry on 20 September. Duisberg, as chairman of the organization, must have been sure that he had a majority of businessmen behind him. Clearly, he propounded the thesis that the RDI could not exist opposed to or along side of the German state, but only within it. Thus he openly rejected crisis politics.[47] Heavy industrialists such as Vögler and Thyssen who supported Hugenberg, disagreed with Duisberg and the industries that backed him. Tensions between the iron and coaling interests and the electrochemical interests seemed very sharp, but not even the entire Ruhr advocated Hugenberg's radicalism. Reusch, the chairman of the *Langnam Verein*, privately dubbed the plebiscitary appeal "a great stupidity."[48] Nevertheless, except for Paul Silverberg, the chairman of Germany's largest lignite mining firm, none of the leaders of the Ruhr publicly opposed the plebiscite.[49]

The second large economic interest from which the Reich Committee expected strong support was agriculture. Despite the demagoguery of many agitators in the countryside, responsible agrarian leaders did not believe that the best way to control radicalism was to join it. Agriculturalists were as divided as industry on the problem of the national referendum. Major Arno Kriegsheim, a member of the presidium of the *Landbund*, agreed to oppose the Young Plan and even to support a plebiscite against it, but he refused to enter into total war with the Weimar regime by demanding that those who would accept the new reparations proposal should be jailed.[50] His approach became the official position of the *Landbund*.

On 5 September, Hugenberg met with two leaders in his party, Schiele and Count Westarp, to discuss the position of the agrarians. As president of the *Reichslandbund* as well as a member of the DNVP Reichstag delegation, Schiele promised to work for the approval of the proposed law, but he could not sanction such a move without consulting both the presidium and the executive committee of his organization. Hugenberg promised to postpone publication of the text of his proposal until after these governing boards of the *Landbund* had met. On the evening of 10 September, Hugenberg supposedly telephoned Schiele to confirm the fact that leading members of the agrarian organization had not raised serious objections to the text.[51] Then the full and unaltered legislation proposed by the Reich Committee went to the printers to be set in type and forwarded by Hugenberg's *Wipro* to papers throughout Germany for publication on the morning of 12 September. On the afternoon of 11 September, Hugenberg learned that the executive committee of the *Landbund* had refused to sanction the penal clause.[52] Up to this time, the text of the "Freedom Law" had been kept secret. Rather than halting the presses and thereby risking substantial leaks in the contents of his proposal, which would forearm his opponents, Hugenberg decided to force the *Landbund* to accept the entire proposal.

Certainly the penal provision was not the essence of Hugenberg's assault on the republic, but it did reflect the bitter and uncompromising nature of his opposition to the government. It was one thing to reject the "war-guilt lie" and the Young Plan; it was quite another to demand that agents of the republic who accepted a policy of fulfillment should be jailed. From the beginning, Westarp, in his private dealings with Hugenberg, had objected to this clause. Now the *Reichslandbund* disavowed it. The

RDI had never supported it. Once the proposal was published, some members of the DNVP Reichstag delegation informed Westarp that they, too, could not accept paragraph 4. Even the Stahlhelm did not unanimously favor this controversial paragraph.[53] On the other hand, the National Socialists fully endorsed the demand for criminal punishment of government officials. Hugenberg feared that striking the controversial clause would drive the Nazis from the Reich Committee and would herald defeat of the united bloc he sought.[54] In opting for paragraph 4, the chairman of the DNVP deliberately aligned himself with extremists rather than with moderates. Hugenberg fully recognized the ramifications of the threat confronting him and his campaign to establish a nationalist bloc. He interpreted reaction against paragraph 4 as a conspiracy of moderates attempting to drive him from the political scene by forcing him to depend upon the Hitler party. Prepared to accept the challenge, the German National chairman urged his colleague in the DNVP party office, Nagel, to spare "neither formalities nor costs" in an attempt to enlighten agrarian leaders. He was convinced that in the interest of its continued existence, the DNVP could not "detach itself from the National Socialists."[55]

In the Berlin Sport Palace on 24 September, Hugenberg issued his call for support. The organizer of the Reich Committee explained to the crowds that the law submitted to the public for its initiative rejected the "war-guilt lie" just as Hindenburg had done in his Tannenberg speech. He also protested that Germany's economic condition made the "Paris tribute plan" totally infeasible. Reiterating charges against "international mobile capital," he claimed that the Young Plan would destroy the nation's currency and affect the vital interests of every profession. At the same time, he emphasized that the Reich Committee intended to transcend current partisan interests and establish a "bloc for the formation of the future and the freeing of the Fatherland."[56] In the next three months, the Hugenberg press echoed these themes over and over again. Differences among the groups in the Reich Committee were deliberately glossed over. Again and again his editorialists hammered away at the idea of a single, unified, national front. The Hugenberg syndicate did not build up the NSDAP as the party of the future. As a shrewd entrepreneur, Hugenberg would not invest recklessly in a concern whose board of overseers he could not name. The Scherl concern and its affiliates strongly propagandized the Reich Committee and the development of a national opposition precisely because Hugenberg was in control.[57] A separate press for the publication of propaganda material for the referendum was organized.[58] Free copies of the daily publication, *Volksbegehren*, and the irregularly printed *Fort mit dem Pariser Tributplan* were widely circulated.[59] In addition, the presses of the Reich Committee issued no less than forty-one pamphlets attacking the Young Plan. The intellectual level of these publications ranged from those containing sophisticated economic arguments to those presenting simple pictures and diagrams.[60]

The volume of agitation against the Young Plan alarmed the government. At a cabinet meeting on 3 October, the Socialist minister of the interior, Carl Severing, stressed the need for expenditures to defend the cabinet's position. The ministers of Chancellor Hermann Müller agreed and appropriated M 350,000 for countering the opposition's publicity. The minister of the interior also asserted that government employees would be subject to disciplinary action if they supported the Reich Committee.[61] The Prussian government exerted similar pressure; the Socialist minister president, Otto Braun, used the state-controlled radio to warn civil servants that they were not free to sign the referendum.[62]

Between the emerging national front and the existing republican cabinet stood President von Hindenburg. Both sides solicited his support. The Reich Committee presumed that the field marshal, who had rejected the charges of war-guilt, would favor its position. Because of his oath to support the constitution, the cabinet did not expect strong opposition from the president of the republic. The old field marshal, caught in crossfire, issued a statement to the effect that no one had the right to present his views and that he would personally express his opinion at the appropriate time.[63] The president did inform the cabinet that he considered paragraph 4 to be a "nonfactual and personal political attack," but he would not allow the government to print a poster publicizing this.[64] On the other hand, his action forced the *Ufa* to cease showing its propagandistic film implying his support for the referendum. Hindenburg's position enraged Hugenberg, who charged that the president had turned against those who had elected him and was allowing himself to be used by his "true opponents."[65]

While the field marshal simply refused to take a position, other rightists leaders publicly denounced the Hugenberg proposal. Industrialists and politicians who opposed the Young Plan circulated a petition objecting to the penal provision because it would be "detrimental" to the development of foreign policy. These men bluntly concluded that "a success for the referendum would frustrate all efforts at improving the German situation for the foreseeable future." Leading industrialists—as Abraham Frowein, Clemens Lammers, Carl Friedrich von Siemens, and Paul Silverberg—were joined in this petition by such right-wing politicians as Franz von Papen and Karl Jarres.[66] Aside from Silverberg, heavy industrialists in the Ruhr were apparently so opposed to the Young Plan that not even the independent-minded Reusch felt free to sign the petition. Indeed, the vitriolic old Kirdorf, who even in his retirement had a position of respect in the Ruhr, believed that whoever refused to vote for the referendum forfeited the right to be called a German. Kirdorf, as other Hugenberg admirers, was totally convinced that the DNVP chairman had the leadership qualities necessary to save Germany.[67] Unfortunately for Hugenberg, not all his allies held him in such high esteem. Some Nazi orators boasted that old nationalist leaders, conscious of their insufficiency, had turned to Hitler for assistance. Hitler, they asserted, was giving the orders on the Reich Committee.[68] In view of these factors, Hugenberg conceded that the risk he was taking in sponsoring the referendum was much greater than he had ever anticipated.[69]

Despite these problems, Hugenberg registered an important victory on 2 November. Over ten percent of the electorate had signed the petition for the "Freedom Law." The proposal would now come before the Reichstag and, if that body refused to agree to it, the proposition would be presented to the people for a referendum. Hugenberg never expected the Reichstag to accept his proposal, but he did want his own party to maintain a united position in favor of the bill. A significant number of German Nationals, however, feared that the radical nature of the proposal would frustrate any coalition with nonsocialist parties to the left of the DNVP and bind the party to Nazi radicalism.[70]

THE DIVIDED RIGHT

Both Hugenberg and his opponents knew that the existing party structure could not accommodate their divergent views. The radicalization of the DNVP, coupled with the death of Stresemann in the fall of 1929, amplified the possibility for the emergence of a large bourgeois party to the right of the Center. Undoubtedly, this was the type of nationalist, antisocialist organization desired by military men such as von Schleicher,[71] by industrial leaders such as Duisberg,[72] agrarian leaders such as Kriegsheim, and possibly even right-wing unions such as the DHV. Hugenberg's leadership of the DNVP obviously prevented the German Nationals from developing along such lines. His persistent conclusion was that the DNVP had to pull the parties in the middle of the political spectrum further to the right.[73] A coalition government in which rightists would exercise preponderance could be acceptable, but it would have to reject the Young Plan and follow a more radically nationalist policy. Men such as Vögler, Helmuth Poensgen, and Franz Gürtner, who were loyal to Hugenberg but who feared burning their bridges behind them, apparently urged him to try such a tactic.[74]

Unwilling to leave himself open to the charge that he never attempted a policy of conciliation, Hugenberg, at the end of November, wrote to Monsignor Ludwig Kaas, chairman of the Center Party. He emphasized the criticism of the SPD, which had grown in the ranks of the Center and the DVP, and delineated his own view that an anti-Marxist bloc had to assume power in both the Reich and Prussia. The key that would permit such a development was, he argued, the position of party leaders on the acceptance or rejection of the Young Plan. He lectured Kaas that compliance with the reparations proposal would lead to the economic and cultural collapse of Germany. At the same time, Hugenberg declared that he would refuse to participate in any government which would be burdened with carrying out the financial exactions of the plan. He predicted that a nationalist regime burdened with such a fiscal policy would fall victim to the Socialists on one side and the Nazis on the other—it could not secure popular support.[75] Hugenberg thus justified his radicalism and offered the Center an opportunity to cooperate with him if that party would bow to his leadership.[76] Responsible political leaders, however, avoided identification with the Hugenberg strategy. Negotiations with the Center never materialized. Even the Reich Association of German Industry thought that the reparations payments demanded by the Young Plan could be fulfilled if the government would reorganize its economic and fiscal policies according to the advice of businessmen.[77] For such leaders, Hugenberg's unyielding position was calculated to produce a catastrophe and a sharp break with Weimar; they preferred evolution to counterrevolution.

Within the German National Reichstag delegation, tensions focused on the penal paragraph of the "Freedom Law." When Hugenberg indicated at a party caucus that he wanted all delegates to support the entire bill and that he would demand parliamentary discipline, leaders such as Hans Schlange-Schöningen criticized not merely the proposal, but Hugenberg and his policy.[78] At the party executive committee meeting on 21 November, the chairman noted the sharp criticism levied against him by the parliamentarians. He also produced a letter from one of the most popular and articulate young party leaders, Gottfried Treviranus, soliciting opinion in Bremen on the feasibility of party renewal and the development of a "new form" in which progressive conservative policy would be pursued.[79] Confronted with the rebellious tone of some parliamentary delegates, the executive committee rallied behind Hugenberg and demanded that "from all sections of the party an unreserved support of the law in all its sections is expected."[80] At the DNVP party day on 22 November at Kassel, Hugenberg reiterated his prediction that if any moderate government accepted or sought to implement the plan, the Nazis or Socialists would gain control of the state. He argued that "factual policy was impossible under the Weimar regime and consequently one was forced to drive out the devil with Beelzebub."[81] Party moderates less willing to sup with satanic forces remained silent and avoided a public confrontation.[82]

Behind the scenes, the dual problem of the penal paragraph and the move against Treviranus produced continued conflict. Finally, as the number of dissenters continued to grow, Hugenberg and his adversaries reached a compromise whereby he agreed to tolerate their absence or abstention from voting on the penal provision and they agreed not to publish their reasons for so acting. In the Reichstag on 30 November, fourteen German Nationals, including Treviranus and his supporters, refrained from voting. Then three delegates—Hartwig, Lambach, and Hülser—released a statement defining their opposition and affirming their support for Treviranus.[83] Hugenberg summoned the party executive committee and demanded expulsion of the three. Once more the entire problem of Hugenberg's leadership was heatedly discussed. The executive committee upheld the party chairman.[84] Westarp tried to prevent a growing secession, but Hugenberg refused to cooperate. In all, a total of twelve delegates left the party.[85] The count maintained his membership but resigned as chairman of the Reichstag delegation.[86] The rifts that had torn the party since the elections of May 1928 and the Lambach case had climaxed in a final irremediable rupture.

The failure of Hugenberg to establish a united radical front in his own party reflected the crisis in the entire German right. Aside from the Pan-Germans, the only significant opposition group to give its unqualified support to the "Freedom Law" was the Hitler party. This adamancy of the Nazis allowed them to stand in the vanguard of radical opposition to the Weimar regime and gain votes in the municipal elections at the end of the year. Hugenberg, nonetheless, remained confident that he had chosen the correct course. As far as he was concerned, moderate nationalists would suffocate in the mishmash of the middle. "They could not prevent the success of the national opposition." He claimed that the masses would repudiate the Reichstag's rejection of the "Freedom Law" and form a united bloc to oppose the republican system.[87]

In the last weeks before the plebiscite, the Hugenberg papers continually ran front-page ads, glaring headlines, emotional cartoons—all summoning nationalists to support the "Freedom Law."[88] Only 5,838,000 voters registered their approval of the Hugenberg proposal. This was not only less than the combined vote of the parties of the national opposition in the 1928 Reichstag elections, but also markedly less than the response to the plebiscite organized by leftist groups for the appropriation of royal and princely property in 1926.[89]

The mass base for a unified national bloc failed to materialize, and the Reich Committee itself began to crumble. The *Reichslandbund* leader, Schiele, resigned from the organization claiming that its purpose had been fulfilled.[90] Hugenberg, of course, had not organized the group merely to conduct this plebiscite, and he refused to give up his campaign. The other members of the committee remained united and assumed the title of the Freedom Bloc.[91] On 7 January, he and Seldte wrote to Chancellor Hermann Müller arguing that the total vote in the referendum was 6,293,109 and, since only 337,109 had voted against the bill, the "Freedom Law" should be promulgated. Müller simply rejected this position as an improper interpretation of the constitution.[92]

On 6 January, the Reich president had an interview with the DNVP chairman in which they discussed the possibilities of reorganizing the government in late February or March. Because he and his advisers expected a crisis over financial reforms, Hindenburg believed that the opportunity would then exist for the creation of an "antiparliamentary and anti-Marxist" government. Hugenberg would not promise either direct or indirect support for such a regime and seemed prepared to resist a cabinet that would still have to carry the burden of the Young Plan. Hindenburg was grieved by Hugenberg's position and summoned Westarp for consultation nine days later. Westarp explained that he himself thought that the party would have to sustain a cabinet which decisively excluded the SPD, but he could give no assurance that Hugenberg would countenance such support. He also indicated that prospects for a change in party leadership were dim, since the local party associations backed Hugenberg. While there were pockets of resistance to Hugenberg and while about thirty of the Reichstag delegates favored a more moderate position, they were by no means a majority. Only the DNVP delegate, Schiele, who had his own basis of power in the *Reichslandbund*, could definitely be counted on to support such a projected government.[93]

Hugenberg's fundamental policy had been clear, and his position hardened after the Hague conference had been forced to consider the possibility of nonpayment on the part of a nationalist government.[94] The final agreement did not sanction occupation in case of default, but provided for international adjudication.[95] This point infuriated Hugenberg as did the German-Polish Liquidation Agreement settling claims arising from the transfer of territory in the East.[96] The chairman of the DNVP fulminated that not only would the "tribute policy" burden Germany with impossible debts, but the treaty with Poland would mean a loss of two billion marks to the already suffering farmers of Germany. Publicly, he asserted that it would be a mistake to believe that the bogie of responsibility might induce him to join a government so heavily burdened.[97]

When the legislation necessary for the implementation of the Young Plan and the Hague agreements came before the Reichstag, Hugenberg stepped to the speaker's rostrum.[98] For the first time since the National Assembly, he directly confronted his opponents in the stronghold of the republic. In the face of the world economic crisis and particularly in view of increasing unemployment at home, Hugenberg's emotional presentation bespoke a firm conviction that acquiescence to the Young Plan and the Hague agreements would be extremely detrimental to the future of the nation. His key question was: "How could Germany pay reparations?"[99] This was the same problem that had bothered Heinrich Brüning and his Center Party.[100] The difference between Hugenberg's and Brüning's concern hinged on the former's ideological attack not only on the economic provisions of the plan, but also on the probity of his opponents in the Reichstag. After all, the legislation that Hugenberg had sponsored for the last half year would have placed those who were about to accept the Young Plan into penal institutions.[101]

As Hugenberg's opponents were quick to point out, ideological rejection of the government freed him from the burden of proposing a realistic alternative. Given the current international situation, the government parties argued that Germany could not afford the luxury of negativism, which Hugenberg proposed, but rather had to look to the advantages of the Young Plan and accept these as a marked improvement over the situation that had existed under the Dawes Plan.[102] The vote in favor of the proposed legislation received substantial support. After the last reading of the bill on 12 March, the final count was 266 to 193. Hugenberg had lost. Hindenburg signed the laws.[103]

As the president and his advisers had foreseen, the continuing economic crisis produced a governmental crisis. The problem of financing unemployment insurance divided the SPD and the DVP; the coalition collapsed. Despite the fact that the new government would be clearly non-Marxist and follow a conservative economic policy, which would include agricultural assistance, Hugenberg remained adamant in his opposition and embarked on a course that prevented his party from accepting any government that tolerated the status quo. Not even conflict among the remaining members of the Reich Committee could convince him of the danger of crisis politics.[104] Two specific factors convinced him that his ideological opposition was correct. First, the Young legislation would hamper the economic and social policies of the new cabinet, and, second, the Socialist-Centrist coalition in the largest federal state, Prussia, would limit antisocialist measures. Accordingly, those bourgeois leaders who wanted to form a viable government under the current constitutional order would have to do so not only without Hugenberg, but also against Hugenberg.

On 27 March 1930, Müller resigned as chancellor. The following day, President von Hindenburg commissioned Brüning to form a government. Negotiations for the new cabinet did not follow the usual method of party consultation; the ministers acted as individuals.[105] Although seven of the ministers from the Müller cabinet remained, divisions in the German National camp opened the way for collaboration with anti-Hugenberg, anti-Nazi, conservative leaders. Treviranus and the conservatives about him had organized to form the Popular Conservative Union (*Volkskonservative Vereinigung*), and he, as the champion of the new party, entered the Brüning government.[106] Similarly, Schiele and the *Landbund* leaders eager to secure legislation for agrarian interests were also willing to collaborate in a non-Socialist regime. Indeed, President Hindenburg specifically requested that Brüning include these two men in his cabinet.[107] Their participation threatened the viability of the DNVP.

Both Treviranus and Schiele had significant followings among German Nationals. The Hugenberg machine could discredit Treviranus and his party as turncoats and collaborators with trade unionists because of their connections with Lambach and the DHV and with Brüning and the Christian unions, but Schiele was a different case. As the respected leader of the *Reichslandbund*—an intimate DNVP ally in rightist causes—the agrarian leader could be portrayed neither as a leftist nor as a republican. Schiele informed Hugenberg that agriculture could best be served by his

(Schiele's) participation in the new cabinet. He made it extremely difficult for Hugenberg, a champion of agrarian interests, to oppose the new regime.[108]

German Nationals accused the government of trying to split the right and drive Hugenberg from the political field.[109] Indeed, the DNVP leader had run afoul of General von Schleicher, the confidant of Hindenburg who had helped to engineer the current political design.[110] The general preferred a more subtle and gradual reorientation to the right than that espoused by Hugenberg. Brüning and Treviranus also favored a gradual transition to a more conservative governmental form. This bourgeois cabinet, armed with the support of President von Hindenburg, possessed not only a substantive program with which to challenge Hugenberg, but the tactical and psychological advantage as well.[111]

With the party apparatus and his vast newspaper syndicate on his side, the DNVP leader remained a formidable opponent. Brüning and his associates, however, held some trumps which they now played against Hugenberg. Burdened with grave economic difficulties, the new regime called for increased taxes to pay for reparations required by the Young Plan and unemployment compensation. At the same time, an agricultural assistance program would be introduced to help farmers whose plight had become critical. Hugenberg wanted to reject the government completely and rely upon new elections to clarify the issues.[112] Some German National representatives of agrarian and industrial interests, however, were determined to vote for the cabinet in spite of Hugenberg.[113] Count Westarp and other DNVP delegates predicted another party split and argued that abandoned by agriculture the DNVP would experience grave difficulties in an election. Fifteen minutes before the opening of the Reichstag session, Hugenberg and his staff arrived in the party caucus-room. He requested parliamentary discipline for the maintenance of unity in the next weeks and then read a statement outlining his rather reluctant acceptance of the government.[114] The party chairman allowed no time to debate either of these issues; the delegation had to leave immediately for the Reichstag meeting.[115]

Hugenberg's speech was greeted with derisive laughter. He defended his vote for the government but then excoriated the cabinet for perpetuating the policy of fulfillment and tolerating the coalition in "red Prussia."[116] The National Socialists immediately accused him of "going to Canossa" and of practicing pork barrel politics.[117] Hitler resigned from the Reich Committee.[118] Publicly, the Nazi leader asserted that the DNVP had reached a peak in its campaign against the Young Plan, but the future now belonged to the NSDAP.[119] Hugenberg rejected Hitler's reasoning. He argued that a strong agricultural base was necessary for the nation, that agrarians had cooperated in the campaign against the Young Plan, and that without agriculture "national reconstruction" would be unthinkable.[120]

Despite Hugenberg, moderate agrarian and industrial leaders wanted to support the non-Socialist, Hindenburg cabinet. Brüning exploited this situation by linking aid to agriculture with new taxes; this *Junctim* demanded that both parts of the legislation be passed together. Rejection of the *Junctim*, the chancellor threatened, would mean taxes by decree and no agricultural assistance program.[121] In the Reichstag voting on 12 and 14 April, the DNVP split its vote 31–23 and 32–20. On both occasions, Hugenberg and his followers stood in the minority as German National dissidents, including representatives from heavy industry such as Reichert, joined agrarians in opposing the party leader.[122] A less determined man might have surrendered the chairmanship. Even the Pan-German League was critical of him.[123] Hugenberg stood trapped between the radicalism he had fostered and the moderation he would not accept. Still, he determined to salvage whatever he could from a deteriorating situation. The party executive committee solidly supported him and opposed the "Westarp group," which had voted with the government.[124]

In an attempt to hold the National Socialists in line, Hugenberg reminded Hitler that the Nazi vote was not essential for the crucial decisions in the Reichstag, and so the NSDAP left him alone to bear the responsibility. He lectured the National Socialist leader that the governmental attempt to split the DNVP was in the interest of neither the "common struggle for freedom" nor "parliamentary opposition." Cryptically, Hugenberg concluded his letter:

> I presume after the discussion I had with you several days ago, that—despite the publications of the National Socialist

press, the tone of which is certainly not compatible with
cooperation in the Reich Committee—you will hold firm to
the orally-expressed wishes regarding your letter: "as in the
proposal of two weeks ago."[125]

Precisely what Hugenberg meant by this reference is not clear.
Apparently he had reason to believe that he had some claim on
Hitler's loyalty. The situation was reminiscent of the older theme
of DNVP–DVP collaboration in which Hugenberg and Vögler
saw both parties marching separately but working for the same
goals. To what extent Hugenberg supported the idea of financial
assistance for both parties in the radical national front remains a
problem. The hope that the Nazis would win votes from the SPD
was fondly cherished not only by Hugenberg, but also by Kirdorf
and Thyssen. Hugenberg could not afford to abandon the Nazis
now that he had begun his campaign. He could use them just as
they could use money from his *Wirtschaftsvereinigung*. Unfortunately for him, neither financial power nor press power in-
sured political power. Goebbels fully understood this when he
described Hugenberg as

> The type of bourgeois calculator who had become impor-
> tant in industry and who in the last attempt undertakes the
> replacement of the eternal powers of politics with patriotic
> mechanics and formulas.[126]

The chairman of the DNVP lacked the charisma so valuable in
inspiring confidence. He needed a "drummer" to rally the
masses. He could not afford to alienate Hitler; he could try to buy
him.[127]

THE SECOND SPLIT IN THE DNVP AND THE ELECTION OF 1930

The struggle between the Hugenberg and the Westarp groups
in the Reichstag delegation was one of political life-or-death. The
newspaper magnate and his supporters made it clear that delegates who had voted for the *Junctim* would not receive the support
of the party office.[128] Disunity in the DNVP intensified. Even
those who admired the German National leader began to argue,
"Hugenberg will do something brilliant as a dictator, but he cannot be party leader and he cannot make party policy."[129] Still, his
dedicated followers saw him as the man who could bring about a

rebirth in Germany. These devotees rejected Nazism because of its socialistic tendencies and repudiated the compromise of the "middle parties." They invested in Hugenberg "not only the fate of the party, but the fate of a nation."[130] Doubtless such reverence buoyed Hugenberg and convinced him that increased efforts would ultimately be rewarded.

To recoup his strength, the chairman of the German National party developed several appeals. He continued to promote the thesis that the Brüning government was only a transitional cabinet which would assume the responsibility for the taxation necessary to fulfill the Young Plan; once this bourgeois group with its tight fiscal program had alienated the people, the Socialists would be able to take full control of the government. As an alternative, Hugenberg offered racidal nationalist solutions to the problems of the economy. He argued that agriculture needed protection from foreign competition, and, therefore, an entirely new trade policy based on the principle of autonomous tariffs had to be introduced. Similarly, to protect agricultural interests, Hugenberg proposed the establishment of a special banking agency to ensure the farmer profitable sale of his produce.[131] His most daring proposal called for the imposition of a "reparations duty" on all goods coming into the state. In this way, he concluded that 50 percent of the burden of the Young Plan would be placed upon foreign nations trading with Germany.[132] Finally, Hugenberg developed the theme that a party supporting the interests of only one economic group could not survive. Since only 20 per cent of the voting population consisted of independent farmers, the DNVP had to appeal to all vocational groups interested in the fatherland and form a spirit of community on the right.[133]

While Hugenberg was developing these themes, the Brüning government, beset by a continuing economic crisis, proposed new taxes to ease the deficit caused by the depression. The chancellor warned that if the Reichstag did not approve the new tax legislation, it would be passed under Article 48. Hugenberg and his associates opposed the taxes, but Westarp and the more moderate Reichstag delegates were prepared to accept them. To prevent another split, some of the German Nationals sought to have Brüning promulgate the new taxes by presidential decree while the Reichstag was adjourned. The chancellor had no inten-

tion of doing Hugenberg such a "favor."[134] The opposition
caused Brüning to carry out his threat of using Article 48 to enact
the new taxes by decree while the Reichstag was still in session.
Socialists immediately introduced a motion demanding the
revocation of this legislation.[135] Again Hugenberg was confronted with a dilemma.

With the delegates around Count Westarp determined to bolt
the party, this was not a propitious time for Hugenberg to wage
an electoral campaign. To gain as much political capital as possible from this situation, Hugenberg requested a meeting with
Brüning. The two protagonists, accompanied by their associates
Ernst Oberfohren and Hermann Dietrich, met on the evening of
17 July. Hugenberg spoke about his hope for a government that
would fully repudiate Marxism and the Young Plan. He expressed his desire for a change in the governmental coalition in
Prussia, a change in the Reich government, and alterations in
trade policy. Specifically, Hugenberg wanted the vote on the SPD
motion against the new taxes to be delayed until the fall.[136]

The DNVP leader had a fairly strong bargaining position. The
government parties, despite the backing of Hindenburg, were
not in an optimal position to face an election. The chancellor
conceded that he had always desired a coalition with the DNVP
in Prussia, and he pledged himself and Kaas to produce a change
by the fall. Negotiations could begin immediately, the chancellor
indicated, if the DNVP would accept the tax proposals. Hugenberg demanded the coalition first.[137] In effect, the German National leader refused to make any concessions. Brüning only
agreed to discuss the proposition of delaying the vote with his
colleagues in the cabinet. Hugenberg left the meeting with
valuable gains—he would later claim that he offered to save the
government and even to accept responsibility in the cabinet.[138]

After discussing Hugenberg's proposals with Schiele, Treviranus, and others, the chancellor firmly rejected delaying the
vote on the SPD motion.[139] Treviranus seems to have encouraged
the chancellor to hope that once more the Westarp group within
the DNVP might give the government a majority.[140] Even
Hugenberg was unsure of what would happen. When the decision on the government had to be made the next day, twen-
ty-five delegates under Count Westarp refused to vote against the
cabinet and left the Hugenberg party. The government lacked a

majority by only fifteen votes, and the Reichstag was dissolved.[141]

Hugenberg had once more taken a position against a bourgeois government that enjoyed Hindenburg's favor. The DNVP chairman had desired "to teach the Center a lesson,"[142] but now he had to salvage what he could of his own party. The disintegration immanent in the DNVP was not peculiar to that party. All of Germany was in turmoil. The impact of the depression was making itself clearly felt. Unemployment had spread. Radicalism flourished on the left as well as on the right. The German bourgeoisie was torn apart by conflicting ideologies, confronted by demands for the preservation of social status, and harried by fears of greater economic suffering. The old party structure of the bourgeois classes crumbled, and traditional party leaders could not agree on any substitute.[143] The scene was set for unscrupulous demagoguery to triumph. Because the DNVP had played such an important role in manufacturing the one-sided shibbolths of the right and because his own press had been so active in propagandizing simplistic, nationalistic slogans, Hugenberg and his associates had confidently expected to reap their share of the radical harvest and recoup their losses from the two secessions in the party. After the local electoral victories of the Nazis in Thuringia and Saxony, however, German National leaders could not be overly sanguine about the prospects of monopolizing the radical vote, but they were far from despondent.[144]

Hugenberg could secure solid support from neither industry nor agriculture, from neither the traditional nobility nor the threatened lower-middle classes. While leaders of the RDI reflected the near panic-ridden fears of German industry and summoned all industrialists to play a role in the elections, the association supported no particular party. Industry, as before, showered its largess on all bourgeois parties.[145] In agricultural circles, economic pressures had created a more drastic situation. Many agrarian leaders flocked to the radical NSDAP. At the same time, others supported their own interest parties, the newly organized splinter factions, or traditional parties. Similarly, the traditional nobility was hopelessly divided. Some, as Count Reventlow, went to the Nazis; others, as von Oldenburg-Januschau, rallied behind Hugenberg; still others, as Count Westarp, supported the newly organized parties of the right. The military, the bureaucracy, and other groups were all splintered. Traditional elites provided no unified leaderships; each man considered himself a leader. The electorate had over thirty parties to choose from.

The bloc, which Hugenberg had set out to organize, stood in shambles. Not even the Stahlhelm solidly supported him.[146] Thrust on the defensive at the meeting of the party executive committee on 24 July, Hugenberg admitted, "The danger of the National Socialist movement is fully clear to me."[147] Pan-German optimists like Bang, however, asserted that the party's return to a firm position on 18 July constituted a definite threat to the appeal of the Nazis. Others argued that the advance of the NSDAP was only temporary and that the momentum gathered by the Nazi drive would soon aid the DNVP. Hugenberg himself was of this opinion and believed that the National Socialists should be given governmental responsibility so that they could demonstrate their strengths and weaknesses. He concluded that "throughout the country we have to build up a strong, powerful, national, anti-Marxist party. As uncomfortable as it is to me that a National Socialist movement has developed, we must still take it into account."[148]

Hugenberg found himself attacked on all sides. Not only did his party have to campaign against the Weimar coalition and the communists, but in a more subtle way he had to deal with the National Socialist threat. In the last months, the Nazis had rejected collaboration with the DNVP and gloated that their former ally entered the electoral campaign "broken, torn, incapable of any true activity"[149] Despite such attacks, Hugenberg formulated an offensive rather than a defensive campaign.[150] He refused to accept responsibility for the development of Nazi radicalism. His party's appeal for industrial support flatly asserted:

> If after years the tempo of National Socialism becomes increasingly more rapid, that is not the result of a "manufacture" [Mache], but a natural and irresistible reaction to the policy of the middle....[151]

Nevertheless, Hugenberg had difficulties in securing funds from some heavy industrialists. The men who had articulated the interests of heavy industry in the DNVP—Reichert, Hasslacher,

Leopold, and Rademacher—had all seceded.[152] The party did have thirteen industrial candidates on its ballot, but apparently none of them directly represented the Ruhr. Businessmen who continued to support Hugenberg came from the radical fringe; they were either Pan-Germans, like Gok and his boss Rudolf Blohm; radical ideologues, like Thyssen; or reactionaries, like Winkhaus and Wiskott from the coaling community.[153]

The position of the *Ruhrlade* was unclear. Blank's correspondence with Springorum and Reusch indicated that the organization was prepared to support all parties, from the State Party to the DNVP, but that these gentlemen wanted Hugenberg to maintain no contact with the NSDAP. They wanted the bourgeois parties to unite as much as possible, and they did not want Hugenberg to attack conservative, rightist groups.[154] None of these goals was achieved. That the members of the *Ruhrlade* were able to maintain a unified position is highly dubious. Thyssen, who strongly supported Hugenberg's tactics, had been labeled "more radical than Hugenberg."[155] Vögler, who was to negotiate with Hugenberg on this approach, had threatened in the spring to support the Nazis if the DNVP split.[156] Possibly this was an idle threat. Nevertheless, this background, coupled with the apparent nonexistence of details on the distribution of funds, permits me to draw no conclusion with regard to financial support for the NSDAP.[157] This group certainly assisted the DNVP. Given the attitude of industrial radicals like Thyssen and Kirdorf and given the financial resources available to Hugenberg directly from Scherl and from the coaling interests in the *Wirtschaftsvereinigung*, I am convinced that Hugenberg had adequate funds at his disposal not only to subsidize the German Nationals, but also to assist the National Socialists.

Hugenberg ordered Weiss to begin the campaign early in August rather than wait until the customary four weeks before the balloting.[158] Through Scherl, Hugenberg agreed to give party collaborators free subscriptions to *Der Tag* during the campaign period. The *Ufa* prepared short films for use at party rallies. The party presses turned out large numbers of pamphlets and special bulletins appealing to all groups.[159] Hugenberg also encouraged the use of loudspeakers and airplane advertising;[160] he would omit no means of attracting the voters. For him anti-Marxism was the key issue; the SPD had corrupted the state and had created a giant welfare system to prepare for bolshevism. Similarly, Marxist theory had inspired all socialists to destroy the middle class and to engender a revolutionary situation. He believed that the voters had to reject not only the SPD and the KPD, but also their "fellow travellers" in the Center and other "middle parties."[161] German National propagandists argued that socialist philosophy had also influenced the NSDAP. The Nazis, especially the economist Gottfried Feder, were ambivalent in their attitude toward private property. The Hitler party could help the state only if it purged this socialistic tendency. Then a freedom movement could be organized on a broad front; the Nazis could save the workers from Marxism, and the DNVP, the farmers.[162]

After losing so many voters to the NSDAP in local elections and after collaborating with Hitler against the Young Plan, the DNVP could certainly not outrightly oppose the Nazi movement. In its approach to National Socialism, Hugenberg's party dealt in conciliatory terms, which it had fully rejected in its relations with Treviranus and Westarp. General accord united the DNVP and the NSDAP on such issues as "culture and religion, the attitude toward Jewry and the will toward the reconstruction in individual social and economic questions...." German National leaders argued that the conflict between the two parties was the type of fratricidal war which foreign adversaries had incited since the time of Hermann.[163] As far as Hugenberg was concerned, the nation needed a synthesis of Nazi drive and German National experience.[164] The man to produce this synthesis and unite the nation was, in the view of the DNVP, Hugenberg himself.[165]

Curiously, Hugenberg, who had always preferred to work behind the scenes, felt extremely awkward in leading his first major DNVP electoral campaign. He had reservations about personal propaganda and even obstructed circulation of Wegener's pamphlet praising him.[166] Clearly, Hugenberg was not a political leader and did not belong in the position which he held.[167] His supporters argued that only devotion to duty urged him on. A more objective appraisal would dismiss altruism as a Hugenberg characteristic and emphasize his constant drive for power and excellence. Undoubtedly, the encouragement of Wegener and Class strengthened his self-confidence, but their support could not have kept Hugenberg in the forefront of politics unless he himself had wanted to be there.[168] Some psychologists might argue that the cocky self-assurance of a short and stocky self-made man, who found interpersonal relations extremely difficult, demanded that he demonstrate his righteousness.

Hugenberg was publicized not as a man of words but as a man of action. The leader who had created a great national press to oppose the "Jewish infiltrated leftist press" would steer Germany triumphantly through the Scylla and Charybdis of Versailles and Marxism. To youth, he extended his hand over the generation gap. To farmers, he offered guarantees of independence and profit; to the middle classes, protection against proletarianization; to the workers, a secure future. To all who promised to make the right wing strong, he promised to rebuild the state.[169] His supporters wrote that their "Third Reich" would end socialist experiments and class divisions in Germany, for Hugenberg knew "new ways which lead out of the economic and governmental crisis to the organic reorganization of a vitally powerful economy in a free state."[170] The building stone of this new Reich was to be each individual—fortified by the principles of self-help and united in an organic community.[171]

The electorate rejected Hugenberg's vision of the future. Condemned as a reactionary by both the Nazis and the parties to the left of him, the former Krupp director proved unable to attract not only the young voters who came to the polls for the first time, but even the older voters who had just begun to exercise their parliamentary perogative.[172] The Hugenberg party received only 41 seats in the new Reichstag—37 less than the DNVP had won in May 1928. The NSDAP secured 107 seats—a gigantic increase over its 12 mandates in the last election.[173] Hugenberg had been overwhelmed by his own propaganda. Throughout the past fourteen months his syndicate had blurred the distinction between the two parties, encouraging support for radical nationalism. When the voters went to the polls they selected the NSDAP to represent this national opposition. The radical seed sown by the Reich Committee against the Young Plan was reaped by the Nazis in these September elections.[174]

4 The National Opposition and the Harzburg Front

The election of 1930 strengthened radicalism in the Reichstag and fostered an aura of cooperation among nationalists united against Brüning and the Weimar "system." In this alliance, Hugenberg believed that his party was superior since men of education and property had a natural right to govern the state. Hitler, however, refused to follow Hugenberg's tutelage, and Stahlhelm leaders refused to play a subordinate role. The attempt to rally rightist forces at Bad Harzburg heralded not a unified *Sammlung*, but the amplification of conflict in the national opposition.

THE NATIONAL OPPOSITION AGAINST BRÜNING

The outcome of the 1930 election both surprised and frustrated Hugenberg. The DNVP had campaigned under his banner, "Make the right wing strong."[1] His allies in the ADV, however, advised against greeting the returns as a victory for the right. As Class carefully observed, certain leaders in the NSDAP would object to being labeled rightist. Not the right, but the "national opposition" had been strengthened by the election.[2] With a flair for hyperbole, Hugenberg's aides still proclaimed the election a triumph; *Der Tag* rejoiced in a victory over the Marxists.[3] Nevertheless, Hugenberg was realistic enough to realize that there were three ways that he could gain power. First, he might secure greater influence over the Reich president; second, he might succeed in controlling the National Socialists; or third, he might build up his own party. He tried all three.

Through Hindenburg's neighbor at Neudeck, Elard von Oldenburg-Januschau, Hugenberg hoped to prejudice the president against Brüning. The party leader made certain that the "old Januschauer," as a new German National Reichstag delegate, fully understood the DNVP's policy. Because the country would have to choose between Marxism and a rejuvenated nationalism, Hugenberg argued that he had successfully aroused youth. The "cowardly and irresponsible" policy of moderates had, however, split the DNVP and provided an opportunity for the electoral victory of National Socialism. In his hubris, Hugenberg asserted, "It will be my responsibility, in the event of difficulties which could arise from the present preponderance of the National Socialists, to master the situation."[4] As he sought "to unburden his conscience," the party leader emphasized his willingness to cooperate in a rightist regime which would not be bound by the Centrist-Socialist coalition in Prussia. Instead of listening to false advisers, Hugenberg challenged the president to choose between Marxism and nationalism. In the face of imminent catastrophe, he insisted that the president would have no alternative but the DNVP.[5]

Hindenberg, counseled by his entourage, realized that the government demanded by Hugenberg would precipitate a social, economic, and constitutional convulsion. Personally affronted by Hugenberg's refusal to support a bourgeois cabinet, he continued to support Brüning. Rejection of the radical approach had a personal as well as a political basis—the president felt that in their infrequent interviews, Hugenberg had treated him like a schoolboy.[6] In contrast, his relationship with Brüning, a veteran of the western front, was based on mutual respect. Both Hindenberg and his chancellor agreed that "one could help Germany only through peace and factual work;"[7] they rejected the argument that the DNVP and the NSDAP should be given power in order to end negative nationalist propaganda.[8] Hugenberg's policy seemed to them neither peaceful nor constructive.

Even as he attempted to influence the president, Hugenberg tried to maintain accord with the National Socialists. His press argued that the "national wave" which had begun with the campaign against the Young Plan had grown in the last election and had broken the strength of the "middle parties." The National Socialists, *Der Tag* pointed out, had reaped the fruit sown in this earlier campaign, for they had never been burdened with ministerial responsibility. The Hugenberg paper praised the "will to sacrifice" and the "courage of battle" that defined the youthful appeal of the NSDAP. Nevertheless, *Der Tag* counseled that youth had little interest in economic policy and that this aspect of the nationalist program had better be left to the DNVP.[9]

Hugenberg and his allies de-emphasized incongruities and insisted that the only differences between the parties on the extreme right lay in "temperament and disposition."[10] The DNVP and the NSDAP fought side by side in foreign affairs, but domestically the older party had much to teach the Nazis. The Hugenberg party considered itself the source of "schooled, conservative, constructive, youthfully strong determination."[11] Even after the Nazis displaced the German Nationals from their seats on the extreme right-wing of the Reichstag, Hugenberg claimed the right to lead the national opposition. His intimates believed that their champion was comparable to Baron vom Stein, the great Prussian reformer of the early nineteenth century.[12]

Understandably, the Hugenberg press never showered attention on the NSDAP. Though editorial policy was friendly and positive, Hitler and his party rarely made the headlines. Klitzsch, the director of Scherl, was very aware that collaboration was playing with fire. Not only were the Nazis competing with the German Nationals politically, but the papers of the Eher *Verlag* threatened Scherl. In his estimate, "The excessively 'affectionate' treatment, allotted to the National Socialists by many German National press organs, has frequently exceeded the bonds of political wisdom." He wanted some of that fervor directed toward Hugenberg as a leader.[13]

Publicly, Hugenberg remained optimistic. True, the Reichstag delegates of the two parties could not yet form a common bond.[14] True, the time was "not yet ripe for talk" of reorganizing the Reich Committee.[15] True, the DNVP would prefer the Nazis to limit their appeal to cities where they could lure the workers from socialist parties.[16] Yet the people had finally been aroused against the republican system.[17] When a moderate nationalist like Otto Gessler warned that the Nazis were an extremist party like the KPD, Hugenberg's supporters replied that they would rather work with the NSDAP than with a democratic group.[18]

On 26 November 1930, Chancellor Brüning had a long discussion with the German National leader. For three hours, the chancellor carefully explained his economic policy, detailing the cabinet's fiscal conservatism and its willingness to assist agriculture. Hugenberg focused on constitutional problems and, finally, rejected the chancellor's attempt to establish either personal rapport or political understanding, with the statement:

I am more convinced than ever, that I have always been right. Germany is standing right before the collapse which I have predicted. After your detailed presentation, that is clearer to me than ever. Therefore, I must fight you and the entire system.[19]

The breach between moderate nationalists and radicals was clear. Brüning hoped to prevent, confine, or moderate any crisis. Hugenberg welcomed crisis as a fuse to explode democracy and disgrace socialism.

Willingness to collaborate with National Socialists was exemplified not only in Hugenberg's support for the Ulm officers, who had sought to win military backing for Nazism,[20] but also in his attitude toward Prussia. Despite the fact that new elections would mean losses for the DNVP and gains for the Hitler movement, German Nationals preferred this to the existing coalition led by the Socialists. Hugenberg and his allies calculated that if the elections could return fifty to sixty of the seventy German National delegates in the Landtag and then increase the representation of the Nazis from six to about one hundred, Prussia would have a strong nationalist government.[21] In such a patriotic atmosphere, he was sure that the DNVP, despite its numerical inferiority, would dominate the national opposition.[22] Downplaying conflicts with some Nazi lieutenants, German National leaders felt that friendly personal relations with Hitler would facilitate manipulation of the NSDAP.[23] Hugenberg and his entourage apparently believed that Hitler owed them something—whether this claim was moral or financial, or both, is not clear.[24]

Enthusiasm for radical political polarization caused the DNVP to follow the National Socialists out of the Reichstag on 10 February 1931.[25] When opponents admonished the DNVP for dereliction of duty and refusal to accept reality, Hugenberg replied that he would accept responsibility only under certain conditions.[26] He argued that by leaving the Reichstag he removed the veil shielding the collaboration between the SPD and Brüning's bourgeois government, thus revealing the "hypocritical system" in which the bourgeois Reich government collaborated with "Red Prussia."[27] Even when Hindenberg publicly requested the DNVP's cooperation in the cabinet's proposals for agricultural assistance, Hugenberg resisted.[28] He was convinced that the na-

tional opposition had chosen the correct tactics and would succeed in ultimately destroying what his press labeled the "majority of cowardice," the tolerant majority extending from
former DNVP members to Socialists.[29] Moderate nationalists
retorted that the Hugenberg party could be excluded even from
a more radical nationalist regime and thus had no choice but to
follow the Nazi line.[30]

To strengthen his power base, the German National leader
had already begun the third phase of his program—the effort to
improve the position of his own party. The DNVP organization
attributed its losses in the September elections to three basic
causes: the secession of the "left-wing" groups, the ignorance of
the electorate, and the youthful vitality of the National Socialists.
Hugenberg directed his resources toward each of these
problems. The party central office concentrated on local chap-
ters in order to fill the gaps left by the secessionists. Weiss, one of
the key electoral strategists in the party central office, referred
the DNVP's regional leaders to the example of the Nazi organization as a model for development. To attract new constituents
Weiss planned a "November wave" of party rallies.[31]

Typically, Hugenberg believed that better organization would
rally the masses. He undertook two important reforms within
the party—an attempt to place younger men in influencial positions and a drive to reform party finances. Every local party
organization had to extend its executive board by 20 percent.
Men under 30 were to fill half the positions thus created, and
men between the ages of 30 and 40 were to fill the other half. At
the same time, the DNVP executive committee insisted that local
organizations would have to put their finances in order and
establish regular checks upon themselves.[32] Here the problem
was more than financial. Dues collecting, as in the NSDAP and
even the SPD, brought the membership closer together and
usually resulted in "self-sacrificing devotion" to the party.[33]
Hugenberg had learned that a newspaper concern and large
contributions from wealthy reactionaries were inadequate
substitutes for the commitment engendered by each party
worker contributing his own share.[34]

This focus on expansion and reorganization, however, exposed the dilemma the DNVP had created for itself by devaluing
the party concept. As an independent political force, the party

leadership might have readily developed a more appealing youth organization. Subordinating party egotism to the idea of a broad national front, however, created serious problems. To expand the already existing youth organization, the *Bismarckbund*, into something like the National Socialist SA or the Young Stahlhelm would immediately arouse the antagonism of the NSDAP and the veterans' organization. Thus Hugenberg hesitated to sanction expansion of the youth group.[35] Not until late in the spring of 1931 did the party leadership begin to request local leaders to form such units. For these youth groups there was to be no central organization, no standard uniform; regional distinctions were to be encouraged.[36]

Hugenberg and party leaders were gradually convinced that street rallies, aided by militant, activist units, attracted the politically concerned youth in these radical times. Rejecting consensus, extremist parties thrived on crisis and sought to exploit it as a means of imposing their ideological aspirations on society. This growing radicalism alarmed industry. The strong moderate bourgeois party, favored by the majority of the RDI, had not emerged.[37] Treviranus's Popular Conservatives, on which many had placed fond hopes, made a poor showing at the polls; the numerous bourgeois parties articulating particular interests seemed incapable of establishing any real unity.[38] Most industrial leaders were extremely skeptical of the NSDAP as a movement, particularly because of its anticapitalist, populist demagoguery.[39] At the same time, Hugenberg's DNVP did not represent industrial groups. After the election of 1930, there was not one major industrialist in the party's Reichstag delegation.[40] German National relations with the RDI, which tended to support Brüning, were strained, if not downright hostile. Rather than stressing the needs of industry and the industrial worker, Hugenberg reasserted that the cure for the nation's economic woes must begin with a financially secure native agriculture.[41] Such emphasis on the basic demands of the domestic market clashed with the trade policies of the electrical and chemical industries and even with those of the iron producers. Some Ruhr leaders, however, favored the Hugenberg approach.

Heavy industry's sympathy for the agricultural community was not a new development. The ideals of Friedrich List and the tariff policy established in the Bismarckian Reich had cemented this collaboration. Hugenberg's own economic and political policy reflected this view. In this tradition, some heavy industrialists voiced grave reservations about the RDI's tolerance of the Brüning government. Hugenberg's friend Vögler, of the United Steel combine, informed Duisberg that he could not speak before the association because he felt "somewhat strange in the *Reichsverband*."[42] When the RDI invited the chancellor to explain his economic policies to the main committee of its association, Fritz Thyssen was the first speaker to criticize the regime and argue that meaningful reform was impossible unless the chancellor was able to secure the support of "all national circles."[43]

Thyssen's sympathy for the NSDAP at this time is indisputable. Precisely how this can be measured in terms of financial contributions is unresolved, but there is no doubt that he had hoped the Nazis might affect federal policy.[44] As a member of the DNVP, Thyssen did not hesitate to admonish the party leader:

> I would thus like to raise my warning voice loudly and clearly; all of us here want the German National Party to remain in close contact with the National Socialists and not disturb this movement.[45]

That Hitler did not have the support of "all" Rhur industrialists was undoubtedly known to Hugenberg. The Nazi leader had recently spoken to leaders of heavy industry at the home of Hugenberg's friend, Kirdorf. Reportedly, Hitler made a "strong impression" on these men, but Ernst Poensgen of the steel combine had criticized the Nazis for not supporting the Brüning regime. Obviously, heavy industry was divided.[46]

Radicalism in the Ruhr was best exemplified by leaders of the coaling community, with whom Hugenberg had remained in close contact. Tensions between western mining industrialists and the RDI were so strong that Ernst Brandi, chairman of the *Bergbaulicher Verein*, apparently considered removing his association from the RDI.[47] The moderate approach of the RDI leadership evinced the willingness of many industrialists to work within the existing state. Radicals in the Ruhr, however, were willing to use the economic crisis as a means of ending the republic and destroying the intervention of unions and government in industry. Hugenberg, radical industrialists, and the Nazis were united in a negative consensus opposing the SPD and its allies, the "unionist,"—Brüning, the Center Party, and all democrats.[48] The secession of the coaling interests from the RDI never materialized, but the tensions which had existed since the dispute over the Young Plan could not be easily dissipated.[49]

Economic unrest had also radicalized many farmers, who either formed their own parties or turned to the Nazis.[50] In December 1930, Hugenberg presented a two-pronged program to rehabilitate the agrarian economy and rally the "green front" behind the DNVP. First he demanded the introduction of a more rigorous tariff-and-quota system to protect native produce and expand the domestic market. Then he proposed a new agrarian credit system which would allow the government to guarantee mortgage payments and permit the farmer to begin amortization of his loans.[51] Critics of this plan charged that it would encourage inflation and cost the government millions. Hugenberg retorted that it was "not too much" to pay for saving the foundations of the national economy.[52]

Moreover, Hugenberg proposed that government and industry could save millions by reforming the social welfare system. Emphasizing individualism, he argued that self-help rather than state assistance would save the worker. Socialist theory misinterpreted the natural harmony which existed between employer and employee. Instead of larger sums allotted to house administrators and to pay bureaucrats, a true capitalist system had to be developed in order to provide for "the creation, maintenance, and increase of small property in the city and in the country and the protection of individual small entrepreneurs."[53]

At the tenth party day of the DNVP in September 1931, Hugenberg presented his foreign policy. His proposals, he believed, would revitalize Germany and ensure progress for the entire West. According to Hugenberg, the economic crisis was the result of an erroneous concept of world economy. Blind faith in gold and the system of "international capital," coupled with the reparations clause of the Treaty of Versailles, threatened to enslave the German economy and reduce Germany to a colony. "A misunderstood capitalism combined with destructive Marxist teaching" had produced chaos and resulted in the application of colonial techniques to inappropriate areas of the world. But one could not colonize "great free-born peoples" without jeopardizing the colonist. Reparations and credit in the context of an international market forced concentration upon exports rather than on development of the domestic market. This was the cardinal error. For Hugenberg, individual national economies, self-contained and autonomous, formed the kernel of a healthy world order. A nation had to produce its own capital and organize the distribution of wealth within its borders. "To stop the progressive cultural bankruptcy of the civilized world" and to restore the solvency of all great nations, Germany, as the foremost victim of international economic blundering, had the solution. What Germany needed was an area in which it could develop its natural economy. The Germans were a *Volk ohne Raum*, a "people without space." This deficiency could be overcome by again giving Germany a colonial empire in Africa and by opening up territory on Germany's eastern frontier. Thus the economic crisis would be terminated and a "spirit of freedom in the fullest meaning of the word" would be established.[54]

For Hugenberg, liberalism and socialism in both foreign affairs and international finance still constituted the nation's chief political enemy. This view of a common foe, coupled with belief in the communion of the German with his native soil, which fortified the "blood" of the nation, tended to bind the ultranationalists. His optimism—based upon the ability of the wind, the weather, the woods, water, and the climate, to help the people remain true to the traditions of their fathers—enabled Hugenberg to approach all nationalists as men desirous of organizing a new Reich.[55] Yet, *völkisch* sentiment was insubstantial cement for a patriotic bloc, and unity among groups in the national oppostion remained elusive.

Not only the NSDAP, but also the Stahlhelm challenged Hugenberg's claim to leadership. As economic and social conditions continued to deteriorate, Duesterberg and Seldte emphasized their nonpartisanship and then began to act directly in the political sphere. At the end of 1930, these Stahlhelm leaders organized a plebiscite for the dissolution of the Prussian Landtag.[56] The veterans had apparently learned that they, too, could use the idea of a national opposition to coerce their allies into supporting a particular tactic. Manipulating the idea of an antidemocratic referendum, Jenö von Egan-Krieger, the Stanhlhelm coordinator for the plebiscite, calculated that the

DNVP could lure Catholic voters from the Center Party and the Nazis could win workers from the Socialists.[57] Neither nationalist party, however, anticipated success for the referendum, and their endorsement was only half-hearted. The Nazis flaunted their disinterest. Hitler did not come to the February meeting before the announcement of the proposal, and Frick never attended the April meeting at Rohbraken.[58] Hitler had Seldte bluntly informed that Nazi support would be dependent on the size of the financial subsidies provided.[59] Hugenberg ordered the party to participate but insisted that the DNVP save essential funds for itself.[60]

In cooperating, Hugenberg sought to make himself and the DNVP the essential link in the national opposition. Though the Nazis refused to attend the February meeting, the German National leader had already had "a rather lengthy and not unsatisfactory exchange of views" with Hitler.[61] Similarly, before the Rohbraken meeting in April, the two party leaders had agreed not to support any candidate for the position of Reich president without mutual consent. The Stahlhelm leaders accepted this agreement later.[62] Obviously, each group was attempting to manipulate and upstage the other. When plans for the initiative were completed in March 1931, Duesterberg complained that neither party had exerted itself.[63] Hugenberg angrily claimed that the Stahlhelm had exploited the German National organization and then charged the party with lack of support.[64] Both men were right.

Hugenberg wanted the plebiscitary agitation to propagandize his ideas and rally support for his party in the next election.[65] He was furious when local party organizations incurred debts for financing rallies for the plebiscite.[66] These additional financial burdens came at a time when the party was attempting to develop and maintain an independently solvent organization. The central party office had cut the budget for 1931 by 37 percent.[67] Still the party was not self-supporting. Hugenberg had threatened to resign if the party membership could not resolve this fiscal crisis.[68] He argued that the "development of the party and the national movement depends on the solution of this problem."[69] Though he had continually opposed the idea of partisanship, Hugenberg as chairman of the DNVP was forced to depend on the structure of a traditional party. In criticizing the party state, his propaganda weakened his own political base. Even some of Hugenberg's intimate collaborators noted that it was too late to model the DNVP on the SPD and that voters tired of parliamentarism turned to the Nazis or the Communists.[70]

The depression and its results were certainly major factors in the financial plight of the DNVP. Contributing to a political party—especially one whose influence seemed to be waning—was not a high priority on restricted budgets. In addition, Hugenberg's refusal to support the non-Socialist Brüning cabinet sharply circumscribed the number of industrialists willing to finance his political radicalism. The net result was that the DNVP became more dependent than ever on the Hugenberg concern. Obviously the syndicate could provide favorable press coverage of the party. Indeed, since the election of Hugenberg as party chairman in 1928, the Scherl papers published in Berlin and the publications in cities like Augsburg, Munich, Hanover, Detmold, etc., had rapidly become a party press mirroring his policies.[71]

The use of the Hugenberg press to bolster rightist radicalism had at least the tacit backing of the firm's supporters in the coaling industry. The syndicate, however, did not totally abandon the profit motive in order to become the propaganda division of the party. This was most clearly the case with the *Ufa* film concern. Preoccupation with the introduction of sound, pressures of international competition, and the financial risk in producing a profitable film left little room for a purely partisan point of view. Of the total number of films made at Neu Babelsberg in 1930–1932, only a limited number—such as *Flötenkonzert von Sans Souci, Im Geheimdienst,* and, most particularly, *Yorck* and *Morgenrot*—had a calculatedly strong national appeal which the DNVP could exploit.[72] Moreover, the *Ufa*, with its large number of Jewish employees and international contacts, was not a pure asset for the Hugenberg party.[73] Klitzsch, the general director of the concern, had, however, made this corporation a profitable enterprise.[74]

Profit remained important for the Hugenberg concern because, in the interlocking directorate of corporations presided over by Hugenberg and the men of the *Wirtschaftsvereinigung*, new funds for subsidizing political enterprises had apparently become scarce. Nevertheless, the coaling interests allowed dividends derived from the several corporations of the concern to be used for political purposes. In 1930, a year in which profit was still rather high, Hugenberg had a political slush fund of M 600,000 at his disposal. This enabled him to provide a regular monthly subsidy of M 4,600 to the DNVP and an estimated M 7,500 monthly for special party expenses.[75] Since the central party budget for 1930 was almost M 600,000, the funds at Hugenberg's disposal—provided he subsidized no other political or paramilitary movement—would have been more than sufficient to cover the total expenses of the main office. This would have meant, however, that no other contributions had helped to balance party expenses. Such a conclusion is improbable.[76] Industrial magnates, such as Thyssen, Kirdorf, Vögler, and Springorum, viewed the DNVP in 1930–1931 as the bastion of social and fiscal responsibility in the national opposition.[77] Even in a tight money market, the probability that these men and, especially, their coaling subsidiaries united with Brandi in the *Bergbaulicher Verein* and *Zechenverband*, would have contributed to the party is—in my opinion—very high.[78] Moreover, despite the financial bind of the German National organization, the party did not monopolize the funds at Hugenberg's disposal. His factotum, Mann, indicated that Hugenberg had specific financial obligations to the DNVP and additional undefined political obligations of M 450,000.[79] Hugenberg apparently helped subsidize the Young Stahlhelm, and he definitely patronized the work of Professor I. F. Coar who championed an end to reparations.[80] That Hugenberg also used a portion of these funds to finance the National Socialists is, in my opinion, highly probable. Thyssen, who was privy to many of the financial details of the Hugenberg concern, supposedly claimed that Hugenberg "placed about one-fifth of the donated amounts at the disposal of the National Socialist party".[81] Though the exact testimony attributed to Thyssen has been legitimately questioned,[82] I believe that the entire modus operandi of Hugenberg indicates that subventions to the Nazis were made during this period. Since the *Wirtschaftsvereinigung* was disposed to help all rightist parties and since the coaling industry favored a radicalization of political life, the conclusion that Hugenberg contributed substantially to Nazi coffers seems definitely justifiable.

Such benefactions would have become much more difficult in 1931 when the profits of the Hugenberg concern declined. Mann indicated that instead of M 600,000 only M 270,000 would be available from the profits of the various corporations. Political expenditure beyond this figure would have to come from the principal.[83] This obviously accounts for Hugenberg's almost panicky insistence that the DNVP become more financially self-sufficient. His concern was not in the red—neither the Berlin papers nor the *Ufa* experienced deficits—but total profits dropped almost 30 percent in the Scherl corporation. Circulation of *Der Tag* fluctuated from 66,845 in 1930, to 67,009 in 1931, to 60,450 in 1932. The *Berliner Lokal-Anzeiger*, which on a weekday ran as many as thirty-eight pages of advertising, lost some of its ads, and its morning and afternoon editions fell from an average of 211,693 copies in 1930 to 188,843 in 1932. The *Berliner Nachtausgabe* increased its circulation to 210,000 in 1930 but then fell to 209,000 in 1931 and to 184,000 in 1932.[84] A much graver problem lay in the deficits incurred by regional publications. In 1929 and 1930, the *Vera* had been forced to subsidize these papers. The situation became so critical during the winter of 1930–1931 that Hugenberg was compelled to reorganize the corporations dealing with the provincial press.[85] Still, papers such as the *Süddeutsche Zeitung* in Stuttgart and the *München-Augsburger Abendzeitung* continued to lose money.[86] By the end of 1931 he seriously considered closing down the latter.[87] Apparently, tieing the press to the party had benefitted neither. When the presses of Hugenberg's *Münchener Druck-und Verlagshaus* began printing the photogravure section of the Nazis' *Völkischer Beobachter*, his critics hastened to gloat that the NSDAP was ruining him.[88]

Hugenberg was determined to be neither ruined nor manipulated. Through Jacob Goldschmidt, a director of the Darmstädter and National Bank (Danat Bank), Mann negotiated an American loan for the concern. A line of credit amounting to almost four million marks had been available, but now the dollar equivalent of this was secured and a formal loan to the Hugenberg controlled *Deutsche Gewerbehaus A.G.* was concluded in May 1931.[89] Despite the anti-Semitic propaganda which he tolerated and the anti-internationalism which he preached, Hugenberg was well prepared to deal with Goldschmidt and seek foreign funds at the lowest possible interest rate.[90] That the coaling interests behind the *Wirtschaftsvereinigung* did not provide this money, as a subsidy for the firm, indicated their own economic difficulties during the depression and hesitancy to make sacrifices for the Hugenberg syndicate.[91] Nevertheless, Hugenberg pressured and cajoled his friends in the Ruhr for financial assistance.[92] The bourgeois leaders of these corporations, afraid of Nazi radicalism, looked to the DNVP to establish "sound" social and financial policies in the ranks of the national opposition. Their own firms and their investments through the *Wirtschaftsvereinigung* would be adversely affected if Hugenberg's business or political interests should fail. These were intangible assets which Mann could not list in his reports, and it is a measure of Hugenberg's determination that he exploited them fully.

THE HARZBURG FRONT

During the summer of 1931, when social discord and financial adversity threatened the state and mandated the cooperation of all politically constructive forces, Hugenberg continually placed obstacles in the chancellor's path. The DNVP denounced the Hoover moratorium on international payments as a temporizing measure which sustained the Young Plan and evaded the issue of revision.[93] Despite the fact that political instability would intensify the economic crisis, Hugenberg and Hitler declared on 9 July that "the national opposition will introduce and carry out a decisive battle for the destruction of the present system."[94] While Brüning was in London attempting to inspire confidence in the German economy among its creditors, German Nationals joined with the NSDAP and the Stahlhelm in announcing that the national opposition would refuse to consider as "legally binding" any further French demands.[95]

The DNVP, of course, rejected the idea that its leader was pursuing crisis politics. Hugenberg himself insisted that he was a trustworthy statesman and would accept responsibility if a thorough "change of course" guaranteed the opposition "absolute, full power."[96] When they met in the beginning of August, not even Hindenburg could persuade Hugenberg to moderate his stance. The German National leader insisted that his tactics had forced the SPD to accept responsibility and that his cooperation with the National Socialists had rescued the nation from a socialist government.[97] When Hindenburg later arranged a meeting between Hugenberg and Brüning, the DNVP leader maintained the same position. Cooperation was impossible.

Hugenberg was confident that he would eventually guide the national opposition to power.[98] He preferred to collaborate more closely with Hitler and apparently viewed the conference with Brüning as an attempt to sabotage radical unity.[99]

Calculatedly, Hugenberg plotted that the radicalization of the electorate, caused by the continuing depression and particularly the bank crash in July of 1931, would win support for a nationalist *Sammlung*. Radical unity could then influence the presidential election mandated for 1932. Control of the presidency and success in new Reichstag and Landtag elections could ultimately secure Hugenberg the power he wanted. Concrete negotiations for the rejuvenation of a common front and a joint rally to demonstrate its strength began at the end of August. In the Bavarian village of Kreuth, Hugenberg met with Hitler and began discussion of the next presidential election. The Nazi leader indicated that he himself would not seek the presidency; several potential candidates were discussed. No definite agreement was reached, but the common groundwork of opposition to the current regime was reemphasized.[100]

Subsequently, Hugenberg and his associates continued negotiations with other nationalist leaders. A discussion of problems with Wilhelm Frick and Gregor Strasser ran smoothly. German National optimism flourished. In the quiet of the Bavarian Alps, Hugenberg and Schmidt-Hannover even managed to bring Seldte to a *volte face*. The first leader of the Stahlhelm had favored a more moderate position than the DNVP's; now he willingly accepted the plan for a common rally.[101] Duesterberg, however, had reservations about the probity of the NSDAP and urged Seldte to drop the arrangements. Hugenberg's intervention allayed the fears of the second leader of the Stahlhelm and convinced him that it would be better to collaborate in this endeavor rather than split his organization.[102] Once the leaders had agreed on general guidelines, a working committee of Schmidt-Hannover for the DNVP, Frick for the NSDAP, and Major Siegfried Wagner for the Stahlhelm, set about finalizing the plans for a joint rally.[103] The national opposition seemed on the brink of a potent, unified campaign.

Just as everything began to move smoothly for Hugenberg, the Nazi Führer denounced the DNVP for the policy of its local party in Braunschweig. Because of its nationalist coalition, this was the very province where Hugenberg had proposed to hold the rally. The NSDAP minister in the provincial government had seceded from the party, and his nationalist colleagues tolerated his continuance in office rather than immediately replacing him with a loyal Nazi. Hitler condemned this in strong language and brashly asked Hugenberg if the DNVP would take similar advantage of the NSDAP in a national cabinet. The Führer raged that such collaboration with the bourgeois right strangled his party; the Center could not treat the National Socialists more shabbily; possibly Hugenberg would value him more as an enemy than as a friend.[104]

Hugenberg immediately communicated his dismay that Hitler would threaten him "so rashly with a division." Such tactics, he remonstrated, might be appropriate for enemies but their deployment against fellow members of the national opposition would make the acquisition of power "extraordinarily doubtful." He chidingly suggested that, possibly, elements in the NSDAP harbored opposition to a unified national front and Hitler was unable to control them. As for the specific problem in Braunschweig, Hugenberg replied that he knew nothing of it but would intervene to correct the situation.[105] Two days later, he could write to Hitler that the local DNVP had agreed to replace the secessionist minister with an NSDAP member.[106] Harmony was restored, and the provincial resort of Bad Harzburg in Braunschweig was judged an ideal setting in which to exhibit the unity of the national forces.

Despite his reassuring rhetoric about the national opposition, Hugenberg had already recognized that the only constant factor upon which he could rely was the DNVP itself. Like his friend Class, Hugenberg must have observed that Hitler, as a self-appointed "savior of Germany," was not only a classic example of "megalomania, but also of uncontrollability, imprudence, and lack of judgement."[107] Even while Hugenberg tried to manipulate such a man, he could never fully depend on him. To demonstrate his own strength and to exhibit the revitalization of the German National party, he planned a mass party rally. Stettin, a Pomeranian city east of the Elbe where the DNVP had remained relatively strong, was chosen as the setting.

Hugenberg staged a spectacle in the style of a Nazi party rally. The DNVP press emphasized the numbers present and described

Hugenberg's enthusiastic reception. For his followers, the party chairman had become not only the "intellectual leader of the national opposition," but also a figure of international stature.[108] At the opening meeting, Hugenberg surrounded himself with nationalist leaders from every walk of life. The presence of Prince Oskar of Prussia satisfied the monarchists; the prominence of General von Mackensen and Admiral Schroeder delighted the militarists. At the same time, Count Kalkreuth represented the importance of agricultural interests, and Fritz Thyssen did the same for industry.[109] "Extended applause and rousing cheers" repeatedly greeted Hugenberg in this demonstration that the DNVP was the "only party with unified will."[110] A torchlight procession of workers climaxed the events in a grandiose display of the party's universal appeal.[111] The DNVP had become a "Hugenberg movement."[112]

In his speech on the second day of the meeting, Hugenberg aggressively defended his policy of the last two years. He charged that only an "artful and unconstitutional" manipulation of power had prevented the complete triumph of the national opposition. Claiming that the nationalists already represented a majority of the people, he condemned the Brüning government and argued that the timidity of moderates had fostered the intrusion of bolshevist nationalism. Young and thoughtless proponents of such nationalism, according to Hugenberg, needed the strong and friendly hand of a good leadership. He offered them this. Nevertheless he noted:

> With bitter earnestness I add warningly and threateningly: I dare say that in the most extreme emergency every man among us would prefer this so-called national bolshevism to either Marxian bolshevism or foreign domination. If you have to die once, it is after all better to die in honor than in disgrace.[113]

While Hugenberg spoke publicly of the possibility of such an honorable death, he was by no means prepared to give up the ghost so easily. At closed meetings with the party leaders, he castigated the hostile tactics of some Nazis and urged German Nationals to reply in kind. DNVP combat units were to be expanded and to maintain full independence from other paramilitary groups, including those of the Stahlhelm. He again insisted that the party must become solvent. Finally, to maximize policy coordination within the party, Hugenberg requested and received far-reaching powers which would limit the autonomy of the local party organizations.[114] Armed with complete authority and bedecked with laurels from his supporters, Hugenberg was confident he would dominate the rally at Bad Harzburg.

As the German Nationalist leader had foreseen, rightist pressure on the Brüning cabinet had increased throughout September. The leading entrepreneurial associations of the state demanded strict adherence to the principles of classical economics.[115] In a joint statement, these organizations—including those representing the traditional middle classes—argued that there was no middle ground in economic policy because "a politically dictated system which staggers back and forth between capitalism and socialism ... has the result that capitalism is burdened with the failures of socialism."[116] Brüning was as alarmed by such a warning as he was disconcerted by the impending Harzburg reunion. However, the chancellor was far from powerless. His opponents were not monolithic, and he had only to stress their differences.

Hugenberg had anticipated industrial support for the Harzburg rally, and western leaders like Springorum were shrewdly invited. Through Treviranus, however, Brüning warned Ruhr leaders that governmental policy would be affected by the participation of industrial leaders at the rally.[117] In an uncertain political situation, many heavy industrialists could afford to alienate neither Brüning nor Hugenberg. With the very same rationale, they were loathe to oppose the strongest nationalist party leader, Hitler.[118] Capitalizing on his assets, Brüning engineered a two-pronged plan to exploit the weaknesses of Hugenberg's strategy. First he mended his bridges with industry, and then he joined the bourgeois leaders wooing Hitler. On 7 October 1931, the chancellor resigned. Retaining the confidence of Hindenburg, he was immediately charged with reorganizing the cabinet to create an opening to the right.[119] The appointment of Hermann Warmbold, who had contacts with the I. G. Farben trust, as minister of finance helped erode the appeal of Harzburg to industry.[120] Similarly, to counter Hugenberg's attempt to organize a united opposition, Brüning arranged the first meeting of President Hindenburg with ex-corporal Hitler on the day before the Harzburg rally.[121] Courted by both moderate and radical nationalists, Hitler stressed the independence of his movement and refused to be manipulated by either side.[122]

At Bad Harzburg on 11 October 1931, the other members of the national opposition were confounded by Hitler's conduct at the rally. The Nazi leader arrived too late to participate in discussions of the parade route, and he ignored the ecumenical field service held that Sunday morning. When the paramilitary groups did parade, Hitler remained just long enough to review the SA from his auto. He avoided the common banquet that had been arranged. Later in the day, he even threatened not to speak to the general assembly convoked by the national opposition. He and Hugenberg remained closeted in one of the private rooms of the spa hall, and only with difficulty did the chairman of the DNVP and Schmidt-Hannover convince him to join them in addressing the nationalists, who were awaiting their arrival.[123]

Hugenberg, who chaired the meeting, began by announcing that a common agreement on the Reich presidential election would be announced at the proper time. He then proceeded to delineate his estimate of the world situation, declaring that between bolshevism and nationalism there was no middle road. For him, the power expressed in this common meeting would propel the nation toward a new Germany. He concluded his talk with a reading of a joint resolution denouncing Marxism, cultural bolshevism, and the Treaty of Versailles, condemning inequality in arms, and demanding the resignations of Reich Chancellor Brüning and Prussian Minister President Braun.[124] After Hugenberg, Hitler continued in the same vein; Seldte and Duesterberg followed.[125] More significant than the familiar litany of these speeches was the address of the former president of the Reichsbank, Hjalmar Schacht, repudiating Brüning's economic policy.[126] His inclusion in the program emphasized the attempt of the radicals to counteract the charge of crisis politics and indict the current cabinet as the real cause of Germany's woes.

Harzburg, however, was no more able to unite the national opposition than was the Reich Committee against the Young Plan. The Hugenberg syndicate played the same role it had in the earlier campaign; it propagandized the cause of unity and sought to create a snowballing effect among rightists. The list of participants, as presented in the Hugenberg press, calculatedly emphasized the significance and diversity of the various elitists who attended. The Pan-Germans were represented by Class, von Vietinghoff-Scheel, and Prince zu Salm-Horstmar. *Reichslandbund* President Count Kalkreuth, Director von Sybel, and Dr. Wendhausen indicated the approval of the agricultural community. General von Seekt, General von Einem, Admiral von Trotha, and Admiral von Levetzow lent military prestige to the meeting. Count von der Goltz led the United Fatherland Associations to the event. From the circle of the imperial and royal family came Prince Eitel Friedrich, Prince Oskar, the Crown Prince, and General von Dommes. Alongside parliamentary delegates from the DNVP and the NSDAP came representatives from the DVP and the Economic Party.

Hugenberg's Munich paper specifically listed the names of industrialists who reportedly attended the meeting. It included: Dr. Brandi from the *Bergbaulicher Verein*, Dr. Schlenker from the *Langnam Verein*, Dr. Vögler from the steel combine, General Director Moellers, Geheimrat Kreth, General Director Gottstein, Director Gosse, General Director Meydenbauer, Director Gok, Dr. Blank, Dr. Grauert, Geheimrat Poensgen, General Director Middendorf, Winnacker, Blohm-Hamburg, Krüger-Wintershall, Geheimrat Ravené, Paul Rhode, Geheimrat Boringer, Reineker, Dr. Regedanz, Hütten-director Cuber, Dr. Sogemaier, Dr. Meesmann-Mainz, Delius-Bielefeld, and General Director Hohn from the *Langman Verein*.[127] The publication of such a detailed list in this haphazard way indicated the desire of the Hugenberg syndicate to create the impression that industry overwhelmingly supported the rally and thus to pressure the noncommitted. Simple readers might be impressed, but, clearly, the ambivalent attitude of industry helped to frustrate a *Sammlung* at Harzburg. Conspicuous by their absence were some of the key leaders of the Ruhr, in which Hugenberg supposedly had a firm base of power. Neither the new president of the RDI, Krupp von Bohlen, nor the president of the *Langnam Verein,* Springorum, were present.[128] Undoubtedly such men did not want to commit themselves. Brüning's anti-Harzburg attitude was clear; Hitler's unpredictability was becoming infamous. Schacht, who understood the mentality of the industrial magnates, emphasized rightist fears when he wrote to Reusch, "Continuing collaboration with the present system and lack of courage of conviction will cost industry its inmost life."[129]

While the tacit refusal of industry to rally behind Harzburg indicated the unsuccessfulness of Hugenberg's attempt to unite the right, Hitler's overt obstruction made the effort a colossal failure. Harzburg was not the first step toward a more unified national opposition, but rather the beginning of open conflict among the members of the national bloc.[130] Hitler offered an excuse for each of his uncooperative actions[131] Essentially, however, NSDAP leaders were convinced that they no longer had to depend exclusively on allies in the national opposition. German Nationals blamed Brüning for Hitler's recalcitrance,[132] but the Hitler-Hindenburg meeting affected no substantial change in Hitler's policy. The Nazi leader was fully aware that he controlled three times as many votes in the Reichstag as the DNVP and that his popularity had continued to grow after the election of September 1930. He might well have judged that by openly aligning himself with the conservative forces in society he would weaken his appeal to the poor and the lower-middle classes. The NSDAP attracted the masses. Regardless of Brüning's tactics, elementary logic would assure Hitler that bourgeois leaders at Harzburg needed the NSDAP more than it needed them.[133]

The Nazi leader played his cards well. In subsequent weeks, the relationship between the Center and the NSDAP became decidedly less hostile.[134] Right-wing union leaders, like Max Habermann of the DHV, began talking about a Brüning-Hitler alliance.[135] Goebbels's Der Angriff in bold headlines posed the question, "The Position of the NSDAP: Harzburg or Brüning?"[136] The parties of the middle as well as the DNVP were bidding for National Socialist favor. With his lieutenants supporting varied policies, Hitler's political stock soared.[137] Since the Nazis had never shared ministerial responsibility and had compromised their propagandistic line, Hitler could stand Janus-like between opposing forces, offering hope to everyone and cooperation to none.[138] Obdurate against the "middle," Hugenberg's options were more limited. Indeed, as Westarp had noted, the German National leader was more dependent on Hitler than the Nazi leader was on Hugenberg.[139]

In the ensuing struggle for political leverage, the DNVP had none of the advantages of the NSDAP. Hugenberg had never sought to conciliate interest groups. He had continually preached that politics must transcend the demands of particular pressure groups and respond only to the needs of the nation. In his own words, the German National leader had never put his party "up for sale."[140] But at the same time, Hugenberg failed to win popular support. As a public speaker his style was pedestrian, his delivery uninspiring. His taciturn manner and aggressive policies conveyed the image of an arrogant, unapproachable demigod. His wealth, his power, his former association with heavy industry made it almost impossible for him to emerge as a popular leader. Uncompromising determination in business and politics earned him the nickname "Cross Spider" and "Silver Fox." Observing the brush-cut hair, the handlebar mustache, and the high Victorian collar which topped his short and rotund frame, caustic Berliners mockingly called him "The Hamster."[141] Such caricatures bared his vulnerable political image.

At the German National party meeting in early December, Hugenberg responded to Nazi tactics. He repudiated the label of social reactionary, which the NSDAP had used against him, and he encouraged his followers to fight back with the same weapons as their opponent. The German National leader admonished his followers not to refer to the Harzburg Front as the ultimate panacea, "We have to fight for the party and nothing else."[142] The attitude of industry, in particular, disturbed Hugenberg. Representatives of I. G. Farben and other industrial leaders, like Silverberg, allegedly negotiated with the Nazis.[143] Karl Scheibe, leader of the German National industrial committee, warned entrepreneurs that although the National Socialists had won many votes from the DNVP in 1930, the field was now clearing and German Nationals and the Stahlhelm were gaining ground. DNVP leaders reminded industry that their party was the only constant and vigilant sentinel against socialism and they would never entrust this duty to Hitler.[144]

Nevertheless, the DNVP lost ground in industrial circles that respected Nazi power more than they feared National Socialist economic attitudes.[145] The meeting of German National industrialists in Berlin later that year was a bitter disappointment for Hugenberg, especially since Thyssen, formerly a stalwart champion of Hugenberg's tactics, rejected the German Nationals.[146] The steel magnate arranged for Hitler to speak at the Düsseldorf Industrial Club on 27 January 1932. Hitler did not convert the Ruhr, but he certainly made an impression. The day after Hitler's speech in Düsseldorf, Thyssen resigned from the DNVP and abandoned his position on the party's executive board. He charged the German Nationals with working against Hitler and claimed that DNVP demands upon the NSDAP were in inverse ratio to the popular strength of the two parties. His support for the DNVP, he argued, had been conditioned by the demand that German Nationals and National Socialists cooperate. Since, he concluded, DNVP leadership obstructed this and since the number of "men on Hitler's side, who think intelligently in economic affairs, has in the interim grown significantly," the steel magnate repudiated Hugenberg.[147]

Though the weakness of his position became apparent to Hugenberg during the winter of 1931–1932, he refused to change his policy. In response to a letter from Carl Goerdeler discussing various political alternatives, Hugenberg still demanded ideology and rejected compromise. Convinced that any amelioration of Germany's plight through collaboration would preserve the parliamentary system and "the unions—the major supporters of this reigning idiocy"—Hugenberg believed: "This is the decisive point of the development. If Brüning succeeds, with the help of these powers, in saving himself and along with that the basic system of collaboration with Social Democracy, then every peril and every sacrifice is once more in vain." Confident in his ultimate goal, he clearly expressed his tactics: "Battle against the opposing unobjective system and struggle for the reestablishment of a system of objectivity. But so long as we have neither power nor responsibility, our primary aim continues to be overthrow of the opposition."[148]

5 Conflict and Compromise

The period from January 1932 through January 1933 epitomizes the ambivalent relationship between the German Nationals and the National Socialists. The tension generated at the Harzburg rally rapidly deteriorated into open rivalry and, ultimately, into direct confrontation. The traditional right and the young radicals disagreed vehemently. When other alternatives to provide a strong nationalist regime failed, Hugenberg compromised his principles and returned to his original plan to manipulate Hitler. The cabinet appointed on 30 January 1933 was the result of this reversal in tactics.

THE PRESIDENTIAL ELECTION

The presidential election mandated for 1932 afforded nationalists an opportunity to redefine their tactics. Chancellor Brüning wanted to avoid an election campaign and sought a two-thirds majority in the Reichstag in order to extend Hindenburg's term through constitutional revision.[1] Continuing his policy of dividing the national opposition, Brüning met first with Hitler on 6 January and sought to win Nazi support for this scheme.[2] Wary of trading Hugenberg's patronage for that of Brüning or Schleicher, Hitler delayed his answer. On 10 January Hugenberg directly repudiated the chancellor's proposal.[3] The German National leader anticipated that the impending election would provide a perfect opportunity for wheedling concessions from Hindenburg in return for nationalist support. The old field marshall would be loathe to run on a ticket backed by the weak middle parties, the Center and SPD—the very parties that had opposed him in 1925. Meeting on 11 January, both Hitler and Hugenberg were unwilling to forego the propagandistic value of opposition. They formally agreed to reject the chancellor's proposal.[4] A whirlwind of political discussions ensued.

The latitude which Hugenberg had hoped to enjoy during this period was significantly curtailed by several factors. Not the least of these was the personal enmity which his intransigence and the hostility of his press had inspired in the aged Hindenburg.[5] Similarly, many nationalists whom the German National had alienated and whom Hitler could never attract would support the field marshall in spite of the national opposition. General Rudolf von Horn, the leader of the *Kyffhäuserbund*, a prestigious veterans' organization less formally organized than the Stahlhelm, pledged his support for Hindenburg.[6] By mid-February, Heinrich Sahm, the mayor of Berlin, and Westarp, the former chairman of the DNVP, enlisted the support of over three million nationalists for the Reich president.[7] Brüning's struggle against overwhelming odds had earned the chancellor a significant measure of respect and undermined the DNVP's bargaining position. Unable to influence moderates, Hugenberg was equally incapable of controlling radicals. Hitler, more determined than ever to be free of Hugenberg's tutelage, refused to commit himself to any candidate. Nazi leaders considered introducing their own presidential contender; Frick and Hitler were discussed as possibilities.[8] The Stahlhelm was in a quandary. Seldte, in particular, found it anomalous for the veterans' organization to enter a campaign against the highest ranking and most respected veteran in the country. Hugenberg's friend, Wegener, was convinced the German National leader would secure "more votes than Hitler in the first campaign" and "would win in the second election."[9] Not precluding his own candidacy until the middle of February, Hugenberg groped about for some leader who could elicit a DNVP-dominated consensus.[10] But none of the prominent names that had been discussed—General von Below, Baron von Lüninck, Albert Vögler, Prince Oskar of Prussia, etc.—could inspire unity.[11] Radical nationalism had never appeared so undefined, fragmented, and self-seeking.

Hoping to amplify this dissonance among nationalist leaders, Brüning twice offered to resign his post; Hindenburg remained steadfast and declined both offers.[12] The old man stood by as Hitler, Hugenberg, and the Stahlhelm explored every alternative but could not come to terms. In negotiations for a new cabinet, the nonnegotiable demands of the National Socialists for the chancellorship and pivotal portfolios in a nationalist government collided with intractable opposition from the Stahlhelm, the DNVP, and Hindenburg.[13] Similarly, Hitler refused to subject his constituents to a Hugenberg government.[14] The German National leader could not ignore the NSDAP, for exclusion of Hitler would necessitate collaboration with the middle parties—a rapprochement he had consistently repulsed. Another scheme which Hugenberg hoped would destroy the Brüning government was foiled when Hindenburg rejected the DVNP proposal to call a Reichstag election before the presidential election.[15] The frantic activity of the German Nationals proved futile. Hindenburg could later write:

> The "Harzburg Front" is still only a fiction, more properly said, has never de facto existed.... I have not been an obstacle for such a development [a right-wing government] and neither has the Reich Chancellor Brüning, but *only the disunity of the right,* their inability to come together even on the main points....[16]

Torn between desire to unseat Brüning and reluctance to oppose their honorary chairman, Seldte and Duesterberg tried to convince the president that he should not run in this campaign but should let some other candidate clear the field and reserve himself for the second election.[17] Nevertheless, on 15 February Hindenburg's office announced that by popular request the field marshall would again present himself as a candidate.[18] This decision set off a second wave of activity among the members of the "national opposition."

As early as 4 February at a meeting in Munich, Hitler had suggested to Hugenberg that each of the three major groups field its own candidate. In a subsequent conference, Hugenberg himself was said to have made a similar proposition,[19] but he still hoped to persuade the Stahlhelm to support a candidate of his choice, possibly even his own candidacy.[20] At a meeting with Wagner of the Stahlhelm on 15 February, Hugenberg vehemently protested the inappropriateness of veterans' campaigning against their comrade Hindenburg.[21] Wagner, however, affirmed that the Stahlhelm would sponsor its own candidate and requested Hugenberg to delay action.[22]

Resigned to this lack of control over the national opposition, Hugenberg worked with Wagner to bind the Stahlhelm to the DNVP. A formal contract of collaboration guaranteed German

National support for the Stahlhelm nominee and ceded Hugenberg leadership in political negotiations during the entire course of the presidential campaign. The veterans also promised not to act as a party in the later Prussian elections.[23] Prominent members of their organization would be given leading positions of the DNVP electoral lists. The Stahlhelm would then support the full panoply of German National candidates.[24]

The first campaign revealed Hugenberg not as the grand strategist of *Sammlung*, but as a party boss struggling to maintain national influence. He could not support Hindenburg; he would not support a National Socialist. By accepting a Stahlhelm candidate, Hugenberg believed he still might force Hindenburg's hand. If there had to be a run-off election, as everyone expected, it would open the way for further negotiations.[25] At the same time, supporting a Stahlhelm candidate would bolster his own party and could lead to success in the Prussian election.

Hugenberg did not wish to totally estrange the NSDAP. Some vestige of the Harzburg Front had to be maintained for the future struggle against the Socialists and their allies. Anxious to avoid unnecessary clashes between the DNVP and the NSDAP and thus arouse the "ambition" of the Nazis,[26] Hugenberg sent Quaatz to Braunschweig in order to expedite Nazi attempts to secure Reich citizenship for Hitler.[27] Thus he removed the final obstacle to Hitler's presidential candidacy. A week after Hindenburg had announced his decision to campaign again, Goebbels informed a tumultuous audience in Berlin that Hitler would enter the lists against him.[28] Then the Stahlhelm and DNVP declared that Duesterberg, the second leader of the veterans' organization, would be their candidate.

Hugenberg and his Stahlhelm allies campaigned in a common front—"The Battle Bloc Black-White-Red"—with platitudes that distracted little attention from the fatherly image of the war hero and the charismatic stature of the Nazi.[29] The Hugenberg press campaigned enthusiastically for Duesterberg. When Nazis charged that the DNVP and the Stahlhelm had conspired against the possibility of one mutually acceptable candidate from the national opposition, the Battle Bloc countered that Hitler's demands for absolute authority were insupportable.[30] Despite this antagonism, the Hugenberg syndicate never directly attacked the Nazis as it did Hindenburg's adherents. Headlines rallied readers against the system and for Duesterberg—never directly against Hitler. A subheadline of the *München-Augsburger Abendzeitung* reiterated the old theme, "March separately but strike together!"[31] Neither the DNVP nor the Stahlhelm expected Duesterberg to win. They merely wanted to demonstrate the power of their own radical appeal by frustrating the election of Hindenburg or Hitler.

When the officials tallied the first ballot, Duesterberg had received only 6.8 percent of the votes and Hitler 30.1 percent. The NSDAP had proven that it was the dominant force in the national opposition. Hugenberg's strategy seemed successful only inasmuch as the Duesterberg candidacy had impeded a definite choice. Hindenburg had received a plurality of the votes cast, 49.6 percent, but not the majority that he needed for constitutional election.[32] Hugenberg immediately proposed that the Reichstag accept Hindenburg's plurality as a majority; new Reichstag elections could then follow the forthcoming Prussian elections.[33] Despite his detestation of the Reichstag, Hugenberg had conceived this tactic as a means of wheedling concessions from Hindenburg and obviating the second campaign. His grandstanding went unapplauded, and once again Hugenberg was denied the saviour role. He then considered proposing the crown prince as a candidate against the field marshall.[34] This plan, too, was ill-advised. In Doorn, Wilhelm, as the head of the imperial family, emphasized his own legitimate claims and scorned the idea of restoration through a republican election as "absolute idiocy."[35] In Berlin, Hitler determined to campaign a second time, and the crown prince publicly supported him.[36]

Hugenberg's strategy led him into a blind alley. He could accept neither candidate. With his arsenal depleted, the German National leader ordered his followers to stand "at ease" and hold themselves in readiness for the Prussian electoral campaign.[37] He warned his party not to be personally involved in the Hitler campaign, for then they would be linked with the Nazi failure.[38] The Hugenberg press maintained a neutral stance. Indeed, only a very careful reader could discern that a national electoral campaign was dividing the country.[39] Anxious to alleviate hostility, Hugenberg wrote to Hitler detailing his rationale for not supporting him and yet requesting continued cooperation. The DNVP leader pointed out that the National Socialist campaign would be fruitless—Hitler could not defeat Hindenburg. This second election, Hugenberg believed, could only hurt the national opposition; if this were not the case, he would "act differently." He explained the necessity of cooperation and asserted that events since Harzburg had menaced the spirit of unity. He argued that Hitler's demands for full power were totally unacceptable in German society; it had never been so under any "emperor or king in Germanic lands." Moderation was a part of wisdom, pleaded Hugenberg; success demanded collaboration.[40] Hitler ignored this would-be mentor. With the reelection of Hindenburg on 10 April 1932, the weakness of Hugenberg's position was apparent to all. Over thirty-six percent of the voters chose Hitler, and fifty-three percent elected Hindenburg.[41] Even Hugenberg's allies had rejected his leadership. The ADV urged its membership to vote for Hitler;[42] the Stahlhelm leader, Duesterberg, bequeathed his votes to Hindenburg.[43] Neither industry nor agriculture rallied behind Hugenberg.[44] The impact of the second presidential campaign was devastating for his idea of *Sammlung*. By refusing to support Hitler's candidacy, Hugenberg had forfeited any moral claim on Nazi allegiance.

As a final blow to his ideal of a national bloc, the Stahlhelm complained that its close association with Hugenberg in the first campaign had proven a liability.[45] Arguing that they preferred a nonpartisan position and consequently could not support a single party in the Prussian elections, Stahlhelm leaders broke their agreement with the DNVP.[46] Apparently Seldte and Duesterberg realized that many of their followers would vote for Hitler and, consequently, close alliance with Hugenberg could destroy their own organization. In a meeting of Stahlhelm leaders, Major Wagner revealed the attitude of many younger veterans toward Hugenberg when he added insult to injury. The major mockingly pointed out that it was intolerable for a soldier to esteem "the little man—naturally always formally attired—with the big belly and short little legs and arms with which he could not even reach his neck to scratch himself."[47] The wistful vision of molding this veterans' organization into a German National SA totally dissolved.[48]

Lack of nationalist unity alarmed some industrial leaders. Yearning for a strong bourgeois, antisocialist party, men such as Paul Reusch searched for alternative means to influence national politics. Hoping to affect Nazi policy, he and his colleagues in the *Ruhrlade* agreed to subsidize Hjalmar Schacht's proposal for an office (*Arbeitsstelle*) to protect industrial interests and "influence National Socialist economic ideas in a sensible direction."[49] While there was relative unanimity on this course of action among the controllers of heavy industry, reactions to Hugenberg's leadership of the DNVP varied. Reusch, who had personal as well as political objections to Hugenberg's rule of the party, insisted that the German leader would have to resign. He pledged to withhold all financial support for the DNVP until the party chose a leader able to attract and unify the bourgeoisie.[50]

Reusch's contention was shared by Krupp's brother-in-law, Baron Thilo von Wilmowsky, a prominent figure in agricultural as well as industrial circles. In fact, Wilmowsky seems to have been the principal organizer of the movement to eliminate Hugenberg. Oldenburg-Januschau, who had broken German National ranks to support the election of his friend, Hindenburg, joined this move and sought to convince Hugenberg to resign.[51] Hanoverian industrial circles tried to achieve the same goal by offering M 100,000 to subsidize a united bourgeois front without Hugenberg.[52] On the other hand, Springorum, chairman of the *Langnam Verein* and treasurer of the *Ruhrlade*, rejected this approach. He argued that the DNVP was so bound to its leader and so dedicated to the ideals of bourgeois conservatism that it already was the consensus party that Reusch and the others demanded. A split with Hugenberg and the possible fragmentation of this last strong bourgeois party would lead to the complete frustration of industry's political aspirations.[53] Others apparently shared Springorum's view, and the idea of eliminating Hugenberg before the Prussian elections had to be abandoned.[54]

Intractable as ever, Hugenberg rejected any pressure for his resignation, but he did move toward a slightly more conciliatory posture. In a series of articles circulated throughout his syndicate, he appealed for unity on the right. He claimed that since the secession two years earlier, the DNVP had been so strengthened that it could now afford to reincorporate earlier dissidents. To avoid squandering votes, he urged all rightist parties to collaborate with German Nationals in organizing a Reich list of candidates. This would capitalize on the surplus votes left over from regional constituencies.[55] At the same time he hoped to reconcile the Nazis by explaining his reasoning for not supporting Hitler in the presidential campaign and urging the NSDAP to cooperate in "a new Harzburg of common political work."[56] Essentially, Hugenberg once more resurrected his idea of *Sammlung* and urged the "national and bourgeois world to unite around us."[57]

The Prussian and provincial elections at the end of April, Hugenberg argued, would be the true index of his success. He believed that the Prussians who opposed both the dictatorial inclinations of Hitler and the weak policy of Hindenburg would flock to the German Nationals.[58] At least that was his public position. In his innermost soul, as revealed to his confidant, Wegener, Hugenberg was less optimistic. He was uncertain of the outcome of the campaign and indicated that he felt dissident rightists were making him the scapegoat for their failure to win elections.[59] National Socialist success during the presidential campaigns, coupled with what the Hugenberg circles referred to as Nazi megalomania,[60] made the German National leader more emphatic in stressing the distinction between the DNVP and the NSDAP. As he expressed it to a rally in the Berlin Sport Palace on 21 April:

> We owe it to youth and to our children, to stress loudly and clearly in this campaign that we are not National Socialists and that the National Socialists alone on their own and without us are unable to solve the problems of our time.[61]

Hugenberg continually stressed that a strong, principled DNVP was necessary. He hoped that together the German Nationals and the Nazis would secure a majority and oust the Weimar coalition, which had continued to govern Prussia. Repeatedly, he and his press pointed to the example of Mecklenburg-Strelitz, the small state in which the NSDAP and the DNVP controlled the government, as one of the best examples of good government.[62] This was the model he had in mind for Prussia; the voters rejected it. When the ballots of 24 April were counted, the Hugenberg party suffered losses in every province. The German National delegation fell from second to fifth place; it lost 56 percent of its votes. Even the party press was forced to admit that the DNVP did not receive the votes it had expected.[63] Radical nationalists had once more turned to the NSDAP and increased its representation in the Landtag from 8 to 162 delegates. Together, the two radical national parties did not secure a majority and the anticipated collaboration never developed.

HUGENBERG AND PRESIDIAL GOVERNMENT

After his reelection as president, Hindenburg felt increasingly uneasy with the Brüning cabinet. Disaffection among the soldiers and veterans and the complaints of Junker friends disheartened the old man. His weakened physical and mental health made him vulnerable to the machinations of ambitious men like von Schleicher, who planned to form a more rightist cabinet. The general set the stage by betraying his close friend, General von Groener, minister of interior and minister of defense, who had acted against the Nazi paramilitary units and yet tolerated the accusedly red-dominated *Reichsbanner*.[64] The climax in this political melodrama was contrived when the plan for agrarian settlement encountered sharp criticism. Opposition was led by Count Kalkreuth of the *Reichslandbund* as well as influential agrarian experts, such as Baron von Gayl and Hans-Joachim von Rohr, who supported the DNVP.[65] Schleicher groomed the rightist Center politician, Franz von Papen, to be Brüning's successor.[66]

In directing this movement to the right, the general expected greater support from the national opposition. Hitler wanted the cabinet's recent prohibition against the SA lifted and new elections for the Reichstag. As the Nazi Führer told Hindenburg on the evening of 30 May, the formation of a national government in accord with these ideas would find his movement cooperative.[67] Hugenberg, too, indicated that he could support a stronger, nonsocialist cabinet that deferred to presidential authority rather than partisan interests—providing the new chancellor were acceptable. Somewhat prophetically the German National leader also confided to the president his skepticism regarding Hitler's intentions of supporting such a government. He believed that the National Socialist leader would change his position after the elections for the new Reichstag.[68] Despite the warning and the fact that this move to the right would embitter the Center and totally alienate the SPD, Hindenburg commissioned von Papen to form a government. The "cabinet of barons" represented a clear break with the parliamentary system. Cabinet members had no direct connections with parties and the chancellor depended solely on the use of Article 48. At least three of these ministers were members of the Hugenberg party,[69] who had entered the cabinet without fully discussing the matter with their party leader.[70] Thus Hindenburg took the step to the right that Hugenberg desired, but he excluded the German National chairman from his plans. The new elections scheduled for July could hardly increase support for the DNVP.

Exclusion from the post-Brüning cabinet, after the severe losses suffered in the Prussian election, created a mood of unrelieved failure in the DNVP leadership.[71] Reacting uncharacteristically to disaffection with his leadership, Hugenberg actually considered retiring completely from politics. His good friend Wegener attempted to buoy his spirits by calling Hugenberg "the true Ekkehard" needed by the nation and urging him at least to remain in the Reichstag. Argued Wegener, "Your career is still on the rise. Just when you no longer appear in partisan conflict, the love of the people will gather around you very rapidly."[72] As a member of the Reichstag, Hugenberg would be recognized as "father of the people" and would soon evoke the "love of the nation."[73] If Hugenberg had been courting the people's love, he must have been disconsolate indeed. Not only had the masses remained passive, but the middle classes and the traditional ruling elite were also unimpressed. As his opponents on the right explained, Hugenberg's failure emanated not merely from poor public relations, but from the very personality of the man. As Schleicher's confidant, General von Bredow noted, Hugenberg's "appearance, his speeches, his intractability" readily lent themselves to the formation of a broad front against him.[74]

Capitalizing on Hugenberg's increasing isolation, opponents on the right renewed their demands for his resignation as party leader. Again, Baron Wilmowsky led this drive with encouragement from men like Goerdeler. Dissident German Nationals like Count Westarp, Schiele, and Treviranus indicated they might return to the party if Hugenberg were replaced.[75] The new minister of the interior, von Gayl, favored the move against Hugenberg as did the German National mayors of Halle and Düsseldorf. The industrialist Reusch encouraged such defections, and party leaders in Stuttgart and East Prussia jumped on the bandwagon.[76] Hugo Stinnes, the son of the great entrepreneur, respectfully wrote to his father's friend that large groups of his former associates "would be very grateful, if you were to make the sacrifice for the common cause."[77] Ironically, Hugenberg's quondam allies saw him as the major obstacle to the formation of a unified nationalist opposition. Under this momentum, the DNVP leader might have stepped aside, but the imminency of the July elections for the Reichstag prevented this. As Oldenburg-Januschau cautioned Wilmowsky, the German National party was so dependent on the Hugenberg concern that transfer of leadership on the eve of the campaign would cause grave problems.[78]

Indeed, dividends from Scherl and *Ufa* had continually flowed into party coffers via the *Werbegemeinschaft* and the *Aussendienst*.[79] But while the Berlin-centred media persisted in reaping profits, the provincial press and even the *Ala* continued to lose money and gradually pulled the entire concern deeply into debt. Only a careful manipulation of funds from one corporation to the other permitted Hugenberg and Mann to keep the total enterprise operational.[80] Mann and Klitzsch tapped every possible resource for political purposes. Electoral contributions could help liberate both the party and the concern from fiscal plight. Despite the aversion of many businessmen to its leader, the DNVP could expect sizable contributions from industry. After all, the party still remained the most viable non-Nazi, ant-Socialist party on the right.[81] Even industrialists such as Reusch, who desired a strong bourgeois, nationalist party, could not oppose the German Nationals.

Despite his former opposition to Hindenburg and the personal snub he had received in the formation of the new regime, the DNVP leader gradually moved to support the new chancellor. Policies pursued by the von Papen cabinet—especially the suppression of the Prussian regime on 20 July—encouraged Hugenberg to believe that the new chancellor had begun dismantling the Weimar "system" and constructing a new state. On 23 July, he wrote to von Papen hailing the action against Prussia and indicating that he would not oppose the regime. The German National leader also declared that he felt a certain "co-responsibility for the national movement" and thus he criticized the chancellor for agreeing at Lausanne to make one final reparations payment. Pointing out that a government which did not rely upon the Reichstag still had to maintain contact "with the great national currents in the country," Hugenberg criticized the government's domestic economic program and informed the chancellor that he intended to make additional proposals in the future.[82] Anxious to keep the government free of parties, von Papen did not answer the letter himself. He encouraged Hugenberg's positive attitude, but he had no intention of limiting himself to the partisan support of the DNVP.[83]

Somewhat heartened by the policy of the cabinet, Hugenberg entered the fourth major campaign that year asserting that the prestigious Hindenburg favored the German National program.[84] While he continued to pay lip service to the idea of a "national opposition," Hugenberg warned his adherents that the party had to be revitalized in order to prevent a coalition of the NSDAP and the Center. In effect, the DNVP entered the campaign not as an ally of the National Socialists, but as an opponent. Hugenberg conjured up the dreadful prospect of a dictatorship by a brown-black coalition. Such a regime, he argued, would destroy the DNVP and all that it stood for.[85]

Extolling individualism and denigrating socialism, Hugenberg—in contrast to his previous ideas on the development of the middle classes—now asserted that mechanization would permit the greater expansion of small shops.[86] Such a plank was calculated to cut into the National vote. The DNVP maintained that nationalism and socialism were totally incompatible and that all antisocialists had to gravitate to the German Nationals.[87] There was no direct criticism of Hitler, but at times Hugenberg himself openly criticized "many leaders of the NSDAP."[88] There is no specific documentation detailing financial relations between the two party leaders, but I believe that any subsidies provided by Hugenberg and his *Wirtschaftsvereinigung* for the NSDAP were either terminated or reduced to insignificance during 1932. The attitude of heavy industry toward these parties as well as the financial plight of the Hugenberg concern and the conflict between the DNVP and the NSDAP, in my estimation, justify this conclusion.

To clarify the position of the German Nationals, two of Hugenberg's closest collaborators, Quaatz and Bang, prepared a brochure outlining "The Freedom Program of the German National People's Party." Emphasizing the individual personality as the source of progress, Quaatz and Bang advocated the ascendency of the talented and proposed an open society within which a gifted man could rise to the top. They wanted not only legislation to protect the middle classes from proletarianization, but the opportunity for people of moderate means to improve their condition. Self-help would replace welfare legislation. State intervention in the economy had to be minimized.[89] From provincial village to the federal capital, there had to be a clear definition of power and responsibility, emphasizing the principle of subsidiarity. They proposed a foreign policy based upon "national egotism" and demanded *Lebensraum*, area in which the population could expand and develop its economy free of foreign dictates.[90]

Anxious to court industry and to minimize conflicts on the traditional right, Hugenberg and the authors of this pamphlet omitted any reference to his agricultural assistance program.[91] This facilitated the conclusion of an electoral alliance between the DNVP and the DVP. The growing radicalization of the latter party, after the death of Stresemann, and the alienation of the DNVP from the NSDAP during the spring stimulated this rapprochement which entrepreneurial interests fearful of Nazi socialism encouraged.[92] The two leaders, Eduard Dingeldey and Hugenberg, agreed to form a common Reich list to avoid the loss of votes under the system of proportional representation. According to their agreement, the DNVP would have the first twelve places on the list and the DVP, the next eight. Deputies would still represent their own parties.[93]

Because the DNVP and the DVP were the only major Reichstag parties through which conservatives could support von Papen's cabinet, Hugenberg intended the election not only to strengthen the German Nationals, but also to make von Papen somewhat dependent on his party. The DNVP press sought to create the image of Hugenberg as an economic authority who had much to teach the chancellor in foreign affairs.[94] This strategy failed to increase the voting power of the party on 31 July. The DNVP won only 5.9 percent of the vote and lost four of the forty-one seats it had held since 1930.[95] On the other hand, Hitler's party more than doubled its strength to acquire 230 seats in the Reichstag. Nazi voting power was more than six times greater than that of the DNVP. Hopes of creating a conservative counterpoise to the National Socialists suffered a severe setback.

Similarly, the ill-conceived attempts of von Papen and von Schleicher to secure Nazi cooperation with their regime failed. When Hindenburg met with Hitler on 13 August, the National Socialist leader demanded authority commensurate with his strength as head of the largest party in the Reichstag. This Hindenburg refused to grant.[96] Papen's dream of a compliant majority in the Reichstag evaporated. Still trying to salvage something from the interview of the field marshall and the corporal, he immediately dispatched a report of the meeting to the press. Hitler was portrayed as a man who had not only refused the requests of the president, but had done so in an impertinent, ungentlemanly manner. In thus depicting Hitler, the chancellor opened an almost unbridgeable chasm between his government and the Nazis. The Hugenberg syndicate gave this news release banner headlines but, at the same time, carried the official Nazi version of the meeting.[97]

Hugenberg, who had continually sought not to alienate the leader of the NSDAP, might have provided some link between the cabinet and the Nazi government. But when the National Socialists explored the possibility of forming a coalition government with the Center Party, Hugenberg became one of the chancellor's strongest supporters. While conciliatory German Nationalists like Goerdeler would have preferred including the Nazis in a broad-based coalition, Hugenberg totally rejected such a return to parliamentary government.[98] The German National leader had only attempted to form a "national bloc" as a means of securing popular support to eliminate the "system." Once reform came from "above," the need for a mass base "below" became less necessary. Increasingly distrustful of the National Socialists and the megalomaniacal tendencies of Hitler, Hugenberg became an outspoken proponent of a dictatorial form of government based upon the power of the Reich president.[99] He encouraged cabinet leaders and particularly the minister of the Reichswehr, von Schleicher, to act radically by proscribing the Communist Party and avoiding new elections.[100] Realizing that von Hindenburg—who had sworn to protect the constitution— could not countenance such a blatant violation of his sworn trust, the regime was reluctant to proceed so arbitrarily.

The DNVP nevertheless emerged as the strongest bulwark of von Papen's nonparliamentary cabinet. Leading officials such as

Foreign Minister von Neurath and Minister of the Interior von Gayl confidentially discussed their policies with Hugenberg and solicited his support.[101] The German National leader used this leverage to advocate approval for his economic proposals. Before the new Reichstag opened, Hugenberg informed the chancellor that if the economy were to be saved, the German National program would have to be implemented.[102] In a conciliatory reply, von Papen informed Hugenberg that he was "thoroughly at one with his judgment of the situation" and that the cabinet was preparing its legislation.[103] The government, however, had been pressed by industry to block autarkic demands to establish a quota system on agricultural imports.[104] Consequently, Hugenberg's advocacy of strict protective legislation for native produce was a barrier between him and industrial supporters of the Papen regime.[105] The cabinet's program of 4 September accepted industry's demands and did not include German National demands for agriculture. Hugenberg claimed that it was merely a step in the right direction and prophesied that only the inclusion of his agrarian program could prevent continued economic hardship.[106]

OPEN CONFLICT BETWEEN THE DNVP AND NSDAP

When the Reichstag convened on 12 September, Hermann Göring was the presiding officer. In a tragicomic scene, he refused to accept the dissolution decree presented by the chancellor and entertained the motion of nonconfidence introduced by the Communists. The overwhelming rejection of the von Papen government by a vote of 512 to 42 humiliated not only the "cabinet of barons," but also the Hugenberg party.[107] The Reichstag was dissolved once more—the nation braced itself for the fifth major election of the year.

Once again many rightists thought the time ripe for establishing a more comprehensive bourgeois party than the Hugenberg DNVP. There were suggestions that the appeal of the NSDAP might have peaked. Failure to attain power, coupled with Hindenburg's rebuke of Hitler on 13 August, could halt its momentum.[108] Rather than organize a separate presidial party behind the cabinet, elitist nationalists viewed the German National organization as a possible unifying force. Reusch and his friends intensified efforts to force or persuade Hugenberg to step aside.[109] Jarres, the former presidential candidate and a leader of the DVP, advised Hugenberg that his departure would facilitate a real union of the two parties.[110] Reportedly, Schleicher spoke with Hugenberg about this possibility; von Gayl supported it.[111] The young Stinnes summarized the attitude of many industrialists when he wrote Vögler, Hugenberg "is certainly right, but he cannot inspire enthusiasm and that's what it's all about."[112]

Industrialists refrained from making their debate over German National leadership a public issue. Most of these men, after all, were not democrats and believed that popular opinion regarding the selection of party chairman was un-informed, irrelevant, and partially damaging for bourgeois unity.[113] Hugenberg was not the kindly paternal figure many might have chosen as the image of an older statesman. Nor did his portly gait fit the ideal of the dynamic, youthful leader others might have preferred. Nevertheless he still wielded significant power. Millions of German Nationals remained loyal to their leader and were convinced of his rectitude. His intimates were convinced that the future election would see him reap the fruits of his labors over the past four years.[114]

Cognizant of industrialist sentiment, Hugenberg stressed that he intended the DNVP to be the consensus party of the bourgeois right. The German Nationals, he reiterated, were not an ordinary party in the republican sense—they were "the bearers of the desired national community." Numbers were not essential; only superior ability and indomitable will mattered. His goal had always been "the deliverance of the country and the nation from the 'system'—from parliamentarism, from the party state, from Marxist corruption, from internationalism, and from economic pauperization." Only a mission of such magnitude had prompted his initial alliance with the National Socialists; it had never been his intention "to allow ourselves to be devoured by them." He conceded that the NSDAP had a good organization but stated clearly that his strategy had always been to exploit them and not to bring them to power. Unequivocally he wrote, "Their policy was corrupted the moment they fundamentally refused to listen to our advice. That happened on the day before Harzburg." All of this appeared on the first page of his papers.[115]

Hugenberg's stance possibly helped to ease the financial plight of his syndicate. Through the *Aussendienst G.m.b.H.*, the coaling interests agreed to a sale of profitable *Ufa* stocks from the *Deutsches Gewerbehaus A.G.* to Scherl. This shift within the concern enabled the latter corporation to reorganize and extend its credit with the Dresdener Bank; ultimately, the move prevented Scherl from ending the year with a loss.[116] To secure approval for this transfer, Hugenberg had to pledge the press's right to the use of the title of the *Berliner Lokal-Anzeiger* to the *Aussendienst*.[117] There was also a provision in the agreement dealing with the political policy of the Scherl press, but the coaling interests agreed to raise no objection in this area so long as Hugenberg and Klitzsch remained in control of the firm.[118] In the following weeks, Scherl sharply attacked various elements in the NSDAP but never directly attacked the Nazi leader. Whether this is precisely what the mining interests wanted—or merely tolerated—is not clear.

On 19 October 1932, leaders of the RDI and the cabinet arranged a conference to centralize collection and distribution of funds. Fearful of the growing power of the KPD and distrustful of the SPD, the primary goal of this group was the maintenance of the present government. Obviously the DNVP as well as the DVP had to be subsidized, but the cabinet neither expected nor desired a positive majority in the Reichstag. A fund of two million marks was established to ensure the perpetuation of a rightist government.[119] Industrialists, unsure of the future, were unwilling to alienate the NSDAP. Vögler, who was to meet later with Hitler, thought that some understanding might be reached with the Nazis before the election. But industry could not control the tactics of partisan leaders.

Nazi criticism of the Hugenberg party and its identification with the Papen government had begun even before the campaign. Hitler condemned Hugenberg as reactionary,[120] and he described his own movement as new wine which could not be placed in old sacks made before 1914.[121] While the Nazis dismissed the German Nationals as an aged and effete clique, the DNVP launched a scathing counterattack. German Nationals branded the Nazis as preservers of the constitutional "system," traitors to the cause of national opposition, and opponents of Hindenburg's presidial government.[122] Hugenberg and his allies complained that it was they who had first given the National Socialists the opportunity to join in attacking the Weimar

Republic, but Nazi instability had resulted in a betrayal of the national opposition.[123] Long-standing differences in economic policy were also stressed, as the DNVP criticized the capriciousness that characterized the "unalterable" NSDAP program.[124] In contrast, the DNVP projected itself as the paragon of wisdom and steadfastness. Ignoring his earlier propaganda against Hindenburg, Hugenberg stressed support for a nonparliamentary cabinet based on presidential power. German Nationals boasted of their refusal to collaborate with those who had aligned with the Socialists, as the Center had done. Similarly, the DNVP vaunted its faithfulness to the Harzburg ideal.[125] As the "bearer of the greatly desired people's community," the DNVP would no longer shout "Heil Hugenberg!" but "Heil Deutschland!"[126]

The National Socialists responded with more than propaganda. Goebbels organized a strike at the Scherl press. *Der Angriff* charged Hugenberg with "throwing workers on the street without wages" and claimed that he was cooperating with Communist strike breakers.[127] Later, the Nazi *Gauleiter* of Berlin initiated a boycott of Scherl publications.[128] So intent was Goebbels on destroying the Hugenberg party that scarcely a day passed without some negative comment about the DNVP in *Der Angriff*. The German Nationals were depicted as the party of reaction and the Nazis as the protectors of the little man battling against the hydra of capitalism and Marxism.[129] To further exploit anti-Semitism, *Der Angriff* listed the nationalists of Jewish origin employed at Scherl and charged that the party which had supported the "Jew Duesterberg" had no right to claim leadership in Germany.[130] The Hugenberg press countered that over fifty Nazi leaders had been previously convicted of criminal and moral misconduct.[131] The brown-shirted SA, of course, had been contributing its particular talent to the NSDAP by disrupting German National rallies with the cries, "Heil Hitler!" and "Hugenzwerg verrecke!"[132] Throughout the country, the small German National paramilitary units were either threatened or mugged by their former allies in the national opposition.[133] A classic example of the disruptive tactics employed by the NSDAP against the DNVP in this campaign was the debate between two lieutenants of Hugenberg and Hitler, Schmidt-Hannover and Goebbels. The Nazi propagandist had requested an open discussion in the huge Berlin Sport Palace; the German

Nationals proposed a smaller gathering. Goebbels agreed, but, as he later bragged, "craftily" arranged that the NSDAP would control the meeting. Under his aegis, thousands of tickets were forged and distributed to Nazis. Even before the debate began, the auditorium and its environs rang with confusion and disorder. Neither Schmidt-Hannover nor his colleague, Lothar Steuer, were able to speak without constant interruption. Goebbels, in his turn, spoke longer than the time allotted to him[134] and castigated the DNVP as a "class" party that had participated in republican cabinets on two occasions.[135]

The campaign inflamed contempt and hostility between German Nationals and the Nazis. The DNVP was rooted in the attitudes and traditions of the nineteenth century. It comprised men of property and education who patronized inferiors while scorning democratic idealism and loathing socialistic egalitarianism. Older men raised in the prewar era of peace and prosperity, the German Nationals identified their superiority as social, intellectual, and racial. Hugenberg, himself, typified their Pan-Germanic idealism and expansionism. Hitler and the Nazis were products of the twentieth century. Alienated and deprived, enured by the hardships of the war, the frustrations of inflation, and the humiliation of the depression, these were men of action. No Spenglerian historicizing for them; power was the goal. Hitler and his SA felt that polite bourgeois civilities had castrated the earlier generations; Nazis would not be so easily subdued.

One factor tempered this enmity between the two parties; both leaders publicly avoided personal attacks on one another. Under pressure from Vögler, Hugenberg even agreed to a secret meeting with Hitler.[136] There is no indication that the meeting took place—but the intention was clear. Undoubtedly, Vögler and some other industrialists did not wish to see the divorce finalized. For his part, Hugenberg hoped that the success of presidial government would defuse Nazi power and restrict the National Socialist threat. His hope proved sterile.

Hugenberg's harvest in the election of 6 November amounted to an increase of 800,000 votes for a total of fifty-two delegates, fifteen more than he had in the previous Reichstag.[137] His supporters had gained in all thirty-five electoral districts, especially in the Catholic urban areas of the West.[138] Such a meager increase was insufficient for the government to rely upon, but real success for the German Nationals lay in the fact that the Hitler party had suffered its first electoral setback. These losses made it impossible for the National Socialists to form a majority coalition with the Center Party.[139]

After von Schleicher had prompted von Papen to offer his resignation to the president on 17 November,[140] Hindenburg met with the party leaders to determine the degree of support that he could expect for continuing a presidial cabinet. In his interview with Hindenburg, Hugenberg reaffirmed that such a nonparliamentary regime was the best for Germany and estimated that the present impasse was merely the "frenzied struggle" of the Center and the Nazis to regain power. He argued that the Nazis could incite civil war just as readily as the Marxists; the only safeguard would be presidial government. As far as the economy was concerned, Hugenberg expressed his confidence that the worst was over and that the government, by implementing his policies, would improve the situation. Once the financial crisis had been overcome, Hugenberg counseled, the government could deal with constitutional problems. When asked his impression of a possible Hitler cabinet, Hugenberg replied that he had cooperated with the NSDAP Führer before Harzburg on the assumption that the Nazis would accede neither to the presidency nor to the chancellorship. Then Hitler sought both positions. Hugenberg concluded:

> I have not found Hitler to be very loyal to agreements: his whole manner of handling political affairs makes it very difficult to be able to entrust Hitler with political leadership; I would have very grave reservations against this.[141]

Despite the urging of some industrialists,[142] Hindenburg, after meeting with party leaders, refused to entrust Hitler with the chancellorship of a presidial government. Since the Center could reach no agreement with the National Socialists and the other parties, the president determined to summon von Papen again.[143] General von Schleicher, however, had other plans and virtually forced the old field marshal to give him the chancellorship. Schleicher, through a change in cabinet policy, expected to win over the various union leaders and moderate nationalists. This support, coupled with his hope to rally the Strasser wing of the Hitler party, would provide him with the backing that he needed.[144] During the war, army leaders and union officials had developed a degree of successful cooperation.[145] Now, the Strasser wing of the NSDAP demanded social reform and was disenchanted with Hitler's failure to accept anything but total power. If unionists and Strasserites could be engineered into supporting his cabinet, Schleicher would be a success. The new chancellor was a skilled manipulator of political factions, and nationalist politicians bided their time before directly attacking him.

THE FORMATION OF THE HITLER CABINET

In Hugenberg's view, the appointment of the general reinforced the parliamentary system, weakened the office of the president, and delayed important reform measures.[146] Political uncertainty did not inspire economic confidence. Industrialists, shopkeepers and small farmers, entrepreneurs and professional men—all felt threatened. The new chancellor had neither the charisma nor the practical policies which could rally these forces. His cabinet merely bought time for the regrouping of factions.

At the beginning of December, leaders in the Ruhr were unsure of the new government, just as some were unsure of the Hitler movement. The anti-Marxist stance of the Nazis had encouraged some industrialists to support Hitler's claim to chancellorship. Indeed, some businessmen had petitioned Hindenburg to turn over "the responsible leadership of a presidial cabinet filled with the best professional and political strength to the leader of the strongest national group," that is, Hitler. These industrialists were not advocating a totally Nazi cabinet, but they wanted the Nazis to be granted power in accordance with their "factual and political strength."[147] Men like Schacht and the Cologne banker, Kurt von Schröder, enthusiastically supported the NSDAP. They wanted not an arbitrary Hitlerian dictatorship, but a period of calm predictability in which Germany, under a strong rightist cabinet, could redevelop its economy. Industrial opponents of this proposal, men like Reusch and Springorum, feared the socialist thrust of Nazi policy and distrusted the totalitarian claims of the NSDAP. They did not directly oppose Hitler, but they lacked confidence in his movement and suspected that supporting a single party would weaken the influence of industry.[148] As an old conservative shocked by the demagoguery of Nazism, Hindenburg empathized with such men and refused to sponsor a Nazi-dominated cabinet. The president's appointment of von Schleicher, however, did not win the positive support of industrial leaders. The new chancellor's social and economic policies indicated a greater amount of state intervention and aroused the suspicion, if not the outright hostility, of some large corporations.[149] With six million workers unemployed, bourgeois circles blamed socialist experimentation for the economic slump. Hugenberg and Reichert observed that the country and the world had reached the end of the economic crisis and the spiral would soon begin its upward trend.[150] Rightists feared that governmental intervention—be it ever so moderate—might hinder the upswing; radicals dreaded an improvement in the economy before they could exploit the crisis. Industrialists demanded that the state avoided a zigzag course in economic policy; a clear distinction had to be made between the functions of the state and those of the private economy.[151] The RDI had had such a policy throughout the Weimar era, but now on the brink of economic improvement, industrialists demanded that government accept these principles. The *Langnam Verein* stressed this view at its annual meeting on 23 November 1932.[152] Krupp and the board of directors of the RDI repeated it on 25 November.[153]

By excoriating any manifestation of socialism, industry reemphasized its own basis for unity and groped for cooperation with agricultural leaders. The vigorous demands of the *Reichslandbund* and Hugenberg for governmental intervention on behalf of agriculture had emphasized the sharp divisions separating the two basic pillars of the traditional "producing classes" (*schaffende Stände*). Hugenberg's conflict with the RDI had developed because of this divergence. During the two Reichstag campaigns of 1932, antagonisms persisted. In the von Papen cabinet, von Braun, as the spokesman for agriculture, and Warmbold, as the representative of industry, disagreed on economic policy. Schleicher's maintenance of the two men in office sustained this dichotomy.[154] The Ruhr had traditionally encouraged an alliance between heavy industry and agriculture. At the turn of the year, Krupp as president of the RDI was particularly disturbed by the personal attacks of agricultural leaders on the policy of organized industry.[155] He had no desire to alienate the agrarian elite, especially since he believed that "the consolidation of political conditions is urgently necessary from the standpoint of the total economy and it [consolidation] cannot be achieved rapidly enough."[156] RDI leadership emphasized that economic unrest was "extremely dangerous" and that an unambiguous policy along the lines demanded by private industry was the only solution to the economic crisis.[157]

Conflict between industry and agriculture reached a climax over the problem of trade treaties to be negotiated with Holland and other states in 1933.[158] A key figure in neither the RDI nor the *Landbund*, Hugenberg nevertheless understood the mentalities of men involved and the need for a unified governmental economic policy.[159] Industrialists anxious for stability might be willing to accept a champion of agriculture familiar with the needs of industry. In a series of editorials published in the middle of December, the German National leader sought to convey his image as the experienced authority eminently able to guide the country out of the economic crisis. He emphasized that strong, determined leadership could reconcile agriculture and industry; a coherent policy would terminate disputes between ministries and place the good of the nation over special interests. In this area as well as in the field of international economics, Hugenberg indicated that he held the key.[160]

Unwilling to alienate the Schleicher regime, Hugenberg bided his time and explored his options. If the DNVP were to gain power, it could only be through a dictatorial regime or through a more broadly based coalition with other nationalist forces. The possibility of Hindenburg's selecting him to form a ministry was slim, but Hugenberg was prepared to accept this responsibility. At the same time, he believed that his party still had to consider cooperation with the National Socialists. The greatest danger, as he envisioned it, would be the exclusion of the DNVP from an agreement between Hindenburg and Hitler granting the Nazi the chancellorship and calling for new elections.[161] Unable to determine or predict the political outcome, Hugenberg planned for any eventuality.

Plans for a presidial cabinet dominated by German Nationals were drawn up. In view of his personal conflicts with Hindenburg and the attempt to remove him from the leadership of the DNVP during 1932, Hugenberg thought of the popular mayor of

Leipzig, Carl Goerdeler, as a suitable candidate for the chancellorship. In this "shadow cabinet," Hugenberg wanted to be the "economic dictator" controlling the ministries, which would permit him to activate his plans for economic and social development.[162] To ensure success, Hugenberg and his colleagues prepared a series of thirteen "Urgent Measures" to inaugurate totalitarian controls over German society. The DNVP leader willingly embraced severity because "every clemency here costs blood and time." The bureaucracy and in particular the police were to be purged of hostile elements. Strikes were to be declared illegal, and measures to prevent a general strike were outlined. Opposition was to be considered treason, and public opinion was to be controlled. "Ring leaders" were to be immediately arrested "at the least sign of unrest," and those who were parliamentarians were to be taken into "protective custody."[163] Hugenberg's view that "something unnational" (etwas unvölkisches) infected the German people apparently justified such draconic measures, which "paramilitary organizations" (bündische Gemeinschaften) would have to help enforce.[164]

Since Hugenberg's German Nationals had neither the prestige nor the numerical strength to enforce such extremist action, the sketchy nature of the "shadow cabinet" outlined by Schmidt-Hannover and the "preparations for a possible cabinet formation" could readily be applied to a nationalist government including National Socialists. A man of Hugenberg's experience knew that the antisocialist regime he desired necessitated some Nazi collaboration. Despite the conflicts of the past campaign and the public contempt of Nazis for him in the Reichstag,[165] Hugenberg took the initiative in restoring unity in the national opposition. He wrote to Hitler emphasizing the dangers of a coalition government including the Center Party and pointed to the German Nationals' experience in 1925 and 1927 to exemplify the detrimental effect such collaboration could have on a party of ideological opposition. Hugenberg was convinced that:

> As soon as the Center gains the central position on the scale, Marxism which had long ago been defeated internally, will gain new strength. It was and is not necessary, that the Center should regain the lost key position.... But if that is

> not to be, if everything that has been gained up to now is not to be gambled away, there must of course be unity within the national movement.[166]

In the coming weeks, this letter was a valuable aid to Hitler as the Nazis negotiated for the formation of a new cabinet.

Hugenberg's attempt to reconcile Hitler after the bitter confrontation of their parties in the November elections apparently arose not solely from his need for popular support, but also from his attempt to conciliate industrialists partial to the Nazi cause. In the middle of December, ex-chancellor von Papen contacted the Nazi banker, Baron von Schröder, and began arrangements for the famous Hitler-Papen meeting at the home of the banker at Cologne.[167] The former chancellor also arranged a conference with key leaders in heavy industry after his discussions with Hitler. Undoubtedly elitists such as Springorum, Vögler, Reusch, Krupp, and von Papen, were seeking some sort of middle ground in their attempt to reconcile Nazi claims with traditionalist forces.[168] All of these men were apparently willing to accept Hitler as a junior partner in a coalition government under the leadership of von Papen. Certainly, this is the possible development which the industrialists discussed with the ex-chancellor. Quite probably, Hugenberg learned some of the details of this conference through his contacts in the Ruhr. Both Springorum and Vögler had a strong sense of loyalty to him, and both were intimately involved in his concern.[169]

That the magnates of the Ruhr desired a strong bourgeois *Sammlung* is obvious, but Hitler's precise role in such a ministry remains a matter of dispute. In November, Vögler had been willing to accept the Nazi as chancellor—perhaps that is what he still thought was best in January. Reusch, however, wrote shortly after the meeting with von Papen that Hitler seemed to have innerly adjusted to surrendering the chancellorship.[170] The political solution apparently favored by some men of the *Ruhrlade* was the united bourgeois front which Reusch, Wilmowsky, and, presumably, Krupp and Goerdeler had sought throughout the middle of 1932.[171] In this view, Hugenberg, if not an obstacle, was surely very expendable. The German National Party, however, was a significant power base which a more attractive figure, such as von Papen, might lead. The idea of a Catholic presiding over a strong, rightist party introduced the very appealing prospect of unifying all Christian opponents of Marxism.

While non-Nazi industrialists conspired to mitigate differences with the NSDAP, the Nazi Thyssen, directly threatened the German National leader. His corporation had been part of the consortium which ensured Hugenberg's control of the *Ufa* film company. Precondition for Thyssen's purchase of M 500,000 worth of stocks had been the possible fostering of "collaboration in various fields." He now judged that "this precondition has proven to be false" and informed Hugenberg that he intended to sell.[172] Hugenberg feared that Thyssen would use the stock to help the Nazis.[173] Obviously, Thyssen's objections to the lack of collaboration indicated his anger at the rivalry which split the DNVP and the NSDAP into opposing factions in the last election. Conversely, greater collaboration might ensure Thyssen's maintenance of the stock.

After four years of intense political campaigning coupled with the administrative burdens of his concern, the sixty-seven-year-old Hugenberg was depressed over the financial plight of his concern and his party.[174] He wrote to his friend Wegener, "I see the difficulties growing all around ... I myself am growing older and often do not know how the difficulties should be overcome."[175] Constitutionally, however, Hugenberg's entire personality rejected defeat. Emotionally, the support of devotees such as Wegener undoubtedly bolstered his belief in his own economic genius. To destroy socialism, to eliminate the "treasonous" Center Party, and to create a Germany based on the principles of individualism had been Hugenberg's overwhelming ambition. Despite his mood of depression, he was still reluctant to surrender his position—especially since the need for a political leader capable of inspiring the confidence of both industry and agriculture became more and more apparent in the first weeks of the new year.

On 11 January, leaders of the *Reichslandbund* met personally with President von Hindenburg and presented their objections to the cabinet's agrarian policy.[176] Since Hugenberg possessed the confidence of many agriculturalists, his political stock rose. Two days later on 13 January, Hugenberg spoke with Chancellor von Schleicher and clearly developed his favorite idea of a "crisis ministry." Such a cabinet post would unite the ministries of economics and agriculture in the Reich and Prussia under an "economic dictator."[177] This was the post Hugenberg wanted; it was his overriding goal throughout these critical weeks. To secure this position, the German National leader hesitated to alienate von Schleicher and, at the same time, sought to conciliate the Nazis and the industrialists who favored a cabinet of national unity.

With greater numbers than the DNVP, the NSDAP was in a more secure political position. However, the heterogeneous, populist nature of Nazism indicated that the movement might collapse as rapidly as it had grown. Propagandistically, the nimbus of the movement had already been broken by the loss of votes in the November election. Despite Hitler's frustration of von Schleicher's attempt to divide the party, new victories were necessary if the dynamic image of Nazism was to be perpetuated. The provincial elections in Lippe offered the Nazis an opportunity to recapture this dynamism.[178]

In this province, which included Hugenberg's electoral district, the German National leader had his estate. In its capital he controlled the *Lippische Tages-Zeitung*, which was read by the prosperous farmers of the community. In such an atmosphere there could have been sharp conflict between Nazis and German Nationals, between Hitler and Hugenberg. There was none. Hugenberg's hand-written proposal for a pamphlet, "National Socialist Agitation Against Dr. Hugenberg," was apparently never published.[179] Instead of attacking the "false, vile, and odious campaign tactics" of the NSDAP, Hugenberg delivered a mild speech on 11 January repeating hackneyed shibboleths against the "system."[180] Although his letterheads indicate that he was at Rohbraken during this campaign, the only other Hugenberg speech was a closed presentation to the party faithful.[181] His newspaper supported the DNVP, but there was none of the spirited attack on the NSDAP which had characterized the last Reichstag elections. Indeed, the local German National organization had entered into a truce (*Burgfrieden*) with the NSDAP.[182] The result was that the German Nationals lost more than 4,000 votes and the Nazis gained over 5,000.[183] The Detmold paper headlined the fact that the way was now open for a nationalist government in the province.[184] In view of the economic pressures on Hugen-

berg and his own desire to conciliate the Nazis, the logical con-
clusion seems to be that Hugenberg sought more than peace in
Lippe. He and the industrialists who supported von Papen
wanted Nazi collaboration. The termination of the DNVP-
NSDAP electoral conflict may well have been the price
Hugenberg paid to prove his goodwill.

Despite Hugenberg's change in tactics, many German Nationals
remained hostile to the Nazi movement. Oberfohren, the chairman of the German National Reichstag delegation, expressed
the sentiments of many party members when he said that the
Nazis were not fit to govern and the powers of the Reich president would have to be used against them.[185] Such sentiment did
not permit a complete and rapid *volte-face* in dealings with Hitler.
Official party circulars indicated that losses in the Lippe elections
were due to the inefficiency of local party leaders; there was no
mention of a general policy of reconciliation.[186] Official reports
of the Hugenberg-Hitler meeting on 17 January gave no positive
indication of a new tactic. Publicly, the two men merely expressed their common antipathy for the current cabinet.[187]

Hugenberg was still anxious to prevent a Nazi-dominated
regime. After the German Nationals had learned that
Kriegsheim of the *Reichslandbund* would support a Hitler chancellorship, Schmidt-Hannover—possibly as Hugenberg's emissary—urged von Schleicher to clarify his policy. The German Nationals wanted him to establish a firm "social, political, and
economic course and thus take the wind out of the Nazi sails."[188]
Neither Hugenberg nor Schleicher, however, were to be the chief
architects of a strong rightist regime. The manipulator who
would bring diverse nationalist factions together was von Papen.

Having won the friendship of the president, the ex-chancellor
used his leverage to work against his successor. The friendly attitude of industry secured him powerful supporters among men
who wanted stability and predictability to characterize the German regime at home and abroad.[189] Nazi success in the Lippe
election indicated that the coming political constellation would
not be a combination of Strasser and Schleicher, but of Hitler
and Papen. This last alternative could be harmonized with
Hugenberg's concept of a Goerdeler cabinet uniting DNVP and
NSDAP. A former member of the Center, von Papen possessed a
certain attractiveness for a broad strata of bourgeois nationalists.

The ex-chancellor could readily replace the mayor of Leipzig in Hugenberg's calculations. The necessity of collaborating with von Papen was clearly brought home to Hugenberg when on 22 January he learned that President von Hindenburg would not be against a Hitler chancellorship, provided that it had a broad parliamentary base.[190]

Von Papen's polish and tact, coupled with his apparent willingness to lie glibly, has made it impossible to follow his negotiations precisely. He had no intention of splitting the NSDAP, as von Schleicher had unsuccessfully attempted to do.[191] Having readily manipulated von Hindenburg, Papen expected to control Hitler and the Nazis just as easily. His approach was thus a return to Hugenberg's policy before Harzburg. His problem after the 4 January meeting was to find some way to satisfy Hitler's demands without giving the Nazis total power. The resulting negotiations were conducted in such an atmosphere of secrecy and intrigue that right up until the official inauguration of the new cabinet on 30 January 1933, conditions for the formulation of the new government remained unclear.

Hugenberg was not included in all of the meetings and schemes that went on in the background. Like most elitists from the ranks of agriculture and industry, the chairman of the DNVP apparently remained uninformed of the secret negotiations between the ex-chancellor and the Nazis at the home of Joachim von Ribbentrop.[192] Nevertheless, his tolerant and even benevolent attitude—like that of Oldenburg-Januschau and Vögler—undoubtedly assisted von Papen.[193] On 24 January, Duesterberg informed Hugenberg that Seldte had been negotiating with Hitler, and on the following day, Dr. Stadtler reported that Hitler had a long discussion with von Papen and Schacht. Nevertheless, Hugenberg's conversations on 25 January with Frick and Göring and then with Seldte and Duesterberg apparently enabled him to learn little about the status of these negotiations.[194] Hugenberg was, however, willing to compromise with Hitler; his tactics since 28 December make that abundantly clear. As his editorialists expressed it, their party leader would accept a Hitler chancellorship, but not a Nazi dictatorship.[195]

Hitler had arranged a meeting with Hugenberg for the afternoon of 27 January. Frick, Göring, and Schmidt-Hannover were also present. Göring claimed that von Papen had "unambiguously agreed" to propose to Hindenburg the appointment of Hitler as chancellor and that Seldte had recognized Hitler's claim to leadership. Confronted with what was apparently a clear decision, Hugenberg could either remain in the opposition or join with von Papen in an attempt to "frame Hitler in." He chose the latter alternative and fought to prevent Nazi control of key ministries and to reject the demand for new Reichstag elections.[196]

On 28 January, Hugenberg met with von Papen immediately after he had received his commission to form a new government. Hugenberg was informed that the Nazis would be offered not merely the chancellorship, but also the Reich and the Prussian Ministries of the Interior. Von Papen would serve as vice-chancellor. The decision had been made. Hitler would be chancellor, and the NSDAP would control the Prussian police. For Hugenberg to refuse cooperation would mean that all his work over the past four years as party chairman and over the last thirteen as an engineer of counterrevolution would be unrewarded. Collaboration, on the other hand, could mean that his ideas might be implemented. In addition, his firm was deeply in debt, and cooperation with von Papen could help solve this problem. Up to the last minute, he sought to influence Seldte and the Reich president to change their support for Nazi control of the police and for new elections, but he placed no irremovable obstacle in von Papen's path.[197]

On 29 January, the former chancellor informed the German National leader that the defense ministry would go to General Werner von Blomberg and the Ministry of Labor to Seldte. Most of the other ministers would remain at their posts. The "president" was prepared to offer Hugenberg four important economic portfolios in the Reich and Prussia. Hugenberg would become the key man in the formulation of the total economic policy of the state. This was, in Schmidt-Hannover's words, "an attractive offer." When Seldte indicated that he would prefer a portfolio dealing with the training of youth and the development of labor service, the German National leader persuaded him to accept the position as minister of labor and transfer to the "crisis ministry" the department dealing with social policy and labor law. Hugenberg thus ensured greater support for von Papen's plan and assured the strengthening of his own position as "economic dictator."[198] He would now have the opportunity to implement his grand design for the reorganization of the German economy.[199]

A few minutes before the new cabinet's reception by Hindenburg on 30 January, the question of new Reichstag elections resurfaced. In a corner of Meissner's office, the discussion became heated as Hugenberg declared new elections unnecessary. Time to debate this issue was limited. Meissner informed the new ministers that they were already late for their appointment with von Hindenburg. Hitler protested that the new elections would not affect the structure of the cabinet, that the same men would remain in control. Nevertheless Hugenberg continued to object. Finally, von Papen intervened and Hugenberg reluctantly agreed to leave the formal decision on new elections to von Hindenburg. A few minutes later the Reich president commissioned the new government.[200]

The Hitler cabinet was not a Nazi cabinet; indeed, only three of the eleven ministers were members of the National Socialist party. Nazis held the chancellorship with Hitler and the Ministry of the Interior with Frick; in addition, Göring was minister without portfolio. The dependency of the cabinet upon President von Hindenburg provided an additional guarantee that the NSDAP would not take over full power. Hitler was not even to speak with the old field marshal unless the vice-chancellor, von Papen, was present. To prevent National Socialist experiments in the economy, Hugenberg occupied the posts of Reich minister of economy, Reich minister of food and agriculture, Kommissar for the *Osthilfe*, Prussian minister of economics, and Prussian minister of agriculture and forestry.

Hitler himself later boasted the political structure was contrived to make the situation "anything but simple" for him and his party.[201] Hugenberg had reason to believe that the Nazis could be "tamed." He returned to his office and confidently announced: "Now the catastrophe is over."[202] His syndicate reflected his confidence. The *Lippische Tages-Zeitung* commented that the total situation in Germany would improve because Hugenberg, "who possibly alone in Germany perceived the interrelationships of economic life, will have the opportunity to realize his plans."[203] The *Berliner Lokal-Anzeiger* claimed that Hugenberg had the best position in the cabinet.[204]

For many observers of the German scene, the greatest threat
was not the Nazis. As Mussolini expressed it, there was no
necessity to fear Hitler, who was "malleable," but rather
"Hugenberg and the Junkers of the old Germany."[205] Hugenberg's principled intransigence in internal affairs and his plans
for national economic development seemed to present the
greatest threat to the status quo. In classical understatement, the
French ambassador had voiced this same concept when he informed his foreign office that "in the association of the three
men (Hitler, Papen, and Hugenberg) ... the least dangerous, the
least troublesome is certainly not M. Hugenberg."[206] Similarly,
Germany's eastern neighbour, Poland, was less disturbed by the
appointment of Hitler to power than by "his connection with
Hugenberg" whom the Poles viewed as "the more dangerous
threat."[207] Even within Germany itself, "the impression of a German National preponderance" was widespread.[208]

At the first meeting of the new cabinet, Hugenberg was indeed
more radical than Hitler. To prevent new elections to the
Reichstag, Hugenberg argued that the Communist Party should
be proscribed. Through such a measure, he asserted, the government could gain a majority in the Reichstag and possibly even
secure the passage of an enabling act. In contrast to such an
openly repressive measure, Hitler and Göring argued in favor of
a more constitutional approach—negotiations with the Center
and new elections. Both these tactics threatened Hugenberg's
position. The Nazis further protested that the outlawing of six
million voters would disrupt the economy and possibly produce
a general strike. The National Socialists preferred preserving the
semblance of legalism. The chancellor, however, reassured the
ministers that new elections would not affect the composition of
the cabinet.[209] In this meeting and in a further discussion of the
same problem on the next day,[210] the Nazis had outmaneuvered
Hugenberg and he knew it. He could only comment to Goerdeler, "Yesterday I made the biggest mistake of my life—I concluded an alliance with the worst demagogue in history."[211]

Dr. Leo Wegener, Hugenberg's friend and adviser. *(Courtesy Bundesarchiv Koblenz.)*

Hugenberg, Klitzsch, and Mann examining the silver plaque presented to Hugenberg by his associates on his seventy-fifth birthday. *(Courtesy of the Hugenberg family.)*

Hugenberg and his family watching peasants celebrate the harvest festival at his estate, Rohbraken. *(Courtesy of the Hugenberg family.)*

Uniformed protesters organized to campaign against the Young Plan. *(Courtesy of the Hugenberg family.)*

Schmidt-Hannover and Hugenberg (foreground left to right) arriving at Bad Harzburg. Behind them are Dr. Weiss of the party central office and Hugenberg's executive secretary, Wolfgang Vogelsang. *(Courtesy of the Hugenberg family.)*

der Nationalen Opposition in Bad Harzburg am 11. Oktober 1931

Dr. Frick   Hitler   Dr. Hugenberg   Schmidt-Hannover   Duesterberg   Seldte

Postcard commemorating the meeting of the forces in the national opposition on 11 October 1931. *(Courtesy of the Hugenberg family.)*

Hugenberg and traditional radicals at Bad Harzburg in October 1931. *(Courtesy of the Hugenberg family.)*

Minister Hugenberg addressing a group of "Green Shirts" early in 1933. *(Courtesy of the Hugenberg family.)*

Hugenberg and his wife, Gertrud, at an old-age home after the Second World War. *(Courtesy of the Hugenberg family.)*

6 Nazism Triumphant

The carefully contrived "cabinet of national concentration" had been planned to manipulate Hitler. Conservatives, convinced that society should be subject to the state and that the regime could control the state, thought they had outwitted the Nazis. In their hubris, Hugenberg and his associates could not imagine a revolution from below. Ensconced in his ministry, Hugenberg believed he could remodel Germany. Within five months, he was forced to admit that he had totally misjudged the political scene. The manipulators had become the manipulated. German Nationalism and its leader were obsolete.

The Election of a Nationalist Reichstag

On 2 February the cabinet issued a proclamation summoning the electorate to the polls and stating the unified goals of the new government. The ministers argued that the loss of "honor and freedom" of the last fourteen years had to be reversed and the spiritual regeneration of Germany had to be their first task. The maintenance of Christian principles, protection of the farmer, and the termination of unemployment constituted their expressed guidelines for future policy. Such goals, coupled with the "utilization of individual initiative," formed the best protection for a secure currency that would not be threatened by dangerous experiments.[1] Certainly the counterrevolutionary DNVP could stand solidly behind such rhetoric. The manifesto issued by the Hitler cabinet said what conservative nationalists wanted to hear. But if Chancellor Hitler supported such a platform, all nationals could support the NSDAP. If the "party state" had been overcome, the German National party was superfluous.

In the party press, Hugenberg and his supporters established their rather ambiguous basis for the necessity of the DNVP. His syndicate argued that a stronger party was more necessary than ever in order to give Hugenberg the support he needed—especially since his task of reorganizing the economy was the most difficult and most important function of the new cabinet. Furthermore, the DNVP had to ensure the "Christian-conservative way of life" against the incursions of "atheism and liberalism, socialism and Marxism" and, at the same time had to lead the way back to a "pure state" free of party influence "according to the Prussian tradition." Burdened with such a responsibility, German Nationals could not be "indifferent" to governmental party. Nevertheless, the DNVP asserted that "the party is nothing, the state everything."[2] The paradox that there were to be no parties, but that a German National party was necessary, led Hugenberg and his followers into a dead-end street.

Privately, the German Nationals presented a more familiar argument—that the DNVP had to continue because the Nazi movement was unreliable. The central party office warned its membership that "the common battle against the opposing front of the left must not lead to a watering down of the difference" in the "political principles and concepts" of the DNVP and the NSDAP. Hugenberg's supporters had to work against the Nazis because they had "not unambiguously recognized the principles of private economy." Moreover, the NSDAP placed greater stock in "political agitation than in political responsibility to the state" and did not always recognize the necessity of a "professional civil service."[3] Finally, the German Nationals maintained that men of property and education had to have a strong enough base to influence the unprincipled and inexperienced National Socialists.

Because a campaign against the Nazis based "less on the character of hostility than on the spirit of political differentiation"[4] did not offer a clear choice to the people, one of the party leaders suggested an agreement with the NSDAP whereby the two parties would set up one list on which every third candidate would be a German National.[5] The central party office rejected this for two reasons. First, Hugenberg's advisers realized that a Nazi rejection of this offer could be used against the DNVP in the campaign, and, second, they believed that the "enthusiasm for torchlight processions" would pass and the DNVP would be seen as the true governmental bulwark against Socialism.[6] The party was determined to enter the campaign as a muted opponent of National Socialism. There was another alternative to the total independence of the DNVP—the development of a suprapartisan, nationalist, bourgeois front. This is precisely the type of organization men such as Reusch and Wilmowsky had desired in 1932. Vice-chancellor von Papen, who knew of this plan and who had presumably engineered the cabinet so that a group such as this could manipulate Hitler, proposed the formation of such a united bloc.[7] Hugenberg rejected the prospect of making electoral concessions that might result in the loss to the Reichstag of some of his own men, just as they seemed so near the goal of effectively manipulating the government.[8] He did, however, accept a compromise in the form comparable to the alliance of the Stahlhelm and the DNVP in the first presidential campaign. Von Papen and Seldte joined with him in endorsing the "Battle Front Black-White-Red."[9] Obviously, Hugenberg hoped to exploit Papen's and Seldte's support in order to strengthen his own hand.

On 11 February, the DNVP cancelled the party rally it had planned—or rather, changed the structure of the demonstration and announced the formation of the new front. With von Papen and Seldte at his side, Hugenberg proudly proclaimed to an enthusiastic audience that Germany under Field Marshall von Hindenburg had the opportunity to overcome its internal dissensions by rallying the "good old forces of the nation."[10] Hugenberg later asserted that the national movement advanced in two columns toward the same goal. On the one hand, there was the National Socialist group, and on the other, there was "the proper right, the Battle Front Black-White-Red, the national bourgeoisie of the best tradition."[11]

In the campaign, the new cabinet used every means possible, from placing placards in public buildings to manipulating the government controlled radio, in order to secure popular ratification of its powers. The DNVP could profit from such techniques but certainly not to the extent that the National Socialists could. With similar determination, the Nazis turned to industry for financial support. Hitler knew that industry desired a firm, stable government which would not experiment with the economy. These were the preconditions which the presidium of the RDI in its meetings on 16 and 17 February had set down for its support of the government.[12] When he met with industrial leaders on 21 February, Hitler told them what they wanted to hear. He assured them that there would be no experiments and asserted that his fundamental position in the political battle of the last fourteen years had always been based on respect for individualism and private property. Krupp, as chairman of the RDI, thanked the chancellor.[13]

Hitler then left, and Göring moved to the business of the day—electoral contributions. The Nazi propaganda chief and Schacht proposed the establishment of a three-million-mark fund. All agreed that western iron and coaling interests would provide one million; the chemical and potash industries another, and finally the lignite, machine, and electrical corporations the third.[14] Hugenberg, who had not been present at the meeting, must have been ambivalent about its results. His conflict with the RDI had once more reaped bitter fruit. The industrial fund was to be distributed among the NSDAP, the DNVP, and other right-wing groups proportionately. German Nationals would hardly receive the lion's share.

The DNVP expected to receive a quarter of the funds collected and, supposedly, planned its budget accordingly;[15] but Schacht, who administered these contributions, informed Scheibe, the DNVP treasurer, that most industries favored a ratio of 80:20. Only contributions from heavy industry and some others who directly expressed a preference for the formula 75:25 would be distributed according to this more favorable percentage.[16] Hugenberg was peeved at this determination and wrote Schacht to be sure that all segments of industry paid their share directly to the DNVP and not to other organizations like the Stahlhelm.[17] The chemical industry, however, refused to support Hugenberg and demanded that from its contribution of M 500,000 twenty percent should go directly into an account under von Papen's control. The Stahlhelm was also to recieve assistance from this special Papen fund, which amounted to at least M 162,500.[18] In sum, the German National treasurer concluded that his party would only receive approximately M 587,000 from the three million marks collected for the campaign.[19] Presumably, both national parties involved in the fund had other sources of income. For example, Hugenberg secured a safe seat for the industrialist Rademacher, who had seceded from the DNVP in 1933. Reportedly, the party received at least M 300,000 as the price of reconciliation.[20] In a separate report, presumably to the members of the Wirtschaftsvereinigung, Hugenberg detailed the expenditure of M 284,277.50 in contributions placed at his discretion.[21]

Obviously, the DNVP had sufficient resources to wage a spirited electoral campaign. Contributions to the party bolstered the Hugenberg concern and strengthened the symbiotic relationship between the two. In manipulating propaganda, Hugenberg and his supporters determined that movies were "the most effective" form of propaganda and the cinema would consequently have to be used "in far greater proportion" than had been the case before.[22] One of the most important ways that the *Ufa* could help was through its control of the weekly newsreels shown in German theaters. In the film clips, reserved for this period, the German National position was continually evident. The necessity of the DNVP and the importance of Hugenberg's work were depicted as having greater significance than the radicalism of the Nazis. The very first news reel of the new cabinet emphasized that the regime was one of "national concentration." The cameras, of course, showed Hitler and all the ministers, but the clip ended by focusing on von Papen talking with Hugenberg.[23] The intimation was obvious.

There was no doubt that the German National party leader intended to use the full weight of his concern in order to strengthen his position in the cabinet. Films with a distinct nationalist appeal were to be rented to the party and used at political rallies held right in the 97 *Ufa* theaters spread over 47 cities across Germany.[24] In addition, the Scherl *Verlag* offered subscriptions to *Der Tag* at reduced prices to members of the DNVP, and the party press made its anti-Nazi literature readily available.[25] This propaganda base was further amplified by the use of radio, which brought Hugenberg's speeches to thousands of homes.[26] His discussion of the necessity of economic adjustment and the lowering of interest rates, so as to emphasize national development of a bulwark against international bolshevism, was heard and seen by millions.[27]

The campaign emphasis of nationalism versus socialism was amplified by the deliberate burning of the Reichstag—a case of arson, which the government used to indict the entire left. Hugenberg's speech on the eve of the election reinforced this polarization. The DNVP leader spoke of the necessity of "draconic measures" and of "exterminating the hotbeds in which bolshevism can flourish;" he argued that "in these earnest times there can no longer be any half measures ... no compromise, no cowardice."[28] Had Hugenberg not continued with an appeal for the DNVP, his speech could have been delivered by any member of the Hitler party. The results of the elections of 5 March were a bitter disappointment. The party admitted that the Battle Front Black-White-Red was a "failure" and that the voters who had cast their ballots for the DNVP in November had now turned to the NSDAP.[29] Of the total electorate, seventeen million chose the Nazis and only 3.1 million, the German Nationals.[30] The national government, with 288 seats for the National Socialists and 52 for the German Nationals, now controlled a majority in the Reichstag.[31]

To ensure appropriate propagandistic support for the formal Reichstag opening, Hitler pushed through the cabinet the appointment of Goebbels as minister of propaganda.[32] German Nationals participated in this grandiose display of national power, but Hugenberg and his "Green Shirts" were buried in "a brown sea."[33] Once more the Nazis had outmaneuvered Hugenberg and pushed him to the sidelines. Rather than allowing the old Germany to express itself in new forms, the ceremonies gave the signal for "the younger [generation] to evict the senior."[34] Potsdam symbolized the overwhelming of elitist traditions by the vulgar exuberance of Nazism.

The most important business on the agenda of the new Reichstag was the passage of an enabling act granting extensive powers to the Hitler cabinet. After Hugenberg had not opposed the Emergency Decree of 28 February which, in the wake of the Reichstag fire, gave the cabinet very extensive powers,[35] he would find it difficult to reject this new legislation. Moreover, the National Socialists had used this previous decree to arrest Communist Reichstag delegates. Thus, even without the DNVP, Hitler had a majority in the Reichstag.[36] The proposed enabling act would, however, be a constitutional reform and needed a two-thirds vote. Hugenberg, convinced that he could not prevent the passage of the act, hoped that certain checks on National Socialist power might be included. When Frick spoke about the legislation in the cabinet, Hugenberg proposed that the Reich president be called upon to cooperate in the passage of laws under the new proposal.[37] Meissner, however, interjected that

Hindenburg's cooperation was not necessary and the president would not request it.[38] At a later meeting of the cabinet, Hitler, in reply to von Papen's suggestion that under the new legislation the Reichstag become a form of National Assembly, stated that he had already promised delegates of the Center Party that such could be the case. Hugenberg seized this opportunity to propose that this idea should be incorporated into the enabling act. Göring immediately replied that he had already studied such a proposition and dismissed Hugenberg's proposal.[39]

Disconcerted by the new legislation, Hugenberg contacted the Centrist leader, Brüning, about the possibility of including an amendment whereby "civil and political freedom would be guaranteed." The two men agreed, but on the day that the legislation came before the Reichstag, the amendment never materialized because they feared an open confrontation. On the one hand, the decree of 28 February had already been used to outlaw one party, and some members of the Center and of the DNVP feared that the Nazis could use it against them. On the other hand, pressures within and without the Reichstag chamber were great. Twenty-three DNVP delegates literally adhering to Hugenberg's antiparliamentary principles threatened to resign and join the NSDAP if the amendment were introduced.[40] Moreover, as a member of the cabinet which had produced the bill, Hugenberg would have had to have made a full *volte face* in order to modify the antiparliamentary legislation introduced by the government.

Caught between his own antiparliamentary rhetoric and manipulation by the National Socialists, Hugenberg had only one guarantee upon which he could rely. The Enabling Act secured extraordinary powers for the "present government."[41] Hugenberg believed that this legislation depended on his continuance in office. Accordingly, the minister dedicated himself more than ever to his role as "economic dictator."

THE MINISTER AND THE PARTY

Since the formation of the government, Hugenberg believed that his work in the cabinet for the economic reconstruction of Germany far outweighed the importance of his role as active party leader. He nevertheless refused to surrender ultimate authority and merely named the chairman of the German National delegation to the Prussian Landtag, Friedrich von Winter-feld, as his deputy.[42] The "economic dictator" firmly believed that his restructuring of the economy could produce the Ger-many he had always desired. But if Hugenberg and the non-Nazi ministers were to "tame" the National Socialists, they would have to coordinate their endeavors. Apparently von Papen had planned that he would be the majordomo of the cabinet, but he had neither the personal strength nor the political backing in the Reichstag to play such a role. Hugenberg, on the other hand, had these assets. He was a meticulous and consistent worker who sometimes ate his lunch in his office and devoted as many as fourteen hours of the day to his ministerial tasks. Hugenberg, however, was a difficult man to work with.[43] His gruff, taciturn personality and his total absorption in economic revitalization alienated some of his colleagues and obviated his emergence as cabinet leader.[44]

As soon as he entered the government, Hugenberg had two of his lieutenants made state secretaries in the ministries he con-trolled. Paul Bang, the ADV economic expert, assumed this posi-tion in the Ministry of Economics. His autarkic ideals and racist fanaticism had never endeared him to the leaders of the RDI,[45] and he did little to aid industry or improve his image.[46] With his small-minded ideological approach, Bang was apparently one of the first men in the new regime to propose direct anti-Semitic legislation.[47] He added little to Hugenberg's prestige. On the other hand, Hansjoachim von Rohr, who assumed the parallel post in the Ministry of Agriculture, was a member of the Reichslandbund and an agrarian leader in his native Pomerania.[48] Though von Rohr emerged as a persistent opponent of the Nazi agrarian policies, the Pomeranian had not been one of Hugen-berg's intimates, and he found it sometimes difficult to work with the "economic dictator" who closeted himself for long hours and painstakingly wrote out long legislative proposals in his own hand.[49]

Hugenberg remained convinced that if farming, the weakest link in Germany's economic chain, could be strengthened, the downward spiral of the economy would be reversed.[50] Accord-ingly, he and von Rohr worked out a vast number of decrees and legislative proposals for agricultural assistance.[51] Hugenberg intended not only to make the farmer a more prosperous member of society, capable of buying the products that German industry produced, but he also wanted to make Germany as independent as possible of foreign imports. Two most important measures capped Hugenberg's endeavors for agrarian assistance, the Law on Fats and the Law on Debts and Settlement. The first was a grandiose scheme to protect the German dairy industry and curb the production of margarine by limiting the the importation of such oleaginous materials as butter and soybeans.[52] With this scheme, Hugenberg expected to help equalize prices between agrarian and industrial products and so establish an organic relationship that would benefit employment because of increased demand.[53] The second law was essentially Hugenberg's proposal of December 1931, aimed at preventing foreclosure and allowing the farmer to get out from under the burden of debt. With this plan, farmers would pay a new decentralized governmental agency a reduced interest rate of 4.5 percent the remainder of the interest would be paid by the government. Farmers could agree to pay anywhere from .5 percent to 5 percent of the principal to their mortgagors through the same agency, and the government would accept in lieu of cash payment other lands which the agrarians might wish to transfer in order to pay their debts. Through such a process, the minister hoped to prevent unprofitable foreclosure and increase the number of small farmers. Farms and estates that were not good risks could be taken over for settlement.[54]

The struggle for this last law made Hugenberg more aware than ever of the disruptive Nazi forces that existed in the countryside turning many farmers against the German Nationals. Darré and his National Socialist agrarian organization had taken control of the major agrarian organizations, and he demanded a two percent interest rate as opposed to the four and a half percent or even four percent acceptable to Hugenberg.[55] The minister's view prevailed, and Hugenberg continued to believe that his factual work would undermine the juvenile attitudes and the not so juvenile delinquency of the National Socialists. Gradually, however, most German Nationals realized that it would take more than grandiose planning to compete with Nazism. There had to be a two-fold drive. Legal reorganization was necessary, but equal importance had to be given to securing power in the civil service and in business organizations.

Traditionalist conservatives, however, were not prepared to seize the initiative, and the minister immersed in administrative work did not provide leadership. Confronted with the aggressive tactics of Nazi officials, German Nationals were confounded. Local party members complained that Hugenberg "had become invisible for mortals"[56] and that even their contacts with the ministry of economics were "extraordinarily scarce."[57] At the same time, officials of the central party office complained that, while National Socialists acted, German Nationals waited for orders from above and then acted hesitantly.[58]

In fact, a revolution was engulfing Germany, and neither Hugenberg nor his followers were prepared to stem the tide. Despite their rejection of liberalism, most members of the DNVP adhered to the principles of the *Rechtsstaat,* a state governed by laws. Committed to the use of normal channels, German Nationals were frequently confronted with a *fait accompli* which they were powerless to change. During March, sustained terror gathered momentum throughout Germany. German Nationals in Frankfurt am Main, in Hanover, and in Kiel listed specific grievances and demanded federal leadership in combatting the Nazi drive.[59] Finally when the SA began to kidnap the German National members of the local chambers of commerce, Hugenberg protested in the cabinet. Göring replied that the current membership of these groups did not reflect the present conditions in Germany, and thus he could not hold back the SA.[60]

The disillusionment of the German Nationals intensified when Nazi lawlessness threatened even national figures. Herbert von Bismarck, the leader of the German National youth group, was hounded because of his monarchic sentiments and prevented from speaking over the radio. Ultimately, he left his post in the Prussian ministry of interior because he did not wish to bear responsibility for the illegal acts perpetrated in the name of the government.[61] Even more shocking for the German Nationals was the case of Dr. Oberfohren, who had developed a deep mistrust of the Nazis and had argued against Hugenberg's entrance into the cabinet on 30 January.[62] Despite his immunity as a member of the Reichstag, Nazis searched his home in Kiel and jailed his Reichstag secretary.[63] National Socialists ignored his complaint and claimed that among his papers they had found circulars criticizing Hugenberg. Oberfohren denied this, but

Hugenberg never came to his assistance. The party leader argued that Oberfohren's actions, coupled with his resignation from the Reichstag, had made it "internally impossible" for him (Hugenberg) to take any steps against this violation of parliamentary immunity.[64]

In the face of such persecution, Hugenberg and the party office determined that the German Nationals would have to extend their influence in society. To symbolize the end of the "reign of parties," the DNVP in March changed its name to the German National Front (DNF). In a flurry of activity, German National offices organized cell work in every aspect of life. The goal was to win champions for conservative German Nationalism and at the same time frustrate the radical demands of the National Socialist masses for a social revolution.[65] The increased activity of Hugenberg's followers merely substantiated the Nazi charge that, despite the name change, the German Nationals remained a party in opposition to the NSDAP.

In their policy during this period, Hugenberg's supporters perpetuated his distinction between the leadership of the NSDAP and the radical masses that flocked to the swastika. German Nationals argued that Hitler had taken over many of their ideas and had moderated his own demands, particularly in the economic field, but the Nazi masses were still not attuned to the change. As a result, the DNVP continued to rely on its liaison with Hitler rather than on any nationwide collaboration of the German Nationals and the National Socialists.[66] Hugenberg, however, never succeeded in having Hitler positively affect Nazi conduct toward German Nationals. The "economic dictator's" only recourse was to bolster the spirits of his followers by informing them that they were equal partners in the new government and thus had equal rights.[67] The minister could appeal to bravery, but the average bourgeois, anxious to preserve his position in society and fearful of physical assault, found minimal security in support for the German National Front.

Hugenberg left even the editors in his press syndicate without clear guidelines. The result was that some German National politicians accused the Scherl editorial staff of suffering from a "strong Nazi psychosis." The writers were incensed and charged that party leaders had a "drunkenlike and hazy conception of the present situation."[68] The policy of Goebbels's propaganda ministry had created such anxiety among German National newspapermen that they feared a Nazi monopoly would force them out of business.[69] Even editors such as Kriegk, who had continually vaunted Hugenberg's policy, claimed that no one at Scherl or in the party office clearly enunciated the party leader's current tactics in connection with either "the formation of a definite relationship to the NSDAP" or "the evolution of personal contacts with Hitler and Göring."[70] Such cries for clear and strong leadership were ignored.

Hugenberg's approach was more wish than policy. Hitler, the political manipulator par excellence, readily perceived the timid tactics of the DNF and had nothing but contempt for the "grovelling" of the German Nationals.[71] Rather than ending attacks, the Nazis unleashed a massive campaign against Hugenberg himself. National Socialist newspapers and party rallies throughout the countryside called for the resignation of the minister.[72] Even in the cabinet, Hugenberg himself felt the opposition of the Nazis. The appointment of Göring as minister president of Prussia had, in effect, revived a distinct Prussian cabinet, which revamped the von Papen approach initiated after 20 July 1932. Hugenberg proposed a treaty (*Staatsvertrag*) uniting the economic ministries of the Reich and Prussia.[73] Göring not only avoided any action on this but also sanctioned a law on entailed estates without even consulting Hugenberg.[74] The German National leader had also wanted to make Schmidt-Hannover his personal state secretary for the joint ministries under his control, but the Nazis frustrated this.[75]

Such developments caused many German Nationals to despair. From the beginning of the government there had been those who argued in favor of a merger with the NSDAP as a means of influencing it from within. Now the frustrations of German Nationals in public life encouraged this tendency.[76] The subordination of the RDI to the Hitler movement and the increased strength of the Nazis in agricultural circles added to this impetus. If industrialists, agrarians, and civil servants could not achieve their purposes through the DNF, they might have a better chance in the NSDAP.[77] At the end of April, these ideas, coupled with the reality of repression, caused the DNVP in Braunschweig to dissolve itself and join the NSDAP.[78] This action

and the suicide of Oberfohren on 7 May, under rather questionable circumstances, provoked the continuous disintegration of the
party.[79]

The interview of Hugenberg and von Winterfeld with the
Reich president on 17 May pointed out the German National
dilemma. Winterfeld explained that DNVP officials in state
governments were being forced out of their posts and that
professional men in every area were being pressured into desert-
ing the German National party and joining the NSDAP. He implored the field marshall to intercede for the rights of German
Nationals. Hugenberg followed with a longer exposition which
emphasized his difficulties in dealing with Darré and the Nazi
commissars disrupting the economy. He also indicated his
problems with Göring in securing control of the Prussian ministries. Hugenberg, however, was careful to make a distinction between Hitler and the Nazi masses. Although he pressured Hindenburg by threatening that the "common front" formed on 30
January might break, he gave the president an easy reply when
he stated, "In the countryside—not on the part of the Reich
chancellor himself—there is an evident attempt to gather total
power in the hands of the NSDAP and to shove all other national
men to the side." The field marshall replied with an expression
of confidence in Hitler. He was convinced "that the Reich chancellor has the best intentions and with clean hands works in the
interest of the fatherland and in the spirit of justice." Some local
Nazis might act over zealously, but this was a "critical time" and
one should not forget "what a national upsurge the new movement has brought us." The president agreed to speak with the
chancellor about these things and was convinced that Hitler had
"the will gradually to produce an amelioration here."[80]

HUGENBERG'S RESIGNATION AND THE DISSOLUTION OF THE DNVP

Extraordinary pressure upon Hugenberg and his supporters
reinforced the minister's determination to concentrate upon his
cabinet functions. This seemed the only power base from which
a countermanding influence might be exerted. Hugenberg still
hoped that, with a continued upswing in the economy, the
public and his opponents would recognize the indispensability of
German National officials.[81] By further implementing his

economic proposals through international agreement at the
World Economic Conference, he expected to accelerate the improvement in Germany's financial situation.

Hugenberg's tactics for dealing with the London conference
began long before June.[82] In the beginning of March, he proposed that the interest rate on international private loans be
lowered to a rate compatible with Germany's export surplus.[83]
In a memorandum to Hitler, Hugenberg defended his plan for
the use of tariffs and quotas by arguing that Germany had to
gain for itself not only "tactical freedom of action and of decision," but also a "*preferential position* to facilitate the gradual dis-
charge of its debts." The nation would have to be granted the
position of an "*autonomous ... regime operative as against all other
countries.*" What this meant was that the cabinet would decree
special tariffs on imports "irrespective of her customs duties and
obligations under trade agreements" and that the revenues from
these imports would then be used to promote exports. In such a
scheme, Germany, as "the heart of Central Europe," would
grant special rebates to other states in "the middle of the con-
tinent."[84] Single-minded as ever, Hugenberg proposed that Germany, on the basis of economic necessity, express demands very
similar to the Pan-German war aims advocated before 1918.

When the Economic Policy Committee discussed these ideas
on 24 April, Hitler himself raised some doubt as to the value of
Hugenberg's plan. The chancellor argued that despite the fact
that the national economies of the world were the starting point
for international economic order, there were also existing international agreements that had to be considered. Von Neurath objected to Hugenberg's proposals because he believed that
retaliatory measures of other states would make the scheme infeasible. Vice-chancellor von Papen joined the chorus of dissent
by arguing that such a program would lead to a planned
economy. The meeting was discouraging for Hugenberg; the
"economic dictator" could not act freely in outlining international economic policy. Schacht, as president of the Reichsbank,
and von Neurath, as foreign minister, would also determine Germany's position at the London conference.[85] Hugenberg's plans
suffered a further setback at the cabinet meeting of 5 May. The
United States had proposed that all states adopt a tariff truce
before the opening of the conference. Hugenberg wanted to reject the proposal out of hand. Von Neurath, von Blomberg, and

von Papen opposed the "economic dictator" and argued that such action would undermine Germany's international position by making it appear that the Germans "wanted to sabotage the World Economic Conference."[86] A week later, after the international "organizing committee" for the conference had proposed a formula for eliminating new tariffs, yet permitting "*certain* measures," von Neurath requested that the cabinet accept the proposal. Again, Hugenberg objected and proposed that Germany's "intolerable" situation be cited as justification for full "freedom of decision."[87] The cabinet compromised by accepting the proposal presented by von Neurath but stating the Hugenberg argument that Germany was in a "fundamentally different" position because it was the "most burdened country in the world."[88]

Hugenberg's autarkic ideology had obviously brought him into conflict with the non-Nazi ministers of the cabinet—particularly von Neurath, who feared that Hugenberg's harsh policy would alienate Germany's neighbors and diminish its poor bargaining position.[89] Hungarian and Italian reaction to Hugenberg's policy confirmed this fear.[90] Neurath's policy apparently had some support in organized industry. Krupp's brother-in-law, Baron Wilmowsky, feared that the "quiet boycott" of German goods by states in southeastern Europe was not due to Nazi anti-Semitic antics, but to Germany's agricultural policy. He implored the foreign office to impress upon Hugenberg the need for cooperation.[91] Hitler, who favored a conciliatory foreign policy during this era, sided with von Neurath. It was no surprise when the cabinet approved Hitler's decision to place the delegation attending the world conference under the foreign minister.[92] Neurath, realizing that his position would place Hugenberg in a secondary role at the conference, informed his colleague that the decision corresponded with "international custom." Quite bluntly the foreign minister indicated that he also wrote to the minister of economics so that "no misunderstanding would arise." Hugenberg was to represent the purely economic interests of the government at the London meeting.[93] The note was unambiguous, but polite. The German National leader emphasized its conciliatory tone and later claimed that von Neurath had assured him that the conference was primarily a matter for the Ministry of Economics and that the Foreign Office would keep its hands out of the negotiations as much as possible.[94] Before departing for London, Hugenberg successfully secured the agreement of the cabinet that the government would not "allow itself to be pushed in the direction of the destruction of the protection of German agriculture."[95]

At the World Economic Conference on 16 June, Hugenberg delivered a memorandum expressing his principles on national and international economic development. He argued that the basis of all economics was the principle of "free exchange of services." This was defined as the concept of reciprocity whereby "for every service there must be a corresponding service in return." Hugenberg pointed out that if one section of the economy, such as agriculture, did not receive this corresponding service, the entire economy of the state would collapse. Similarly, if one country, such as Germany, was required only to give, international economic order would be disrupted, and the national economies of the world would suffer. In addition, he argued that international investments disturbed the world order and were an "offense against the economy of nations." Hugenberg concluded his speech with the thesis that only "two impartial steps" could make Germany solvent. One would be "to give Germany a colonial empire again in Africa," the other would be to "open up to the 'nation without space' (*'Volk ohne Raum'*) areas in which it could provide space for the settlement of its vigorous race and construct great works of peace." Only thus, he believed, could the destructive processes which threatened the civilized world be eliminated.[96]

The "Hugenberg Memorandum" set off a flurry of activity. The German delegation informed the committee that the ideas presented did not represent the official governmental position, but were merely the "private work of a member of the German delegation" expressed merely as a means of engendering debate.[97] When Hugenberg learned of this just before his departure from London, he had an interview with a reporter from the *Telegraphen-Union* and countered that there was no disagreement in the German delegation and his memorandum did indeed express the ideals of the German government.[98] Von Neurath, as soon as he learned of the substance of this interview, sought to have it suppressed.[99] Hugenberg was furious and, in the cabinet, objected to the entire procedure. Both von Neurath and Schacht formally filed statements indicating that they had not fully approved the Hugenberg proposal for publication.[100] Neurath further argued that Hugenberg's interview, asserting that the delegation was indeed unified, contradicted the official position taken by the foreign minister and, since these comments did not have prior approval, the Foreign Office had them suppressed throughout Germany.[101] The "economic dictator" claimed that von Neurath's statements were false.[102]

In retrospect, what happened was relatively simple but immensely important. In the tradition of the foreign office, von Neurath believed in the primacy of foreign policy. Undoubtedly among the ardent nationalists who comprised the delegation, Hugenberg's memorandum found a sympathetic hearing, but von Neurath himself expressed diplomatic reservations about the timeliness of its presentation. Nevertheless, Hugenberg presented his proposal, which aroused the hostility of France and Russia and won the sympathy of no one. Neurath then chided Hugenberg that "a single member cannot simply overlook the reservations of others." Under such conditions, German policy would not only be "ridiculous," but a detriment to the nation. Neurath claimed that Hugenberg "either did not understand these objections, which were naturally clothed in polite form, or he did not want to understand them."[103] Rather than permit the interests of state to be harmed, von Neurath humiliated Hugenberg.

Since Hugenberg knew that there was cabinet opposition to his economic proposals, his public presentation of them implied political suicide. He indicated this in his denazification proceedings when he wrote, "it was a matter between Hitler and me of who was going to seize the initiative."[104] The leader of the German National Front saw his organization crumbling. On the very day that he left for London, a group of his followers, including the prestigious Reichstag delegate Martin Spahn, went over to the Nazis. Spahn argued that he could not serve two leaders and that the organization of the German Nationalist movement was now superfluous.[105] In the face of such developments, Hugenberg was desperate. His continued frustration in the cabinet, coupled with his inability to maintain or win confidence in the countryside, caused him to consider "whether I should not put an end to this game through my departure from the Prussian and Reich cabinet."[106] Rather than abjectly depart from office, Hugenberg sought some great diplomatic and national success through a defiant expression of his principles. He might thus prove that his economic genius and his international prestige were indispensible and, consequently, the German Nationalist movement was still a vital necessity for the "new Germany."[107] Such a tactic was undoubtedly a gamble, but apparently Hugenberg calculated that, no matter what the result was, he personally would win. He would strengthen his position or, more likely, the conflict would give him an opportunity to leave the cabinet and save his reputation.[108]

Hugenberg had not coordinated his attempt to trump Hitler's nationalist demands with either Neurath or Schacht. Possibly, he hoped that by presenting them with his speech as a *fait accompli* he would force them to accept his position. Hugenberg's radicalism, however, aided the Nazis rather than the conservatives. The Hitler cabinet could not easily change its membership without upsetting the political balance in Germany. The elimination of the DNF and the curtailment of Hugenberg's independence had to take place in a way that would not arouse the suspicions of other non-Nazis in the cabinet or of the Reich president. The National Socialists thus exploited Hugenberg's lack of tact to destroy his influence in the government.

When he returned to Berlin, Hugenberg immediately argued in the cabinet that his memorandum "had in no way contributed toward aggravating the feeling against Germany." Neurath conceded that the speech had not added to the "general ill will prevailing against Germany" and now claimed that the refusal of the press to publish Hugenberg's repudiation of the official position taken by the delegation was a "mistake" by a member of the press department. Obviously, the foreign minister did not wish to debate the issue. When neither Schacht nor Schwerin von Krosigk spoke in support of Hugenberg, Hitler attempted to brush the whole incident aside with the comment, "What was past and had already happened was no longer of any interest." Hugenberg, however, refused to let the matter rest—his reputation was at stake. He persisted in his complaints and demanded then that the ministerial director, Dr. Posse, who had disagreed with him on principle, be replaced at the continuing negotiations in London. By making such a demand, Hugenberg alienated the non-Nazis who disagreed with his economic principles. Neurath denied that there was any difference in the views of Hugenberg and Posse—another diplomatic lie (one that

gave Hugenberg an opportunity to drop the matter). Hugenberg, however, insisted that he disagreed with Posse and stated
that if necessary he would have to return to London. Hitler
replied that only von Neurath, as the head of the delegation,
could make such a decision. Finally, von Papen, von Neurath,
Schwerin von Krosigk, and Schacht—all non-Nazis—joined in rejecting Hugenberg's demand for the immediate removal of
Posse. Hugenberg had sought to appeal over the heads of the
other ministers to the nation and to the world; he succeeded only
in alienating himself from his colleagues.[109]

Hugenberg's isolation in the cabinet was reflected in the
vulnerability of the DNVP. In the Free City of Danzig, the electoral campaign at the end of May had been a hard fought battle
in which the NSDAP attacked the local DNVP with particular
vehemence.[110] Once the ballots had been counted, the Nazis
formed a government alliance, not with their fellow nationalists,
but with the Danzig Center Party.[111] Clearly, the NSDAP wanted
to break the spirit of the German Nationals and destroy their independent position. Despite the arguments of Schmidt-Hannover, the new chairman of the DNVP Reichstag delegation,
asserting that Hugenberg, "the man who saved the press" and
"made the DNVP into a national revolutionary party of attack,"
was not the man to form an opposition,[112] the Nazis exploited the
situation in Danzig to charge that the German Nationalist harbored oppositional tendencies. Issues of the party journal were
confiscated,[113] and party meetings were continually disrupted.[114]
Under such conditions the continued existence of the front
became more and more intolerable.

The section of the DNF that most provoked the National
Socialists was the *Kampfring,* the paramilitary group sponsored by
the German Nationalists. Since the dissolution of the *Reichsbanner*
and other non-Nazi organizations, National Socialist leaders
charged that opponents of the NSDAP apparently flocked to the
"Green Shirts" as a means of expressing their opposition to the
Nazis. Despite local agreements seeking to terminate the feud
between the SA and the *Kampfring,* Nazi leaders continued to
challenge the nationalist loyalty of the German National units.[115]
Hugenberg himself disputed National Socialist statistics on the
number of "nonassimilable elements" from Marxist groups and
personally assumed responsibility for this paramilitary forma-

tion.[116] Hitler, however, refused to tolerate its existence. As early as March, local units had already been banned by Nazi authorities,[117] and, while Hugenberg was in London, Göring decreed that the entire Prussian organization had to be dissolved. The leader of the "Green Shirts," von Bismarck, was taken off to the Berlin police station by the SA, and even one of Hugenberg's own relatives was arrested.[118]

Hugenberg had no further illusions. He had never had mass support. Now he failed not only to win the allegiance of ministers in the Reich and Prussian cabinet but also to maintain and secure the backing of powerful pressure groups. In agricultural circles, where he had hoped to inspire the greatest appreciation, Darré's organization had frustrated the emergence of a Hugenberg movement. Even the *Reichslandbund* had directly undercut Hugenberg's attempt to maintain control of the Prussian portfolios which he ministered. Count Kalkreuth, the agrarian leader, had argued that the peasants could not support the one-man "crisis ministry" which Hugenberg had demanded. He and his organization had proposed that the Nazi, Werner Willikens, become the spokesman for agriculture in the Prussian regime.[119] Unable to maintain the allegiance of agrarians, whom he had helped, the minister was less able to win the support of industrialists, whom he had largely ignored. Despite the attempts of his friend, Vögler, to involve him in the needs of the iron industry,[120] Hugenberg delayed action on this area of the economy and concentrated on agrarian legislation. His partisanship for domestic production and his consequent demand for tariff protection alienated industrialists, who feared reprisals in world commerce.[121] Even the reorganization of the RDI and the VDAGV, the two key organizations of industry, received little attention from Hugenberg.[122] Hitler and his followers, on the other hand, sought to conciliate business leaders.

Despite the fact that the anti-Semitic campaign of the NSDAP evoked strong reactions around the world and hurt business, many industrialists believed that the best way to influence the Hitler movement was through penetration rather than opposition. The total capitulation of the RDI under Krupp indicated that organized industry would be incapable of effective opposition—even if some magnates had wanted it. Any strong industrialist challenge to the Nazis in 1933 was, however, very doubtful. The anticommunist, antisocialist, and antiunionist tactics of Hitler hardly displeased organized industry. On the National Day of Labor, 1 May, the once "socialist" publication of Goebbels, *Der Angriff,* was a giant volume filled with ads from key concerns and major banks.[123] Not opposition, but support would win the favor of the Nazis—so industrialists hoped.[124]

By the end of May, a movement was started among some businessmen to oust Hugenberg from the Ministry of Economics. Wilhelm Keppler, one of Hitler's key contact men with industry, circulated the idea that the chancellor and other key Nazis were fearful that Hugenberg's concentration on agriculture would leave an opening for leftist elements in the national movement to force a change in the cabinet. The "orphaned ministry" needed greater attention than Hugenberg gave it, but Hitler, feeling bound by his pledge that there would be no change of ministers, could not simply act against Hugenberg. On the other hand, if a significant number of industrial leaders petitioned him to do so, the chancellor might repress his reservations.[125] This move never matured—in part, because some industrial leaders feared that if Hugenberg left, a radical Nazi might get his post and really damage the economy—in part, because some leaders of heavy industry felt a sense of allegiance to Hugenberg as a national leader.[126]

Hugenberg's failure to inspire a strongly committed following among the two key groups he supposedly represented was matched by the flight of less important, but more numerous, socioeconomic interests traditionally associated with the Pan-German movement. Teachers, civil servants, and white-collar workers felt that unless they joined the NSDAP or at least ceased supporting the DNF their livelihoods would be endangered. Small businessmen felt that Hugenberg's policies did not offer them adequate protection, and they feared Nazi reprisals if they did not support the NSDAP.[127] Not even the Lutheran Church, which had largely supported the monarchial conservatism of the DNVP, could be protected by German Nationals. At the end of May, church leaders chose Friedrich von Bodelschwingh, a theologian of international renown, to be Reich bishop. The "German Christians" under the Nazi chaplain, Ludwig Müller, objected and demanded that the people had rights in the election. Hitler refused to receive Bodelschwingh, and the Reich president gave the new bishop no support.[128] The policy of *Gleichschaltung* could tolerate no possible sanctuary for dissident conservatives. Bodelschwingh was forced to resign, and the Prussian minister of culture, Bernhard Rust, appointed a National Socialist commissar for the Lutheran Church in Prussia.[129]

The decision of the Stahlhelm to enter the NSDAP further dramatized the weakness of the German National position.[130] Only the direct intervention of the Reich president might have changed the situation, but von Hindenburg never acted to save the "economic dictator" or his party. This culmination of events in June led to a two-fold development. First, Hugenberg, judging his position in the cabinet to be untenable, determined that he could no longer bear responsibility for developments. By 24 June, he had made an "unalterable" decision to resign from the cabinet.[131] Second, leaders of the party pondering their position began to consider dissolving the DNF.

As deputy party chairman, von Winterfeld summoned a special meeting of party leaders, the *Reichsführerstab,* to explore alternatives. Hugenberg, even though he was in the same building, refused to attend the meeting and refused to discuss the rationale he would give for his resignation. Gravely concerned that the policy of *Gleichschaltung* would cause severe difficulties for a large number of loyal German Nationals, some party leaders wanted the minister to remain in the cabinet or to base his resignation on the Nazi frustration of a united national opposition rather than on the difficulties he encountered in the cabinet. Though these party leaders had strongly supported Hugenberg over the last five years, a tone of frustrated anger ran through their discussion. Some felt that the minister belonged at their meeting, that he "viewed things too much from the viewpoint of a chairman of the board of overseers and that he had not helped us politically." Fearful that Hugenberg's resignation would be interpreted as the formal beginning of political opposition to the NSDAP and unwilling to make any firm decisions in the absence of their leader, these German Nationals explored three options—joining the NSDAP, dissolving the party, or simply waiting for further developments. The first alternative remained totally unacceptable; the third fostered the danger that continued Nazi attacks would destroy the livelihood of numerous German Nationals and ultimately lead to a forced dissolution.

Thus self-dissolution emerged as the most realistic option. No vote was taken, but von Winterfeld requested Freytagh-Loringhoven to talk informally with Frick. Hergt was to explain to Hugenberg that the group wanted him to base his resignation on broad political developments.[132]

Hugenberg continued to act independently. He had not asked the party's permission to join the cabinet, and he would not deal with it when he decided to leave it. He arranged to have Brosius, his press chief, deliver his letter of resignation to von Hindenburg at Neudeck at the exact same time that he himself would meet with Hitler and inform the chancellor of this decision.[133] As he expressed it to the president, the request to be relieved from his offices stemmed not "from the concern for the offices entrusted to me as from the responsibility of fidelity to my friends and (the responsibility of) protecting my own name." Hugenberg argued that the opposition of the National Socialists had made his work impossible. In the cabinet, they had not kept the agreement to turn over the control of employees' rights and social policy to him, they had not permitted him to reorganize his ministries with the type of men he needed, and they had frustrated his policy at the World Economic Conference. Similarly, they had disbanded the German Nationalist youth organizations. He concluded that for himself and his friends there was no defense against such actions, despite his membership in the cabinet.[134]

When Hugenberg presented these ideas to Hitler, the chancellor was conciliatory at first. He praised Hugenberg's work in the past and requested him to forget recent events, but the resignation of Hugenberg, coupled with the continued existence of the DNF, meant that *ipso facto* a national opposition would be created. The chancellor could not permit this. Hugenberg, Hitler argued, should stay in the cabinet but should replace von Rohr with a National Socialist and dissolve the DNF. In such a case, the police could release the German Nationalist prisoners that it held. The mention of dissolution supposedly caught Hugenberg off guard, and he informed Hitler that Freytagh-Loringhoven was already negotiating with Frick on this.[135] The minister argued that he had no intention of going over to the opposition and that as soon as Hitler decided to act against "leftist elements" in National Socialist organizations he would again be

available for office. At this Hitler changed his tactics and began
to lash out at Hugenberg for bringing up the counterrevolutionary (i.e., anti-Nazi) theme which he claimed was the motivation of
the German Nationals. Hitler raged that he had requested the
minister three times to remain in office and still Hugenberg
refused. Concluded the Nazi Führer, this meant an open battle—
thousands of German Nationals would lose their jobs and others
would find themselves in most unfortunate circumstances. The
battle in the political arena would extend to the press and film,
and in only three days Hugenberg would be a broken man.
Hugenberg remarked that if Hitler depicted these threatening
dangers to the German Nationalists they would probably dissolve
the organization, but then, he asked, why would Hitler want him
to continue in the cabinet? The meeting ended on this note of
estrangement.[136] Hugenberg immediately composed a second
letter to von Hindenburg informing him of Hitler's threats and
requesting the president to remember that "well-meaning" German Nationals respected him and his government and that they
had no intention of going over to the "opposition."[137]

On 27 June, the party executive committee met twice. Hugenberg arrived late but then presided at the first meeting. He read
his letter of resignation to von Hindenburg and briefed the
members on his meeting with Hitler earlier that day. The deputy
chairman, von Winterfeld, then explained that the previous
meeting had been called without Hugenberg's approval; he had
felt compelled as deputy leader to summon the committee
because the party no longer enjoyed "freedom of decision."
Winterfeld believed that the unrest in the country had become
too great and that the DNF stood under the threat of forced dis-
bandment which would endanger the position of active and
retired civil servants and everyone who had supported the party.
Freytagh reported that his discussions with Frick and then with
Hitler indicated that the Nazis were willing to negotiate on
relatively generous terms. Hugenberg added that a general
agreement on personal affairs could probably be made but that
"Scherl and *Ufa* would probably be controlled (*gleichgeschaltet*) by
the National Socialists." Though he wanted to maintain the DNF
as an active group, Hugenberg presented no clear plan for a
modus vivendi with the Nazis. Indeed, he clearly repeated the
threats which Hitler had made. The party leader protested that

"he had not formulated any resolution for dissolution" but requested that the body vote on whether negotiations on dissolution should be continued. Only six of the approximately sixty leaders present disagreed. Winterfeld, Freytagh-Loringhoven, and Helmuth Poensgen were commissioned to represent the party.[138]

Hitler rapidly came to a written agreement with the German Nationals. The Nazi leader personally guaranteed that the members of the DNF, especially civil servants, would be recognized as "full and legally equal cofighters" and that those held in jail would be unconditionally released. The DNF agreed, in turn, to dissolve itself. Party officals in the Reichstag and the various provincial legislatures would be absorbed into the governing bodies of the NSDAP. Hitler also promised to do his best to find equivalent positions for party employees. In addition, Scherl and *Ufa* would be permitted to continue their work "in the spirit of the present Germany."[139]

When the party executive committee reconvened at 10:30 that evening, von Winterfeld presented the agreement to the members, and they accepted it. Only after this did Hugenberg arrive at the meeting. Divested of the pride that had continually characterized him, Hugenberg saw his lifetime plans for the organization of Germany shattered. He could only despondently comment:

> I am indeed of the opinion that we all have cause to go home and to crawl into our closets or go into the woods. In the last days and weeks it has been my chief goal to remain respectable in every way and not to allow my good name to be marred. I would hope that in a difficult situation I have succeeded in this and would find for that reason a great peace and relief. You don't know what you ought to say in days like these, but one thought has gone through my mind in these hours and I would still like to add it: if anyone should hear that I have committed suicide, do not believe it at all. I would not do it and I do not believe in suicide.[140]

Postscript: Hugenberg in the Third Reich and Postwar Period

That Hugenberg had failed to manipulate the Nazis is manifest. That he had aided and abetted their cause, even as he opposed some of their policies, is obvious. These two factors plagued Hugenberg in the last years of his life. In the Third Reich he was deprived of the political and economic influence he had so ardently desired. At the same time, the security of his financial investments was gravely threatened by the totalitarian policies of the NSDAP. Ultimately, Hugenberg secured the financial future of his family, but his press and film concerns were devoured by the Hitler state. After 1945, British occupation forces and German denazification proceedings again threatened the economic security of Hugenberg and his heirs. To avoid the hardships that he and his mother had confronted after the death of his father, Hugenberg and his allies tailored arguments to fit the regime. To the Nazis, they stressed his contributions to the development of the Third Reich;[1] to the postwar authorities, they emphasized his differences with Hitler.[2]

In the summer of 1933, Hugenberg feared that the Nazi policy of *Gleichschaltung* would destroy his concern and his personal assets.[3] The fact that important coaling interests had invested so heavily in his syndicate, coupled with Hitler's gentlemen's agreement with the German Nationals, provided some guarantee for the continued existence of the concern, but more than ever before, Hugenberg distrusted the arbitrariness of the Nazis.[4] The forced sale of the *Telegraphen-Union* and the *Ala* in the winter of 1933 did not bode well for his ability to maintain control over the other corporations involved in the media.[5] Fearful of Nazi vindictiveness, Hugenberg nominally transferred his assets to his son and three daughters. Technically, he did not even own Rohbraken.[6] In practice, however, he maintained iron-handed control over the enterprises he had founded. His son, Gerhard, gained a seat on the board of overseers of the *Deutsches Gewer-*

behaus A.G. and on the twelve-man *Wirtschaftsvereinigung,* but it was his talented son-in-law, Henning von Boehmer, who was groomed as the chief administrator of the concern.[7]

In the fall of 1933, when Frick offered Hugenberg the opportunity to be a nonpartisan member of the Reichstag, the old man did not decline.[8] Obviously he did not wish to alienate the Nazis any further.[9] As a delegate, he would have some pledge of personal immunity, he could better protect investments in his concern, and, possibly, he could even influence national policy. Realistically, the first two expectations were stronger; Hugenberg had no impact whatsoever on the decision-making forces of the Third Reich. Direct contact with Hitler was apparently limited to a few friendly letters exchanged during the Christmas season in 1933–1934 and a discussion in February 1935.[10] Hugenberg used the interview as a means of promoting his pet plan for private ownership of homes. In collaboration with his advisers from Scherl, he published a book dealing with architectural and legislative proposals for urban renewal.[11] Specifically, old "rental barracks" were to be demolished and high-rise condominiums, based on the idea of a cooperative association, were to replace them.[12] Such a proposal, however, had as little affect on the regime as his desire to maintain the existence of his concern. By the end of 1935, Hugenberg had been forced to sell everything but Scherl and *Ufa* to the Nazis.[13] The film, however, was too important a propagandistic weapon to leave in private hands. After complex negotiations, Hugenberg and his allies were forced to sell their shares. At this point, Hugenberg returned the "trust fund" which the *Zechenverband* had placed at his disposal. The *Wirtschaftsvereinigung zur Förderung der geistigen Wiederaufbaukräfte* was dissolved.[14] In accordance with the laws of the Third Reich, the Scherl *Verlag* became a *Kommanditgesellschaft,* with Hugenberg personally responsible for its publication.[15]

In effect, the Nazis did not persecute Hugenberg, but they circumscribed his power. Germany's new rulers treated him gently, as a superfluous, elder statesman.[16] Through his investments, primarily in Scherl, Hugenberg earned approximately M 500,000 annually during the period 1933–1943.[17] Scherl publications, the *Illustrierte Nachtausgabe* and *Der Adler,* were well respected and widely circulated.[18] On the twenty-fifth anniversary of the founding of the *Ufa,* Goebbels presented Hugenberg with the Order of the Eagle for his work with the film concern.[19] Even when the Nazis refused to transfer control of Scherl to his family in 1943 and later demanded that Hugenberg surrender control of the firm, National Socialist officialdom treated him kindly. In September 1944, Hitler's minister of economics, Walther Funk, basically agreed to Hugenberg's terms for the sale and guaranteed payment in accordance with his demands.[20] The old man was not happy to lose a family controlled corporation, but comforted himself with the fact that there would only have been losses if he had been able to keep the firm.[21] Shortly after the sale, allied bombing greatly destroyed the Scherl complex in Berlin.[22]

Rohbraken had been untouched by the war, but in 1945 Hugenberg could only view the future with uncertainty—his son was lost on the Russian front;[23] his beloved Germany lay in ruins. British occupation forces in Lippe did not immediately act against the aged man even though old enemies denounced him. Hugenberg drew attention to himself by developing a program for the reconstruction of German cities.[24] On 27 September 1946, British soldiers summarily arrested Hugenberg and interred him at Staumühle. The following day, relatives and friends were forced to leave his estate. Family assets were frozen.[25] Hugenberg spent the remaining five years of his life in a persistent battle to prove his righteousness. After nine months in the mass prison barracks in Staumühle, the British transferred him to German authorities for denazification. Still not permitted to return to his estate, he and his wife lived in an old-age home at Bad Meinberg until a special house was built for them on the edge of their land.[26]

Hugenberg rejected the charges that he was the "Lord of Press and Film" and a lackey who had helped Hitler grasp the reins of power.[27] Nevertheless, the local denazification committee of Lemgo labeled him one of the "lesser evildoers" of the Nazi regime.[28] German officials thus collaborated with the British in denying Hugenberg the opportunity to travel or to involve hiself in politics. More important for the eighty-two-year-old man was the legal obstacle which this decision placed on his investment accounts. Since he had never been a member of the party and had left the cabinet in June 1933, Hugenberg successfully appealed this judgment. A decision rendered in Detmold on 18 July 1949 advised that because of his continued membership in the

Reichstag, Hugenberg be labeled a "fellow-traveller" and be placed in a less culpable category. The special commissioner for North Rhine Westphalia approved this judgment but refused to allow Hugenberg to be active in political life.[29] Though he still could not return to his estate house, his assets were now technically free, and he began preparing the court cases which ultimately (in 1970) secured for his heirs full compensation for the forced sale of Scherl. At the same time, Hugenberg was determined to salvage his reputation from the stigma of Nazism and anxious to point out the fallacy of the denazification proceedings. As the result of a further appeal, the Detmold Denazification Committee, on the basis of legal technicalities and in consideration of Hugenberg's advanced age, categorized him as one of those "not tainted" (*Unbelastete*) with the guilt of the Nazis.[30]

To the very end, Hugenberg symbolized par excellence the Pan-German who claimed to be misunderstood and persecuted. He insisted that had his leadership been properly followed events for Germany and the world would have been very different.[31] Such hypotheses, however, can never be proven or disproven. Only what has actually happened—*wie es eigentlich gewesen*—counts. Even his former collaborators admitted that "the excessive confidence of Hugenberg in Hitler was one of the greatest mistakes"[32] and empathized with the "inner doubts" Hugenberg must have had in his last years.[33] He and his public defenders, however, continually claimed that there was no guilt—there had merely been errors of political judgment. If Hugenberg suffered torments of conscience because of his political tactics, he bore them silently. Throughout his life, Hugenberg rarely dealt with emotion and avoided any sign of weakness. His taciturn, rational, aloof personality left little time for intimacy. He approached death with the same businesslike determination that had characterized his life. In his death throes he deliberately isolated himself from all members of his family. Only a nurse ministered to him.[34] He died on 12 March 1951.

Conclusion

References to Alfred Hugenberg often bear the outlines of political stereotypes. Descriptions of him as the former director of Krupp's conjure up the figure of the quintessential imperialist conspiring for the control of Germany by monopolistic capitalists. Labels dubbing him the "Lord of Press and Film" imply exclusive manipulation of newspapers and cinema, which strangled opposition. The title of "Hitler's *Steigbügelhalter*" creates the illusion of a lackey submissively standing aside the stallion of power and assisting the Nazis to mount in triumph. Impressions of him as an *Einzelgänger* foster the image of a solitary and steadfast idealist absolutely repudiating political compromise. Each of these interpretations contains an element of truth, but each is too simplistic to explain the full significance of Hugenberg's impact on the German state in the first third of this century.

The span of his political activity from the formation of the Pan-German League in 1890 through his participation in the Hitler cabinet in 1933 bridges the Wilhelminian era and the Third Reich. Critical of both regimes, Hugenberg is nevertheless a significant figure marking the tortuous transition from one to the other. His national liberalism was not the economic and political competition of free forces, but the social Darwinistic struggle of elitists to maintain and amplify their power. Theoretically, access to money and power remained open to all, but, practically, the triumph of the industrial bourgeoisie at the end of the nineteenth century delimited mobility to only a few talented and ambitious men from the nontraditional middle class. At first opposed to the Junkers and their reactionary agricultural techniques, Hugenberg like many bourgeois gradually accepted the ideal of feudal-industrial control of Germany. His own development of Rohbraken and his attempt to secure a landed estate for each of his children bear eloquent testimony to the marriage of industrial elitism with traditional aristocracy.

Similarly, Hugenberg's social Darwinism attested to the continuance of the radical nationalist tradition from the 1890s through 1933. Such nationalism was not a cultural cement uniting men of the same language and customs, but a badge of racial superiority entitling a dynamic state to expand. Inaction was inferiority; imperialism characterized progressive states. Energized by national capitalism, Germany would find her "place in the sun." Any citizen willing to accept these ideals and work for the fatherland could call himself a German. In contrast to this view, vulgar publicists who sought to return to an idealized past or condemned capitalism as a Jewish invention fostered nationalism at the expense of its modern spirit. Such ignorant racists, in Hugenberg's view, could be manipulated, for power belonged to the elite who had proven their ability to survive in the modern world. In short, Hugenberg's mentality was Pan-German. Cultural dynamism, propelled by the eruption of industrial expansion, entitled Germany to a greater control of the world's resources.

This radical nationalism, which Hugenberg and official members of the Pan-German League fostered before 1918, infected large numbers of Germans who had no official contact with the *Alldeutscher Verband*. The league merely promulgated a pervasive sentiment; ideological commitment and not numerical strength explains the role of the Pan-German League in preparing the way for Nazism. The rejection of political liberalism, the condemnation of socialism, the glorification of militarism, the manipulation of propaganda, the demand for colonial expansion, the call for a strong national leader—all of these themes are documented in Pan-German literature. Official members of the league or not, many in the German upper classes subscribed to these notions. Hugenberg represented neither the industrialist who funded this group in order to sell more steel nor the Junker who advocated its ideas in order to secure his domain. Rather, he typified the ideologue who championed autarkic development of a German empire. Expansion would guarantee autarky and perpetuate elitist rule. The ideals of economic and nationalist imperialism were unique to neither Germany as a state nor to Hugenberg as an individual. Hugenberg's genius was not that of creator or leader, but that of the administrator. His managerial talent made him the executor of the Pan-German patrimony and allowed him to preserve and disseminate this estate of elitist ideals and traditions throughout the Weimar era.

Knowledge of corporate law and the principles of capital investment enabled Hugenberg to build limited financial assets into a powerful and profitable enterprise. His early activity in the cooperative movement and in the Prussian Ministry of Finance confirmed his belief that power derived not from the democratic organization of men on behalf of an idea, but from the ability to structure a bloc which manipulated the masses and pressured political leaders to execute the plans of an elitist group. In the last years of the Wilhelminian era, the Ruhr's concentration of political funds in Hugenberg's hands increased his conviction that political and social change could result only from such tactics. Hubris fostered by personal success facilitated his condemnation of unionists, Marxists, democrats, and internationalists who disagreed with either his goals or his tactics.

During the war, the dramatic struggle for survival convinced Hugenberg that bureaucratic control and the coordination of pressure groups provided an inadequate power base. The manipulation of propaganda to produce a united nationalist bloc—a tactic which dated back to Bismarck—had to be revised and radicalized. Differences between elitists and democrats, capitalists and socialists, militarists and pacifists, had to be simplified. Concentrating on bureaucratic control of the media and collaborating in funding antirepublican forces, Hugenberg approached new issues with traditional tactics. Loss of the war enabled Pan-Germans to amplify their condemnation of opponents by labeling them as the cause of the defeat. The old regime was condemned for being too mild; the new republic was rejected as a national betrayal. Basing his power on the development of his syndicate, Hugenberg emerged as a somewhat independent lobbyist championing Pan-German, nationalist, capitalist views. Counterrevolutionaries would produce a *Sammlung* when the time was ripe. Meanwhile, all nationalist forces would be patronized; preference was for those like the DVP and the DNVP which favored the elite.

Bourgeois acceptance of the republic, as encouraged by Stresemann, threatened the elitist ideals of the Pan-Germans. The greater the success of Weimar, the more dangerous the threat. As burgeoning support repudiated counterrevolution,

neoconservatism sought a new political organization which
would perpetuate nationalism and capitalism in a new form.
When some elements in this movement began developing a
"Tory-like" conservatism, Hugenberg demanded a radical
change in the political course of the right. Believing that inevitable catastrophe would result from democracy and socialism,
Hugenberg and his allies expected that the republic would
destroy itself. When it did not, these men who had awaited a
crisis encouraged one. Deliberately reversing his earlier repudiation of racism, Hugenberg sought the help of the criminal element in a campaign against moderation. Hitler and the Nazis
were to be incorporated into a new national bloc. With his
bureaucratic mentality, the chairman of the DNVP expected to
manipulate political factions as readily as he had controlled
boards of overseers in his concern. Hugenberg was neither a
politician who could arouse the populace nor a statesman who
could confront reality. He was an unlikely and unwieldy combination of ideologue and administrator.

Antiquated social Darwinism and bureaucratic expertise
hardly provided Hugenberg with the charisma to create a new
bloc. Unable to force moderate nationalists to accept his leadership, he failed to control the rabid element which he had helped
to unleash in his campaign against the Young Plan. Constant
refusal to cooperate with the non-Socialist regime of Brüning did
not demonstrate adamant idealism; it merely emphasized his
negativism. As chairman of the DNVP, Hugenberg not merely
frustrated the development of that party into a dynamic conservative movement, but also inhibited the coalescence of a broad-
based moderate rightist bloc. In the organization of the Reich
Committee against the Young Plan, in the election of 1930 and in
January 1933, Hugenberg demonstrated none of the ideological
adamancy which characterized his approach to Brüning's conservative regime. His radical Pan-German inclinations fostered
compromise with Nazism. Even when he opposed the election of
Hitler as Reich president, Hugenberg facilitated this candidacy by
helping Hitler to become a German citizen.

That Hugenberg cooperated with Hitler is clear; that he
wanted Nazism to triumph is not—despite his contributions to
the development of Hitlerism through the encouragement of
radicalism in the media and, I believe, through financial con-

tributions to Nazis. Hugenberg opposed the independence of the Hitler movement. With arrogance typical of the Pan-Germans, the DNVP leader expected to manipulate National Socialism as conservatism before the war had exploited other rightist movements. The Reich Committee against the Young Plan, the Harzburg Front, and the Hitler cabinet had each been structured so that elitists could frame in the NSDAP. Prewar radicalism, however, had spawned an ungrateful and unmanageable movement. The manipulator became the manipulated; propaganda became reality. The mob proclaimed itself the new elite. Hugenberg and the new Pan-Germans spoke of radical tactics; Hitler and the Nazis implemented them. Despite their reluctant tolerance of the NSDAP, Hugenberg and his allies were among the first to be devoured by the totalitarian appetite of the Nazis.

Neither the counterrevolutionary rhetoric of the Hugenberg press nor the financial contributions which, I believe, Hugenberg provided could be deemed sufficient cause for the triumph of Nazism. Undoubtedly, the attitudes fostered by the Hugenberg syndicate undermined the republic; there was a market for venom, and his publications encouraged it. Yet a vast majority of the newspapers published in the Weimar era were not influenced by his concern. Similarly, monetary aid could not have produced the voting power of National Socialism. If money could have bought votes, the Hugenberg party would have been much stronger than it was. As important as Hugenberg's role was in the destruction of the republic, it can in no way be labeled the decisive factor in the triumph of German fascism. Nevertheless, in the deliberate campaign to frustrate political and economic democracy, Hugenberg and the Pan-Germans must bear a large portion of the historic responsibility for the rise of Nazism. Hugenberg's narrowly rigid point of view catered to the most selfish and unenlightened tendencies of men. Not justice for all, but power for the few was his goal.

Hitler's peculiar perversion of the Pan-German ideal was not Hugenberg's legal responsibility. But that Nazism could reap such a harvest of followers was certainly nurtured by his radical strategy.[1] Hugenberg and all Germany were victimized by that pied piper which the Pan-German dream had fostered. That dream became a nightmare when the nation was led not to the summit of Germanic glory but into the abyss of the Nazi cataclysm. Up to his death, Hugenberg refused to admit his responsibility for the development of Nazism; history must disagree.

Notes

Introduction

1. Bueck's condemnation of all forms of liberalism, as well as socialism and clericalism, set a distinct tone among some leaders in heavy industry. See BA Koblenz, R13I/11, Clemens Klein, Geschichte des Vereins Deutscher Eisen- und Stahlindustrieller, especially Bueck's "swan song," pp. 285–86.

2. Alfred Hugenberg, *Bank und Kreditwirtschaft des deutschen Mittelstandes* (Munich, 1906). Hugenberg's views on the middle classes and on capitalist development are distorted by Denkwart Guratzsch (*Macht durch Organization: Die Grundlegung des Hugenbergschen Presseimperiums* [Düsseldorf, 1974] pp. 54–55, 107) with the result that his views appear more *völkisch* than they actually were.

3. See Fritz Fischer, *Krieg der Illusionen: Die deutsche Politik von 1911 bis 1914* (Düsseldorf, 1969); and Dirk Stegmann, *Die Erben Bismarcks: Parteien und Verbände in der Spätphase des Wilhelminischen Deutschlands* (Cologne and Berlin, 1970).

Chapter 1

1. In AH Rohbraken, E 4, there are two chronological outlines detailing Hugenberg's early life, "Lebensdaten Alfred Hugenbergs nach Aufzeichnungen von Fräulein Margarete Hugenberg" and "Lebensdaten Alfred Hugenbergs und Meilensteine seines vaterländischen Wollens und Wirkens." In his later life Hugenberg noted that after the death of his father, his mother "had become familiar with all the cares of life." AH Rohbraken, M 27, "Aus den Aufzeichnungen Dr. Hugenbergs. Rohbraken." There is no date on this document, but its placement with Hugenberg's tax records indicates that it stems from 1933 or 1935. The library at Rohbraken preserved a copy of Hugenberg's drama "Stahleck," poetic notes, and his personal correspondence with the poet Otto Erich Hartleben during their school years. AH Rohbraken, XXIV. Many of his poems, which indirectly reveal his lack of interest in formal religion and his ardent love for Germany, were published in Karl Henckell, Arthur Gutheil, Otto Erich Hartleben, and Alfred Hugenberg, *Quartett* (Hamburg, 1886).

2. Alfred Hugenberg, *Innere Colonisation im Nordwesten Deutschlands* (Strassburg, 1891), pp. 400–18, 451–52.

3. For details see the chronologies of his life in AH Rohbraken, E 4. See also Leo Wegener, *Hugenberg: eine Plauderei* (Solln-Munich, 1930), pp. 11–16; Freiherr (Axel) von Freytagh-Loringhoven, *Deutschnationale Volkspartei* (Berlin, 1931), p. 45; Friedrich Swart ed. *Aus Leo Wegeners Lebensarbeit* (Posen, 1938), pp. 8–9; Ludwig

Bernhard, *Der Hugenberg Konzern: Psychologie und Technik einer Grossorganization der Presse* (Berlin, 1928), pp. 1–7.

4. Hugenberg, *Bank und Kreditwirtschaft*, pp. 1, 2, 22–23, 26, 32, 70, 87, 107–13.

5. See the minutes of ministerial conferences dealing with this in AH Rohbraken, WP 2, and note Hanne-Lore Land, *Die Konservativen und die Preussische Polenpolitik: 1866–1912* (Berlin, 1963), pp. 61–98.

6. Alfred Hugenberg, *Streiflichter aus Vergangenheit und Gegenwart* (Berlin, 1927), Hugenberg to Forester, 13 September 1907, pp. 222–24.

7. Ibid.; also Dr. Wahrmund [pseud.], *Gericht über Hugenberg* (Dillingen, 1932), p. 16. As the pseudonym indicates, the author was most critical of Hugenberg; he charged that the mayor of Frankfurt, Hugenberg's father-in-law, Franz Adickes, was instrumental in having this offer made. The move apparently improved Hugenberg's financial status—the bank guaranteed him an annual salary of M 15,000. See his contract with the bank in AH Rohbraken, A 1.

8. Gert von Klass, *Krupps*, trans. James Cleugh (London, 1954), p. 297. The author is very defensive of the Krupp firm and de-emphasizes the role of Hugenberg.

9. A clear analysis of Hugenberg's role at Krupp's is hampered by a lack of documentation. The public relations director of the firm informed me that material from this period had not been organized for archival usage, that the ravages of war had left large gaps in documentation, and that the retirement of Dr. Ernst Schröder in 1972 had left the firm without any archival staff. Georg-Volkmar Graf Zedwitz-Arnim to the Author, 29 March 1972. Guratzsch was apparently allowed limited access to only two files (the signatures of which indicate a definite arrangement by provenance). Despite the lack of documentation, the count instructed Guratzsch that under Krupp von Bohlen directors of the firm never had a strong determinative influence on policy. Guratzsch, pp. 66, 445. In the Kornwalzer affair, Hugenberg indicated the exact reverse. Guratzsch, p. 66. Hugenberg is obviously not seen as an asset in Krupp's public relations.

10. *Jahrbuch für den Oberbergamtsbezirk Dortmund: 1912–1913* (Essen, 1913), p. 425.

11. Interview with members of the Hugenberg family, 30 December 1971. Tilo Freiherr von Wilmowsky, *Rückblickend möchte ich sagen ...: An der Schwelle des 150 jährigen Krupp-Jubiläums* (Oldenburg and Hamburg), p. 105.

12. Bernhard Menne, *Krupp* (London, 1937), p. 282.

13. Georg Bernhard, *Meister und Dilettanten am Kapitalismus im Reich der Hohenzollern* (Amsterdam, 1936), pp. 243–44. See also Hartmut Kaelble, *Industrielle Interessenpolitik in der Wilhelminischen Gesellschaft: Centralverband deutscher Industrieller 1895–1914* (Berlin, 1967), pp. 72–74.

14. See Wilmowsky, p. 105; and Guratzsch, p. 67.

15. AH Rohbraken, E 4, "Lebensdaten... Meilensteine"

16. Kurt Stenkewitz, *Gegen Bayonette und Dividende: Die politische Krise in Deutschland am Vorabend des ersten Weltkrieges* (Berlin, 1960), pp. 184–85. Hugenberg had already indicated his ideas on the *Werksgemeinschaft* in *Bank und Kreditwirtschaft*, p. 113.

17. For instance, the average daily wage in Krupp's steel mills in Essen was M 5.44 at the end of 1913 and only forty-six pfennigs higher at the end of 1913—

not much, especially if one considers that in the same period, dividends went from ten to fourteen percent. For these and similar statistics on hours and living conditions see *Jahrbuch für den Oberbergamtsbezirk Dortmund: 1912–1913*, pp. 242, 421; and Wolfram Fischer, *Herz des Reviers: 125 Jahre Wirtschaftsgeschichte des Industrie- und Handelskammerbezirks Essen–Mühlheim–Oberhausen* (Essen, 1965), p. 91.

18. "Zur Hundertjahrfeier der Firma Krupp: 1812–1912," Sonderausgabe der Kruppschen Mitteilungen, pp. 86–89. Fifty years later, Wilmowsky (p. 105) termed the speech a "masterpiece." Krupp had planned an elaborate medieval pageant to celebrate the event, but a mining accident caused this to be cancelled. A beautifully bound copy of "Kruppianer," including members of the Hugenberg family in medieval costumes, is preserved in the library at Rohbraken.

19. Germany, *Stenographische Berichte der Verhandlungen des deutschen Reichstages* (hereafter cited as *Reichstag-Protokolle*), 289, 18 April 1913, p. 4911. Liebknecht wanted the investigation continued into the central administration at Essen and not limited to the Berlin office and peripheral areas. *Reichstag-Protokolle*, 290, 11 May 1914, pp. 8705–06. Also cf. von Klass (p. 304) with the more critical analysis of Menne (pp. 267–76).

20. The same corporations controlled both groups; distinctions between the two associations were essentially juridical and functional. *Glückauf*, no. 48, 7 December 1912, p. 2020, and "6. ordentliche Hauptversammlung des Zechenverbandes ... den 26. April 1913." In his inaugural speech as chairman of the BbV, Hugenberg proudly noted that the association was not merely an economic pressure group, "but also a unique structure of unified determination and intense bourgeois strength." Hugenberg, *Streiflichter*, p. 207.

21. Fischer, *Herz des Reviers*, p. 403.

22. BA Koblenz, R13I/51, "Sitzung des Direktoriums des Centralverbandes deutscher Industrieller in Berlin am 27. April 1911." He was also elected to the committee of the *Verein zur Wahrung der gemeinschaftlichen Interessen im Rheinland und Westfalen (Langnam Verein)* on 5 May 1911. See "XL. ordentliche Hauptversammlung des Vereins ..." in *Langnam Mitteilungen* (1911), p. 121.

23. Correspondence preserved at Rohbraken makes this obvious. Note also Hugenberg's eulogy of Stinnes in *Streiflichter*, pp. 101–04; and Guratzsch, pp. 100–10.

24. BA Koblenz, R13I/52, "Niederschrift über die Sitzung des Direktoriums des Centralverbandes ... am 15. February 1912." Note also Stegmann, p. 358; Bernhard, p. 54; and Guratzsch, pp. 99–109.

25. See Fischer, *Krieg der Illusionen*, pp. 384–412.

26. Valeska Dietrich (*Alfred Hugenberg: Ein Manager in der Publizistik* [Berlin, 1960]), was the first to depict the managerial genius of Hugenberg. Guratzsch's study of Hugenberg's activity to 1918 emphasizes the same point; the only weakness of his work is its failure to elucidate Hugenberg's very definite political motivation and thus place his activity within its historical context.

27. Guratzsch, p. 203.

28. "Erklärung der Werke" cited in Guratzsch, p. 207.

29. See the letter of Hugenberg to Class, 8 May 1908, as cited in Annelise Thimme, *Flucht in den Mythos: Die Deutschnationale Volkspartei und die Niederlage von*

1918 (Göttingen, 1969), pp. 171–72, n 48.

30. Alfred Kruck, *Geschichte des Alldeutschen Verbandes 1890–1939* (Wiesbaden, 1959), p. 8; Otto Bonhard, *Geschichte des Alldeutschen Verbandes* (Leipzig, 1920), pp. 240–47; Heinrich Class, *Wider den Strom* (Leipzig, 1932), p. 46. The last author, a continued collaborator of Hugenberg, claimed that Hugenberg was the "real father" of the organization. He certainly played a major role, but this claim might well have been propaganda for the 1932 elections.

31. Class, *Wider den Strom*, pp. 81–82; Alldeutsche Verband, *Zwanzig Jahre Alldeutscher Arbeit und Kämpfe* (Leipzig, 1910) pp. 62–67; "Edgar Hartwig, Alldeutscher Verband (ADV)," in Dieter Fricke, ed., *Die bürgerlichen Parteien in Deutschland* (Berlin, 1968), 1: 9–10.

32. Felix-Heinrich Gentzen, "Deutscher Ostmarkenverein (DOV) 1894–1935," in Fricke, 1: 503–07; and Kruck, p. 17.

33. See Dieter Fricke, "Reichsverband gegen die Sozialdemokratie (RgS) 1904–1918," in Fricke, 2: 620–30.

34. Heinrich Class, *Denkschrift betreffend die national und sozialpolitischen Ziele des deutschen Volkes im gegenwärtigen Kriege* (Als Handschrift Gedruckt). There is extensive correspondence between Hugenberg and Class on the problem of war aims in DZA Potsdam, Akten des Alldeutschen Verbandes (ADV), 179/1.

35. Fritz Fischer, *Germany's Aims in the First World War* (New York, 1967), pp. 95–98. Note also the biography of the chancellor by Conrad Jarausch, *The Enigmatic Chancellor: Bethmann Hollweg and the Hubris of Imperial Germany* (New Haven and London, 1973).

36. Class, *Wider den Strom*, pp. 326–55.

37. Ibid., pp. 354–55.

38. Hugenberg, *Streiflichter*, p. 203. The move was particularly bold since Class was under house arrest and his mail was censored.

39. AH Rohrbraken, WP 18, Bund der Landwirte, Deutscher Bauernbund, Centralverband deutscher Industrieller, Bund der Industriellen, Hansabund und Reichsdeutscher Mittelstandsverband to the Reichstag, 10 March 1915; and the same groups (except the Hansabund) to the chancellor, 20 May 1915.

40. Guratzsch, p. 323.

41. Ibid.

42. Guratzsch, p. 325 n 760, and note the excellent graphs on p. 330–31.

43. Guratzsch, pp. 178–80, 322.

44. Guratzsch, pp. 324–28. Since the purpose of the *Wirtschaftliche Gesellschaft* was to promote the social and economic policies of the *Zechenverband*, the distinction between the four major investors and the coaling association is fundamentally a juridical one. Since so much came directly from Krupp, it would be hard to argue that von Bohlen opposed this attempt to infiltrate the press. That Hugenberg was the guiding hand behind this move is apparent from the documentation preserved at Rohbraken (e.g. WP 19, "Wirtschaftliche Gesellschaften"). The social and political tendencies of this group, and most especially of Hugenberg, manifest themselves through the close collaboration which was maintained with Class. See their correspondence in DZA Potsdam, ADV, 179/1. Hugenberg and Kirdorf were instrumental in establishing the *Norddeutsche Verlags- und Treuhandgesellschaft m.b.H.*, which published the Pan-Ger-

man *Deutsche Zeitung.* See BA Koblenz, R431/892, Class circular of 30 November 1916; AH Rohbraken, M 1, Kirdorf to Hugenberg, 9 January 1917 and Hugenberg to Kirdorf, 19 March 1917; also M 25, Class to Hirsch, 11 January 1917.

45. AH Rohbraken, O 2, "Aufzeichnung über des Verwaltungsausschusses der August Scherl G.m.b.H. vom 27. Juli 1916." See also Bernhard, p. 72; and Günther Heidorn, *Monopole—Presse—Krieg: Die Rolle der Presse bei Vorbereitung des ersten Weltkrieges* (Berlin, 1960), p. 45. For an understanding of Scherl see Peter de Mendelssohn, *Zeitungsstadt Berlin: Menschen und Mächte in der Geschichte der deutschen Presse* (Berlin, 1959), pp. 82–92; and Hans Erman, *August Scherl: Daemonie und Erfolg in Wilhelminischer Zeit* (Berlin, 1954).

46. For instance, during the Bülow era, Scherl's general director received a letter of recommendation from the chancellor in order to sell Scherl stock to Krupp. AH Rohbraken, O 2, [?] to Hugenberg, 10 February 1914. See also Stegmann, p. 174.

47. Heidorn, pp. 52–53; Stegmann, p. 174; and Guratzsch, p. 277. The members of the association are listed in a document preserved in AH Rohbraken, O 2, which is reprinted with a sociological analysis of the membership in Guratzsch, pp. 421–27.

48. AH Rohbraken, "Geschäfts-Bericht des Deutschen Verlag-Vereins zu Düsseldorf für das Geschäftsjahr 1916." See also Bernhard, pp. 67–68.

49. Guratzsch, pp. 288–89, 429–31. See Hugenberg's undated list, "Vorzugsanteile" in AH Rohbraken, O 2. The funds possibly invested by the Prussian government were later the source of a parliamentary investigation to determine whether these were a loan or a free grant to the firm. Unfortunately, it was found that the pertinent documents of the Prussian *Domänenbank* had been torn from the files. See Andreas Weitenwerber, "Herr über Presse und Film: Hugenbergs Aufstieg, Glück und Ende," Sonderdruck aus der *Journalist* (n.p., 1957). Guratzsch makes excellent use of the report, but fails to mention the cause of the inquiry.

50. The extensive correspondence dealing with the sale and control of Scherl in AH Rohbraken, O 2 and WP 19, leaves no doubt that Hugenberg was the key figure in these dealings.

51. AH Rohbraken, O 2, "Aufzeichnung über die Sitzung des Verwaltungsausschusses der August Scherl G.m.b.H. vom 27. Juli 1916."

52. AH Rohbraken, O 2, Wegener to Hugenberg, 14 November 1916.

53. The chancellor who had been influential in bringing the Ruhr industrialists into the Scherl concern felt threatened by the change in editorial policy which Neumann fostered. BA Koblenz, Bauer Papers, 16, "Aktennotiz" of Bauer's discussion with State Secretary Zimmermann on 29 June 1917.

54. Otto Groth, *Die Zeitung: Ein System der Zeitungskunde (Journalistik)* (Mannheim, 1928–30), 2: 541–42.

55. Wilhelm Hermann, *Die Geschichte der ALA: Eine Zeitungswissenschaftliche Studie* (Frankfurt/M, 1938), p. 20. Despite the superficial Nazi bias, this is an excellent mongraph which reveals a careful study of pertinent archival sources.

56. Groth, 2: 588–89; Bernhard, pp. 78–81.

57. Hugenberg, *Streiflichter*, "Schreiben des Bergbauvereins und Handelskammer zu Essen vom 26. März 1918 an die Herren von Hindenburg und Ludendorff," pp. 190–91; and see Willi Boelcke, *Krupp und die Hohenzollern: Aus*

der Korrespondenz der Familie Krupp: 1850–1916 (Berlin, 1956), von Gayl to von Valentini, 23 June 1915, pp. 143–45; and Wilhelm Groener, *Lebenserinnerungen: Jugend–Generalstab–Weltkrieg*, ed. Friedrich Freiherr Hiller von Gaertringen (Göttingen, 1957), pp. 368–70.

58. AH Rohbraken, A 24, Schiele (Deutsche Vaterlandspartei) to Hugenberg, 4 October 1917; and Wolfgang Kapp to Hugenberg, 15 October 1917.

59. See the pioneer work of Hans Gatzke, *Germany's Drive to the West: A Study of Germany's Western War Aims During the First World War* (Baltimore, 1950), p. 155.

60. HA, GHH, 300 193 90/17, Hugenberg to Reusch, 28 November 1917. Guratzsch, pp. 365, 370–71.

61. For a closer examination of the nature and intent of these corporations see Guratzsch, pp. 363–78; and Bernhard, pp. 17–25.

62. Hugenberg did suffer periods of depression, but his spirit was sustained by men who thought as he did. For example, see AH Rohbraken, M 7, Vögler to Hugenberg, 31 October 1919. Despite the opportunities Hugenberg had for meeting stimulating intellectuals of conflicting views, he never took time to enjoy them. He almost never encountered the intelligentsia of Berlin, and he rarely attended the theater or the cinema. His working hours—most of the day—were compulsively regular. During the Weimar era, when he was not at his house in Dahlem, he was at Rohbraken or on a business trip. After his friend Wegener had established *Haus Sonnenschein* in Kreuth (Upper Bavaria), Hugenberg usually visited him twice a year. At other times he would visit Bad Kissingen and take the cure for obesity. In effect, he led the life of a stolid burgher surrounded by business associates, family, and friends who reinforced his basic ideas.

63. There seems to be little substance to the charge that Hugenberg became *persona non grata* with Krupp because of his advocacy of expansionist war aims. Hugenberg's assertion that he had determined to leave the firm well before the events of November 1918 (and thus was not discharged) seems substantiated by the development of his interests in the media, especially after 1916. See Ernst Schroeder, *Otto Wiedfeldt* (Essen, 1964), p. 94; and Hugenberg's statement in the *Berliner Lokal-Anzeiger*, 14 March 1926. Hugenberg received a pension from Krupp and exchanged friendly, if infrequent, letters with him after 1918. See the correspondence in AH Rohbraken, A 7 and A 16.

64. Hugenberg was not merely a figurehead; he participated in the negotiations producing the Stinnes-Legien agreement and continued to direct the affairs of these associations. See Gerald Feldman, "The Origins of the Stinnes-Legien Agreement," in Gerhard Ritter, ed., *Entstehung und Wandel der modernen Gesellschaft: Festschrift für Hans Rosenberg zum 65. Geburtstag* (Berlin, 1970), pp. 312–41; and Hugenberg's correspondence with von Loewenstein in AH Rohbraken, A 17.

65. WA Bayer, Leverkusen, 62/10.1, "Auszug aus dem Briefe ..." Oppenheim to Duisberg, 28 February 1919; *Mitteilungen des Deutschen Industrierates*, no. 25 (12 April 1919), p. 3490; and Danielson report to Duisberg, 8 April 1919. See also AH Rohbraken, A 22, Sorge to Hugenberg, 10 May 1919. For a history of the association, see Fritz Günther and Manfred Ohlsen, "Reichsverband der Deutschen Industrie (RDI) 1919–1933," in Fricke, 2: 580–619.

66. Hugenberg's correspondence makes this obvious. For example, see AH

Rohbraken, M 7, Vögler to Hugenberg, 22 December 1922; and HA, GHH, 300 193 90/17, Hugenberg to Reusch, 23 June 1922.

67. Funds from Hugenberg's office helped establish Martin Spahn's Political College and the Evangelical Social School; they also helped develop the National Club in Berlin and Heinrich von Gleichen's June Club. Hugenberg was a member of the Gäa (the *Gemeinsamer Ausschuss*), and provided subsidies for the radical paramilitary group, the Organization Escherich, in Bavaria. Hugenberg and his Pan-German friends associated with the *Deutschvölkischer Schutz- und Trutzbund* were interested in the Austrian anti-Semite, Adolf Hitler, as a popular orator. See the Hugenberg-Vögler correspondence in AH Rohbraken, M 7; Oswald Spengler, *Briefe 1913–1936*, ed. Anton M. Koktanek and Manfred Schröter (Munich, 1963), p. 236; Uwe Lohalm, *Völkischer Radikalismus: Die Geschichte des Deutschvölkischen Schutz- und Trutzbundes 1919–1923* (Hamburg, 1970), p. 287; and AH Rohbraken, A 24, Traub Memorandum (n.d.).

68. AH Rohbraken, M 27, "Satzungen des nicht rechtsfähigen Vereins 'Wirtschaftsvereinigung zur Forderung der geistigen Wiederaufbaukräfte' im Sinne des Paragraphen 54 des Bürgerlichen Gesetzbuches."

69. AH Rohbraken, M 7, Vögler to Hugenberg, 22 December 1922; HA, GHH 300 193 90/17, Hugenberg to Reusch, 17 December 1921, and Reusch to Hugenberg, 31 December 1921.

70. See Thimme, *Flucht in den Mythos*, pp. 107–41.

71. See Groth, 2:588.

72. See the excellent work of Kurt Koszyk, *Deutsche Presse: 1914–1915* (Berlin, 1972), p. 228; and AH Rohbraken, A 17, Hugenberg to Lindeiner-Wildau, 17 November 1923, and Lindeiner-Wildau to Hugenberg, 19 December 1923. Because of later disagreements with the Stresemann party, the *Alterum* was later eclipsed by the *Vera* and the *Mutuum*. See Bernhard, pp. 81–82.

73. These included the *Oppelner Nachrichten*, the *Oberschlesischer Tageszeitung*, the *München-Augsburger Abendzeitung*, the *Süddeutsche Zeitung* (Stuttgart), the *Hessische Landes-Zeitung* (Darmstadt), the *Bergisch-Märkische Zeitung* (Elberfeld), the *Magdeburger Tageszeitung*, the *Lippesche Tageszeitung* (Detmold), the *Göttinger Tageblatt*, the *Allensteiner Zeitung* and the *Niederdeutsche Zeitung* (Hannover). See AH Rohbraken, P 17, Gnoyke (Vera) to Mann, 13 June 1932, and M 8, Traub to Hugenberg, 23 September 1922. And in Amsterdam ISH, see Braun Papers, 452, Grezinski to Braun, 5 June 1926. Also note Groth, 2: 592. Determining the circulation and influence of these publications would require exacting regional studies of the cities in which these appeared and analyses of the press such as Arno Schroeder *Geschichte des Zeitungswesens in Lippe [Detmold, 1932])* provides. Broadsides narrowly based on the editorial policy of a single paper—e.g., Christian Schmaling, *Der Berliner Lokal-Anzeiger als Beispiel einer Vorbereitung des Nationalsozialismus* (Berlin, 1968)—are of little use.

74. The *Handbuch der deutschen Tagespresse* (pp. 11–17) indicates that the number of newspapers in Germany was as high as 4,500 and that about 70 percent of these were small town publications dependent on regional and national news syndicates. In his defense of Hugenberg during denazification proceedings, Dr. Borchmeyer relied on the *Handbuch der Weltpresse* and emphasized that there were 3,553 daily newspapers. See *Hugenbergs Ringen in deutschen Schicksalsstunden:*

Tatsachen und Entscheidungen in den Verfahren zu Detmold und Düsseldorf (Detmold, 1949–1950), 2: 37.

75. Bernhard, pp. 84–85. The federal government gave an annual subsidy to the Wolf Telegraph Bureau; see BA Koblenz, R43I/2526, Zechlin to Pünder, 16 January 1929.

76. HA, GHH, 300 193 20/0, "Niederschrift über die Sitzung des Vorstandes des Reichsverbands der Deutschen Industrie am Mittwoch, den 9. Juli 1920."

77. AH Rohbraken, A 23, Schwerin to Hugenberg, 8 November 1919, and M 7, Vögler to Hugenberg, 28 August 1920.

78. Bernhard, pp. 87–88; and Groth, 2:607–08.

79. The last general director of the corporation, Otto Mejer, claimed that the *TU* was not and could not be used for political purposes. AH Rohbraken, E 4, Mejer to Meesmann, 27 June 1949 and 29 June 1949. Since 1920, however, every editor within the *TU* had unambiguously contracted to support "the political and economic reconstruction of Germany *on a national basis* without partisan or other obligation." AH Rohbraken, P 17, "Kurze Denkschrift über die Notwendigkeit der Beibehaltung zweier grosser Nachrichtenbüros in Deutschland." This memo, composed in 1933, pointed out that "*all National Socialist newspapers* have worked *exclusively with the services of the TU.*" Schmidt-Hannover's great interest in this service is evident in his diary of 28 January 1932 to 4 August 1932. S 21 Hannover.

80. Groth, 2:520–21, 604.

81. Groth, 2:605–06. For a practical example of this, see the correspondence dealing with the conflict of the Cuno government with the *TU* in 1923. BA Koblenz, R43I/2475 and 2478. In 1923, Klitzsch lamented that the directors of the *TU* viewed the dispatch service "chiefly as a political instrument," and consequently the commercial aspects of the firm suffered. BA Koblenz, Hugenberg Papers, 589, Klitzsch to Hugenberg, 12 June 1923.

82. See the Hugenberg-Klitzsch correspondence on the development of this firm and the conflict over its function with Stinnes. BA Koblenz, Hugenberg Papers, 200. Also note Bernhard, pp. 82–83.

83. Groth, 1:470.

84. Groth, 2:608–09.

85. Dietrich, p. 60.

86. Bernhard, p. 83.

87. Most of the original members of the *Deutscher Verlags-Verein* abandoned their interest in the firm. AH Rohbraken, O 2, Wehr to Hugenberg, 26 March 1921 and 29 April 1921; BA Koblenz, Hugenberg Papers, 250, "Niederschrift über die Sitzung des Verwaltungsausschusses der Firma August Scherl G.m.b.H. am 26. Juni 1922." Though the association had lost control, it remained a factor until after Neumann, as its chairman, agreed to turn over its M 8,750,000 worth of shares to the *Ostdeutsche Bank A.G.* and the *Aussendienst G.m.b.H.* (two Hugenberg firms) in 1924. BA Koblenz, Hugenberg Papers, 368, "Nr. 306 des Notariatsregisters."

88. BA Koblenz, Hugenberg Papers, 590, "Vertrag vom 20. Dezember 1919."

89. It later peaked at 300,000 to 400,000 copies daily. AH Rohbraken, E 4, "Vertriebspropaganda-Bericht ..." cited in Wahlert to Meesmann, 9 July 1949;

and AH Rohbraken, E 4, "Denkschrift von Dr. Klitzsch."

90. AH Rohbraken, A 20, Klitzsch to Hugenberg, 9 September 1922; and Bernhard, p. 73.

91. Enclosure in AH Rohbraken, E 4, Wahlert to Meesmann, 2 July 1949.

92. BA Koblenz, Wegener Papers, Wegener to Traub, 6 January 1930; and AH Rohbraken, GB 10, "Denkschrift vom 22.1.30." Hugenberg's *Roggenrentenbank A.G.*, *Landbank A.G.*, and *Ostbank für Handel und Gewerbe*—as well as his collaboration with the *Reichsverband der landwirtschaftlichen Genossenschaften*—were all originally grounded in this vision. See BA Koblenz, Wegener Papers, 21.

93. His *Landbank* failed in 1925 and the *Ostbank* collapsed in 1929. In both cases Hugenberg blamed the Prussian government for not properly supporting investment in the East; see *Berliner Börsen Zeitung*, 10 December 1925, and AH Rohbraken, "Denkschrift vom 22.1.30." His opponents claimed that he had used the funds in these banks to bolster his ventures in the media, see *Vossische Zeitung*, 24 December 1925. Klaus Peter Hoepke claims that Hugenberg gave up his involvement in the *Roggenrentenbank* in order to purchase shares in the Universum Film A.G. See his "Alfred Hugenberg als Vermittler zwischen grossindustriellen Interessen und Deutschnationale Volkspartei," in Hans Mommsen, Dieter Petzina, and Bernd Weissbrod, *Industrielles System und politische Entwicklung in der Weimarar Republik* (Düsseldorf, 1974), p. 910.

94. The *Ostdeutsche Privatbank*, *Neuland*, and the *Roggenrentenbank* had an interlocking council which allowed members of the boards of overseers to coordinate their plans. *Neuland* not only lent money directly to Scherl and served as a major shareholder in the *Mutuum Darlehns A.G.* and the *Alterum Kredit A.G.*, but also helped to back the *Revisions und Treuhandgesellschaft des Reichsverbands der deutschen landwirtschaftlichen Genossenschaften m.b.H.*, the major shareholder in the early days of the *Ostdeutsche Privatbank*. BA Koblenz, Wegener Papers, 21, "Reise Berlin: 9–14. Juli 1923." Also note the pertinent documents in BA Koblenz, Hugenberg Papers, 378, 435, and 436.

95. HA, GHH, 400 101 10/2, "... Gesellschaftversammlung der Deutschen Gewerbehaus G.m.b.H. am 1. Juli 1927 ..."

96. HA, GHH, 400 101 2007/10, undated notes from ca. March 1926.

97. HA, GHH, 400 101 200/0, Hugenberg to Haniel, 6 January 1925, and Donner to Haniel, 30 May 1925 in Haniel to Reusch, 2 June 1925. The latter speaks of Hugenberg's "impudence" in making this claim.

98. HA, GHH, 400 101 200/0, Haniel to Hugenberg, 11 February 1925; and see HA, GHH, 400 101 290/89, Loewenstein to Reusch, 13 July 1925.

99. The legal briefs are preserved in HA, GHH, 400 ·10110/2. The GHH claimed that the Hugenberg people proposed to dissolve the *Deutscher-Verlags Verein* for tax purposes and for fear of state intervention, but that the real reason for the dissolution—the sale of the association's stocks in Scherl to the *Opriba*—was kept secret.

100. See HA, GHH, 400 101 2000/1, Haniel to Reusch, 1 February 1927; 400 101 2007/14, Reusch to Thyssen, 9 September 1927; 400 101 2000/2 Reusch to Haniel, 16 December 1927.

101. HA, GHH, 400 101 290/37. Vögler to Reusch, 18 December 1926.

102. HA, GHH, 400 101 10/2, "Mitgliederversammlung des Deutschen Verlags-Vereins in Berlin am 1.7. 1927." Cf. above, n 87.

103. HA, GHH, 400 101 2007/14, Reusch to Thyssen, 13 September 1927, and 400 101 2000/2, Reusch to Haniel, 16 December 1927. Hugenberg had also prepared a court case against Haniel; both men withdrew their threat to sue.

104. HA, GHH, 400 101 2007/10, undated notes from ca. March 1926.

105. HA, GHH, 400 101 2007/14, Reusch to Thyssen, 13 September 1927. Thyssen acted as mediator here and suggested that Haniel continue acting as the trustee for the *Zechenverband's* investments in Knorr and Hirth.

106. Bernhard, p. 59.

107. See HA, GHH, 400 101 2024/4, the correspondence of Blank and Reusch in 1928. Also Richard Lewinsohn (Morus), *Das Geld in der Politik* (Berlin, 1931), p. 185; and Koszyk, pp. 225–26. Earlier, Oskar Hergt of the DNVP had apparently been one of the twelve. See the notes on membership in BA Koblenz, Wegener Papers, 37. According to Hugenberg's undated notations in 1933, three members were replaced. Neumann and Winkhaus had died; Witthoeft had apparently resigned. The new members were Paul Bang of the ADV, *Rittergutsbesitzer* von Goldacker, and Fritz Springorum of the Hoesch concern. AH Rohbraken, P 17.

108. BA Koblenz, Hugenberg Papers, 230, unsigned notes [presumably by Hugenberg], 22 May 1940.

109. Bernhard, p. 97.

110. After the grant of M 264,000 in 1931, the sums fell to M 33,100 in 1932, and M 28,200 in 1933; see AH Rohbraken, P 17, Hugenberg to Werbegemeinschaft, 5 December 1933. Complete records of this association are not available, but in 1925 this *Werbegemeinschaft* received M 300,000 from Scherl and M 325,000 from the firm in the years 1926–1929. BA Koblenz, Hugenberg Papers, 317, "Brutto-Überschuss und Verwendung desselben 1910–1913, 1924–1929."

111. In the period 1925 through 1927, Scherl paid a dividend of 10 percent on common shares. Hugenberg personally owned M 225,000 worth of stock. When his fees for services on the board of overseers were included, his income from Scherl alone was M 167,500 in 1925, and M 154,500 in 1926. AH Rohbraken, A 23, Scherl to Hugenberg, 4 May 1925 and 27 March 1926. Through additional recompense to the other boards of the concern and, most likely, a guaranteed salary for his coordination of the entire syndicate, Hugenberg began to accumulate a private fortune. See the pertinent documents in AH Rohbraken, A 19. Hugenberg also received handsome stipends for his nominal service to the boards of overseers of the *Gelsenkirchener Bergwerks A.G.* and the *Deutsch-Luxemburgische Bergwerks- und Hütten A.G.*; see BA Koblenz, Hugenberg Papers, 14.

112. Not all of Hugenberg's personal funds were invested in Scherl. He developed his estate, increased the holdings of a family concern (the *Familien Verwaltungs Gesellschaft m.b.H.*), and borrowed M 200,000 from Scherl to secure an estate for his heirs at Uhsmannsdorf in Silesia. AH Rohbraken, volumes dealing with Rohbraken, FVG, and Uhsmannsdorf.

113. AH Rohbraken, M 27, "Aus den Aufzeichnungen Dr. Hugenbergs: Rohbraken."

114. Bernhard, pp. 93, 96. On the involvement of heavy industry, see "Filmindustrie," *Ruhr und Rhein*, 11, no. 29 (18 July 1930): 959. This article boasted

that the determined action of "German industrial circles" prevented an alien
group from taking control of the *Ufa*. Such participation is further substantiated by the figures involved in the sale of the firm in 1937. See AH Rohbraken,
O 15, "Durchsicht der in Hannover befindlichen Ufa-Aktien-Paketes im Jahre
1937." In addition, the new board of overseers in 1927 included Paul Silverberg
of the lignite industry and Fritz Thyssen, scion of the famous Duisberg industrial family. BA Koblenz, R109/1035, "Nr. 38 des Notariatregisters für
1927."

115. See Siegfried Kracauer, *From Caligari to Hitler: A Psychological History of the
German Film* (Princeton, N.J., 1947) and the study commissioned by the
Spitzenorganization der deutschen Filmindustrie in 1925—Walther Plugge, "Film und
Gesetzgebung: Die kulturelle, politische und wirtschaftliche Bedeutung der
deutschen Filmindustrie ..." in BA Koblenz, R431/2498.

116. For greater detail see the notarized statements on control of *Ufa* shares
in BA Koblenz, R109/1035; and BA Koblenz, Hugenberg Papers, 454, 458.

117. On the origins of this fund, see Kaelble, p. 217. In the course of 1918,
Hugenberg urged that this campaign chest be strengthened in anticipation of
elections. He collaborated intimately with industrialists such as Beukenberg,
Springorum, and Vögler in collecting money and with Johannes Flathmann,
the executive secretary in charge of the fund, in the disbursement of subsidies.
See AH Rohbraken, WP 18.

118. Siemens, p. 130. And see Werner Fritzsch and Heinz Herz, "Deutsche
Demokratische Partei (DDP) 1918–1933," in Fricke, 1:308–10.

119. Henry A. Turner, *Stresemann and the Politics of the Weimar Republic* (Princeton, N.J., 1963), p. 29; and Wolfgang Hartenstein, *Die Anfänge der Deutschen
Volkspartei 1918–20* (Düsseldorf, 1962), p. 99.

120. On the formation of the DNVP see Werner Liebe, *Die Deutschnationale
Volkspartei: 1918–1924* (Düsseldorf, 1956); and Lewis Hertzman, *DNVP: Right
Wing Opposition in the Weimar Republic 1918–1924* (Lincoln, 1963).

121. The concept of a *Sammlung* remained paramount in Hugenberg's think-
ing no matter how the political structure evolved. He believed that "the support of a single mass party cannot be of use to industry, just as generally the
splitting of those elements of a nationalist right-wing character among the
various political parties can only lead to an absence of political influence. Instead, industry has the task of infiltrating as many parties as possible in accordance with the variegated character of its composition, and then of working
toward a political consolidation so that we can finally suceed in having, a party
structure capable of ruling and maintaining the state." Hugenberg's letter to
the Vereinigung von Handelskammern des Industriebezirks Essen, 20 February 1920, as cited in Feldman, "Big Business and the Kapp Putsch," p. 105.
Vögler agreed with Hugenberg and believed that the times demanded that
they "undertake the necessity of collaboration separately." AH Rohbraken, M
7, Vögler to Hugenberg, 27 October 1919.

122. Nevertheless, membership in the National Assembly and influence in a
political party constituted only one aspect of the total power necessary for
counterrevolutionary success. HA, GHH, 300 193 90/17, Hugenberg to Reusch,
5 April 1919. For an even more pessimistic approach to German politics during

this period, see Emil Kirdorf, *Erinnerungen 1847–1930* (private printing), pp. 90–91.

123. See Hugenberg, *Streiflichter*, "Die Deutschnationalen—eine Reformpartei," p. 123.

124. The diverse factions even had difficulty in agreeing on a name. It was the Christian Socialists who proposed the name DNVP; the conservative Count Kuno Westarp, preferred the title *Staatspartei*. See WP, "Konservative Politik in der Republik: 1918–1932", pp. 16–17.

125. Hertzman, p. 48. Wahrmund (pp. 35–36), asserted that industrialists wanted Hugenberg to go into the DVP, but the Stresemann party could only offer him a seat in the Düsseldorf area which was heavily populated with workers, and so he opted for the DNVP. There seems to be no factual basis for his assertion.

126. *Reichstag-Protokolle*, 331, 9 December 1919, pp. 3932–39.

127. Ibid., p. 3947.

128. Ibid., p. 3937.

129. Alfred Hugenberg, *Wirtschaftsfragen der Zukunft: Rede auf dem Parteitage der Deutschnationalen Volkspartei in Berlin: am 12. u. 13. Juli 1919* (Berlin 1919), p. 13; and Hugenberg's comments at the *12. ordentliche Hauptversammlung des Zechen-Verbands: am 30. Juni 1919* (n.p., n.d.), p. 16.

130. Hugenberg, *Streiflichter*, "Die Deutschnationalen—eine Reformpartei," p. 123.

131. Hugenberg, *Streiflichter*, "Auszug aus einer Ansprache vom 28. Juli 1920, (vor der Generalversammlung des Bergbauvereins zu Essen)," p. 131. In 1934, an official historian of the coaling community emphasized this statement and used it to boast that the Ruhr mining interests had acted like a John the Baptist preparing the way for the Nazi savior. Paul Osthold, *Die Geschichte des Zechenverbandes 1908–1933: Ein Beitrag zur deutschen Sozialgeschichte* Berlin, 1934), p. iii.

132. Hugenberg, *Streiflichter*, "Etwas mehr Treue (Auszug aus einer Ansprache an Herrn Geheimrat Emil Kirdorf zu seinem 75. Geburtstag (1922)," p.109.

133. Wegener, p. 85.

134. See the publications of this association and the unpublished minutes of its meetings in WA Bayer, Leverkusen.

135. For example, see his correspondence with Flathmann and with Gottfried von Dryander, treasurer of the DNVP, in AH Rohbraken, A 10.

136. Hertzman, pp. 101, 137, 147.

137. D. Traub, "Der völkische Gedanke," *München-Augsburger Abendzeitung*, 29 November 1923. Hugenberg secured this post for Traub and used him to be certain that the paper would follow the proper editorial policy. BA Koblenz, Traub Papers, 5 (unpublished memoirs).

138. Nationalist Jews played an important role in his press concern and an even more important one in the *Ufa*. Even in political life, one of the men most intimately associated with Hugenberg, Reinhold Quaatz, was reportedly the cousin of Ludwig Hollander, the chairman of the Central Association of Germans of the Jewish Faith. See *Dresdener Neuester Nachrichten*, 4 and 6 December 1924; and S 5 Hannover, undated *Anlage* (apparently to one of the *Parteimitteilungen*).

139. "Hitler–Mussolini," *Lippische Tages-Zeitung*, 10 November 1923.

140. D. Traub, "Gerechtigkeit," *München-Augsburger Abendzeitung*, 14 November 1923. Traub believed that Hitler had "gone to peices," but remained "irreplaceable as drummer." He believed that it would be a miscalculation "simply to turn against the Hitler people as a whole." AH Rohbraken, A 24, Traub Memorandum (n.d.). There is an implication here that the Nazis were receiving some sort of support from the Hugenberg syndicate or industry.

141. See the prejudicial coverage of the Hitler trial in the *Berliner Lokal-Anzeiger*, *Der Tag*, and the *München-Augsburger Abendzeitung*.

142. (Elard) von Oldenburg-Januschau, "Was nun?" *Berliner Lokal-Anzeiger*, 22 November 1923.

143. BA Freiburg, N 253 (Tirpitz Papers), 300, Tirpitz to Hugenberg, 14 September 1923.

144. Friedrich Hussong, "Die Putsch und seine Nutzniesser," *Berliner Lokal-Anzeiger*, 10 November 1923, and "Nun erst Recht: Schwarz-Weiss-Rot," *München-Augsburger Abendzeitung*, 13 November 1923, and the same in *Lippische Tages-Zeitung*, 19 November 1923. Hugenberg considered Stresemann to be "the misfortune of the bourgeoisie." Hugenberg, *Streiflichter*, "Unglück des deutschen Bügertums, (*Der Tag*, 9 Januar 1926)," p. 80.

145. Manfred Dörr, *Die Deutschnationale Volkspartei 1925 bis 1928* (Marburg/Lahn, 1964), p. 63; see also [Karl] Helfferich and [J. W.] Reichert, *Das zweite Versailles: Das Reparationsgutachten der allierten Experten* (Berlin, 1924).

146. See the party platform as printed in the *Lippische Tages-Zeitung*, 23 March 1924.

147. Dörr, pp. 63–64; and Wilhelm Dittmann, *Das politische Deutschland vor Hitler* (Zurich and New York, 1945), p. 4.

148. Dörr, pp. 66–69; and Georg W. F. Hallgarten and Joachim Radkau, *Deutsche Industrie und Politik von Bismarck bis heute* (Frankfurt/M, 1974), pp. 182–83.

149. He further argued that the country needed "more Germanic pride instead of low half-breed opinion (*Mischlingsgeist*)." Hugenberg, *Streiflichter*, "Umstellung (*Der Tag*, 27. Juli 1924)," p. 98.

150. AH Rohbraken, O 17, Meesmann to Liebe, 19 November 1953. Meesmann was in a good position to know because his service with Hugenberg had been preceded by intimate activity with the RDI and Duisberg. He lists the other dissidents as Thyssen, Reusch, and Ernst von Borsig.

151. Osthold, p. i.

152. *Berliner Lokal-Anzeiger*, 16 May 1924, 1 June 1924; and *Lippische Tages-Zeitung*, 17 August 1924. The party's tactics are carefully detailed in Tirpitz's attempt to inform Bavarian business leaders that the DNVP did not intend to leave them in an "extraordinary difficult economic situation." BA Freiburg, Tirpitz Papers, 60, Tirpitz to Baerwolff, 12 June 1924. Tirpitz ultimately voted for the Dawes legislation.

153. *Berliner Lokal-Anzeiger*, 1 June 1924; *Lippische Tages-Zeitung*, 27 August 1924; and *München-Augsburger Abendzeitung*, 28 August 1924.

154. Hugenberg, *Streiflichter*, Hugenberg to Hergt, 26 August 1924, pp. 96–97.

155. Hergt's seven-page statement defending his position provides an excellent description of the party's split. BA Freiburg, Tirpitz Papers, 60, Hergt to

the East Prussian (DNVP) Regional Association in Baerwolff to Tirpitz, 15 September 1924.

156. Hertzman, pp. 220–23. The best analysis of the political struggle to accept the plan is in Michael Stürmer, *Koalition und Opposition in der Weimarer Republik 1924–1928* (Düsseldorf, 1967), pp. 38–73.

157. *München-Augsburger Abendzeitung*, 30 August 1924. The syndicate also published a conciliatory essay by Gottfired Treviranus debating the issue (*Lippische Tages-Zeitung*, 31 August 1924) and a smarting attack by Hussong (*Berliner Lokal-Anzeiger*, 30 August 1924).

158. Hertzman, p. 223.

159. BA Freiburg, Tirpitz Papers, 311, Mann to Tirpitz, 4 September 1924.

Chapter 2

1. Dörr, pp. 80–82; and see Friedrich Hussong, "Herunter die Maske!" *Berliner Lokal-Anzeiger*, 30 November 1924; and "Schulter," *Berliner Lokal-Anzeiger*, 4 December 1924.

2. Hugenberg's electoral speech at Bünde (Westfalia) in *Berliner Lokal-Anzeiger*, 5 December 1924.

3. Dörr, pp. 83–86. After the election, Dr. Fritz Tänzler, executive secretary of the Union of German Employers' Associations (VDAV) summarized the attitude of most leading industrialists when he wrote that the stabilization of the mark led to a "stabilization of opinion among ordinary citizens" at the expense of the radical fringe. He indicated that his association, which had participated in the elections more than in the past, was concerned not with parties, but with "national economic interests (*volkswirtschaftliche Interesse*)." Fritz Tänzler, "Nach dem Wahl," *Der Arbeitgeber* 14 (1924): 513–14. Tänzler was a member of Hugenberg's ADI. Mitteilung der VDAV, Nr. 11, 30 April 1925.

4. German Nationals indicated their interests by taking control of the Ministries of Agriculture, Economics, and Finance, Dörr, pp. 87–96; and Stürmer, pp. 84–87.

5. Erich Schwarzer, "Luther und Braun," *Der Tag*, 18 January 1925. A similarly qualified position was taken by Johannes Hirsch, "Keine Kampfkabinett," *Berliner Lokal-Anzeiger*, 20 January 1925.

6. *München-Augsburger Abendzeitung*, 21 January 1925, cited in Dörr, pp. 94–95, n 88.

7. Hugenberg claimed that the essays were not immediately published because "the strength and internal unity of the rightist government at that time did not seem to me even in the early part of 1925 to be strong enough to be able to bear wide-ranging factual demands." He entitled the six articles "Decline in Filth or Spiritual Reconstruction?" Hugenberg, *Streiflichter*, pp. 51–72.

8. Hugenberg, *Streiflichter*, "Der springende Punkt," p. 52.

9. Hugenberg, *Streiflichter*, "Nationalisierung der Wirtschaft," p. 55.

10. Hugenberg, *Streiflichter*, "Arbeiterwohnungen" and "Werkaktien," pp. 60–67.

11. Hugenberg, *Streiflichter*, "Am Ende der Flegeljahre," p. 70.

12. Hugenberg, *Streiflichter*, p. 68.

13. Erich Schwarzer, "Jarres," *Der Tag*, 15 March 1925.

14. "Haltet Disziplin," *Der Tag*, 22 March 1925. The author was critical of Ludendorff's candidacy and presented the Hugenberg argument that unity was necessary. Anyone who did not support the *Reichsblock* was a "deserter of the whole national movement."

15. Otto Schmidt-Hannover, *Umdenken oder Anarchie* (Göttingen, 1959), pp. 187–95.

16. Once Hindenburg was elected, rightists hoped to remove State Secretary Otto Meissner and put their own men in positions of power around the field marshal. See . ibid.; and HA, GHH, 400 101 2024/2, Blank to Reusch, 2 May 1925.

17. *Lippische Tages-Zeitung*, 9, 12, 17, and 20 April 1925; and see Dörr, pp. 125, 126–33.

18. See WP, "Stellungnahme ... zur Auftwertungsfrage," ADI circular of 4 June 1925.

19. A. Hugenberg, "Eine ungehaltene Rede," WA Bayer, Leverkusen, Du VIIIa/42. Duisberg thanked Hugenberg for sending him a copy of this pamphlet and congratulated him for noting the "lack of responsibility of the Reichstag." WA Bayer, Leverkusen, VIIIa/42 Duisberg to Hugenberg, 18 July 1925. Hugenberg did not let the summer pass, however, without firing one fully public volley at the economic policy he detested. See Alfred Hugenberg, "Die grosse Lüge," *Süddeutsche Zeitung*, 3 August 1925.

20. For an example of the interparty bitterness evoked by this division, see von Keudell's description,of one of the delegation's debates on the subject. BA Freiburg, Tirpitz Papers, N 253/312.

21. HA, GHH, 400 101 200/1, Haniel to Reusch, 11 November 1925.

22. WA Bayer, Leverkusen, 62/10. 3a, Kastl to Duisberg, 14 November 1925. For the concern of the RDI in the formulation of trade treaties, see WA Bayer, Leverkusen, 62/10. 4a, "Stenographischer Bericht über die Präsidial-und Vorstands-Sitzung des Reichsverbands der Deutschen Industrie vom 23. Juni 1925"; and HA, GHH, 400 101 220/1b, Herle and Ramhorst to Members of the Presidium, 12 August 1925. As with most issues, industrialists were not united on the Locarno policy. Even those who belonged to the DNVP had different positions. Quaatz supported the ideological opposition. Ernst von Borsig, a member of the RDI presidium and chairman of the German National Industrial Committee in Berlin agreed with Kastl. A. Scheibe, the executive secretary of the ADI agreed with Hugenberg and the radicals. See WP, circular of the ADI, "Zu Locarno," 12 November 1925. Two other industrial delegates, Leopold and Reichert, disagreed with a strong condemnation of Locarno but were unwilling to support Stresemann's policy. WA Bayer, AS Duisberg, Kastl to Duisberg, 4 November 1925. Admiral Tirpitz sought to use his personal influence with von Hindenburg to have the president remove Luther and frustrate the treaties. BA Freiburg, Tirpitz Papers, N 253/186, Tirpitz to Hindenburg, 25 October 1925, and N 253/313, Tirpitz to Oldenburg-Januschau, 17 December 1925.

23. *Der Tag*, 17 November 1925. To prevent an open split in the party, the Reichstag delegation passed a series of resolutions limiting the independence of a representative to express in the Reichstag a position diverging from that of

his colleagues and delimiting the rights of delegates to reject decisions made by a party caucus. BA Freiburg, Tirpitz Papers, N 253/60, Mitteilung Nr. 18 and Mitteilung Nr. 20 of March 1926.

24. See BA Freiburg, Tirpitz Papers, N 253/314, Keudell to Westarp, 1 March 1926.

25. For analyses of Westarp's political approach, see Dörr, pp. 466–88; and Thimme, pp. 45–50.

26. Bernhard, p. 54.

27. Interview with members of the Hugenberg family, 30 December 1971.

28. Alfred Hugenberg, "Parteien und Parlamentarismus," *Eiserne Blätter*, 17 January 1926, p. 46. This article is sharply critical of Stresemann for disrupting the unity of the nationalist bourgeoisie.

29. The new editions of Class's "Kaiser Book" left no doubt about that. See Daniel Frymann (Heinrich Class), *Das Kaiserbuch: Politische Wahrheiten und Notwendigkeiten*, 7th ed. (Leipzig, 1925).

30. Discussion of this plan was not even recorded in the unpublished minutes of the ADV. The report simply refers to discussion of a highly influential matter. DZA Potsdam, ADV, 143, GA Verhandlungsbericht, Bremen, 10 April 1926.

31. Radicals had been attempting to influence the president through his Junker cronies, Oldenburg-Januschau and Berg-Markinien, as well as General Wilhelm von Dommes, a representative of the imperial household, Admiral Ludwig von Schroeder, and the field marshall's son, Oskar von Hindenburg. BA Freiburg, Tirpitz Papers, N 253/313, Tirpitz to Oldenburg-Januschau, 17 December 1925, and 253/314, von Keudell to Westarp, 1 March 1926; and for particulars on the entire putsch plan and its consequences see "Abschrift der Oberreichsanwalt, Leipzig Ci, den 13. Juli 1927, 12 J 57/26," in ISH Amsterdam, Grzesinski Papers, 1465, and "Material für die Landtagsverhandlungen über das Untersuchungsverfahren gegen Justizrat Class wegen Vorbereitung eines hochverrätischen Unternehmens," ibid., 1460.

32. ISH Amsterdam, Grzesinski Papers, 1465. See also WP, Schmidt report on the putsch plans, 12 May 1926. For an excellent account of the putsch, see Brewster S. Chamberlin, "The Enemy on the Right: the Alldeutsche Verband in the Weimar Republic, 1918–1926" (Ph.D. diss., University of Maryland, 1972), pp. 342–91.

33. ISH Amsterdam, Grzesinski Papers, 1465; and *Deutsche Zeitung*, 19 May 1926.

34. One of the informers, Konrad Dietz, who had a personal grudge against Hugenberg because of business dealings with the syndicate's *Bergisch-Märkische Zeitung*, later changed his story. Another informer associated with Arthur Mahraun, leader of the *Jungdeutscher Orden*, was angered by the refusal of Hugenberg's *Ostdeutsche Bank* to grant a loan for the order's newspaper. ISH Amsterdam, Grzesinski Papers, 1465; Arthur Mahraun, *Gegen getarnte Gewalten: Weg und Kampf einer Volksbewegung* (Berlin, 1928), pp. 129–51; and *Berliner Lokal-Anzeiger*, 9 September 1927.

35. See the semiofficial Pan-German repudiation of guilt, E. Fritz Baer, *Putsch-Gefahr und Hochverrat* (n.p., n.d.).

36. ISH Amsterdam, Grzesinski Papers, 1460.

37. Alfred Hugenberg, "Putsch und Kabinettskrise, *Berliner Lokal-Anzeiger*, 15 May 1926; *Der Tag*, 29 May 1926; *Lippische Tages-Zeitung*, 15 May 1926, p. 2; and Dr. Traub, "Polizeiwillkür," *München-Augsburger Abendzeitung*, 22 August 1926.

38. Baer, pp. 6, 18; ISH Amsterdam, Grzesinski Papers, 1465.

39. Bernhardt, pp. 46, 54–59, 66–69, 93, 94–102. Despite these prejudices, *Der Hugenberg-Konzern: Psychologie und Technik einer Grossorganization der Presse* remained the standard work on the Hugenberg syndicate until the Hugenberg Papers became available.

40. BA Koblenz, Wegener Papers, 20, Klitzsch to Wegener, 12 January 1926.

41. See BA Koblenz, Wegener Papers, 63–67.

42. See BA Koblenz, Wegener Papers. Members of the Hugenberg family claim that Frau Hugenberg was totally apolitical. Interview with members of the Hugenberg family, 30 December 1971. On the basis of material preserved in the *Forschungsstelle für die Geschichte des Nationalsozialismus* in Hamburg, Chamberlin (pp. 345–46), claims that Class enlisted her support in securing her husband's agreement to assume a leading role in politics. Wegener also collaborated closely with Class. Both believed that Hugenberg possessed the ability to lead Germany into a new era. See especially, BA Koblenz, Wegener Papers, 23, Wegener to Class, 17 September 1927.

43. Interview with members of the Hugenberg family, 30 December 1971.

44. Wegener, *Plauderei*, pp. 11–21; and see "Hugenberg," *Eiserne Blätter*, 3 April 1927, pp. 226–28.

45. This was the position planned for Hugenberg in Class's plans. ISH Amsterdam, Grzesinski Papers, 1465. (This was also the idea which Hugenberg's supporters stressed when he entered the Hitler cabinet in 1933.)

46. Hayessen claimed that Hugenberg directly told him that such were his reasons for not moving into the center of the political stage. BA Koblenz, Wegener Papers, 11, Hayessen to Wegener, 9 January 1926. Chamberlin (pp. 345–46) also asserts that Hugenberg was reluctant to assume a leadership role because he "considered only his family and property important...." This assertion certainly fits Hugenberg's character.

47. BA Koblenz, Wegener Papers, 20, Klitzsch to Wegener, 12 March 1926.

48. BA Koblenz, Wegener Papers, 24, Wegener to Traub, 23 November 1927.

49. He and other traditionalists were alarmed when a leader in the lignite coal industry, Paul Silverberg, argued at the 1926 RDI convention that "there should be no government without Social Democracy...." Apparently Blohm and Vögler directly challenged Silverberg; Sorge agreed and added that "with the unions and Social Democracy no understanding is possible, we must manage without them." Nevertheless, the leaders of the RDI avoided open confrontation on this issue. See WA Bayer, Leverkusen, 62/10. 4b, "Protokolle der Vorstandssitzung des Reichsverbands ... den 14. Oktober 1926"; and ibid., "Endgültige Fassung einer von Präsidium und Vorstand zu fassenden Entschliessung."

50. Hugenberg, "Der springende Punkt," *Streiflichter*, p. 53.

51. *Berliner Lokal-Anzeiger*, 15 November 1925. Hugenberg remained a member of the RDI presidium but took less and less interest in its activities. He did not play any significant role in the attempts of this association to collaborate

with agrarian leaders in order to develop a joint economic policy. See the lists of the leaders involved in HA, GHH, 400 101 2024/3a, Blank to Reusch, 1 and 17 December 1926. Through his involvement in agricultural cooperatives, Hugenberg had earlier sought election to the board of directors of the *Reichslandbund.* Hugenberg blamed Count Kalkreuth and other agrarian leaders for the failure of his negotiations for the development of an office complex for the agrarian association. Since the building and the election were apparently linked, both failed. See S 38 Hannover, Hugenberg to Kalkreuth, 22 December 1925.

52. See Dörr, p. 269, n 14.

53. The DNVP had continually flaunted its monarchial ideal. Wilhelm Mommsen, ed., *Deutsche Parteiprogramme* (Munich, 1960), p. 536.

54. For the attitude of Freytagh-Loringhoven see his extensive letters to Otto von Sethe. BA Koblenz, Kleine Erwerbung, 293; also Axel von Freytagh-Loringhoven, *Deutschnationale Volkspartei* (Berlin, 1931). General von Dommes was so disconcerted by party policy that he wanted to form a "special group" within the DNVP to support his views. WP, Meyer to Westarp, 1 September 1927, and Westarp to von Dommes, 6 September 1927. Tirpitz was greatly disenchanted with parliamentary life in general and, even before the party reentered the cabinet, had hoped that the party congress of the previous fall in Cologne had given the party leader enough backbone to be of use. BA Freiburg, Tirpitz Papers, N 253/314, Tirpitz to Oldenburg-Januschau, 8 December 1926.

55. WP, Hugenberg to Westarp, 15 January 1927 and 2 March 1927.

56. Dörr, pp. 303–06. Conflict within the DNVP was clearly brought out in the meeting of the party executive committee, which discussed the acceptance of this law. See BA Freiburg, Tirpitz Papers, N 253/60, "Sitzung des Parteivorstandes (der DNVP) am 2. Juni 1927. . . ."

57. BA Koblenz, Traub Papers, 50, Traub to Schiele-Naumberg, 21 May 1927.

58. DZA Potsdam, ADV, 146, GA Verhandlungsbericht 12 and 13 January 1927. And see, Stürmer, p. 72.

59. Hugenberg, *Streiflichter,* "Rathaus," pp. 1–19. Class and the members of the ADV publicly bemoaned the fact that a man who had such "ability, objectivity, and training" did not have more influence. *Alldeutsche Blätter,* 2 April 1927, p. 60. Albert Scheibe, editor of the naval journal, *Nauticus,* and Hugenberg's collaborator in the German National Industrial Committee, praised the positive note of the book and concluded that it revealed the "nature of a leader." *Unsere Partei,* 1 February 1927, p. 24.

60. On the young conservative movement, see Arnim Mohler, *Die Konservative Revolution in Deutschland: 1918–1932* (Stuttgart, 1950); and especially for the impact of this tendency on the DNVP, see Erasmus Jonas, *Die Volkskonservativen: 1928–1933* (Düsseldorf, 1965), pp. 1–32. For a direct criticism of Hugenberg by this group, see Jungnationaler Ring, ed., *Der Niedergang der nationalen Opposition* (Berlin, 1929).

61. WP, Hugenberg to Westarp, 1 December 1927 and see WP, "Verhandlungsprogramm des Verfassungsausschusses der DNVP nach dem Ergebnis der Generaldebatte am 25. November 1927."

62. Hugenberg's supporters were proud of this letter and saw it not only as proof of their leader's consistent advocacy of principled opposition, but also as one of the first moves that culminated in the reorganization of the party under Hugenberg's leadership. The letter has been reprinted in Jonas, pp. 180–182.

63. WP, Hugenberg to Westarp, 15 November 1927. Each of these men, except Tirpitz and Duesterberg, played an important role in the later election of Hugenberg as party chairman.

64. WP, Hugenberg to Westarp, 15 November 1927, "Anlage," (n.d.).

65. On the structure of the party, see Liebe, pp. 34–39.

66. BA Freiburg, Tirpitz Papers, N 253/60, "Finanzierung der Hauptgeschäftsstelle und der Landsverbände ... den 9. September 1926 ..."

67. Ibid.; and see WP, Feldmann to Westarp, 1 July 1927, and reply, 4 July 1927.

68. Dailies such as the *Neue Preussische (Kreuz-) Zeitung* and the *Deutsche Zeitung* represented disparate factions within the party, such as the old conservatives and the Pan-German League respectively. Weiss, *Nationaler Wille*, p. 11; and see Liebe, p. 43.

69. Hugenberg continually expounded the theme that the press had to be viewed as a business enterprise and could not function as an appendage of the party and thus run the risk of "squandering money unnecessarily." He also reminded the party that its ministers in the government had done nothing to help his syndicate but, rather, had acted as though his publications would have to survive on their own. WP, Hugenberg to Präfke, 8 March 1928. In the period before 1928, he refused to provide free issues of his papers for propaganda purposes on the grounds that the cost would be prohibitive. See WP, Hugenberg to Westarp, 25 January 1927. In the fall of 1927, after he had assumed control of the *Ufa*, Hugenberg was particularly concerned with a reduction of the entertainment tax on theater tickets. Despite the fact that the party was a member of the ruling coalition, little help was forthcoming for the film industry. See BA Koblenz, R109/1026, Minutes of the *Ufa* board of directors for 9 November 1927; and Traub, *Ufa*, p. 75.

70. When the DNVP entered the Marx government in 1927, the editor of *Der Tag*, Baron von der Meydem, asserted that there was no basis for jubilation. He nonetheless hoped that this could be a move in the direction of forming a "true national community" (*Volksgemeinschaft*). "Volksgemeinschaft und Staat," *Der Tag*, 29 January 1927. Hugenberg's papers fairly reported Westarp's reasons for accepting the Law for the Protection of the Republic but left no doubt that his syndicate condemned such a policy. *Der Tag*, 18 May 1927; and see WP, Westarp to Hugenberg, 23 May 1927, in which the count complains of Scherl's strong criticism of the party on this issue. Despite editorial preferences, the Scherl press still encouraged the entire right wing. For instance, the German National foreign policy expert, Otto Hoetzsch, whose position was anathema to the Pan-Germans, had a regular weekly column in *Der Tag*. See the 1928 issues of *Der Tag* until ca. 30 August 1928, when the column apparently ended. Members of the ADV were so opposed to Hoetzsch that Bang objected to running on the same list as him in the 1928 election. See DZA Potsdam, ADV, 151, "Sitzung des Geschäftsfuhrenden Ausschusses," 21 March 1928. In addition, Scherl

publications carried on a personal vendetta with Stresemann but criticized the DVP much less than its leader. Examples are too numerous to detail. See the articles of the staff editorialist G. Schultze-Pfaelzer.

71. WP, Hugenberg to Westarp, 8 June 1927. The count had written to Hugenberg on 23 May complaining of Rumpelstilzchen's (i.e., Adolf Stein's) sharp criticism of the party's actions on the Law for the Protection of the Republic. This same obligation with regard to the Hugenberg syndicate and the right is expressed in BA Koblenz, Hugenberg Papers, 211, Klitzsch and Lehmann to Aussendienst G.m.b.H., 14 October 1932; and Bernhard, p. 59.

72. For instance, Scherl gave good coverage to rightist organizations such as the Stahlhelm and the *Ostmarkenverein*. *Der Tag*, 2 April 1927, 7 May 1927, and 8 May 1927. The paper also celebrated the centenary of Paul de Lagarde's birthday with front-page editorials. (Significantly, his anti-Semitism was not mentioned.) *Der Tag*, 1 November 1927.

73. Figures on exact circulation vary slightly. BA Koblenz, Hugenberg Papers, 201, "Feststellungsauflagen seit 1928"; and the annual business reports of Scherl in ibid., 269–71. The relatively expensive cost of *Der Tag* was said to have effected its circulation. The decision to de-emphasize the political point of view in the *Berliner Lokal-Anzeiger* and leave this to *Der Tag* was considered a prime factor in the former's increase in circulation. BA Koblenz, Hugenberg Papers, 251, 269, business reports.

74. In Weiss, *Nationaler Wille* (p. 346), even a small portion of independent papers is characterized as rightist. It would be very difficult to determine the extent of Hugenberg's influence on these newspapers. It appears safe to presume, however, that through the Hugenberg corporations concerned with provincial publications, a goodly portion of the entire German press was affected by his policies. The total circulation of the nationalist press was estimated at 1,203,420; that of the Center, at 1,309,550; that of liberal and left-wing groups, at 2,231,450; and that of the SPD, at 690,400. The nonparty press was estimated to have a circulation of 4,103,990. Ibid., p. 345; and Weiss, *Politisches Handwörterbuch*, p. 581.

75. For example, see pertinent issues of the *Niederdeutsche Zeitung*, the *Lippische Tages-Zeitung*, and the *München-Augsburger Abendzeitung*.

76. See Hugenberg's debate with Mahraun, leader of the Jungdo in *Lippische Tages-Zeitung*, 17 May 1928. Klaus Peter Hoepke in his biographical article on Hugenberg for the *Neue Deutsche Biographie* (Berlin, 1974), p. 12, accepts this protestation at face value.

77. Traub's role in the *München-Augsburger Abendzeitung* readily documents this. By contractual agreement, Traub was "the responsible middleman for the entire organization (*Gesamthaltung*) of the paper." He stood between the corporate overseers and the editors as the man who would transmit the political policy to be followed. BA Koblenz, Wegener Papers, 24, Traub to Wegener, 31 May 1927.

78. The party treasurer, Widenmann, was shocked that the Hugenberg syndicate would control this news service; he felt that narrow control over this service would be a "Caudine yoke" for the party. WP, Widenmann to Mejer, 12 November 1927. Also Weiss, *Nationaler Wille*, p. 385.

79. The party did not own a publishing house. Presumably, various publications were printed by a press which permitted the party to use the title *Deutschnationale Schriftenvertriebstelle*. BA Freiburg, Tirpitz Papers, N 253/311. Even though the party paid for this service, it would be easy to become reliant on and indebted to the Hugenberg concern.

80. See the correspondence of Philipp with Dr. Friedrich Freiherr Hiller von Gaertringen, which the latter has graciously permitted me to use. (Henceforth cited as Philipp to Hiller von Gaertringen.) Wahrmund (p. 98) claimed: "his [Hugenberg's] trick now was not to provide immediately and fully everything that was due to the party central office. He gave only drop by drop and so made the party bureaucracy, which suffered from chronic monetary deficiency, dependent on him."

81. WP, Kirdorf to Westarp, 26 February 1927.

82. WP, Hugenberg to Westarp, 2 March 1927. Hugenberg wrote expressly to state his "total agreement with the warnings of this letter." The mutual admiration which Kirdorf and Hugenberg had for one another was founded not only on their respect for ability, but also on their common Pan-German idealism and the reactionary views which flourished in the Ruhr coaling industry. On the latter, see Hans Mommsen, "Sozialpolitik in Ruhrbergbau," in Mommsen, Petzina, and Weisbrod, pp. 305–21.

83. WP, Westarp to Kirdorf, 10 March 1927.

84. The steel magnate even contributed M 50,000 directly to the party for propaganda purposes and seemingly promised another M 50,000 later in the year. WP, Westarp to Thyssen, 11 April 1927 and 18 July 1927.

85. WP, Thyssen to Westarp, 23 July 1927. He refused to pay the second M 50,000.

86. On Kirdorf's attitude toward the Nazis, see Henry A. Turner's "Emil Kirdorf and the Nazi Party," pp. 324–44; and "Hitler's Secret Pamphlet for the Industrialists," *Journal of Modern History*, 40 (1968): 348–74; also see Helmut Böhme, "Emil Kirdorf: Überlegungen zu einer Unternehmerbiographie," *Tradition*, 13 (1969): 282–300 and 14 (1969): 21–46. On Thyssen's views, see Fritz Thyssen (with Emery Reves), *I Paid Hitler*, trans. Cesar Saerchinger (New York and Toronto, 1941) and note the excellent critique of specific errors in this work by Henry A. Turner, "Fritz Thyssen und 'I Paid Hitler'," *Vierteljahrshefte für Zeitgeschichte*, 19 (1971): 225–44. See also Dirk Stegmann "Zum Verhältnis von Grossindustrie und Nationalsozialismus: 1930–1933." *Archiv für Sozialgeschichte*. 13 (1973): 412–14.

87. BA Koblenz, Hugenberg Papers, 317, "Brutto-Überschuss und Verwendung desselben: 1910–1913, 1924–1929." All of these payments were in addition to regular dividends. These extensive profits derived not solely from newspapers, but also from address books and various periodicals such as the *Allgemeiner Wegweiser* and *Scherls Magazin* as well as the profits from advertisements in these publications. See the summary of business reports in BA Koblenz, Hugenberg Papers, 222. To date, no record has been found detailing the use of these funds. Unless Hugenberg was an embezzler—an outlandish proposition—his beneficiaries were numerous and/or well subsidized. August Heinrichsbauer, a journalist from the Ruhr, had close contacts with many of the same men who stood behind the Hugenberg concern. In the last years of

the republic, he served as a contact with Hitler. Though he wrote to de-emphasize the financial connections between heavy industry and Hitler, he claimed that Kirdorf in 1927 had placed M 100,000 at Hitler's disposal. See his *Schwerindustrie und Politik* (Essen, 1948), p. 38. The accuracy of his testimony is debated. See Stegmann, "Zum Verhältnis," pp. 412–13; and Turner, "Grossun-ternehmertum und Nationalsozialismus," pp. 31–34. If this amount were given, it is highly probable that Kirdof did not use his own funds but called upon Hugenberg to tap the resources of the Hugenberg concern. Such a contribution would have been wholly within the general plan accepted by the men of the *Wirtschaftsvereinigung*.

88. HA, GHH, 400 101 10/2, Wilmowski to Haniel in Reusch to Haniel, 31 May 1927.

89. Hugenberg's resignation as chairman of the *Zechenverband* and of the *Bergbaulicher Verband* indicated his greater involvement in politics than in the mining associations. See Winkhaus's comments in "18. ordentliche Hauptver-sammlung des Zechenverbandes ... den 26 Februar 1925 ..." Hugenberg's letter of resignation from the RDI in 1928 noted that he "had for a long time no longer been involved in the realm of industry itself, except for the areas of printing, press, and film production." WA Bayer, Leverkusen, 62/10. 4c, "Vorstandssitzung des Reichsverbands der deutschen Industrie, Donnerstag, den 25. Oktober 1928."

90. WP, Widenmann to Westarp, 14 November 1927.

91. See the correspondence on this in WP and HA, GHH, 400 101 293/86.

92. HA, GHH, 400 101 293/86, Brandi to Reusch, 24 December 1927; and a copy of the response, 27 December 1927, in Reusch to Westarp, 28 December 1927. For Reusch's refusal to accept Hugenberg, see HA, GHH, 400 101 290/39, Reusch to Wilmowsky, 10 December 1927.

93. WP, Westarp to Hugenberg, 14 January 1928.

94. AH Rohbraken, WP 3, "Rede des Geheimrats Hugenberg vom 7. Februar 1928, vor dem Arbeitsausschuss deutschnationaler Industrieller."

95. Ibid.

96. See Ellen L. Evans, "The Center Wages Kulturpolitik: Conflict in the Marx-Keudell Cabinet of 1927," *Central European History*, 2 (1969): 139–58.

97. Note Reusch's advocacy of constitutional reform and industrial-agrarian cooperation. See Hans Luther, *Vor dem Abgrund 1930–1933: Reichsbankpräsident in Krisenzeiten* (Berlin, 1964), pp. 35–46; and Heinrich A. Winkler, "Unternehmer-verbände zwischen Ständeideologie und Nationalsozialismus," *Vierteljahrshefte für Zeitgeschichte*, 17 (1969): 354; and see Reusch's correspondence with Luther in HA, GHH, 400 101 290/29 a and b, and the documentation dealing with agrarian contacts in HA, GHH, 400 101 24/0–3. Also Dieter Gessner, "Industrie und Landwirtschaft: 1928–1930" in Mommsen, Petzina, and Weisbrod, pp. 773–77. Stegmann's attempt to underestimate the differences between Hugen-berg and Reusch is misleading. See Dirk Stegmann, "Kapitalismus und Fascismus in Deutschland 1929–1934: These und Materialien zur Restituierung des Primats der Grossindustrie zwischen Weltwirtschaftskrise und beginnender Rüstungskonjunktur," *Gesellschaft: Beiträge zur Marxschen Theorie*, 4 (1976): 31.

98. Dörr, p. 375, n 34.

99. Dörr, pp. 373, 380. The difficulties inherent in the German National posi-

tion are apparent in Tirpitz's correspondence. The old admiral favored an ideological approach but saw the necessity of collaboration. He was in fact one of the "Yea-Sayers." Tirpitz avoided the tactical problems of taking a further position by refusing to run for reelection. He salved his conscience by urging a sharper return to the ideological bases of the party. BA Freiburg, Tirpitz Papers, N 253/60, Tirpitz to Westarp. There are no less than ten drafts of this letter composed between 14 February and 10 March 1928, when it was finally sent. Westarp's response concluded with comments that could have been written by Hugenberg. "Your warnings should always be a spur to the party, not to sink in the daily work of parliament and in partisan struggle, not to be worn out with pure economic cares and battles over particular interests, classes, and orders (*Stände*), but to remain for our people a leader for national unity and for a powerfully united national will." WP, Westarp to Tirpitz, 15 March 1928.

100. The joint meetings of industrialists from the DVP and DNVP had brought the two men into direct contact. See WP, Springorum to Westarp, 11 January 1928, 16 January 1928, and 21 March 1928. On the interest of the men from the *Ruhrlade* in the German National electoral lists, see HA, GHH, 400 101 24/11, Haniel to Reusch, 6 March 1928, and 400 101 2024/4, Blank to Reusch, 24 May 1928. See Turner, "Ruhrlade," pp. 203–07. Though Hugenberg secured a "safe place" for Quaatz on the Reich list and forced industrialists such as Hasslacher and Leopold into a lower slot, these men were still elected to the Reichstag. Cf. Turner, "Ruhrlade," p. 207, n 40; and Dörr, p. 497. (Reinhard Mumm was not one of Hugenberg's select candidates.)

101. The local German National party association in Dresden refused to give Quaatz a place on its electoral lists because of his apparent Jewish ancestry. He was then moved to the Reich list. Hugenberg's demand that Bang be given Quaatz's place in Dresden caused the local party chairman to resign, but Bang got the position. See Westarp to Philipp as cited in *Frankfurter Zeitung*, 3 May 1928. On the haggling over positions, see also WP, Rademacher to Westarp, 27 March 1928, Springorum to Westarp, 21 March 1928; and HA, GHH, 400 101 293/8b, Blank to Reusch, 25 June 1928. The Union of German Employers' Associations excluded Quaatz and Bang from a postelectoral list of party delegates who were "to be characterized as standing close to industry." They were listed in a supplementary category of delegates "belonging to industry in a wider sense." Mitteilungen der Vereinigung der Deutschen Arbeitgeberbände, Nr. 15, 31 July 1928, p. 217.

102. WP, *Kali-Industrie A.G.* to Westarp, 10 April 1928, and *Norddeutsche Cement-Verband G.m.b.H.* to Westarp, 30 April 1928.

103. WP, "Wahletat" for May 1928. Depending on the position secured for the candidate, industrial contributions would be turned over to the regional party association or the central office. Hugenberg thus supported his own constituency in Westphalia-North.

104. Since Hugenberg had at least M 900,000 at his disposal during this election year and was so parsimonious in dealing with the DNVP, it is—in my view—logical to conclude that some of this money went to the "other armies"

which Hugenberg hoped to rally to his "war of movement." Presumably the Nazis would be included in this.

105. WP, Westarp to Hugenberg, 8 May 1928. Westarp's marginalia indicate that this matter was resolved in a telephone conversation. The party's financial status, however, and Hugenberg's role in securing funds remained a cause of strife between the two men and, indirectly, between Hugenberg and Springorum even after the election. See HA, GHH, 400 101 293/8b, Blank to Reusch, 25 June 1928. The conflict apparently arose with the failure of Hugenberg's minion, Quaatz, to pay M 80,000 to the central office for his position on the Reich list. Hugenberg not only supported Quaatz, who had contributed only M 25,000 and still secured a safe place, but also filed a claim for reimbursement of M 50,000 on an advance payment which, at the beginning of March, his office had made for the purpose of electing industrial candidates. WP, Westarp to Hugenberg, 8 May 1928, Mann to Westarp, 2 March 1928, Westarp to Hugenberg, 30 April 1928, and Hugenberg to Westarp, 6 May 1928. This issue was not settled between Westarp and Hugenberg, but between Hugenberg and Springorum. See HA, GHH, 400 101 2024/4, Blank to Reusch, 11 July 1928.

106. See Hugenberg's speech on 10 May in Blomberg. *Lippische Tages-Zeitung*, 12 May 1928; "Hugenberg im Wahlkampf," ibid., 13 May 1928; and Hugenberg's debate with Mahraun, ibid., 17 May 1928. This paper gave particularly good coverage to Hugenberg because it was published in his district.

107. *Lippische Tages-Zeitung*, 22 May 1928; and *Berliner Lokal-Anzeiger*, 21 May 1928.

108. For analyses of the election results, see BA Koblenz, Wegener Papers, 42, "Betrachtungen über die und Folgerungen aus der Reichstagswahl vom 20.5.28." And note the excellent work of Heinrich August Winkler, *Mittelstand, Demokratie und Nationalsozialismus: Die politische Entwicklung von Handwerk und Kleinhandel in der Weimarer Republik* (Cologne, 1972), p. 138; also Dieter Gessner, "Industrie und Landwirtschaft: 1928–1930," in Mommsen, Petzina, and Weisbrod, p. 767.

109. See the minutes of this meeting in BA Koblenz, Schmidt-Hannover Papers, 35, "Dienstag, 12.6.28."

110. Walter Lambach, "Monarchismus," *Politische Wochenschrift*, 14 June 1928, pp. 495–98; reprinted in Dörr, pp. 554–56. For extensive treatment of the Lambach case, see Hamel, pp. 220–23; Dörr, pp. 394–415; Jonas, pp. 33–37. I am indebted to the editors of the *Canadian Journal of History* for permission to incorporate large sections of my article dealing with this problem. "The Election of Alfred Hugenberg as Chairman of the German National People's Party" (1972), pp. 149–71. ˋ

111. The DNVP considered the *Politische Wochenschrift* to be on the right but to be independent. This publication favored the Lambach orientation just as other magazines partial to the party favored different approaches; e.g., *Deutschlands Erneuerung* was under the control of the ADV, and the *Eiserne Blätter*, published by Traub, favored the Hugenberg policy. See Weiss, *Nationaler Wille*, p. 350.

112. Wilhelm Stapel, "Antwort," *Deutsches Volkstum* (July 1928), p. 120. Here

the editor of the journal clearly expresses his ideological affinity for Ullmann and the *Politische Wochenschrift*. The publisher of both journals was the *Hanseatische Verlagsanstalt*, a printing house owned by Lambach's union, the DHV. See Hamel, pp. 126–45; Johann Gildemeister, "Die Politik der Deutschnationalen Volkspartei vom Oktober 1929 bis Mai 1932 mit besonderer Berücksichtigung der Abspaltung der Volkskonservativen" (University of Hamburg, Staatsarbeit, 1951), pp. 81–85; also Georg Quabbe, *Tar a Ri: Variatonen über ein Konservatives Thema* (Berlin, 1927).

113. Their romantic, corporatist approach rejected the Marxian antagonism in favor of a joint collaborative effort that could lead to a "German *Volksgemeinschaft*." Hamel, pp. 204–06, 216. Young conservatives around Lambach and his colleagues enjoyed a strong position in the party organization because of their broad popular appeal to working-class voters.

114. DZA Potsdam, ADV 180, Hugenberg to Frowein, 24 June 1928. Abraham Frowein was the first deputy chairman of the RDI. Similar objections to a policy of moderation and also to the failure of industry to support agrarian reform are expressed in BA Koblenz, Silverberg Papers, 228, Hugenberg to Duisberg, 13 July 1928.

115. Hugenberg's local constituency presented a three-point program calling for a delay in any consideration of proposals for changes in the party structure until after the election of leaders was settled. At the same time, the DNVP was to terminate its transformation into a "parliamentary party." To facilitate this, the third proposal demanded thoroughgoing programmatic and personnel changes so that policies would be coordinated with principles and a balance found between the needs of the economy and the demands of ideology. BA Freiburg, Tirpitz Papers, N 253/60, Westarp to Regional Party Chairman, n.d., in Westarp to Tirpitz, 25 June 1928.

116. HA, GHH, 400 101 2024/4, Blank to Reusch, 10 July 1928, and 11 July 1928.

117. Ibid. The major industrial delegates in the DNVP—Reichert, Hasslacher, Leopold, Rademacher and Klönne—collaborated most closely with Springorum, who conceded that Hugenberg should come to the Ruhr to explain his point of view. Reusch adamantly demanded that Hugenberg speak only before some German National group and not before any industrial association, lest he be viewed as a spokesman for the Ruhr. HA, GHH, 400 101 290/36a, Reusch to Springorum, 11 July 1928. Springorum and Vögler, who were more intimately involved in the Hugenberg concern, were apparently less hostile to Hugenberg than was Reusch. See ibid., Reusch to Springorum, 15 July 1928. Leaders of the RDI were, of course, most anxious to promote Reusch's view of Hugenberg. See HA, GHH, 400 101 220/5, Kastl to Sempel, n.d. (copy dated 4 August 1928). Since Sempel was a director at Krupp's, Kastl apparently considered von Bohlen a key to the entire problem.

118. Whether the money from the mining interests to the *Ruhrlade* was collected and dispersed by the *Zechenverband* via its investments in the Hugenberg concern or whether these funds were generated by a special levy on the *Kohlenseite* and then distributed separately is not fully clear. I believe that the money raised by the mining interests was collected and administered via the

Wirtschaftsvereinigung (i.e., the Hugenberg concern) and that the men of the *Ruhrlade* only had an indirect influence on this fund. It is possible, however, that there was an additional political levy on the coaling interests. This seems to be the case at the very end of the republic. Cf. Turner, "Ruhrlade," pp. 203–05. No definite conclusion is permissible until more data is available. The documents preserved in the *Bergbaubücherei* in Essen will undoubtedly help to clarify this situation. Until these are thoroughly studied, our knowledge of the *Kohlenseite* must remain, as Professor Turner indicates, in the beginning stages. See Henry A. Turner, "Das Verhältnis des Grossunternehmertums zur NSDAP," in Mommsen, Petzina, and Weisbrod, p. 928.

119. Dörr, pp. 401–02. In an attempt to win industrial support, Scheibe of the ADI circulated a report, "Zur Lage (Nr. 9) ... Juli 1928", stressing Hugenberg's social and political policies without naming either Hugenberg or Lambach. Some German Nationals complained that this was agitation which endangered the unity of the party. WP, Rippel (Regional Party Association, Arnsberg) to Westarp, 22 August 1928. (Technically, such a charge was basis for explusion from the party.)

120. *Unsere Partei*, 15 July 1928, pp. 265–66.

121. The retired general had been an excellent choice for leading the attack. As official representative of the House of Hohenzollern, he had intimate contacts with the exiled kaiser and with the crown prince; he also had close contact with Class. DZA Potsdam, ADV 150, GA Verhandlungsbericht 4 March 1928. See also DZA Potsdam, ADV, 254, for further contacts of Class and von Dommes during the leadership crisis in the DNVP. Leaders from at least three other local party groups—Gok from Hamburg, Vagts from Bremen, and von Feldmann from Hannover-South—had participated in Class's meetings when the problem of the DNVP had been examined. Leo Wegener, Hugenberg's close friend, had also been present. DZA Potsdam, ADV, 150, GA Verhandlungsbericht, Berlin, 4 March 1928. Von Feldmann and Gok were also present at the meeting in Eisenach on 21 April 1928; von Feldmann encouraged the ADV to participate in the DNVP so that the party could realize the ideals of Bang and Hugenberg. DZA Potsdam, ADV, 155.

122. WP, Westarp to the Chairman of the Local Party Associations, 12 July 1928.

123. BA Koblenz, Lambach Papers, 10, "Beschluss des Landesvorstandes Potsdam II ..."

124. HA, GHH, 400 101 293/9 Politisch-parlamentarischer Nachrichtendienst für das rheinisch-westfälische Industriegebiet, 24 August 1928, and 400 101 2024/4, Blank to Reusch, 11 July 1928. See also WP, Leopold to Westarp, 12 August 1928; and *Der Tag*, 25 July 1928.

125. Hugenberg argued that agitation against him would make silence impossible for him. Typically, he implied that his offensive posture was really defensive. WP, Hugenberg to Westarp, 14 August 1928. The count refused to agree with Hugenberg's presentation. WP, Westarp to Hugenberg, 20 August 1928.

126. Alfred Hugenberg, "Block oder Brei?" *Der Tag*, 28 August 1928. See also *Berliner Lokal-Anzeiger*, 28 August 1928, and *München-Augsburger Abendzeitung*, 27

and 28 August 1928. A more proper translation of *Brei* would be *gruel*, but I have used the term *mishmash*, because I believe it more fully conveys Hugenberg's concept to English readers.

127. Dörr, p. 425, n 81.

128. NSSA Aurich, 1, von Dommes, "Bericht über die heutige Besprechung in Berlin, Dessauerstrasse 14." The party associations present represented Berlin, Bremen, Grenzmark, Hamburg, Hannover-East, Hannover-South, Hesse Dramstadt, Mecklenburg Schwerin, Oldenburg, Osnabrück, Potsdam (I and II), Westphalia-East, and Westphalia-West. The local organizations of Lübeck and Ostfriesland supported the meeting but were not present. The German National industrialist Reichert claimed that these associations belonged "not to the strongest, but to the numerically weakest of the party." HA, GHH, 2 400 101 293/9, Reichert to Reusch, 22 October 1928.

129. Both men belonged to the dissident right wings. Quaatz was a firm supporter of Hugenberg, and Steinhoff was not only the chairman of the party association that later expelled Lambach from the party, but also a leading member of the von Dommes group.

130. LA Schleswig-Holstein, "Denkschrift zur Reform der Parteiorganization, 1. Oktober 1928."

131. WP, Westarp to the Members of the Party Leadership, 12 October 1928; and BA Koblenz, Wegener Papers, 25, Wegener to Traub, 22 August 1928.

132. LA Schleswig, "Denkschrift."

133. If the troika were to consist of the chairman of the Reichstag delegation, Count Westarp, the chairman of the Prussian Landtag delegation, von Winterfeld, and Hugenberg, there would be a certain logic to the proposal. Winterfeld was closer to Hugenberg than to Westarp, and the radicalization of the party would be assured. WP, Treviranus to Westarp, 7 August 1928; and HA, GHH, 400 101 2024/4b, Blank to Springorum in Blank to Reusch, 8 October 1928. This development would guarantee the newspaper magnate final authority and yet free him from the burden of daily partisan struggle. Wegener thought Hugenberg would find this kind of leadership most acceptable. BA Koblenz, Wegener Papers, 25, Wegener to Traub, 25 June 1928.

134. LA Schleswig, [Westtarp's] "Äusserung über die Denkschrift zur Reform der Parteiorganization," n.d.

135. HA, GHH, 400 101 293/9, Reichert to Reusch, 22 October 1928. According to this industrialist: "Hugenberg had all the members of the party leadership, thus all the organizations and delegates, richly supplied with printed material, which sung his praise and glory. He [Hugenberg] himself traveled for weeks on end throughout the countryside and sent his emissaries to all party members who had any influence. In short, he campaigned as hard as he could for himself and had others campaign for him." He even invited large numbers of party friends to his expanded estate for a "Hundertmännertag." AH Rohbraken, M 27, "Rohbraken."

136. BA Koblenz, Wegener Papers, 23, Wegener to Class, 2 September 1928.

137. BA Koblenz, Wegener Papers, 28, Seldte-Wegener correspondence of September and October 1928. This is a development which had been prepared earlier. Note Stadtler's editorial of 26 May 1928, "Nun erst Recht," reprinted in

Eduard Stadtler, *Seldte-Hitler-Hugenberg!: Die Front der Freiheitsbewegung* (Berlin, 1930).

138. HA, GHH, 400 101 293/9, Scheibe's "Zur Klarstellung" in Winnacker to Reusch, 12 September 1928.

139. NSSA Osnabrück, 16, "Bericht über die heutige Besprechung in Berlin, Dessauerstrasse 14, 8. Oktober 1928." This is only a fragmentary record of the meeting. The entire results are preserved under the same title in the Westarp Papers.

140. WP, "Rede vor der Parteivertretung der DNVP am 20. Oktober 1928."

141. Ibid., the material given out by Hugenberg's supporters included copies of his letter sent to Westarp on 17 September 1927 and reprints of his article "Block oder Brei?" In his preface to this, Hugenberg argued that the problem confronting the party was not one of personalities or economic interest groups, but one of whether the party "should be a great ideological movement as it once was—or whether, under the influence of petty factionalism and party spirit, it should turn into a product of the organized new German parliamentarism, a product without hope and youth." WP, "Hugenberg, Zur Partei Vertretung am 20. Oktober 1928." Westarp had not received a copy of this material before his speech. Copies of Hugenberg's handout are preserved in BA Koblenz, Wegener Papers, 31.

142. *Vossische Zeitung*, 23 October 1928. This paper had received the information from leaks in the party. Most of it is corroborated by the chairman of the party court of honor, Dr. Reinhard Mumm, who later reconciled Hugenberg and von Keudell. See his report in WP, "Betrifft: Differenz zwischen Herrn Reichsminister a.D. von Keudell und Herrn Geheimen Finanzrat Dr. Hugenberg beide Mitglieder der Deutschnationalen Reichstagsfraktion," n.d.

143. See WP, "Erklärung abgegeben von Graf Westarp nach der Rede des Ministern v. Keudell am 20. Oktober 1928."

144. This certainly was Reichert's view. This industrialist leader, who was in the anti-Hugenberg camp, reported to Reusch that Keudell's speech was so outlandish that no one in the hall could have supported him. HA, GHH, 400 101 293/9, Reichert to Reusch, 22 October 1928. This is perhaps one of the best "inside" reports on the election. I am indebted to Professor Larry Jones of Canisius College for first making me aware of it.

145. See Otto Meissner, *Staatssekretär unter Ebert Hindenburg-Hitler*, 3d ed. (Hamburg, 1950), p. 17.

146. WP, Philipp to Hiller von Gaetringen; *Der Tag*, 23 October 1928.

147. According to one news leak, the majority was only five. *Vossische Zeitung*, 23 October 1928. Treviranus claimed that one of the counters confidentially told him that Hugenberg had received his majority by a single vote. Treviranus, p. 99, 408 n 35.

148. As soon as he was elected party leader, Hugenberg resigned as chairman of the "Fachgruppe Bergbau" of the RDI and, consequently, surrendered his seat on the presidium of this industrialist organization. *Jahresbericht des Vereins für die bergbaulichen Interessen* (1928), p. 89.

149. *Berliner Lokal-Anzeiger*, 21 October 1928; *Der Tag*, 23 October 1928; *Unsere Partei*, 1 November 1928, pp. 338–40. NSSA Aurich 1, "Wahlkampftagung der

Deutschnationalen Volkspartei im Reichstag am Montag, dem 22. Oktober 1928." At this meeting, Hugenberg again stressed that the party had to be a movement gathering dynamic strength. As chairman, Hugenberg told Weiss that he wanted to be involved only in major decisions and not details. He pointed out that a "correct and sharp press" would help the party regain its losses and achieve status as a "great party, a strong party, and a united party."

150. *Germania*, 21 October 1928.

151. *Vossische Zeitung*, 23 October 1928.

152. DZA, Potsdam, ADV 153, GA Verhandlungsbericht, Berlin, 1 and 2 December 1928.

153. *Eiserne Blätter*, 4 November 1928, p. 728.

154. *Berliner Lokal-Anzeiger*, 21 October 1928; and *München-Augsburger Abendzeitung*, 22 October 1928.

155. Such criticism not only came from Hugenberg's avowed opponents in the *Politische Wochenschrift* on occasions too numerous to cite, but also from the membership of the DNVP *Evangelischer Ausschuss*. See DZA Potsdam, Mann to von Tilling, 1 September 1930. Ibid., DNVP, 465, a meeting of the Lutheran Committee and its negative comments on the *Nachtausgabe*. For the standard defense of the Hugenberg supporters against such complaints, see the series of articles by Traub in *Eiserne Blätter*, 22 February 1931, pp. 122–24; 1 March 1931, pp. 139–41; 8 March 1931, pp. 154–56; 15 March 1931, pp. 173–76. Even President Hindenburg was concerned with Hugenberg's reputation. When the new party leader first visited him, the president "cautioned him not to promote the interests of industry at the expense of agricultural needs." Dorpalen, p. 149. The very first issue of the party journal after Hugenberg's election stated that Hugenberg was neither a "Geldfürst" nor a plutocrat and indicated that the fanatical attacks on him came from Jewish sources. *Unsere Partei*, 1 November 1928, pp. 343–44.

156. The Bernhard defense had set the theme; it was followed by Freytagh-Loringhoven (p. 47) and Kriegk (pp. 56–57). Wegener (pp. 22–26) presents another image of Hugenberg. The new party leader was a man who did not smoke, play cards, or tell improper jokes, but he still had a Lower Saxon sense of humor; he avoided the banquet circuit and ate vegetarian foods even before the discovery of vitamins.

157. At the same time, he also appointed his adherents to the party central office where the retired Major Nagel of the *Reichslandbund* took charge. Hans Brosius of the *Niederdeutsche Zeitung* became the press chief. *Unsere Partei*, 15 December 1928, p. 402.

158. DZA Potsdam, ADV 154, GA Verhandlungsbericht, Berlin, 19 January 1929.

159. *Unsere Partei*, 1 December 1928, p. 377. Hugenberg's radical approach to the problem of reparations involved him in a direct conflict with the industrialist Reichstag delegate, Reichert, who was a party expert on this issue. As a spokesman for the iron industry, Reichert opposed reparations but took a positive stance in trying to exploit the good that might be derived from the Dawes Plan. Hugenberg and his spokesmen, Quaatz and Bang, totally repudiated any discussion of the positive aspects of this plan and labeled its acceptance

as "criminal carelessness" (*verbrecherischer Leichtsinn*). Reichert feared that such ideological negativism would split the party. WP, Reichert to Hugenberg, 22 December 1928, in Reichert to Westarp, 29 December 1928. This was not the first clash between the two men. See WP, Reichert to Westarp, 18 November 1928.

160. *Unsere Partei*, 1 February 1929, pp. 237–38, and 1 March 1929, p. 77.

161. Gustav Hartz, *Irrwege der deutschen Sozialpolitik* (Berlin, 1928). Hugenberg never identified himself with this book, but there can be little doubt that he agreed with its author. Those close to Hugenberg praised the work. See Traub's advertisement, "Hört nicht Gustav Stresemann sondern Gustav Hartz!" *Eiserne Blätter*, 11 March 1929, on the cover. This ad was repeated for several weeks. On the role of the Scherl *Verlag's* editorial staff in the composition of the book and the attempt to use this to influence particularly the medical profession, see the pertinent documents in Preussisches Geheimes Staatsarchiv Dahlem, Repertorium 92, Robert Wahlert Papers.

162. *Unsere Partei*, 15 April 1929, pp. 127–29.

163. WP, Hugenberg to Westarp, 28 March 1929.

164. See DZA Potsdam, ADV 181, Class to Wegener, 25 March 1929. Class had found Hugenberg depressed not only because of his health, but because "the unionists, the industrialists oriented to the left, and the friends of the government" opposed him.

165. Elisabeth Friedenthal, Volksbegehren und Volksentscheid über den Young-Plan und die Deutschnationale Sezession (Ph.D dissertation, University of Tübingen, 1957), pp. 36–37.

166. WP, Lind to Westarp, 12 May 1929.

167. WP, Quaatz to Westarp, 19 June 1929, and Westarp to Quaatz, 24 June 1929. The final resolution accepted by the party leaders read: "The Party Executive Committee is unanimously of the opinion that it is the right and the duty of the Party Executive Committee and its chairman to determine ultimately the guidelines of party policy. The decision on the question of participating in the government is especially included herein." *Unsere Partei*, 1 July 1929, p. 207.

Chapter 3

1. AH Rohbraken, P 23, "Hugenberg 1931," speech delivered at Detmold, 4 January 1932, in Hugenberg to Brosius, 2 January 1932.

2. The theme of radical unity had permeated editorials in Hugenberg papers such as the *Niederdeutsche Zeitung*; see Hans Brosius, "Nationale Einigung," 8 July 1926, and Otto Schmidt-Hannover, "Vaterländische Bewegung and DNVP," 14 September 1926.

3. See Werner Conze, "Die Krise des Parteienstaates in Deutschland 1929/30," *Historische Zeitschrift*, 178 (1954): pp. 47–83.

4. Volker R. Berghahn, *Der Stahlhelm: Bund der Frontsoldaten* (Düsseldorf, 1966), p. 113.

5. See BA Koblenz, Wegener Papers, 28, Seldte to Wegener, 16 November 1928. Martin Blank, an enthusiastic member of the Stahlhelm, indicated that

his friends in the veterans' organization spoke of a Hugenberg promise to provide M 3,500,00 for propaganda for the plebiscite. For details on the Stahlhelm's preparations for the plebiscite see DZA Potsdam, Stahlhelm, 300, Duesterberg to Wagner, 26 September 1928 and DZA Potsdam, ADV, 497, Stahlhelm circular letter, 21 March 1929.

6. "Sitzung des Parteivorstandes am 15. Juni 1929," *Unsere Partei*, 1 July 1929, pp. 207–10.

7. Ibid., "Hugenberg an die Jugend," p. 205.

8. See Alfred Hugenberg, "Die neue Front: Politischer Rückblick und Ausblick zur Jahreswende," *Lippische Tages-Zeitung*, 1 January 1929. A detailed treatment of the contemporary development of this theme is in the collection of editorials written by Eduard Stadtler, *Seldte-Hitler-Hugenberg: die Front der Freiheitsbewegung*, 1st ed. (Berlin, 1930).

9. See the *Mitteilungen des Vereins zur Wahrung der gemeinsamen Interessen in Rheinland und Westfalen* (1920, 14/15), "Mitgliederversammlung des Vereins ... am 8. Juli 1929," p. 56; and HA, GHH, 400 101 220/6b, Thyssen to RDI, 28 May 1929; and cf. Jon Jacobson, *Locarno Diplomacy: Germany and the West: 1925–1929* (Princeton, N.J., 1972), p. 271.

10. WA Bayer, Leverkusen, 62/10.3a. Kastl to Duisberg, June 1929. Kastl signed not as an official of the RDI, but as an individual representative of Germany.

11. WA Bayer, Leverkusen, 62/10.4c, "Vorstandssitzung des Reichsverbandes der Deutschen Industrie... am 20. June 1929...." The exact wording of the statement unanimously accepted by the RDI read: "The Reich Association of German Industry [expresses its gratitude and recognition to the mebers of the German delegation. It is convinced that each of the experts has endeavoured according to his conscience and with his best expertise to achieve under the current circumstances the best results for the future of the German people; it] understands thoroughly that Dr. Vögler in judging the economic situation has seen fit to announce his resignation. In reference to the economic significance of the Young Plan, the Reich Association maintains the same principle as in its position regarding payments on the basis of the Dawes Plan. [At that time in 1924 the Reich Association declared that the burdens imposed significantly exceeded the ability of Germany to pay. The nature and manner of raising the Dawes payments up to now give no cause to change this view.] In agreement with the German experts, the Reich Association is of the view that the Young Plan loads the German people for a long number of years with burdens which go beyond the ability of the German economy to bear. As the Paris statement declares, the committee of experts has permitted itself to be directed essentially according to political viewpoints. For this reason, the Reich Association reserves its definitive position on acceptance or rejection of the plan until the decision of competent political authorities." DII Cologne, Funcke Papers, RDI 1929, Herle circular of 20 June 1929. The Hugenberg *München-Augsburger Abendzeitung*, 22 June 1929, omitted the sections bracketed above. An abbreviated form can be explained because of lack of space, but it is especially significant here where reference is made to the competence and good will of Kastl.

12. See Max Schlenker, business manager of the *Langnam Verein*, to Reusch, 9 July 1929, and the copies of the Schlenker-Thyssen correspondence enclosed

therein (HA, GHH, 400 101 221/9.).

13. *Langnam Mitteilungen*, no. 14/15 (1929), p. 56.

14. See HA, GHH, 400 101 2024/5, "Aufzeichnung" in Blank to Reusch, 21 May 1929; and WA Bayer, Leverkusen, 62/10. 3a, Kastl to Duisberg, n.d. [June 1929]. Kastl's defense of his role at Paris is in the minutes of the "Vorstandssitzung des Reichsverbands der Deutschen Industrie... den 20. Juni 1929," WA Bayer, Leverkusen, 62/10.4c. At first Duisberg tacitly supported Kastl but then argued against a minority on the executive board of the RDI that Germany could do nothing else because the opposition of the great banks providing loans and supporting the value of the mark would leave the government "completely isolated, alone and deserted." WA Bayer, Leverkusen, 62.10.4d, "Vorstandssitzung des Reichsverbands... den 26. November 1930."

15. The view that German firms would fall under international control is clearly presented in "Auszug aus *Stahl und Eisen*," in BA Koblenz, R131/1038. This argument carried significant weight in the Ruhr and became the essential note of all opposition to the Young Plan. See A. Heinrichsbauer, "Die Konsequenzen aus dem Young Plan," *Ruhr und Rhein*, 5 July 1929, pp. 868–73.

16. For a clear analysis of this position and its dangers, see HA, GHH, 400 101 24/2, von Miquel to Reusch, 18 July 1929. See also WA Bayer, Leverkusen, 62/10.3a, Kastl to Duisberg, n.d. [June 1929]; HA, GHH, 400 101 220/6b, Kastl to Reusch, 28 May 1929; and HA, GHH, 400 101 2024/5, "Aufzeichnung" in Blank to Reusch, 21 May 1929.

17. HA, GHH, 400 101 2024/6, Springorum to Hugenberg, 22 June 1929, enclosed in Blank to Reusch, 27 June 1929. Whether Springorum spoke for the entire group is not clear; he mentioned that he and Vögler were in agreement.

18. Traub corresponded with Hitler. BA Koblenz, Traub Papers 52, Traub to Hitler, 10 August 1922, and n.d. October 1924. He may also have been a channel whereby financial subsidies had been conveyed to Hitler.

19. On this see Konrad Heiden, *Hitler: A Biography* (London, 1936), pp. 232, 244–46. Heiden falsely asserts that Bang was a member of the RDI and seemingly overemphasizes the intimacy of Bang's relations with Hitler. On Dietrich's role, see George W. F. Hallgarten, *Hitler, Reichswehr und Industrie: Zur Geschichte der Jahre: 1918–1933* (Frankfurt/Main, 1955), p. 90. Dietrich was a financial editor for Hugenberg's *München Augsburger Abendzeitung* in 1928. See also Otto Dietrich, *The Hitler I Knew*, trans. Richard and Clara Winston (London, 1957), p. 171. On the early contact of Hitler with Hugenberg's friend, Class, see Stegmann, "Zum Verhältnis," p. 404.

20. The NSDAP press was continually in financial difficulties during this period. The Hugenberg syndicate could provide not only the services of the *Telegraphen-Union* and the *Wipro*, but also advertising subsidies through the *Ala*. (Only the use of the *TU* can be documented.) See Roland V. Layton, "The *Völkischer Beobachter*, 1920–1933: The Nazi Party Newspaper in the Weimar Era," *Central European History*, 3 (1970): 353–82.

21. S 28 Hannover, untitled Hugenberg essay on the end of the republic.

22. *Lippische Tages-Zeitung*, 10 July 1929; *Niederdeutsche Zeitung*, 11 July 1929; *München-Augsburger Abendzeitung*, 11 July 1929.

23. Cf., Heiden, pp. 247–48.

24. *Berliner Lokal-Anzeiger*, 10 July 1929. In the *Lippische Tages-Zeitung*, 10 July

1929, Hitler made the subheadlines, but in the total orientation of the lead article he played a minor role in comparison to the attention showered on Hugenberg and especially on Schiele, who would be an attraction for the agrarian readers of this paper. In the *München-Augsburger Abendzeitung*, 11 July 1929, emphasis was on the establishment of a national offensive and popular movement (*Volksbewegung*); Hitler's name appeared only in the second group listed as supporting the Reich Committee.

25. The idea of a concrete plebiscitary movement became, according to Stahlhelm leaders, a "secondary goal." Morozowicz (Stahlhelm leader) to Blank, 27 July 1929, HA, GHH, 400 101 2024/6. Nevertheless, the unanimous resolution of the group clearly stated that the new committee was assuming responsibility for the constitutional plebiscite proposed by the Stahlhelm. The committee determined, however, to place the struggle against the dual evil of the "war-guilt lie" and the "Paris tribute plan" in the forefront. The Hugenberg syndicate anxiously denied that the original Stahlhelm plan was given up "at the command of Hugenberg." *Niederdeutsche Zeitung*, 11 July 1929.

26. Cf. Helmut Heiber, "Die Republik von Weimar" in *Deutsche Geschichte seit dem Ersten Weltkrieg* (Stuttgart, 1971), p. 157.

27. Hugenberg to Class, 13 July 1929, DZA Potsdam, ADV, 500.

28. Kruck, p. 17.

29. For a critical analysis of Hugenberg's tactics along these lines, see the works of the young conservative, Hermann Ullmann, especially *In der grossen Kurven* (Berlin, 1933), pp. 20ff.

30. As Hugenberg tried to delimit Seldte's moderate tendencies, so he undoubtedly pursued the same tactic in dealing with Schiele. Wegener was convinced that the *Reichslandbund* president should be allowed little influence on the plebiscite. BA Koblenz, Wegener Papers, 6, Wegener to Meydenbauer, 17 July 1929.

31. *Unsere Partei*, 15 July 1929, p. 230.

32. Hugenberg to Class, 13 July 1929, and Hugenberg to Seldte, 13 July 1929, DZA Potsdam, ADV, 500.

33. Hugenberg's calculated delay in securing a position for Count Westarp, chairman of the DNVP Reichstag delegation, on the presidium of the Reich Committee is a typical example of this tactic. WP, Hugenberg-Westarp correspondence, 11 July 1929, 1 August 1929, and 30 September 1929.

34. AH Rohbraken, Hugenberg to Brosius, 14 August 1929, and Brosius to Hugenberg, 17 August 1929. Also DZA Potsdam, ADV, 500, [Class] to Hugenberg, 13 July 1929, and Hugenberg to Class, 13 July 1929.

35. DZA Potsdam, ADV, 501, "Protokoll der ersten Sitzung des Finanzausschusses des Reichsausschussess, 19. July 1929." Both Widenmann, the treasurer of the DNVP, and Mann, Hugenberg's right-hand man in business dealings, played important roles on this committee. Also, DZA Potsdam, ADV, 501, "Niederschrift über die Sitzung des Propaganda-Ausschussess des Reichsausschusses, 19. Juli 1929," where Brosius, the man whom Hugenberg chose to head the DNVP press organization, served as chairman. See AH Rohbraken, P 11, Brosius to Hugenberg, 13 August 1929.

36. DZA Potsdam, ADV, 501, "Protokoll der ersten Sitzung des

Finanzausschusses." The sums discussed for the office-needs of the Reich Committee were very modest, but it was estimated that costs for propagandizing a plebiscite would exceed a million marks. Hugenberg apparently had definite assurances of financial aid from both Thyssen and Vögler. HA, GHH, 400 101 2024/6, Blank to Springorum, 22 July 1929, in Blank to Reusch, 22 July 1929. Though Blank was a confidant of Reusch, he occasionally worked as a liaison with Springorum. He had attended the meetings of the financial subcommittee; he recomended to his superiors that the Reich Committee not be supported at that time and not to the extent of the group's financial expectations.

37. DZA Potsdam, ADV, 501, "Niederschrift über die Sitzung des Propaganda-Ausschusses des Reichsausschusses vom 19. July 1929" and ibid., "... vom 6. August 1929." At the second of these meetings, Brosius pointed out that he thought Hugenberg's Scherl *Verlag* was also ready to help.

38. BA Koblenz, Hugenberg Papers, 317, "Brutto-Überschuss."

39. DZA Potsdam, ADV, 500, Class to Hugenberg, 26 July 1929, and 30 July 1929. See also an eighteen-page study of the problem by a Dr. Wolf, ibid., 29 July 1929.

40. DZA Potsdam, ADV, 500, Class to Hugenberg, 26 July 1929.

41. See "Entwurf 21.8.1929: *Gesetz gegen die Versklavung des Deutschen Volkes*," in WP, Hugenberg to Westarp, 21 August 1929.

42. DZA Potsdam, ADV, 500. This is a proposal dated 14 August 1929.

43. DZA Potsdam, ADV, 500, Lehmann to Class, 13 August 1929. Lehmann charged that Heinz Brauweiler resented Hugenberg for taking the initiative from the Stahlhelm. Brauweiler, who was now the chairman of the juridical subcommittee of the Reich Committee, had favored a plebiscite on constitutional reform. HA, GHH, 400 101 2024/6, Blank to Springorum, 22 July 1929, in Blank to Reusch, 22 July 1929; also Berghahn, pp. 125–29.

44. DZA Potsdam, ADV, 500, Hugenberg to Class, 16 August 1929. Once he and his friends had fundamentally agreed on their proposal for the Reich Committee, Hugenberg sent a copy of the text to Westarp who, as chairman of the DNVP Reichstag delegation, would have to defend the bill in the Reichstag. Hugenberg was prepared to work with the count to a limited extent, but feared that groups in his own party might collaborate with the Center Party to frustrate his proposal. He requested that Westarp treat the matter with utmost confidence. Few of the count's suggested revisions were accepted by Hugenberg. See WP, Hugenberg-Westarp correspondence at end of August 1929.

45. WP, Hugenberg to Westarp, 29 August 1929.

46. The *Niederdeutsche Zeitung* admitted that even though "the front was growing in the *Volk* itself" and surpassing party boundaries and the goals of particular organizations, the Reich Committee was not without its frictions. Opponents were supposedly trying to sow dissension by dubbing the group the "Hugenberg bloc." In line with the general approach, this paper concentrated on the idea that real solidarity could be achieved by concentrating on foreign policy. *Niederdeutsche Zeitung*, 30 August 1929. This lack of consensus among the members of the Reich Committee apparently accounts for the failure of the group to emphasize the role of General Otto von Below, who was seemingly being groomed as a potential counterpoise to Field Marshal von Hindenburg.

See DZA Potsdam, ADV, 500, Lehmann to Hugenberg, 13 July 1929, where the author complained that there had been no mention of the general in the newspapers despite the fact that "the committee has... been organized in good part so that it should act as a springboard for Below." Note also Schmidt-Hannover, pp. 83–97.

47. "Mitgliederversammlung des Reichsverbandes der Deutschen Industrie am 20. und 21. September 1929 in Düsseldorf," *Veröffentlichungen des Reichsverbandes der Deutschen Industrie*, no. 48 (1929), pp. 12, 16, 17.

48. HA, GHH, 400 101 2024/6, Reusch to Blank, 24 July 1929. Reusch had tried to have the meeting of the RDI delayed—presumably because heavy industry might have been forced to bare its divisions. HA, GHH, 400 101 290/35, Reusch to Kastl, 8 August 1929, and the later correspondence in 400 101 220/7.

49. HA, GHH, 400 101 293/9, petition circulated on 18 October 1929.

50. See below, note 51. Hugenberg's friend and adviser, Wegener, was a sharp critic of Kriegsheim. Wegener held the *Landbund* director responsible for the DNVP split on the Dawes vote as well as for the party's entry into the cabinet. He also charged that Kriegsheim had toyed with the idea of organizing a united rightist front from the Center to the left wing of the DNVP, if Hugenberg in the past year had left the party and gone over to the NSDAP. BA Koblenz, Wegener Papers, 30, Wegener to Admiral von Levetzow, 17 July 1929.

51. Schiele argued that he could not and did not give his approval before the meeting of the directors of the agrarian organization. DZA Potsdam, ADV, 500, Schiele to the Members of the Presidium of the Reich Committee, 20 September 1929. Hugenberg, on the other hand, claimed that Schiele promised the approval of the *Landbund* (WP, Hugenberg to Schiele, 30 September 1929).

52. Ibid.; and DZA Potsdam, ADV, 501, Hugenberg to Duesterberg, 14 September 1929. Hugenberg believed that not only Kriegsheim, but also General von Schleicher was involved in this move of the agrarian association against his proposal. DZA Potsdam, ADV, 501, Hugenberg to Duesterberg, 16 September 1929.

53. WP, Westarp to Hugenberg, 17 September 1929 and Westarp to Schultz, 15 September 1929.

54. DZA Potsdam, ADV, 501, Hugenberg to Duesterberg, 14 September 1929; and see ibid., Hugenberg to Members of the Presidium of the Reich Committee, 15 September 1929. The Nazis insisted that the penal paragraph was essential to the entire proposal. DZA Potsdam, ADV, 500, Schmidt-Hannover to Class, 19 September 1929. According to the *Lippische Tages-Zeitung*, 12 September 1929, the text of the "Law Against the Enslavement of the German People" read:

> 1. The Reich government must, in official form, immediately inform foreign powers that the forced acceptance of war-guilt in the Treaty of Versailles contradicts historical truth, rests on false preconceptions, and is is not binding according to international law.
>
> 2. The Reich government must also make sure that the recognition of war-guilt according to Article 231 and also according to Articles 429 and 430 of the Treaty of Versailles will formally be annulled....

3.   In regards foreign powers, new burdens and obligations based upon the war-guilt clause may not be accepted.

4.   Reich chancellors and Reich ministers as also plenipotentiaries of the German government who in violation of paragraph 3 sign treaties with foreign powers are subject to the penalties prescribed in paragraph 93.3 of the penal code.

5.   This law becomes official with its promulgation.

Because of the furor over paragraph 4 and charges that even President Hindenburg would be subject to its all-embracing indictment, Hugenberg and the Reich Committee at a meeting of the presidium on 21 September 1929 made a slight modification in the penal paragraph. The final version read, "Reich chancellors, Reich ministers, and *their* plenipotentiaries..." (emphasis added) *Niederdeutsche Zeitung*, 25 September 1929. Despite its continued objections to this paragraph, the *Landbund* did not resign from the Reich Committee, but agreed to work for the referendum "with the utmost energy." *Niederdeutsche Zeitung*, 25 September 1929, statement of the Federal Executive of the *Reichslandbund*.

55. DZA Potsdam, ADV, 501, Hugenberg to Nagel, 14 September, 1929.

56. "Hugenberg Weckruf," *Unsere Partei*, 1 October 1929, pp. 301–03. Newspaper coverage of the rally in the Hugenberg syndicate paid no attention to the Nazis—see *Niederdeutsche Zeitung*, 26 September 1929.

57. See the relevant issues of Hugenberg's papers *Der Tag, Berliner Lokal-Anzeiger, Niederdeutsche Zeitung, Lippische Tages-Zeitung*, and *München-Augsburger Abendzeitung*.

58. The Scherl *Verlag*, which indirectly controlled the DNVP press, was very flexible. While the title page stated that there was a separate press for the Reich Committee, the strength of the Hugenberg concern's representation on the propaganda subcommittee, the wealth of the Hugenberg concern, the use of the same format and plates in the party press—all leave no doubt that Hugenberg controlled the *Verlag des Reichsausschusses*.

59. For example see BA Koblenz, R43I/1891 and ZSgI/44/2.

60. NSSA Aurich, 1, also has a collection of pamphlets exemplifying this, e.g., *Weisst du die Wahrheit über den Pariser Tributplan* (Berlin, 1929).

61. BA Koblenz, R43I/1439, Minutes of the Reich Cabinet on 3 October 1929. On this issue, see Gotthard Jasper, *Der Schutz der Republik: Studien zur staatlichen Sicherung der Demokratie in der Weimarer Republik: 1922–1930* (Tübingen, 1963), pp. 257–60.

62. He argued that a public official "would contravene his duty as a civil servant, if he supported the initiative." Otto Braun, *Von Weimar zu Hitler*, 2d ed. (New York, 1940), p. 258. The DNVP protested most forcefully against this action, which they called the *Beamtenterror*. Eventually the state court decided against Braun and Severing but maintained that each case had to be decided individually. The decision was rendered only three days before the plebiscite was to take place. See Friedenthal, pp. 91–97. The Prussian regime also sought to hurt Hugenberg financially. In the second part of the campaign, the Prussian Ministry of Justice decreed that Scherl publications would no longer be used for

official announcements because they were "excessively inflammatory and hostile to the government." BA Koblenz, Hugenberg Papers, 570, Decree of the Prussian Ministry of Justice, 5 December 1929.

63. Johannes Hohlfeld, ed., *Dokumente der deutschen Politik und Geschichte* (Berlin, n.d.), 3: 273, Hindenburg to the Reich Chancellor, 16 October 1929. See also Andreas Dorpalen, *Hindenburg and the Weimar Republic* (Princeton, N.J., 1964), p. 159.

64. BA Koblenz, R43I/1439, Minutes of the Reich Cabinet on 18 October 1929.

65. *Berliner Lokal-Anzeiger*, 20 October 1929, Schmidt-Hannover, pp. 245–46; and Friedenthal, p. 77.

66. HA, GHH, 400 101 293/9, Circular of 18 October 1929.

67. Kirdorf, pp. 201, 214; and note Kirdorf to Hitler, 3 January 1929, p. 202, where he wrote: "Your confidence in the success of your work, the salvation of Germany from its total collapse, can only be fulfilled if you line up your movement with that path which leads to the national unity of all German-minded men (*Deutschgesinnten*). Today the basis for this is presented by the DNVP, which under the leadership of Hugenberg can become the true representation of our national interests. If unification does not succeed, then there is no longer any check to the collapse."

68. DZA Potsdam, DNVP, 16, "Hitler und die Knirpse."

69. WP, Hugenberg to Westarp, 4 November 1929.

70. WP, "Ausführungen von Graf Westarp in der Parteivorstandssitzung in Kassel am 21. November," and "Niederschrift des Grafen Westarp über Entstehung und Verlauf der Parteikrise Ende November/Anfang Dezember 1929."

71. Gottfried R. Treviranus, "Zur Rolle und Person Kurt von Schleichers," in Ferdinand A. Hermens and Theodor Schieder, eds., *Staat, Wirtschaft und Politik in der Weimarer Republik: Festschrift für Heinrich Brüning* (Berlin, 1967), pp. 371–73.

72. Duisberg, the chairman of the RDI, was so frustrated with the German National leader's radical policy that he gave Baron Werner von Alvensleben M 20,000 in order to organize opposition to Hugenberg in the DNVP. WA Bayer, Leverkusen, Autographen-Sammlung Duisberg, Alvensleben to Duisberg, 28 November 1929, and reply 29 November 1929.

73. This clearly meant collaboration with the NSDAP, and as Treviranus expressed it, "The psychological orientation of Hugenberg toward the side of the National Socialists is for many well-meaning men an intolerable burden." S 34 Hannover, Treviranus to Ahlefeld, 1 November 1929.

74. Captain Widenmann, the party treasurer and director of Hugenberg's Deutsche Überseedienst G.m.b.H., seems to have been the key figure promoting this approach. BA Freiburg, Widenmann Papers, N 158/17, Widenmann to H. Poensgen, 8 November 1929; Widenmann to Gürtner, 7 November 1929; Widenmann to Hugenberg, 25 November 1929, etc. Hugenberg insisted, however, that any coalition would have to be radically nationalist. His syndicate continually asserted that the DNVP would collaborate with any party willing to assume "a conscious and clear fighting position against Marxism" in both the Reich and Prussia. Hans Brosius, "Neue Wege," *Lippische Tages-Zeitung*, 28 November 1929.

75. AH Rohbraken, P 23, Hugenberg to Kaas, 20 November 1929.

76. Ibid. Another copy of this letter and the reply of 7 January 1930 are in S 30 Hannover. Kaas excused his delay in answering because of illness and necessary travels. As for the content of Hugenberg's proposal, the Center leader indicated that his party would be able to take a definitive position on the Young Plan only after the Hague negotiations were complete. He touched the two weakest points in Hugenberg's argument when he wrote: "The judgment of businessmen and financiers (*der Wirtschaft und Finanz*) regarding the immediate factual results [of acceptance of the Young Plan] is, as you yourself know best, very divided so that the politician can expect, as has frequently been the case, no decisive orientation from this side... if from a government including Social Democrats you fear the accelerated destruction of our economic and cultural conditions, so permit me to indicate that in the front, which you have organized and which, after the departure of a number of personalities especially noteworthy culturally and politically, has been increasingly narrowed, there are forces with which an effective cultural collaboration seems unimaginable."

77. See "Aufstieg oder Niedergang? Deutsche Wirtschafts-und Finanzenreform 1929: eine Denkschrift des Praesidiums der Reichsverbandes der Deutschen Industrie," *Veröffentlichungen des RDIs* 49 (December 1929). Leaders of the association posited, "The view, that under any kind of reparations plan a catastrophe is unavoidable, can only be countermanded through action." Their report presented specific and far-reaching proposals dealing with capital accumulation, the role of the state in the economy, social policy, and tax policy, which in their view would prevent a catastrophe. At the special meeting of the membership of the RDI on 12 December 1929, Duisberg publicly announced, "From the very beginning I would now like to confirm, that German industry (*das deutsche Unternehmertum*) in its totality rejects every purposeful pessimism as well as every aspect of crisis politics...." "Wirtschafts-und Sozialpolitik, Steuer-und Finanzpolitik: Vorträge... gehalten auf der Ausserordentlichen Mitgliederversammlung des Reichsverbandes der Deutschen Industrie am 12. Dezember 1929..." *Veröffentlichungen des RDIs* 50 (1930), p. 5.

78. WP, "Niederschrift des Grafen Westarp über Entstehung und Verlauf der Parteikrise Ende November/Anfang Dezember 1929." On these developments, see also Attila Chanady, "The Disintegration of the German National People's Party: 1924–1930," *Journal of Modern History* 39, no. 1 (1967), pp. 86–87. Erasmus Jonas, *Die Volkskonservativen 1928–1933: Entwicklung, Struktur, Standort und staatspolitische Zielsetzung* (Düsseldorf, 1965), pp. 47–57.

79. S 34 Hannover, Treviranus to Ahlefeld, 1 November 1930. In the letter, Treviranus also noted that "the person of Hugenberg and the tendency of the Pan-Germans is, as is the case with the Reich president, estimated as an insurmountable obstacle." See also WP, "Niederschrift Dezember 1929"; and G. R. Treviranus, "Rückblick."

80. *Die Abtrünnigen*, p. 10.

81. Alfred Hugenberg, *Klare Front zum Freiheitskampf: Rede auf dem 9. Reichsparteitag der DNVP in Kassel am 22. November 1929* (Berlin, 1929), pp. 6–8.

82. Westarp believed that open conflict would only hurt the party. WP, "Niederschrift Dezember 1929."

83. Ibid. The text of their statement is reprinted in *Abtrünnigen*, p. 10.

84. DZA Potsdam, DNVP, 54 and 55, Minutes of the Party Executive Committee. These are undated and incomplete, but intrinsic evidence indicates that they are from the meeting of 3 December.

85. For an excellent treatment of this secession, see Jonas, pp. 47–57.

86. WP, Westarp to Hugenberg, 4 December 1929. Secessionists included: Schlange-Schöningen, an agriculturalist; Mumm, a leader of the Christian Socialists; and Klönne, an industrial representative. All DNVP delegates had signed a declaration (*Verpflichtungserklärung*) in April 1928 agreeing to surrender their parliamentary mandate if they left the party. The secessionists, however, claimed that they were true German Nationalists and refused to turn their seats over to the Hugenberg party. AH Rohbraken, E 4, "Zur Geschichte der DNVP"; and S 34 Hannover, Hugenberg to Klönne, Lambach, and Hartwig, 16 December 1929, and replies.

87. *Unsere Partei*, 15 December 1929, p. 417.

88. The minister of the interior, Carl Severing, had set the date of the plebiscite for 22 December, a Sunday on which stores could remain open for the last rush of Christmas shoppers. Otto Kriegk, *Hugenberg* (Leipzig, 1932), p. 85. The Hugenberg press charged that this was a Socialist trick to make it difficult for the voters to go to the poles but that German mothers would buy their children freedom as this year's special gift. *Lippische Tages-Zeitung*, 22 December 1929.

89. Friedenthal, p. 140.

90. DZA Potsdam, ADV, 501, Schiele to Hugenberg, 23 December 1929. Despite the controversy that had developed between Hugenberg and Schiele, as president of the *Reichslandbund*, the party leader did not wish to alienate the agricultural vote. Hugenberg sent Schiele exuberant greetings for his sixtieth birthday and congratulated him as a "champion not only of the agriculture, but also of the party." The message was published on the first page of the *Berliner Lokal-Anzeiger*, 18 January 1930.

91. BA Koblenz, Wegener Papers, Wegener to Class, 16 January 1930.

92. BA Koblenz, R43I/1889, Hugenberg and Seldte to the Reich Chancellor, 7 January 1930, and his reply, 9 January 1930.

93. WP, "Niederschrift des Grafen Westarp über einen Unterredung mit dem Reichspräsidenten von Hindenburg am 15. Januar 1930."

94. Discussion of this point was probably inevitable, but Hugenberg's critics charged that the recalcitrance of the national opposition threatened Germany's already tenuous credibility in international diplomacy. See the critique of this view in the *Völkischer Beobachter*, Bayernausgabe, 13 February 1929. It is interesting to note that at this time the *VB* places Hugenberg's name before Hitler's. Possibly this was the preeminence coaling funds could buy.

95. Hohlfeld, 3: 283, Article XV of "Das Haager Abkommen vom 20. Januar 1930."

96. Friedenthal, pp. 161–62.

97. *Unsere Partei*, 1 February 1930, pp. 17–18; *Eiserne Blätter*, 2 March 1930, pp. 141–43.

98. The first page of Hugenberg's *Berliner Illustrierter Nachtausgabe*, 11 February

1930, reporting this debate has been preserved. Its pleasing format coupled with its extremely tendentious account make it an an interesting document. This popular paper, more than *Der Tag*, or even the *Berliner Lokal-Anzeiger*, must have had an important impact on the development of the national opposition in the capital. Unfortunately, no significant numbers of this publication seem to have been preserved.

99. *Reichstag-Protokolle* 426 (11 February 1930): 3916–21.

100. Friedenthal, pp. 157–58.

101. See Alfred Hugenberg, "Nun Erst Recht!" *Unsere Partei*, 15 March 1930, pp. 59–60. Here Hugenberg argued that it was the government that was following a policy of catastrophe and that in the crisis the middle parties would ruin themselves. On the right, however: "German hearts stand before an inner revolution. We are with it. We have never felt ourselves to be a 'party' in this 'parliamentary state,' but as the active kernel of the national movement."

102. *Reichstag-Protokolle* 426 (11 February 1930), Curtius's speech, pp. 3921–23.

103. Friedenthal, pp. 158–60. Hindenburg argued that in spite of all the protests that he had received (see, e.g., "Appell der DNVP an Hindenburg," *Der Tag*, 9 March 1930) he believed that the Young Plan was better than the Dawes Plan and that a severe crisis would ensue if he did not sign. The president stated that he accepted his responsibility. He requested that the discussions of the last months end so that Germans of all parties "in a spirit of communal cooperation" could go ahead with "decisive practical work." Hohlfeld, 3: 288–89, "Kundgebung des Reichspräsidenten von Hindenburg zur Annahme des Youngplanes." Hugenberg rejected this plea and protested that an erring Reich president should be criticized as any one else. *Der Tag*, 15 March 1930. Once more Hugenberg was in opposition to the industrial leaders of the RDI, who rallied behind the president. *Geschäftliche Mitteilungen des Reichsverbandes der Deutschen Industrie* 12 (1930): 60.

104. See BA Koblenz, Schmidt-Hannover Papers, 30, Hugenberg to Hitler, 17 March 1930.

105. Karl Dietrich Bracher, *Die Auflösung der Weimarer Republik* 4th ed. (Villingen/Black Forest, 1964), pp. 305–06.

106. Jonas, pp. 58–61, 65.

107. Conze, 81; and Heinrich Brüning, *Memoiren: 1918–1934* (Stuttgart, 1970), pp. 161–62. For an excellent critique of these memoirs see Rudolf Morsey, "Zur Entstehung, Authentizität und Kritik von Brünings' Memoiren: 1918–1934," Rheinisch-Westfälische Akademie der Wissenschaft, Vorträge G 202 (Opladen, 1975), especially p. 43.

108. BA Koblenz, Kleine Erwerbung 436, Schiele to Hugenberg, newspaper clipping, n.d.; also WP, "Niederschrift Graf Westarp, c.6. April 1930." The agrarian leader emphasized the great difference between himself and Hugenberg when he explained to Traub, "Our great goal is not to discern what lies in the distance, but to do what lies before us, to dedicate our strength to the present..." BA Koblenz, Traub Papers, 67, Schiele to Traub, 4 February 1930. The Hugenberg press gave a very fair report of Schiele's position and his reasons for entering the cabinet. *Lippische Tages-Zeitung*, 3 April 1930.

109. *Eiserne Blätter*, 6 April 1930, p. 216. This was the policy which Schleicher

and those about him did encourage. See BA Freiburg, Schleicher Papers, N 42/21 Schulenburg to Schleicher, 6 May 1930.

110. Treviranus, pp. 112–13; Thilo Vogelsang, *Reichswehr, Staat und NSDAP: Beiträge zur deutschen Geschichte 1930–32* (Stuttgart, 1962), pp. 414–15.

111. As far as Hugenberg was concerned, "The new party cabinet, which has been formed against us and with the intention of breaking us up and at the same time misuses the name and respect of the Reich president, is a clumsy attempt to deceive the nation." Alfred Hugenberg, "Aussenpolitischer Protest," in S 36 Hannover. In his memoirs, Brüning rejected the idea that he had sought either to split the DNVP or to drive Hugenberg from the political field. Brüning, pp. 169–70.

112. Alfred Hugenberg, "Das neue Kabinett" in S 26 Hannover.

113. HA, GHH, 400 101 2024/6, Blank to Reusch, 2 April 1930.

114. Technically, Hugenberg and his party did not vote positively for the cabinet; they merely rejected an SPD motion of nonconfidence and thus avoided dissolution of the Reichstag and new elections. Brüning, *Memoiren*, p. 169; and *München-Augsburger Abendzeitung*, 3 April 1930.

115. WP, "Niederschrift April 1930"; and S 35 Hannover, Westarp to Hugenberg, 16 April 1930.

116. *Reichstag-Protokolle* 427 (3 April 1930): 4770–73.

117. *Völkischer Beobachter* (Reichsausgabe), 5 and 30 April 1930.

118. BA Koblenz, Schmidt-Hannover Papers, 30, Hitler to Hugenberg, 3 April 1930.

119. Adolf Hitler, "Zur Krise der Deutschnationalen Volkspartei," *Völkischer Beobachter* (Reichsausgabe), 9 April 1930.

120. BA Koblenz, Schmidt-Hannover Papers, 30, Hugenberg to Hitler, 3 April 1930.

121. See the minutes of the party caucus on this problem in BA Koblenz, Schmidt-Hannover Papers, 35. Also, WP, "Niederschrift Graf Westarp (verfasst zwischen 25. April 1930 und 18. Juli 1930)."

122. Reichert sent out a special circular detailing reasons for the disagreement with Hugenberg. DZA Potsdam, 11, Reichert to Members of the German National Industrial Committee, 16 April 1930. Hugenberg was furious and had a special bulletin prepared to refute Reichert's interpretation. DZA Potsdam, DNVP, 11, Hugenberg to the Main Business Office, 18 April 1930, and Sondermitteilung der Parteizentrale, Nr. 12a, 16 April 1930.

123. *Alldeutsche Blätter*, 12 April 1930.

124. See the minutes of the party executive committee meeting on 25 April 1930. BA Koblenz, Schmidt-Hannover Papers, 35.

125. AH Rohbraken, P 11, Hugenberg to Hitler, n.d.

126. *Der Angriff*, 6 April 1930.

127. Documentation providing absolute proof of financial subsidies to the NSDAP during this period has not been found. Hugenberg's entire method of operation, however, totally convinces me that the German National leader provided the Nazis with monetary support.

128. Through his leadership in the party and through his press, Hugenberg had an enormous advantage over the dissenters. Westarp noted that "the party

chairman and his machine is systematically, publicly and in internal dealings, undermining their [the dissenting Reichstag delegates'] position in the electoral district." WP, "Niederschrift Juli 1930;" there is an extensive exchange of letters between Hugenberg and Westarp on this problem. Agrarians were not idle in their opposition to the party chairman. Men such as Baron von Richthofen-Boguslawitz organized local meetings against him. DZA Potsdam, ADV, 181, Regional Party Manager Ritter to Nagel, 13 May 1930.

129. Cited in DZA Potsdam, ADV, 181, [Bang's] note on 25 May 1930.

130. Ibid.

131. "Warum leidet der Bauer Not? Zwölf Sätze Dr. Hugenbergs," *Unsere Partei*, 1 June 1930, p. 99.

132. "Handelspolitik gegen Tributpolitik," (Hugenberg's speech at Halle) *Unsere Partei*, 15 June 1930, pp. 122–24. The proposal was carefully worked out by Dr. Otto Meesmann in "Vortragsentwurf Nr. 23: Hugenbergs Tributabgabe—der Ausweg aus deutscher Tributnot." AH Rohbraken, WP 20. The German National deputy, Reichert, who was also the executive secretary of the Association of German Iron and Steel Industrialists, totally rejected this approach and wrote a pointed refutation. BA Koblenz, R131/222, "Stellungnahme zur 'Tributaufgabe' auf alle Einfuhrwaren,"; and BA Koblenz, Kastl Papers, 9, J. W. Reichert, "Youngplanrevision auf dem Wege über eine Änderung der Handelspolitik," Sonderdruck aus *Ruhr und Rhein*, 1930.

133. "Das Übel der Berufsparteien" (Hugenberg's speech at Bischofswerda), *Unsere Partei*, 15 July 1930, pp. 134–35. "Appell an die Arbeiterschaft" (Hugenberg's speech at Berlin), ibid., p. 155.

134 BA Koblenz, R43I/1445, Minutes of the Reich Cabinet, 14 July 1930.

135. Bracher, pp. 338–39.

136. BA Koblenz, R43I/2654, "Vermerk von Pünder, 19. Juli 1930"; WP, Mitteilung Nr. 17 der Parteizentrale, 26 July 1930.

137. Brüning, *Memoiren*, pp. 179–81.

138. Ibid. This discussion later led to an extensive debate as to whether or not Hugenberg had actually offered to accept responsibility in the cabinet. See BA Koblenz, R43I/2654, Hugenberg to Brüning, 14 October 1930; and the attitude of the chancellery, ibid., "Ungezeichnete Bemerkungen." That Hugenberg in July was trying to prevent another open split in the party and to delay a decision on elections is apparent from Dietrich's notes on the meeting. BA Koblenz, Dietrich Papers, 254. The government's official rejection of Hugenberg's argument appeared in the *Berliner Börsen Courier*, 15 October 1930. The statement here asserted not only that Hugenberg did not offer to accept responsibility as he had posited, but also that his party, which claimed to have desired and caused the dissolution of the Reichstag, was "on the contrary surprised by it."

139. BA Koblenz, R43I/2654, "Vermerk von Pünder, 19. Juli 1930"; and see Brüning, *Memoiren*, p. 181.

140. See Oberfohren's remarks before the Party Executive Committee meeting on 24 July 1930 in WP, Mitteilung Nr. 17 der Parteizentrale, 26 July 1930.

141. The Hugenberg press de-emphasized the split in the DNVP. *München-Augsburger Abendzeitung*, 18 July 1930; *Lippische Tages-Zeitung*, 19 July 1930. On the

split, see Jonas, pp. 74–79; and Chanady, pp. 88–90. Hugenberg confirmed the count's complaints against his abuse of press power when he wrote to leaders in the party and in his syndicate, "In the immediate future, I request that Count Westarp not be personally attacked, but rather killed with silence." S 35 Hannover, Hugenberg to Schmidt-Hannover, etc., 22 July 1930.

142. WP, Mitteilung Nr. 17 der Parteizentrale, 26 July 1930.

143. On this theme, see the excellent work of Larry E. Jones, "The Dying Middle": Weimar Germany and Failure of Bourgeois Unity, 1924–1930 (Ph.D. dissertation, University of Wisconsin, 1970).

144. DZA Potsdam, ADV, 181, [Bang's] note of 25 May 1930; see also Bracher, p. 335. Some heavy industrialists thought Hugenberg was too optimistic. HA, GHH, 400 101 2024/7, Blank to Reusch, 24 July 1930.

145. See "Industrie und Reichstagswahlen," *Geschäftliche Mitteilungen für Mitglieder des Reichsverbandes der Deutschen Industrie*, 12, no. 21 (1930): 187–88. The association had been accused of collecting political funds and distributing them to various parties through the agency of Hugenberg. The RDI, of course, rejected the charge. Ibid., p. 171. Any one familiar with Hugenberg's conflicts with key business leaders knew this to be virtually impossible. The DNVP's pleas for funds substantiate this. Divergent political approaches would have made it almost impossible for the RDI to centralize political funds. The depression so increased these divergencies, that in the spring of 1930, the very structure of the RDI had to be changed. A special senate was established to reconcile dissidents. See WA Bayer, Leverkusen, 62/10.1, Herle to Members of the Presidium, 15 April 1930.

146. With its aspirations for political leadership, the veterans' organization wanted to alienate no one on the right. When some of its members, as von Keudell and Treviranus, bolted from the DNVP, they were not expelled from the Stahlhelm. *Germania*, 3 May 1930. Among the leaders themselves, Duesterberg had a more radical orientation than Seldte and extremists such as Stadtler challenged moderates like Brauweiler. BA Koblenz, Wegener Papers 31, Schmidt-Hannover to Wegener, 1 May 1930. Also, HA, GHH, 400 101 2024/7, Blank to Reusch, 24 July 1930.

147. WP, Mitteilung Nr. 17 der Parteizentrale, 26 July 1930.

148. Ibid.

149. *Völkischer Beobachter* (Bayernausgabe), 19 July 1930 and 20/21 July 1930.

150. "Es geht um Freiheit und Schicksal der Nation! Der Wahlaufruf des Führers der Deutschnationalen Volkspartei," *Unsere Partei*, Sondernummer, 23 July 1930, p. 157.

151. HA, GHH, 400 101 293/10, "Zur Klarstellung," presumably a circular from Scheibe and the ADI, n.d. The secessionists, of course, rejected Hugenberg's reasons for the radicalization of politics. See BA Freiburg, von Lettow-Vorbeck Papers, N 103/58, "Warum ich aus der Deutschnationalen Volkspartei austrat."

152. HA, GHH, 400 101 293/10, circular from Reichert, Chairman of the Finance Committee of the Popular Conservative Party, 20 August 1930.

153. HA, GHH, 400 101 293 /10, Scheibe's (German National Treasurer's) circulars of 29 July and 29 August 1930. Also, BA Koblenz, Wegener Papers, 53, Wegener to von Loewenstein, 7 September 1930.

154. HA, GHH, 400 101 2024/7, Blank to Springorum in Blank to Reusch, 29 July 1930.

155. HA, GHH, 400 101 2024/6, Reusch to Blank, 10 April 1930. On Thyssen's support for the DNVP see Scheibe's circular of 29 July 1930. HA, GHH, 400 101 293/10.

156. HA, GHH, 400 101 2024/7, Blank to Springorum, 29 July 1930; and Vögler's threat as relayed in HA, GHH, 400 101 2024/6, Reusch to Blank, 17 April 1930.

157. Refusal of the group to support the Nazis did not mean that individuals within that group could not contribute, on their own, to the support of that party. Also, a particular member might refuse the use of his money by a particular party but not object if others—within the general ratio approved by the group—directed their portion of joint funds to that party. For instance, see the attitude of Reusch toward the Hugenberg party in 1932 (below, p. 113) and of industrialists toward the electoral fund administered by Hjalmar Schacht in February 1933 (below, p. 142).

158. BA Koblenz, ZSgI/44/2, Wahlkampfmitteilung Nr. 1.

159. Ibid., and Wahlkampfmitteilung Nr. 2. *Ufa* produced at least three electoral films—"Wohin wir treiben," "Die fremde Faust," and "Tributverlastung." One of Hugenberg's own talks was filmed and then shown in *Ufa* theatres. *Der Tag*, September 1930.

160. BA Koblenz, ZSgI/44/2, Wahlkampfmitteilung Nr. 6.

161. This was a theme that the party repeatedly developed in its propaganda literature. For this and similar topics, see the issues of *Unsere Partei*, the special electoral issue of *Der Tag*, 14 September 1930, and various pamphlet literature in BA Koblenz, ZSgI/44/2, such as the DNVP *Vorwärts!* (an appeal for the workers to vote for Hugenberg), Rüstzeug Nr. 8 against the DVP, Rüstzeug Nr. 23 against Marxism, Rüstzeug Nr. 25 against the *Landvolkpartei*, pamphlet Nr. 359 against the Christian Socialists, and pamphlet Nr. 346 against the middle parties, especially the Center.

162. BA Koblenz, ZSgI/44/2, Rüstzeug Nr. 11, *Nationalsozialisten*, p. 36.

163. Ibid., pp. 5, 7, and 42.

164. *Unsere Partei*, Sondernummer, 23 July 1930. These themes were all carefully developed in Wegener's *Plauderei*, which was specially prepared for this election.

165. BA Koblenz, ZSgI/44/2, Wahlkampfmitteilung Nr. 1.

166. BA Koblenz, Wegener Papers, 31, Nagel to Wegener, 1 September 1930; and BA Koblenz, Wegener Papers, 23, Wegener to Class, 23 December 1930.

167. A. Ebeling summarized the opinion of many rightists when he wrote of Hugenberg, "He has ideals, which we all have—with that he has something right! Aside from that he is [politically] an absolutely incapable man." BA Freiburg, Lettow-Vorbeck Papers, N 103/58, Ebeling to Lettow-Vorbeck, 21 July 1930.

168. Hugenberg delighted in Wegener's support. When he first learned of the *Plauderei*, he affectionately called his friend "a monstrous man." BA Koblenz, Wegener Papers, 53, Hugenberg to Wegener, 1 August 1930.

169. *Unsere Partei*, 15 August 1930, p. 198; and BA Koblenz, ZSgI/44/2, Rüstzeug Nr. 17, *Warum Hugenberg?*

170. Ibid.,p.23.

171. Ibid.,p.29.

172. In 1928, only 75.6 percent of the electorate exercised their suffrage. The percentage of voters increased to 82 percent in 1930. See Bracher, pp. 365–69.

173. Jones, p. 77; and Dittmann, p. 4.

174. In an electoral rally, Schmidt-Hannover had boasted, "The election is a continuation of the plebiscite." *Niederdeutsche Zeitung*, 24 August 1930.

Chapter 4

1. "Sinn und Ziel des Wahlkampfes," *Unsere Partei*, 1 September 1930, p. 234.

2. DZA Potsdam, ADV, 159, GA Verhandlungsbericht, Hannover, 19 September 1930.

3. *Der Tag*, 16 September 1930. At least one of Hugenberg's press associates naively believed that "the result of the election is ... wholly satisfactory." BA Koblenz, Wegener Papers, 18, Mejer to Wegener, 18 September 1930. The director of the *TU* thus revealed the truly radical nature of many men in the Hugenberg syndicate.

4. DZA Potsdam, ADV, 180, Hugenberg to Oldenburg-Januschau, 6 and 11 October 1930. On Oldenburg's attempts to break Hindenburg's confidence in the Brüning government, see Dorpalen, pp. 209–10; and Brüning, pp. 191–92, 200–01.

5. S 32 Hannover, Hugenberg to Oldenburg-Januschau, 16 February 1932.

6. Kruck, p. 176; and see Conze, pp. 78–79.

7. BA Koblenz, R43I/1308, Conference of Ministers on 16 September 1930.

8. Ibid.

9. *Der Tag*, 16 September 1930. However, it became apparent once the Reichstag met that the Nazis were unwilling to defer to the German Nationals even in the area of economics. The NSDAP introduced propagandistic motions calling for confiscation of banking and stock market profits and for compulsory reduction in interest rates. LA Schleswig, DNVP, Mitteilung Nr. 26, 16 October 1930; and see Joseph Goebbels, "Das Wirtschaftsprogramm," *Der Angriff*, 12 October 1929.

10. Freytagh-Loringhoven, p. 82.

11. LA Schleswig, DNVP, Vortragsentwurf Nr. 22 [ca. October 1930].

12. BA Koblenz, Wegener Papers, 23, Wegener to Class, 26 January 1931.

13. BA Koblenz, Wegener Papers, 20, Klitzsch to Wegener, 10 February 1931. Hugenberg was also concerned about the friendly coverage given to the Nazis but worried that the editors of *Der Tag* could not be restrained much more lest they fall into the "opposite extreme." BA Koblenz, Wegener Papers, 58, 17 February 1931.

14. LA Schleswig, DNVP, Mitteilung Nr. 26, 16 October 1930.

15. LA Schleswig, DNVP, Mitteilung Nr. 24, 22 September 1930.

16. DZA Potsdam, DNVP, 370, Vortragsentwurf Nr. 14 [ca. spring 1931].

17. In his speech at Stettin, Hugenberg lauded the idea that the strength of the national movement had been so aroused that its impetus could now drive on and destroy the "net of lies of the November tyrants." *Unsere Partei*, 1 October 1930, pp. 329–30.

18. LA Schleswig, DNVP, Mitteilung Nr. 1, 3 January 1931.

19. Brüning, p. 210. The outcome of the meeting did not absolutely exclude all collaboration. Brüning told Hugenberg he would keep him informed of developments in foreign affairs, and the two men apparently agreed not to attack one another personally but to leave such criticism to their lieutenants. Ibid., p. 211; and S 32 Hannover, Hugenberg to Brüning, n.d. February 1931.

20. Two army lieutenants had traveled throughout Germany encouraging young officers to support the Hitler movement. The paramilitary nature of the SA, which had grown fantastically during the economic crisis, coupled with the revolutionary rhetoric of Nazi leaders suggested that the NSDAP might attempt to seize power forcibly. The campaign to win military support for Nazism was subsequently judged treasonous, and the officers were sentenced to moderate jail terms. Hugenberg appealed directly to Hindenburg to free the men. Once more he lectured the old gentleman that the judgment of the court had "aroused intense emotion and bitter deception in all nationalist (*vaterländisch*) and militantly oriented circles." The trial had proved that "only selfless striving and passionate concern for the maintenance of the military spirit of the Reichswehr, which was confined by the oppressive chains of the system, [had] determined the action of the condemned." The tradition of unconditional obedience, he argued, should be tempered because of the conflict of conscience suffered by dedicated men who might have made a mistake in their choice of means but not in their concept of duty. AH Rohbraken, GB 13, "Telegramm an Hindenburg betr. Beurteilung der Ulmer Offiziere, 11. 10. 1930." See Thilo Vogelsang, *Reichswehr Staat und NSDAP* (Stuttgart, 1962), p. 90.

21. LA Schleswig, DNVP, Mitteilung Nr. 26, 16 October 1930; and AH Rohbraken, P 11, "Die Parolen für 1931," Mitteilungen der DNVP, 28 January 1931.

22. Alfred Hugenberg, "Unsere Aufgaben im Jahre 1931," *Unsere Partei*, 1 January 1931, p. 1.

23. The local DNVP association in Pomerania had sought an electoral alliance with the NSDAP and had encountered difficulties. S 31 Hannover, Zitzewitz to Schmidt, 14 November 1930. Schmidt replied that he would immediately contact Hitler, "who is in thoroughly friendly contact with us. I am convinced that he will scarcely sanction the manner in which his lieutenants in Pomerania carry out national policy, according to your narration." Schmidt was only concerned lest it appear that the DNVP was running after the NSDAP. S 31 Hannover, Schmidt to Zitzewitz, 17 November 1930. The Nazis had a parallel fear. Hitler's deputy, Hess, informed Schmidt that Hitler wanted to concentrate on common enemies and not on conflicts between the parties. At the same time, however, the cooperation desired by the Pomeranian DNVP was rejected. Hitler preferred "not to aim at the presentation of a common list." S 31 Hannover, Hess to Schmidt, 27 November 1930. Obviously each party was trying to manipulate the other for its own advantage.

24. BA Koblenz, Schmidt-Hannover Papers, 30, Hugenberg to Hitler, 13 December 1930; and BA Koblenz, Wegener Papers, 66, Wegener to Hugenberg, 18 July 1931.

25. *Reichstag-Protokolle* 444 (10 February 1931): 875.

26. "Zur Verantwortung bereit," *Unsere Partei*, 15 March 1931, p. 84.

27. "Hugenberg: Hannover Rede am 25. Februar 1931," ibid., p. 82; and "Hugenberg," Landsberg speech on 20 March 1931, *Unsere Partei*, 1 April 1931, p. 97.

28. Wolff Telegraph Bureau, 21 February 1931.

29. "Hugenberg: Braunschweig Rede am 23. Februar," *Unsere Partei*, 15 March 1931, p. 81; Alfred Hugenberg, "Falsche und wahre Freunde der Landwirtschaft," *Unsere Partei*, 1 April 1931, p. 97; and "Von Westarp bis Crispien," *Der Tag*, 9 December 1930. In contrast to the federal government, Hugenberg set up the examples of Braunschweig, Thuringia, and Mecklenburg, where with Nazi participation there were nationalist governments, as models of the "best governed states in Germany." *Unsere Partei*, 15 March 1931, p. 84.

30. Bracher, p. 372; and see Westarp in *Volkskonservative Stimmen*, 14 February 1931. Privately, Hugenberg feared that collaboration between the government and the Nazis—especially on an agrarian program—could destroy his party in the East. AH Rohbraken, M 9, Hugenberg to Wegener, 20 January 1931.

31. LA Schleswig, DNVP, DNVP Main Business Office to the Local and Regional Associations, 29 September 1930; and LA Schleswig, DNVP, Rundschreiben Nr. 33 der Parteizentrale. All of the meetings were to be German National gatherings eschewing slogans like, "With *Hitler* and Hugenberg!"—a rallying call which had apparently been used in some areas during the Reichstag election campaign. Ibid,; and also Rundschreiben Nr. 39 der Parteizentrale, 7 November 1930.

32. LA Schleswig, DNVP, Rundschreiben Nr. 44 der Parteizentrale, 11 December 1930.

33. NSSA Osnabrück, 23, Unidentified Notes from a meeting held during this period. Those present included: Hugenberg; Karl Scheibe, the party treasurer; and Frau Lehmann, DNVP Reichstag delegate.

34. A note of exasperation characterized Hugenberg's comments on this matter. He stated, "I can only fulfill my task if the party throughout the country wants this and is prepared to produce the preconditions for this." NSSA Osnabrück, 23, Circular to the Local Associations, 24 June 1931.

35. A logical leader for such a movement might have been Schmidt-Hannover, who had the confidence of Hugenberg and his intimate associates, such as Wegener. Schmidt, however, was a member of the Stahlhelm. Consequently he typified the dilemma confronting the DNVP; it could neither convert the Stahlhelm into a German National SA nor abandon it to concentrate on developing its own paramilitary unit.

36. In general, however, the *Bismarckbund* was reserved for youth below the voting age; those over 20 could be considered members of a "work association" (*Arbeitsgemeinschaft*) or a "battle association" (*Kampfgemeinschaft*). NSSA Osnabrück, 23, Rundschreiben Nr. 16 der Parteizentrale, 6 June 1931, accompanying letter to the regional associations, 6 June 1931. Interestingly, party headquarters informed the local party units that these organizations were to be carefully controlled so that they would remain fighters and not seek to become a general staff. Even their newspaper was to be characterized by a "certain primitiveness."

37. See "Erwerblosenwahl 1930," *Ruhr und Rhein*. (1930), pp. 1233–34. The conclusion reached by some was that industry would have to become even more involved in politics. Fritz Tänzler, "Wirtschaft und Politik," *Der Arbeitgeber: Zeitschrift der Vereinigung der Deutschen Arbeitgeberverbände*, 15 October 1930, pp. 562–63.

38. See Jonas, pp. 82–103.

39. See "Erwerblosenwahl 1930," pp. 1233–34; and Duisberg's speech, "Der Weg aus der Krise," Geschäftliche Mitteilungen des RDI, Anlage Nr. 27, BA Koblenz, R12I/31.

40. According to the official biographies of Reichstag delegates, the only German Nationals clearly associated with industry were: the Pan-German Gok, of Blohm and Voss; Wilhelm Jaeger, a merchant from Celle; Fritz Klein, a construction contractor from Beuthen (Upper Silesia); and Fritz Wider, a manufacturer from Stuttgart. Bang, Quaatz, and Hugenberg, of course, had contacts with industrial leaders, but on the whole the party had no spokesman from the RDI or from heavy industry. Bureau des Reichstags, *Reichstags-Handbuch: 5. Wahlperiode 1930* (Berlin, 1930). Supposedly, not even Hugenberg viewed himself as a representative of industry. BA Koblenz, Schmidt-Hannover Papers, 57, "Dr. Hugenberg und die Hitler Diktatur." Cf. Struve, p. 223.

41. See the pamphlet, *Entschuldung der Landwirtschaft: Das Hugenberg Programm* (Berlin, 1931).

42. WA Bayer, Leverkusen, 62/10, 5b, Duisberg to Vögler, 8 November 1930, and reply 12 November 1930.

43. WA Bayer, Leverkusen, 62/10, "Reichsverband der Deutschen Industrie, Stenographische Bericht über die Sitzung des Hauptausschusses abgehalten am 27. November 1930." Thyssen's comments were received with "applause and hissing." This parenthetic observation indicating the division among industrialists was omitted in the printed report of the meeting. *Veröffentlichungen des Reichsverbands der Deutschen Industrie* 55 (December 1930): 27.

44. Cf. Thyssen-Reves, pp. 32, 35, 97, 98, and 103; and cf. Turner, "Fritz Thyssen und 'I Paid Hitler'," pp. 225–44.

45. S 43 Hannover, Thyssen [to Hugenberg], 25 December 1930.

46. See BA Koblenz, R13I/1065, Reichert to Schlenker, 4 December 1930. Poensgen placed a similar meeting in November 1931 or 1932. He was, however, possibly writing without notes and his memory, as he himself indicated, was faulty. He certainly erred in suggesting that Hitler first won Kirdorf's support in 1930. Werksarchiv Thyssen, Duisburg, Ernst Poensgen, "Hitler und die Ruhrindustriellen: Ein Rückblick."

47. BA Koblenz, R13I/1065, Reichert to Poensgen and Springorum, 4 December 1930, and Reichert to Schlenker, 4 December 1930. As business manager of the VDESI, Reichert pointed out the ambiguity of the fact that many firms involved in the coaling industry were also involved in the production of iron and steel. He was also concerned that a split in the RDI would affect the employer's association (*Vereinigung der deutschen Arbeitgeberbände*) and the *Langnam Verein*.

48. Brüning, pp. 214, 234–35. Brüning excluded Krupp and Vögler from this radical group. Lack of documentation makes any definite statement impossible,

but a case can be made arguing that Vögler hypocritically masked his radicalism and/or was a weak man who tried to please everyone.

49. BA Koblenz, R13I/1065, Reichert to Poensgen, Springorum, and Schlenker, 6 December 1930; and *Frankfurter Zeitung,* 23 December 1930.

50. For a clear description of the radical impact of the economic crisis on agriculture, see the pertinent sections of Gerhard Stoltenberg, *Politische Strömungen im Schleswig-Holsteinischen Landvolk: 1918–1933* (Düsseldorf, 1962).

51. "Gesetz betreffend Entschuldung der Landwirtschaft," *Der Tag,* 19 December 1930; and Alfred Hugenberg, "Entschuldung," *Der Tag,* 21 December 1930. Also see the pamphlet, *Entschuldung der Landwirtschaft: Das Hugenberg Programm* (Berlin, 1931).

52. See Bruno Buchta, *Die Junker und die Weimarer Republik* (Berlin, 1959), p. 79. Brüning's entire policy opposed inflation and thus sharpened the antagonism between himself (the export industries supporting him) and those Ruhr industrialists who favored Hugenberg and inflation. Brüning, p. 239.

53. "Leitsätze vom Februar 1930" in Hugenberg, *Die Soziale Frage in Deutschland,* p. 23. See also "Hugenberg's klarer Weg," *Unsere Partei,* 15 November 1931, p. 275; "Hugenberg in Berliner Sportpalast am 19 November 1931," *Unsere Partei,* December 1931, p. 283; and "Hugenberg: Rede in Oppeln," *Unsere Partei,* 1 April 1931, p. 98.

54. *Hugenbergs Weltwirtschaftliches Programm: Mahnung an das Ausland* (Berlin, 1931), pp. 4–16.

55. "Hugenberg: Rede in Bückeburg," *Unsere Partei,* May 1931, p. 131.

56. Hugenberg wanted to avoid the impression that the Stahlhelm had the leadership in public affairs. NSSA Osnabrück, 23, Undated Notes, apparently of a meeting of the Party Executive Committee.

57. Berghahn, pp. 161, and 167; and DZA Potsdam, Stahlhelm, 301, "Denkschrift vom 10. Februar 1931." Note also Deutschnationales Rüstzeig Nr. 26, *Kampf um Preussen* (Berlin, 1931), p. 8. Here the Center is sharply criticized for cooperating with the SPD and thus encouraging "cultural bolshevism". Also see NSSA Osnabrück, 23, Anlage 1 zum Rundschreiben der Parteizentrale, 19 February 1931. In this, party faithful are urged to make a clear distinction between the Center Party and the Catholic church.

58. S 43 Hannover, Schmidt-Hannover to Wegener, 7 February 1931; and AH, Rohbraken, P 17, "Aktennotiz", n.d. This is Schmidt's summary of the discussion held on 7 April at the Hugenberg estate. See the Nazi excuse in BA Koblenz, Schmidt-Hannover Papers, 30, Hess to Schmidt, 20 April 1931.

59. DZA Potsdam, Stahlhelm, 301, Kriess (Brown House) to Seldte, 13 March 1931.

60. NSSA Osnabrück, 9, Hugenberg to the Chairman of the Local Associations, 9 March 1931. Once Hugenberg had agreed to support the referendum, he would brook no opposition from dissident elements in the DNVP. The chief mayor of Düsseldorf, Dr. Lehr, favored a moderate position within the party and refused to support the cause. Hugenberg informed him, "There can be no difference of opinion over the fact that it was an indispensable duty of party members and especially those in official positions and in party offices to sign up for the Stahlhelm initiative". For Hugenberg, the demands of the system

necessitated compliance with party discipline even if this might bring some form of personal loss. SA Düsseldorf, Hugenberg to Lehr, 17 July 1931. This letter was first placed at my disposal through the kindness of Dr. Gisbert Gemein, author of *Die DNVP in Düsseldorf: 1918–1933* (Cologne, 1969).

61. S 43 Hannover, Schmidt-Hannover to Wegener, 7 February 1931. Hugenberg, however, was not overly sanguine about Nazi cooperation. He had indirectly reprimanded Hitler for avoiding contact with the other two groups. BA Koblenz, Schmidt-Hannover Papers, 30, Hugenberg to Hitler, 5 February 1931.

62. AH Rohbraken, P 17, "Aktennotiz." Concern about a successor to Hindenburg was a key factor in Hugenberg's political calculations throughout the year. He and Hitler began discussing candidates in April, when they both rejected Cuno as a possibility. AH Rohbraken, P 17, Bucholz (Hugenberg's secretary) to Wegener, 25 April 1931.

63. Berghahn, p. 173.

64. BA Koblenz, Wegener Papers, 66, Hugenberg to Wegener, 11 May 1931.

65. NSSA Osnabrück, 23, Rundschreiben Nr. 6 der Parteizentrale, 11 March 1931; and LA Schleswig, DNVP, Mitteilung Nr. 11, 10 August 1931.

66. NSSA Osnabrück, 9, Hugenberg to the Chairman of the Local Associations, 20 May 1931.

67. It was only M 408,345 as compared to M 594,152 for 1930. NSSA Osnabrück, 23, Undated Notes, apparently of the Executive Committee.

68. Ibid. The threat was apparently serious; the combination of political and economic problems was a heavy burden for a sixty-five-year-old man. As he confidently wrote to Schmidt-Hannover, "Perhaps I can turn these problems over to my successor, because in the total order of things I see no beginning to the overcoming of difficulties." AH Rohbraken, Hugenberg to Schmidt-Hannover, 28 April 1931.

69. NSSA Osnabrück, 9, Hugenberg to the Members of the Party Executive Committee, 9 May 1931.

70. BA Koblenz, Wegener Papers, 6, Meydenbauer to Wegener, 29 May 1931.

71. For example, see the issues of these papers during the plebiscite campaigns and the electoral campaign of 1930.

72. These productions could inspire nationalists of all varieties; they were not specifically intended to assist the Nazis. Films like *Yorck* and *Morgenrot* emphasized traditional nationalist concepts and stressed the advantages of mature leadership as well as the value of youthful exuberance. See the review of *Yorck* in *Lippische Tages-Zeitung*, 25 March 1932, p. 5. (I am particularly grateful to Herr Göbel of the *Friedrich-Wilhelm-Murnau-Stiftung* for the opportunity to view *Morgenrot*.) That such films did not monopolize the energies of finances of the *Ufa* is apparent from the detailed minutes of the board of directors which met frequently throughout 1930–1932. See BA Koblenz, R109/1027. Yet it would be false to argue that the directors were not part of Hugenberg's attempt to develop a sense of strong German Nationalism. In the development of its own biweekly news film with sound (*Tönende Woche*), the board resolved, "The weekly news film (*Wochenschau*) should bear a markedly German character; foreign clips are undesirable" unless there could be a mutual ex-

change of material. Ibid., Minutes, 14 May 1930. The news film was apparently widely used to propagandize rightist candidates for the Prussian Landtag elections of 1932, but the results were not beneficial to the concern, and consequently the directors refused to do the same for the Reichstag elections in July. They did agree, however, to permit rightist parties to rent *Ufa* theaters for showing nationalist films and holding political rallies. (The two had to take place at the same time. Apparently this would prohibit a group such as the Nazis from holding a rally at one time and then showing the conservatively oriented film to an empty theater at another.) Ibid., Minutes, 10 June 1932.

73. Some of the most publicized figures on the *Ufa* payroll—such as Erich Pommer, the director of *Morgenrot*—were of Jewish extraction. Christian Socialists, such as R. Mumm, as well as Pan-Germans, like Lehmann, were critical of this employment of Jews. BA Koblenz, Kleine Erwerbung, 365, Mumm to Heinrich, 19 March 1928; and BA Koblenz, Wegener Papers, 18, Lehmann to Wegener, 21 December 1932. Interestingly, Goebbels, in his fiercest attacks on the Hugenberg concern, concentrated on Scherl; he scarcely mentioned the *Ufa*, which continually advertised in *Der Angriff*. See the relevant issues of October 1932.

74. For a good description of Klitzsch's reorganization of the firm, see Traub, *Ufa*, pp. 68–95. In the period from 1925 to 1930, the *Ufa* paid no dividends. In 1931, 6 percent was paid. AH Rohbraken, O 15, "Merkblatt: Zur Entstehungsgeschichte der Universum Film A.G." In the payment of this dividend, the firms associated with Hugenberg reaped a total profit of M 1,122, 937.80. AH Rohbraken, P 17, Noelle to Vogelsang, 19 October 1931.

75. AH Rohbraken, P 17, Mann to Hugenberg, 19 March 1931. It is not clear if this fund included money made available directly through Scherl.

76. NSSA Osnabrück, 23, Undated Notes, apparently of the DNVP Executive Committee. According to the party treasurer's report, the German National central office was dependent on Hugenberg's monthly contribution of M 4,600 in order to pay the rent and the salaries of party functionaries. Despite some income from local organizations, Reichstag delegates, and lesser contributors, the party still had a deficit of M 14,600 for the first part of 1931. AH Rohbraken, P 17, Scheibe to Hugenberg, 24 June 1931. According to Mann's calculations, the *Victoriastrasse* (i.e., the Hugenberg concern) had contributed a total of M 42,780 to the central office for the first half of 1931. AH Rohbraken, P 17, Mann to Hugenberg, 15 July 1931. Possibly, some of the Hugenberg funds were used to assist the German National regional associations, but there is no record of this.

77. Vögler supported Brüning but, as a member of the *Wirtschaftsvereinigung*, maintained very friendly relations with Hugenberg. HA, GHH, 400 101 2024/8, Blank to Reusch, 27 April 1931. Springorum disagreed with the chancellor and, as chairman of the *Langman Verein*, sought to have that association and the *Ruhrlade* support his opposition. Ibid., Blank to Reusch, 20 April 1931. Springorum unambiguously expressed his support for Hugenberg in a letter to Traub on 10 June 1931. AH Rohbraken, E 3. See also Springorum's criticism of Brüning in the former's speech to the *Langnam Verein*. *Langnam Mitteilung*, 21, no. 20 (1931): 5–9.

78. It was Brandi who had threatened to take the coaling association out of the RDI. At the meeting of 5 May 1931, which prevented the actual secession, Thyssen admonished Duisberg that a "totally different wind" blew in the Ruhr than in Berlin. See the pertinent documents in WA Bayer, Leverkusen, 62/10.8; and HA, GHH, 400 101 290/10. Despite the relatively amicable settlement of differences which helped prepare the way for the election of Krupp to succeed Duisberg (HA, GHH, 400 101 290/27, Reusch to Krupp, 5 May 1931), the strain between the leader of the chemical industry and the heavy industrialists persisted. Ultimately, these differences led to Duisberg's refusal to continue his membership in the Ruhr-dominated *Langnam Verein*. WA Bayer, Leverkusen, Autographen-Sammlung-Duisberg, Springorum to Duisberg, 28 October 1931.

79. AH Rohbraken, P 17, Mann to Hugenberg, 19 March 1931.

80. AH Rohbraken, P 17, Mann to Hugenberg, 29 July 1931.

81. Thyssen-Reves, p. 103.

82. Turner, "Fritz Thyssen und 'I Paid Hitler'," p. 234. The lack of specific documentation in the Hugenberg Papers detailing such contributions need not disprove the existence of subsidies; it might merely demonstrate the incompleteness of the *Nachlass*. See the history of the Hugenberg Papers in the bibliographical essay.

83. AH Rohbraken, P 17, Mann to Hugenberg, 19 March 1931. Hugenberg sought to reorganize some of Mann's actuarial details and ameliorate the situation, but Mann pointed out that the problem was indeed serious. AH Rohbraken, P 17, Hugenberg to Mann, 23 April 1931, and reply, 27 April 1931. Hugenberg's long delay in replying to the first letter was apparently due to an accident in which he had been injured. AH Rohbraken, M 9, Wegener to Hugenberg, 19 April 1931. De facto, the *Werbegemeinschaft* placed only M 264,000 at Hugenberg's disposal for 1931..AH Rohbraken, M 9, Hugenberg to Werbegemeinschaft, 5 December 1933. In 1929, Scherl had turned over M 325,000 to his corporation; this sunk to M 220,000 in 1931. These sums and apparently the funds referred to by Mann were totally separate from the money made available directly from Scherl. BA Koblenz, Hugenberg Papers, 317, "Brutto-Überschuss und Verwendung," and 274, annual report for 1931.

84. BA Koblenz, Hugenberg Papers, 222, summary of annual reports, and 273–276, the annual reports themselves. See also AH Rohbraken, P 16, Klitzsch to Hugenberg, 22 June 1932.

85. HA, GHH, 400 101 2024/8, Blank to Reusch, 13 December 1931, and "Niederschrift über die ordentliche Generalversammlung der Deutschen Gewerbehaus A.G. am 24. Februar 1931 ..." in Blank to Reusch, 25 February 1931.

86. AH Rohbraken, P 17, Mann to Hugenberg, 19 March 1931.

87. The publication was losing approximately M 35,000 a month. AH Rohbraken, P 17, Hugenberg to Traub, 28 April 1931 and 19 November 1931. Even the fate of Traub's *Eiserne Blätter* was in doubt.

88. The firm replied that it was specially equipped to handle illustrated publications and would accept contracts from any nationalist group. *Münchener Post*, 10 June 1931, and *Münchener Abendzeitung*, 15 June 1931. Clippings of both these articles are in BA Koblenz, Wegener Papers, 24.

89. AH Rohbraken, P 17, Mann and Noelle to Hugenberg, 18 July 1931. In a speech at the beginning of the year, Hugenberg had proclaimed: "Foreign loans are new nooses around our neck. Their goal is to make any independent German policy impossible and to maintain at the helm, a system which entangles us ever deeper in dependence and misery." AH Rohbraken, P 11, "Die Parolen für 1931," Mitteilungen der DNVP. Hugenberg's political opponents were aware of the loan, and there was some fear that Brüning might violate the confidentiality of banking transactions and expose the DNVP leader—especially after Quaatz in the Reichstag had attacked the government's financial policy. HA, GHH, 400 101 2024/9, Blank to Reusch, 14 October 1931.

90. Vögler suggested that Scherl become a shareholder in the Danat Bank, and Hugenberg toyed with the idea. Klitzsch, however, thought the venture too risky, partly because "our Rhenish friends—with a few exceptions—have not always proven reliable." AH Rohbraken, P 16, Hugenberg to Klitzsch, 27 October 1931, and reply, 28 October 1931. To obtain funds in another way, Hugenberg also sought to take over the (Berlin) *Deutsche Allgemeine Zeitung*, which industry heavily subsidized. He also attempted to mend his bridges with Paul Reusch and the Haniel family, with an eye to merging their publications in Stuttgart and Munich with his own in order to save money. AH Rohbraken, P 17, Hugenberg to Vögler, 6 November 1931; and HA, GHH, 400 101 2024/9, Blank to Reusch, 27 November 1931.

91. On the connections of Goldschmidt with American banks, see Kurt Gossweiler, *Grossbanken, Industriemonopole, Staat: Ökonomie und Politik des staatsmonopolistischen Kapitalismus in Deutschland: 1914–1932* (Berlin, 1971), pp. 266ff.

92. For an example of such pressure on Springorum, see HA, GHH, 400 101 2024/9, Blank to Reusch, 27 November 1931.

93. "Deutschland bleibt Young-Sklave!" *Unsere Partei*, 1 July 1931, p. 169; and "Deutschland bricht unter dem Young Plan zusammen", *Unsere Partei*, 15 July 1931, p. 181.

94. Ibid.; and see Great Britain, Foreign Office, *Documents on British Foreign Policy: 1919–1939*, 2d series, vol. 2 (1947), Newton to Henderson, 14 July 1931, p. 206.

95. Cited in Berghahn, p. 177, n 3.

96. Hugenberg and Brüning had met on 26 November 1930 at the instigation of bankers and industrialists who hoped that the two men could collaborate; no agreement was reached. Pünder, p. 75. Hugenberg asserted that Brüning had charged him with rejecting an offer of cooperation in the government and that the whole story was a fabrication. "Zur Verantwortung bereit," *Unsere Partei*, 15 March 1931, p. 84. For the official government version of this problem, see the confidential report of Pünder to Schleicher, 3 and 4 December 1930 (Vogelsang), pp. 419–22. See also LA Schleswig, DNVP, Mitteilung Nr. 10, 17 July 1931; and the headlines in *Der Tag*, 17 July 1931: "There is a way out of the crisis! The German National leader knows it: Clear rightist government."

97. BA Koblenz, R43I/2655. At this meeting on 1 August, the president also implored Hugenberg to intercede with the Nazis to cease insulting him; he pointed out that his age and his position made this personally painful. Hugenberg shrugged this off by replying that his own DNVP demonstrations "were

frequently accompanied by National Socialist announcements...." There was nothing he could do about this. See the text of this conference in Hubatsch, pp. 305–07.

98. BA Koblenz, R43I/2655, Meissner to Pünder, 1 August 1931; and DZA Potsdam, ADV, 180, "Empfang von Hugenberg und Quaatz durch Brüning und Kaas am 27.8, 1931—4–7¹/₂ Uhr nachmittags, (Niederschrift nach dem mündlichens Bericht von Quaatz aus der Erinnerung durch Herrn C1)." During this conversation Kaas asked the rather provocative question, "Is it not a pity, Herr Hugenberg, that instead of standing in the locomotive, you are now sitting in the caboose?" Hugenberg replied, "Maybe I will still get on the locomotive."

99. BA Koblenz, Wegener Papers, 73, Hugenberg to Hitler, 1 August 1931, and Buchholz to Hess, 3 August 1931.

100. Schmidt-Hannover, pp. 273–74. See also HSA Düsseldorf, Hugenberg's Denazification Process, Lemgo Protokoll; and *Hugenbergs Ringen*, pp. 14–18, Hugenberg to Borchmeyer, 6 December 1948.

101. Schmidt-Hannover, pp. 274–75.

102. Berghahn, pp. 183–84. According to Stahlhelm records, the two leaders of the veterans' association were to meet with Hitler and Hugenberg on 27 September 1931. Unfortunately, there seems to be no record of this meeting, if it took place.

103. *Der Tag*, 7 October 1931.

104. DZA Potsdam, ADV, 180, Hitler to Hugenberg, 7 September 1931.

105. DZA Potsdam, ADV, 180, Hugenberg to Hitler, 9 September 1931. See also the printed texts of these letters in *Unsere Partei*, 15 October 1932, pp. 341–43.

106. DZA Potsdam, ADV, 180, Hugenberg to Hitler, 11 September 1931. Also see Roloff, pp. 53–63.

107. DZA Potsdam, ADV, 211, Class to Hugenberg, 21 April 1931. The original copy to Hugenberg is in AH Rohbraken, P 16. Class had apparently been incensed by Hitler's reaction to an article in the *Deutsche Zeitung* in April. The Nazi leader claimed that the ADV had tacitly delcared war on the NSDAP and was trying to split his party. Hitler argued that many of his followers would rejoice if all contact with bourgeois nationalists were broken, yet he himself hoped that "national judgment" would obviate such a policy. BA Koblenz, Schmidt-Hannover Papers, 30, Hitler to Lehmann, 13 April 1931.

108. "Geschlossen und Entschlossen," *Der Tag*, 20 September 1931.

109. Wolff Telegraph Bureau, 19 September 1931.

110. *Der Tag*, 20 September 1931; and LA Schleswig, DNVP, Mitteilung Nr. 12, 29 September 1931.

111. "Angriffsparole für die nationale Bewegung," *Der Tag*, 22 September 1931.

112. Hiller von Gaertringen, pp. 553–56.

113. *Hugenbergs Innenpolitisches Programm: Rede gehalten auf dem 10. Parteitag der DNVP am 20. September 1931* (Berlin, 1931), p. 6. The *Berliner Lokal Anzeiger*, 20 September 1931, distinguishing Hugenberg's rhetorical style from that of a demagogue, pointed out that the German National leader avoided cheap

rhetorical tricks, and made no concessions to his listeners but rather demanded concentrated thought. (Everyone knew Hugenberg was a poor speaker.)

114. DZA Potsdam, DNVP, 57, Meeting of the Party Executive Committee on 18 September 1931. Hugenberg again threatened to resign if the party could not improve its financial condition. Between 1 January and 31 August, 1931, the party central office had spent M 304,093. The projected budget for the entire year had been M 408,345. The local party organizations were to contribute M 161,000 but were presently M 85,433 in arrears. The situation nevertheless had improved since 1930 when the provincial party associations had turned in only M 24,184 to the central office. NSSA Osnabrück, 23, "Niederschrift über den Finanzbericht in der Parteivorstandssitzung in Stettin am 18. September 1931." The financial condition of the party had not significantly changed when the Executive Committee met on 2 December 1931. Members were told that, because of the economic situation in the country, contributions from industry were no longer possible. Despite his reelection to the position of party chairman, Hugenberg again threatened to resign unless party finances were improved. NSSA Aurich, 3, Steffens report on the Executive Committee Meeting in "Protokoll über die Vertretertagung der DNVP, Landesverband Ostfriesland, am 13. Dezember 1931." For 1932, the party central office cut its budget figures to M 379,080. NSSA Osnabrück, 22, "Haushaltsplan der Hauptgeschäftsstelle der DNVP für das Jahr 1932."

115. HA, GHH, 400 101 2024/9, Blank to Reusch, 18 September 1931.

116. See the joint statement of the Centralverband des Deutschen Bank und Bankiergewerbes, Deutscher Handwerks und Gewerbekammertag, Deutscher Industrie und Handelstag, Hansabund für Gewerbe, Handel und Industrie, Hauptgemeinschaft des Deutschen Einzelhandels, Reichsgrundbesitzverband, Reichsverband der deutschen Industrie, Reichsverband der Privatversicherung, Reichsverband des Gross und Überseehandels, Reichsverband des Deutschen Handwerks, Vereinigung der Deutschen Arbeitgeberverbände, in HA, GHH, 400 101 220/11, Kastl circular of 29 September 1931.

117. Ibid.; HA, GHH, 400 101 2024/9, Blank to Resuch and Blank to Springorum, 5 October 1931.

118. For instance, Blank scheduled a meeting of Reusch and Springorum with Hitler at the home of the Prince zu Wied. This was to be on the same day that a "small circle" organized by Walther Funk would meet, but the two sessions would not overlap. HA, GHH, 400 101 2024/9, Blank to Reusch, 4 September 1931. The results of these meetings, if they took place, are not recorded. My point is simply that industry could not afford to ignore or totally to alienate Hitler.

119. Ministers Joseph Wirth, Theodor von Guerard, and Julius Curtius, opposed by the nationalists, were dropped. Rumors indicated that men such as Vögler, of the steel combine, Silverberg, of the lignite coal industry, and Karl Goerdeler, German National Mayor of Leipzig, were being considered for cabinet posts. Brüning, *Memoiren*, pp. 425–28; and BA Koblenz, R43I/1453, Minutes of the Reich Cabinet, 7 October 1931. See also Fritz Klein, "Zur Vorbereitung der faschistischen Diktatur durch die deutsche Grossbourgeoisie: 1929–1932" in Gotthard Jasper, ed., *Von Weimar zu Hitler: 1930–1933* (Cologne, 1968).

120. Bracher, pp. 417–21.

121. Vogelsang, p. 135.

122. Brüning took a great risk in arranging a meeting of Hitler with Hindenburg but calculated that it was less dangerous politically than the organization of a united national opposition and the possible establishment of a "shadow cabinet." See Vogelsang, p. 143; and cf. Orlow, p. 235.

123. According to Blank, these leaders were forty minutes late. HA, GHH, 400 101 2024/9, Blank to Reusch, 12 October 1931. Description of this discussion is in S 40 Hannover, "Notizen über Harzburg." The patronizing attitude of the German Nationals toward Hitler as easily manipulatable, weak and undisciplined is patent. See also Schmidt-Hannover, pp. 281–84; Roloff, pp. 69–72; and Berghahn, p. 185.

124. The Hugenberg press gave top coverage to Hugenberg and less attention to Hitler. *Berliner Lokal-Anzeiger*, 12 October 1931; *München-Augsburger Abendzeitung*, 12 October 1931; *Niederdeutsche Zeitung*, 13 October 1931.

125. *Unsere Partei*, 17 October 1931, pp. 245–47. Interestingly, the *Völkischer Beobachter* (Bayernausgabe), 13 October 1931, hardly mentioned Hugenberg's role at the rally; the headline read, in part, "The NSDAP marches in the forefront for the conquest of the ruling system." In Berlin, Goebbel's *Angriff* gave no significant coverage to the meeting at all.

126. Hjalmar Schacht, *Confessions of the Old Wizard*, trans. Diana Pyke (Boston, 1956), pp. 268–69.

127. *München-Augsburger Abendzeitung*, 12 October 1931. The *Lippische Tages-Zeitung*, 11 October 1931, omitted key names such as Vögler, Brandi, Schlenker, and Grauert. Mistakes might be due to faulty reporting; however, the list of those attending might well have been made earlier on the basis of known or anticipated support for the meeting. An examination of the industrial power of these men reveals that aside from Vögler and Poensgen none of those listed were in key positions. (Moreover, the reference to Poensgen is unclear. The man who attended may well have been Helmuth Poensgen, a lesser luminary in the Ruhr who became actively involved in DNVP politics, and not Ernst Poensgen, the deputy chairman of the board of directors of the steel combine.) Brandi, as chairman of the *Bergbaulicher Verein*, was obviously an important man in the Ruhr coaling community, but at the same time he had no independent *Hausmacht*. He was chosen spokesman for the coaling interests, which were intimately associated with the Hugenberg concern. Schlenker and Grauert, as the executive managers of the *Langman Verein* and the Northwest (Ruhr) Group of the Union of German Employers' Associations respectively, were in even less independent positions. The presence of such relatively expendable representatives of the industrial community exemplifies the continuing desire of big business to support all groups on the right without being totally committed to any one political platform. The other figures—except for Louis Ravené, chairman of the board of overseers of the A. G. Deutscher Eisenhandel and Dr. G. W. Regendanz, who played a role in international banking—were all minor leaders.

128. The support of industry for Harzburg is frequently overstressed by historians. The claim that Reusch, Springorum, Vögler, Kirdorf, and Thyssen were present cannot be substantiated. Cf. Gerhard Schulz, *Aufstieg des Na-*

tionalsozialismus: Krise und Revolution in Deutschland (Frankfurt/Main, 1975), p. 662. See also Stegmann, "Zum Verhältnis," p. 421, and the rebuttle to this in Turner, "Grossunternehmertum und Nationalsozialismus," pp. 40–41. Stegmann returns to the same theme in "Kapitalismus und Fascismus," pp. 40–41.

129. HA, GHH, 400 101 290/33, Schacht to Reusch. Note the excellent observation on this meeting in Heiber, p. 85.

130. Leaders in the ADV were among the first to admit this. The *Alldeutsche Blätter* on 24 October could find no great praise for the day, and *Deutschlands Erneuerung* 15 (1931) commented (p. 694) that "only the frictions between the individual rightist organizations seemed to be present." Cf. Czichon, p. 23.

131. He had arrived late because the Berlin police had closed down one of his SA Hostels, and he had to take care of his men. He did not participate in the review of the Stahlhelm because he did not know how to salute them. The veterans had criticized the Nazis for using an "Italian salute," and the NSDAP retorted that the Stahlhelm used a "French salute." Similarly, Hitler explained that he had not participated in the communal meal because he never dined ceremoniously while his men went hungry. Theodore Duesterberg, *Der Stahlhelm und Hitler* (Wolfenbüttel, 1949), pp. 24–28.

132. In the eyes of the DNVP and other nationalist leaders, Hitler had arrived at Harzburg with his self-esteem inflated by his first meeting with Hindenburg. Alfred Hugenberg, "Was war eigentlich die sogenannte Harzburger Front? Wie sie entstand und gleichzeitig entschwand." HSA Düsseldorf, Hugenberg's Denazification Process.

133. The problem was who would exploit whom. In this struggle, the Nazis realized their advantage. Even Frick, upon whom right-wing nationalists believed they could rely, spoke at Harzburg in a manner calculated to allay the "very comprehensible misgivings of his party friends." Frick implied that the NSDAP was using the nationalists just as Mussolini had on his way to power in Italy. *Documents BFP*, vol. 3, Rumbold to Simon, 14 October 1931, p. 297.

134. See the chronological outline of the increasingly friendly contacts of these parties in Wolfgang Bretholz, "Experimental Politik," *Berliner Tageblatt*, 4 November 1931.

135. Hamel, pp. 248–49.

136. *Der Angriff*, 31 October 1931.

137. Even General von Schleicher thought the NSDAP might be malleable. According to Meissner, the general—with the knowledge of Hindenburg—had been trying to find an opening to the right since the spring of 1931 and had met with DNVP and NSDAP leaders. Meissner, p. 212; Treviranus, pp. 291–92.

138. A classic case of duplicity involved Hitler's attitude toward the monarchy. At Harzburg, the rumor had been circulated that Hitler would not appear at the general meeting because Prince Eitel Friedrich appeared in uniform, and Hitler as a convinced republican could not tolerate this. HA, GHH, 400 101 2024/9, Blank to Reusch, 12 October 1931. Two months later in dealing with the conservative Frau von Dirksen, Hitler expostulated, "No German National can be more monarchial than I. I will not marry and want no son because I do not want to have the thought of a successor arise. I want to provide a kaiser for the German people again." Cited in AH Rohbraken, P 23, Brosius to Hugenberg, 25 December 1931.

139. *Volkskonservative Stimmen*, 14 February 1931. And see the anti-Hugenberg publication of secessionist German Nationalists, *Briefe nach Ostdeutschland*, no. 12, 20 December 1931.

140. HSA Düsseldorf, Hugenberg's Denazification Process, Minutes of 26 November 1947.

141. Hermann Rauschning, *Makers of Destruction: Meetings and Talks in Revolutionary Germany*, trans. E. W. Dickes (London, 1942), p. 214; Brüning, p. 272.

142. LA Schleswig, DNVP, Mitteilung Nr. 14, 12 December 1931; "National und Sozial," *Unsere Partei*, 15 December 1931, p. 293. See also *Eiserne Blätter*, 25 September 1932, p. 476; DZA Potsdam, ADV, 163, GA Verhandlungsbericht, Berlin, 20 and 21 February 1932; and DZA Potsdam, ADV, 164, GA Verhandlungsbericht, Berlin, 7 May 1932.

143. LA Schleswig, DNVP, Rundschreiben Nr. 30 der Parteizentrale, 9 December 1931.

144. NSSA Osnabrück, 93, ADI, "Zur Lage," 1 January 1932; see also *Unsere Partei*, 15 December 1931, p. 293.

145. In the German National Party, funds were so scarce, the party treasurer begged party leaders to do everything possible to raise money. "If every individual does not cooperate in the reconstruction of our financial organization, the existence of our party is threatened.... If we do not march forward into the spheres of other parties, discontented elements will completely change over to the National Socialists and with that we will be lost." SA Düsseldorf, Lehr Papers, 7, Scheibe to all delegates in the Reichstag and the several Landtage, 19 December 1931.

146. See BA Koblenz, Schmidt-Hannover Papers, 21, Schmidt to Tetens, 22 February 1950; and AH Rohbraken, P 17, Thyssen to Schmidt-Hannover, 19 December 1931, and Thyssen to Hugenberg, 30 December 1931 and 5 January 1932. Thyssen indicated that Vögler also wanted Hugenberg to cooperate with the Nazis. See also AH Rohbraken, P 17, Thyssen to Hugenberg, 20 January 1932.

147. AH Rohbraken, P 17, Thyssen to Hugenberg, 28 January 1932.

148. AH Rohbraken, P 16, Hugenberg to Goerdeler, 13 November 1931. The terms employed by Hugenberg are difficult to translate meaningfully. In the jargon of the conservative right wing, objectivity (*Sachlichkeit*) referred to its own nonpartisan, factual approach to political and economic problems. Compromises produced by the parliamentary system dealt with issues neither objectively nor factually; such compromises were *parteipolitisch* and *unsachlich*, the result of *Kuhhandel* (logrolling). On this theme, see Thimme, pp. 107–53.

Chapter 5

1. John W. Wheeler-Bennet, *Wooden Titan* (Hamden, London, 1986), p. 361.

2. Brüning, p. 501.

3. Ibid., pp. 453, 502–04. AH Rohbraken, P 23, "Aufzeichnung über Besprechungen Dr. Hugenberg mit Dr. Brüning am 10. Januar 1932."

4. *Der Tag*, 13 January 1932; and *Völkischer Beobachter* (Bayernausgabe), 14 January 1932. Their respective statements are reprinted in Hubatsch, p. 309. The German Nationals sought to capitalize on Hitler's delay in responding by suggesting that the Nazi leader lacked political resolve and was dependent on

Hugenberg. ISH Amsterdam, Braun Papers, 465, "Streng vertrauliche Mitteilung der Deutschnationalen Parteileitung ... (vom 11.1.32)." The Hugenberg
syndicate headlined the decisiveness of the German Nationals and contrasted
this with the continued discussions of the NSDAP. *München-Augsburger
Abendzeitung*, 12 January 1932; and *Niederdeutsche Zeitung*, 13 January 1932.
Government sources, however, indicated that Hugenberg was peeved that
Hitler had been consulted before him. BA Koblenz, R43I/583, "Vermerk (Pün-
ders) vom 8. Januar 1932."

5. See DZA Potsdam, ADV, 163, GA Verhandlungsbericht, Berlin, 20 and 21
February 1932. Class quoted Hindenburg as telling General von Einem of the
DNVP, "Hugenberg I will not accept as chancellor under any circumstances;
the man treats me shabbily."

6. BA Freiburg, Schleicher Papers, 91, Hugenberg to [?]. The German National leader was furious at this move and criticized such organizations on the
right—which claimed to be nonpartisan and then intervened directly in
politics—for destroying rightist unity. The resultant chaos, as he saw it, would
mean victory for the NSDAP, which would then collapse because of internal
dissensions; the ultimate victor would be the left. See also a copy of the same in
DZA Potsdam, Stahlhelm, 281, dated 23 April 1932.

7. "Auszug aus den Erinnerungen, Dr. Heinrich Sahms," Vogelsang, pp.
431–37; and see Bracher, pp. 454–55.

8. BA Koblenz, R43I/583, "Vermerk 29.1.32."

9. BA Koblenz, Wegener Papers, 28, Wegener to Duesterberg, 18 January
1932. Bang and some members of the ADV apparently wanted Hugenberg to
campaign. BA Koblenz, Wegener Papers, 23, Bang to Wegener, 30 December
1931.

10. Hugenberg wrote to Wegener on 23 February that he had chosen the
"more comfortable way"; he would not campaign. AH Rohbraken, P 17. See
also the correspondence of Hugenberg and Herzog Carl Eduard von Sachsen-
Coburg during February in AH Rohbraken, P 16.

11. See DZA Potsdam, Stahlhelm, 295, "Beurteilung der Lage zur
Reichspräsidentenwahl," n.d. [ca. 7 January 1932]; and Dorpalen, p. 273. During this period, Prince Oskar became a member of the DNVP executive committee. *Berliner Lokal-Anzeiger*, 18 February 1932.

12. See Eric Matthias, "Hindenburg zwischen den Fronten," *Vierteljahrshefte
für Zeitgeschichte*, 8 (1960): 75–84.

13. The committee that had set up the Harzburg Front—Schmidt-Hannover,
Wagner, and Frick—tried to reestablish some positive collaboration, but their
leaders could not agree. See DZA Potsdam, ADV, 296, Schmidt-Hannover to
Frick, 28 January 1932. Also see DZA Potsdam, ADV, 295, for the reply to this
letter, a copy of which went to Wagner, 30 January 1932.

14. See BA Koblenz, Wegener Papers, Hugenberg to Wegener, 12 February
1932. For the best analysis of these events, see Berghahn, pp. 199–210. In any
new cabinet, Hindenburg wanted Brüning to maintain control of the Foreign
Ministry and Groener, of the Reichswehr. See the report on the presidential
and Prussian elections in DZA Potsdam, ADV, 181, Schmidt-Hannover to the
Local Party Chairman, June 1932. A copy of this is also in S 32 Hannover.

15. BA Freiburg, Schleicher Papers, N 42/91, notes on the election.

16. Hindenburg to von Berg (Markienen), 25 February 1932, in Matthias, p. 79. See also Hindenburg to Oldenburg-Januschau, 17 and 22 February 1932, in Vogelsang, pp. 442-44.

17. DZA Stahlhelm, 296, Duesterberg to Hindenburg, 11 February 1932.

18. *Der Tag*, 16 February 1932. At the same time, the paper also published a German National announcement stating that leftist democrats were manipulating Hindenburg to the detriment of his good name and Germany's; the party urged that respect for the victor of Tannenberg should not interfere with the conduct of the campaign. Hugenberg's provincial press labeled Hindenburg as the "candidate of the system." *Lippische Tages-Zeitung*, 16 February 1932.

19. S 2 Hannover, Hugenberg to Hitler, 20 March 1932, printed in ADI, "Zur Lage (Nr. 19)," 29 May 1932. See also, Berghahn, pp. 205-06. This suggestion would merely have been a tactical ploy since subsequently Hugenberg continued to block this proposal. DZA Potsdam, Stahlhelm, 296, Hugenberg to Herzog von Coburg-Gotha, 16 February 1932.

20. DZA Potsdam, ADV 181, Schmidt-Hannover to the Chairman of the Local Party Association, June 1932.

21. Berghahn, p. 209.

22. Ibid.; and DZA Potsdam, Stahlhelm, 296, Wagner to Hugenberg, 16 February 1932.

23. BA Koblenz, Schmidt-Hannover Papers, 28, Schmidt to German National Regional Association Koblenz-Trier, 5 March 1932. The contract, dated 18 February 1932, is preserved in BA Koblenz, Schmidt-Hannover Papers, 29.

24. The DNVP also agreed that its regionalized paramilitary groups would not rival the Young Stahlhelm. The *Bismarckbund*, the German National youth organization, was not to be affected by this. There are two essentially similar versions of this agreement in DZA Potsdam, Stahlhelm, 296. As soon as word of the agreement reached regional Stahlhelm leaders, some filed objections. BA Koblenz, Schmidt-Hannover Papers, 28, Stahlhelm circular of 29 February 1932, and Schmidt to Wagner, 7 March 1932.

25. See *Alldeutsche Blätter*, 27 February 1932; and DZA Potsdam, Stahlhelm, 295, "Stahlhelm Landesverbände Westfalen and Westmark, Führerbrief 38," 10 March 1932.

26. AH Rohbraken, P 23, Hugenberg to Brosius, 28 January 1932.

27. As Hugenberg wrote to Hitler, the very minister in Braunschweig about whom the Nazis complained in the fall of 1931 made Hitler's citizenship possible "with my full agreement despite my position on the question of candidates." AH Rohbraken, P 16, Hugenberg to Hitler, 20 March 1932. On this, see Rudolf Morsey, "Hitler als Braunschweiger Regierungsrat," *Vierteljahrshefte für Zeitgeschichte*, 8 (1960): 419-48; and also Roloff, pp. 89-100.

28. Goebbels had continually urged Hitler to campaign himself. The propaganda expert was most critical of the "reactionaries." In his estimation, Hugenberg was "only the fifth wheel on the wagon." See Goebbels, p. 23.

29. See "Wahlaufruf des Kampfblocks Schwarz-Weiss-Rot von 23 Februar 1932," in Hohlfeld, p. 420.

30. *Lippische Tages-Zeitung*, 9 March 1932. See also *Niederdeutsche Zeitung*, 24 February 1932.

31. *München-Augsburger Abendzeitung*, 23 February 1932. See the relevant issues of *Der Tag* and the *Berliner Lokal-Anzeiger*.

32. Bracher, p. 475.

33. *Der Tag*, 15 March 1932.

34. *Documents BFP*, vol. 3, Rumbold to Simon, 16 March 1932, p. 103; and see Bracher, pp. 476–77.

35. GSA Berlin, Dommes Papers 14, Wilhelm to Crown Prince Wilhelm, 5 April 1932, and Wilhelm to his Family Ministers, 15 April 1932.

36. GSA Berlin, Dommes Papers 14, clipping from *Fridericus*, April 1932. See also AH Rohbraken, P 16, Hugenberg to Crown Prince, 26 March 1932. The prince later had Hugenberg informed that though he disagreed with him on the presidential election, he fully concurred on the necessity of having a strong DNVP "in the common assumption of power with the Nazis in Prussia." He urged, "In the leadership of the electoral campaign everything depends on the two parties firmly keeping this common, grand goal in mind and suppressing the conflict over economic and cultural antitheses." AH Rohbraken, P 16, "Herrn General von Dommes verabredungsgemäss übersandt ... 14. April 1932." See also Bracher, p. 459; and Klaus W. Jonas, *Life of Crown Prince William*, trans. Chas. W. Bangert (London, 1961), p. 177.

37. *Eiserne Blätter*, 27 March 1932, p. 149.

38. BA Koblenz, Schmidt-Hannover Papers, 39, Hugenberg to Regional Party Chairman, 23 March 1932.

39. See the relevant issues of *Der Tag*, *Münchener-Augsburger Abendzeitung*, etc.

40. AH Rohbraken, P 16, Hugenberg to Hitler, 20 March 1932. This letter was later published in Traub's *Eiserne Blätter*, 22 May 1932, pp. 241–46, and circulated by the German National Industrial Committee, "Zur Lage (Nr. 19)," 29 May 1932.

41. Bracher, p. 478.

42. *Alldeutsche Blätter*, 30 March 1932; and J. F. Lehmann, "Warum wählt das nationale Deutschland im zweiten Wahlgang Adolf Hitler?" *Deutschlands Erneuerung*, April 1932, pp. 193–95.

43. Duesterberg, pp. 33–34.

44. NSSA Osnabrück, 93, ADI to all Local Party Associations, 24 March 1932; and see, Horst Gies, "The NSDAP and the Agrarian Organizations in the Final Phase of the Weimar Republic," as translated in Henry A. Turner, ed., *Nazism and the Third Reich* (New York, 1972), pp. 68–69.

45. DZA Potsdam, Stahlhelm, 295, "Bericht über die Zusammenarbeit mit der DNVP bei dem 1. Wahlgang des Reichspräsidentwahl 1932."

46. DZA Potsdam, Stahlhelm, 296, Wagner to Hugenberg, 19 March 1932. The final termination of the agreement came on 22 March when leaders of the two groups met at the DNVP central office. Ibid., "Aktennotiz." The Stahlhelm later added a financial problem to this political injury by buying out the *Neue-Preussische (Kreuz-) Zeitung* as its daily organ. Some of those at Scherl thought this might hurt the circulation of *Der Tag*. DZA Potsdam, Stahlhelm, 73, Wagner to Klitzsch, 23 March 1932.

47. BA Koblenz, Schmidt-Hannover Papers, 29, "Bericht über eine am 4. April ... Tagung der Landesleiter, Landeswerbeleiter ..."

48. Officially, the Stahlhelm reiterated its nonpartisan, nationalist position and forbade its membership to campaign officially for any party. BA Koblenz, Schmidt-Hannover Papers, 29, Schmidt to Stahlhelm Federal Office, 5 April 1932, and DNVP circular, 23 May 1932. Schmidt-Hannover expressed the exasperation of German National leaders when he complained that the veterans had set a record for wretchedness, inconsistency, cowardice, and disloyalty. BA Koblenz, Wegener Papers, 31, Schmidt to Wegener, 2 May 1932.

49. Schacht clearly indicated that the genesis of this idea lay in the view that "the hope, that Herr Hugenberg will acquire a decisive influence with the Nazis, is certainly very dubious after the most recent developments." HA, GHH, 400 101 290/3, Schacht to Reusch, 18 March 1932. Reusch replied that in his recent conversation with Hitler, he (Reusch) had expressed an idea very similar to Schacht's; Hitler had no objections to the proposal. Ibid., Reusch to Schacht, 20 March 1932. Ultimately, Springorum, Thyssen, Krupp, and Reusch contributed to the establishment of this *Arbeitsstelle*. HA, GHH, 400 101 290/33, Reusch to Schacht, 9 June 1932. The importance of this foundation and its relationship to the "Keppler Kreis," another attempt of businessmen to influence Hitler, is stressed by Stegmann, "Zum Verhältnis," pp. 425–29. Turner in "Grossunternehmertum und Nationalsozialismus" (pp. 50–56) rejects this interpretation. It is obvious that no one viewed Hugenberg as industry's primary or exclusive contact with Hitler and the NSDAP; indeed, the German National had become a liability in this area.

50. HA, GHH, 400 101 290/39, Reusch to Wilmowsky, 23 March 1932. After a discussion with Hugenberg, Reusch concluded, "A sensible position of the DNVP under the leadership of Herr Hugenberg is unthinkable." HA, GHH, 400 101 290/36b, Reusch to Springorum, 23 March 1932. Among the members of the *Ruhrlade*, Thyssen continued to be an outspoken proponent of Hitler, and he requested Reusch to distribute Nazi pamphlets to the members. Reusch agreed. HA, GHH, 400 101 24/14, Reusch to Fickler et al., 31 March 1932. Distribution did not imply endorsement.

51. HA, GHH, 400 101 290/39, Wilmowsky to Reusch, 25 March 1932. Wilmowsky also sought to involve Goerdeler in this move. Ibid., Wilmowsky to Goerdeler, 1 April 1932.

52. HA, GHH, 400 101 221/11b, Schlenker to Springorum, 23 March 1932. These Hanoverian industrialists wanted to support candidates of the "United National Right" or at least of the "DNVP—United National Right."

53. HA, GHH, 400 101 290/36b, Springorum to Wilmowsky, 22 March 1932.

54. HA, GHH, 400 101 290/39, Wilmowsky to Goerdeler, 1 April 1932.

55. Alfred Hugenberg, "Rumtopf? Neue nationale Wiedergeburt," *Der Tag*, 30 April 1932.

56. Alfred Hugenberg, "Das neue Harzburg," *Berliner Lokal-Anzeiger*, 31 March 1932.

57. Hugenberg, "Rumtopf?" and "Das neue Harzburg." Copies of these articles, as well as a third, "Wohin geht die Jugend?" (printed in the *Berliner Lokal-Anzeiger*, 1 April 1932) were sent directly to Reusch. Undoubtedly, Hugenberg

wanted to counteract the industrialist's opposition to him and at the same time expected Reusch to consider publication of these articles in the southern papers controlled by his firm. HA, GHH, 300 193 90/17, Hugenberg to Reusch, 27 March 1932.

58. "Aufruf Hugenbergs zur Preussenwahl," *Lippische Tages-Zeitung*, 14 April 1932.

59. Hugenberg compared himself to a chicken-ladder ("Sie wissen ja, dass das Leben eine Hühneleiter!") Apparently this is a reference to the German proverb: "Life is a chicken-ladder—shit on from top to bottom." AH Rohbraken, M 9, von Buchholz (for Hugenberg) to Wegener, 15 March 1932. Hugenberg's secretary here cited the beginning of a letter which her boss had begun to dictate but left unfinished.

60. Ibid. In this part of the letter, von Buchholz indicated her own feelings, which undoubtedly mirrored those of Hugenberg's intimates.

61. A copy of this is preserved in S 27 Hannover. Part of the speech is cited in *Hugenbergs Ringen*, 1: 65. Such cautious criticism of the NSDAP was a major theme in DNVP electoral propaganda and foreshadowed the severe conflict of the two parties later in the year. German Nationals were already arguing that a Nazi success would not necessarily end the Weimar system. See "Bayern-Aufruf," *München-Augsburger Abendzeitung*, 12 April 1932; also Professor Lent, "Wir und die Nationalsozialisten," ibid., 19 April 1932.

62. *Niederdeutsche Zeitung*, 5 April 1932; *Lippische Tages-Zeitung*, 6 and 14 April 1932. The state of Braunschweig, which had a similar coalition, was also mentioned in the latter publication.

63. *Unsere Partei*, 1 May 1932, 105–06.

64. See BA Freiburg, Groener Papers, 46/152, Groener to Brüning, 10 April 1932; and "Niederschrift über die Besprechung in der Reichskanzlei über das Verbot der SA," *Berliner Lokal-Anzeiger*, 14 and 17 April 1932; *München-Augsburger Abendzeitung*, 15 April 1932. Note also Brüning, pp. 538–40, 575–89; and Bracher, pp. 481–97.

65. DZA Potsdam, Büro des Reichspräsidenten, 47, Kalkreuth to Hindenburg, 12 May 1932.

66. Analysis of Brüning's fall from power is a complex problem. While Hugenberg and his party cannot be regarded as the one cause for this development, there can be no doubt that the attitude of the party, and especially the actions of some individuals in the party, had an important impact on Hindenburg and on his final decision. See Vogelsang, "Niederschrift aus dem Büro des Reichspräsidenten über die Entwicklung der Krise und Demission des Kabinetts Brüning," pp. 459–66; and Brüning, *Memoiren*, pp. 574–99. Also note Heinrich Muth, "Agrarpolitik und Parteipolitik in Frühjahr: 1932," in Hermens and Schieder, pp. 459ff.

67. DZA Potsdam, Büro des Reichspräsidenten, 47, "Aktennotiz über die Besprechung des Herrn Reichspräsidenten betr. Regierungsbildung am 30. und 31. Mai 1932."

68. Ibid.

69. As a German National, Wilhelm von Gayl had represented East Prussia in

the Reichsrat; Franz Gürtner had been the DNVP minister of justice in Bavaria, and Magnus von Braun, as general director of the *Raiffeisengenossenschaft*, had supported the party. NSSA Aurich 3, Ronneberger report of the meeting of the Party Executive Committee in "Protokoll der Landesverbandsvorstandssitzung am 19. 6. 1932." Also see Hiller von Gaertringen, p. 560, n 2.

70. NSSA Aurich 3, Ronneberger report. The important minister of the interior, von Gayl, later wrote to Hugenberg that an "agreement among the members of the cabinet" had prompted his resignation from the party but he hoped that their cooperation would continue. BA Koblenz, Nachlass Gayl 31, Gayl to Hugenberg, 10 June 1932. The attitude of von Gayl to the DNVP was probably typical. He viewed the party as a means of securing rightist rule and not as a means of ensuring popular sovereignty and parliamentary responsibility. BA Koblenz, Nachlass Gayl 14, clipping from *Ostpreussische Zeitung*, 15 April 1932.

71. Hugenberg was so out of touch with the power centers in the government that he had not even been sure that Brüning would be dropped. AH Rohbraken, M 9, von Buchholz to Wegener, 30 May 1932.

72. AH Rohbraken, P 17, Wegener to Hugenberg, 25 April 1932; and see BA Koblenz, Wegener Papers, 31, Schmidt-Hannover to Wegener, 2 May 1932. Hugenberg decided that if he resigned as chairman, he would also leave the Reichstag. In his depression, he manifested little concern with the idealism which was supposedly his sole motivation. Once out of public life, he indicated he would no longer care what Scherl published, for "in this case the goal pursued by our press undertakings must be counted as finished." BA Koblenz, Wegener Papers, 66, Hugenberg to Wegener, 2 May 1932.

73. AH Rohbraken, P 17, Wegener to Hugenberg, 6 May 1932.

74. BA Freiburg, Bredow Papers, N 97/2, "Vortragsnotiz 6. 12.32."

75. HA, GHH, 400 101 290/39, Wilmowsky to Reusch, 10 June 1932 and 17 June 1932.

76. HA, GHH, 400 101 290/39, Wilmowsky to Reusch, 11 June 1932. Robert Bosch directly approached the Reich president with some form of petition against Hugenberg. HA, GHH, 400 101 290/36b, Springorum to Bosch, 1 June 1932. Goerdeler also presented some form of memorandum to Hindenburg, presumably dealing with necessary changes to create a strongly based bourgeois cabinet. HA, GHH, 400 101 2007/13, 7 June 1932. Goerdeler had refused to participate in the Papen cabinet as minister of labor; he preferred a coalition cabinet including Nazis. According to Papen's minister of agriculture, the Leipzig mayor prepared numerous memos and letters to support this view. Presumably, this was the coalition that Goerdeler and Bosch advocated. Magnus von Braun, *Weg durch vier Zeitepochen*, 3rd rev. ed. (Limburg/Lahn, 1965), pp. 424–43.

77. AH Rohbraken, P 17, Stinnes to Hugenberg, 7 June 1932.

78. HA, GHH, 400 101 290/39, Wilmowsky to Reusch, 17 June 1932. Oldenburg-Januschau indicated, however, that after the elections Hugenberg himself might agree to select a successor. Hugenberg's opponents were considering Baron von Gayl or Mayor Goerdeler for this position. *Ibid.*; and HA, GHH, 400

101 2007/4, Reusch to Cossmann, 16 June 1932. Hugenberg's friend, Wegener had suggested the agrarian leader, Hans-Joachim von Rohr. AH Rohbraken, P 17, Wegener to Hugenberg, 25 April 1925.

79. AH Rohbraken, P 17, Mann to Hugenberg, 14 June 1932 and 16 June 1932; Hugenberg to Klitzsch, 20 June 1932.

80. AH Rohbraken, P 17, Gnoyke to Mann, 13 June 1932, and Mann to Hugenberg, 16 June 1932. Unfortunately correspondence on this matter reveals only part of the difficulty.

81. Political funds from industrial contributors were usually determined by the percentage of votes secured by the several parties. This general rule of thumb, applicable to nonsocialist parties, was frequently disregarded by individuals with particular political preferences. Undoubtedly, Springorum and some of his associates had heavily subsidized the DNVP during the Landtag election. The coaling interests, in particular, backed the party. See AH Rohbraken, P 17, Hugenberg to Mann, 7 May 1932. During the Reichstag campaign in July, Vögler and Brandi apparently made significant contributions to the Hugenberg party. Ibid., Hugenberg to Vögler, 19 August 1932.

82. BA Koblenz, R43I/1457, Hugenberg to von Papen, 23 July 1932. A copy of this is also in BA Freiburg, Schleicher Papers, N42/22. It was also published in *Der Tag*, 18 July 1931. For Hugenberg's criticism of Lausanne and his support for von Papen's intervention in Prussia, see "Plan zur Abdeckung der privaten Auslandsschulden," *Unsere Partei*, 15 July 1932, pp. 205–06; and "Säuberung des Beamtentums in Preussen. Fort mit den Parteibonzen," *Unsere Partei*, 22 July 1932, p. 225.

83. BA Koblenz, R43I/2655, Reich Chancellery to Hugenberg, 26 July 1932.

84. See handbill in BA Koblenz, NSDAP Hauptarchiv 837, which portrays Hindenburg protecting Germany from the Socialists and the National Socialists and encourages the electorate to "vote for him."

85. Hugenberg at the meeting of party leaders on 25 June 1932, *Unsere Partei*, 1 July 1932, pp. 167–69. See *Berliner Lokal-Anzeiger*, 2 July 1932; *Der Tag*, 29 July 1932. In an attempt to win the vote of nationalist Catholics, German Nationals criticized the Center Party more strongly than ever. See Anton Ritthaler, "Die Bundesgenossen des Marxismus," *München-Augsburger Abendzeitung*, 27 June 1932.

86. "Hugenbergs Mittelstandsprogramm," *Lippische Tages-Zeitung*, 13 July 1932.

87. The rallying cry repeated in the Hugenberg syndicate was: "All Germans who do not think socialistically, vote German National." *Niederdeutsche Zeitung*, 3 July 1932; and Eduard Stadtler, "Der Sammelblock der Hugenberg-Bewegung," *Lippische Tages-Zeitung*, 16 July 1932. Hugenberg's lieutenants stressed this in their appeal to industry for support. See the notification announcing Scheibe's speech, "Wirtschaftliche Aufgaben der kommenden nationalen Staates: Wie stehen die Nationalsozialisten?" at the Düsseldorf Industry Club on 8 July 1932. SA Düsseldorf, Lehr Papers, 7, circular of the local party association, Düsseldorf-East, 2 July 1932.

88. *Lippische Tages-Zeitung*, 19 July 1932.

89. R. G. Quaatz and P. Bang, *Das deutschnationale Freiheits-Programm* (Berlin,

[932), pp. 10, 13–18, 19, 21, and 29. Still the state could and should foster internal colonization (p. 16) and, in extreme cases, settle problems of wages and even protect wages (p. 20). Fundamentally, however, the state was to provide an atmosphere in which native capital could be increased; this increment would solve the problem of unemployment and foster the development of social (as opposed to socialist) benefits for all nationals (p. 15).

90. Quaatz and Bang, pp. 7–10, 23–25. The two men favored a restoration of some sort, but this was not a main point emphasized by their much-used bold print. Ibid., p. 9.

91. Despite the fact that these were the policies which he had been promoting for years, Hugenberg gave this manifesto only tenuous public support. In his introduction of the pamphlet, he merely suggested that the only goal was to make the fatherland "free and happy again"—consequently, tactics had to bow to time and circumstances. Quaatz and Bang, Preface, p. 3.

92. Bourgeois unity could also benefit Hugenberg, as his negotiations with Director von Stauss of the *Deutsche Bank* indicated. AH Rohbraken, P 17, Hugenberg to Klitzsch, 20 June 1932.

93. This agreement did not apply to local lists. German National plans for autarkic development prevented closer collaboration between the two parties. Desirous of securing votes and needful of industrial support, Hugenberg was willing to temper his rhetoric but unwilling to alter his policy. BA Koblenz, Dingeldey Papers, 61, Circular Letter of 25 June 1932, and Hugenberg to Dingeldey, 16 July 1932. Also BA Koblenz, R45I/17, "Vereinbarung Hugenberg-Dingeldey betreffend Wahl, Juli 1932." The German Nationals had sought such an alliance in the Prussian election, but Dingeldey had refused. BA Koblenz, Dingeldey Papers, 61, Schmidt-Hannover to Dingeldey, 4 April 1932.

94. *Berliner Lokal-Anzeiger*, 10 and 24 July 1932; *Der Tag*, 24 July 1932. The Hugenberg syndicate also published the Hugenberg-Papen correspondence of 23 and 26 July in a patently calculated attempt to emphasize the leadership qualitites of Hugenberg. *Der Tag*, 28 and 29 July 1932.

95. Dittmann, p. 4.

96. DZA Potsdam, Büro des Reichspräsidenten, 47, "Aufzeichnung über die Besprechung des Herrn Reichspräsidenten mit Adolf Hitler am 13. August 1932 nachmittags 4.15"; and Bracher, p. 616.

97. *Niederdeutsche Zeitung*, 16 August 1932; *Lippische Tages-Zeitung*, 17 August 1932. Scherl papers treated the confrontation over the Beuthener condemnation of the Nazi Potempa murderers in the same factual way, by simply presenting both sides of the issue. *Berliner Lokal-Anzeiger*, 14 August 1932.

98. HA, GHH, 400 101 290/39, Wilmowsky to Reusch, 9 August 1932.

99. AH Rohbraken, P 23, Hugenberg to Brosius, 18 August 1932, Hugenberg to Schleicher, 19 August 1932, and Schmidt-Hannover to Schleicher, 18 August 1932. The original of the latter is in BA Freiburg, Schleicher Papers, N 42/22. In support of this orientation, the ADV once more revived Class's prewar criticism of German society, *Wenn ich der Kaiser wär*, and joined in the support for a right-wing dictatorship. See DZA Potsdam, ADV, 165, GA Verhandlungsbericht, Rudolstadt, 9 September 1932.

100. AH Rohbraken, P 23, Hugenberg to Brosius, 18 August 1932, and P 17, Schmidt-Hannover to Schleicher, 18 August 1932.

101. AH Rohbraken, P 16, "Gespräch mit Freiherrn von Neurath am 1. September 32:11:30–12:55 Uhr," "Gespräch mit Freiherrn von Gayl am 1. September 32:1:10—2 Uhr."

102. BA Koblenz, R43I/2655, Hugenberg to Papen, 2 September 1932.

103. Ibid., Papen to Hugenberg, 3 September 1932. The original is in AH Rohbraken, P 17.

104. BA Koblenz, Silverbeg Papers, "Unterlage für die ausserordentliche Präsidialsitzung (des RDI) am 17. August 1932." For the continued pressure of industry in this matter see HA, GHH, 400 101 220/13b, Kastl to Papen, 7 September 1932, in RDI circular to members of the presidium and executive board, 8 September 1932.

105. For Hugenberg's insistence on the necessity of agrarian assistance, see Alfred Hugenberg, "Die Zeit ist da!" *Der Tag*, 18 August 1932. Here Hugenberg reiterates his thesis that "the born supporter of nonsocialist individualist economy is ... the farmer. Furthermore, the most pronounced individualist of modern history is the vigorous Indo-Germanic *Volk*.... *Volk* and farmer must live—then everything lives." Also see Paul Bang, "Autarkie oder Nationalwirtschaft?" *Der Tag*, 24 August 1932.

106. NSSA Osnabrück, 59, Report of the meeting of German National Reichstag delegates on 8 September 1932 in Hintzmann Report No. 2, 15 September 1932, and "Hugenberg: Reichsführertagung, 6 Oktober," *Unsere Partei*, 8 October 1932, p. 310.

107. Bracher, pp. 627–34; and Vogelsang, pp. 277–80.

108. The abandonment of the NSDAP by such agrarian leaders as Josef Sonntag, editor of the *Grüne Woche*, encouraged such speculation. AH Rohbraken, P 16, "Gespräch mit ... Herrn Josef Sonntag am 31.8.32 ..." See also BA Freiburg, Bredow Papers, N 97/1, "Kurze Orientierung ...," 6 September 1932.

109. HA, GHH, 400 101 2024/10, Blank to Reusch, 17 September 1932 and 21 September 1932. Hugenberg had thought the cabinet would try to establish a new party. BA Koblenz, Wegener Papers, 66, Hugenberg to Wegener, 19 September 1932.

110. HA, GHH, 400 101 293/24, Jarres to Reusch, 22 September 1932; and AH Rohbraken, P 17, Jarres to Vögler, 21 September 1932, in Vögler to Hugenberg, 22 September 1932. From the tone of the letter, Vögler was one of the industrialists who tended to support Hugenberg.

111. Ibid.

112. AH Rohbraken, P 17, Stinnes to Vögler, 19 September 1932.

113. Two days after heavy industrialist leaders discussed the problem of DNVP leadership at Krupp's Villa Hugel, Reusch wrote to the German National mayor of Düsseldorf that the attempt to oust Hugenberg had failed. HA, GHH, 400 101 293/10, Reusch to Lehr, 28 September 1932, and 400 101 290/36b Springorum to Reusch, 22 September 1932. After this meeting, Hugenberg wrote to Vögler as an associate in whom he could confide. AH Rohbraken, P 17, Hugenberg to Vögler, 25 September 1932. Undoubtedly, the German Nationalist leader expected the steel industrialists to subsidize his party, but the gentlemen of the *Ruhrlade* were not totally behind the DNVP. Consequently, Krupp would not personally meet with the German National leader.

HA, GHH, 400 101 290/27, Krupp to Reusch, 3 October 1932.

114. *Eiserne Blätter*, 9 October 1932, p. 502.

115. Alfred Hugenberg, "Partei?" *Berliner Lokal-Anzeiger*, 18 September 1932; *Der Tag*, 18 September 1932. Also, "Aufruf Hugenbergs," *Berliner Lokal-Anzeiger*, 14 September 1932. Goebbels set the tone of the Nazi repudiation of the German National position in his article, " Der Nationalverein des Dritten Reiches," *Der Angriff*, 21 September 1932. The DNVP organization fully supported Hugenberg and resolved: "The gates of the DNVP are opened wide for all Germans who feel themselves bound to the same goals. The party executive committee greets the measures and declarations of the chairman which are aimed at the unification (*Sammlung*) of all truly national forces." *Berliner Lokal-Anzeiger*, 7 October 1932. This attempt to reconcile all rightists to the party went so far as to include Hasslacher, an industrialist who had seceded from the party in 1930, as a candidate for the Reichstag on the DNVP lists in Dresden. Such a move, disheartened some party stalwarts who had adhered stringently to the Hugenberg-line and who now felt the leader was "selling out" to industrial interests. BA Koblenz, Traub 50, Kurt Guratzsch to Traub, 20 October 1932.

116. For details, see BA Koblenz, Hugenberg Papers, 211, 465.

117. Ibid., 211, Klitzsch and Lehmann to Aussendienst G.m.b.H., 14 October 1932.

118. Ibid., 211, Mann (Aussendienst) to Klitzsch, 17 October 1932.

119. HA, GHH, 400 101 2024/10, "Aufzeichnung über Besprechung im Klub von Berlin am Mittwoch, den 10. Oktober 1932 ..." This document is reproduced in Stegmann, "Zum Verhältnis" pp. 468–77.

120. *Völkischer Beobachter* (Bayernausgabe), 30 August 1932. Some of the Centrist politicians used this same theme. See Helmut J. Schorr, *Adam Stegerwald* (Recklinghausen, 1966), p. 251.

121. *Völkischer Beobachter* (Bayernausgabe), 9 September 1932.

122. See the cartoon with the caption: "Every vote for Hitler is a vote for Brüning! If you do not want that, then: German National!" *Unsere Partei*, 24 October 1932. Also *Berliner Lokal-Anzeiger*, 7 October 1932; *Alldeutsche Blätter*, 21 October 1932. Flugschriften des Scherl Verlags, *Der Nationalsozialismus und wir! Weg und Kampf des Scherlverlages* (Berlin, 1932), pp. 6–7. Hugenberg's final electoral appeal ended with the slogan, "With Hindenburg for Germany!" *Der Tag*, 6 November 1932.

123. BA Koblenz, ZSgI/44/2, DNVP "Vorwärts!" (This is German National propaganda disguised in a Socialist format, as the title indicates.) See also Flugschriften des Scherl Verlags, *Wie die Nazi kämpfen* (Hannover, 1932), p. 15; and "Um Harzburg!" *Der Tag*, 21 October 1932.

124. NSSA Osnabrück, 93, ADI, "Zur Lage," 7 September 1932.

125. *Der Nationalsozialismus und wir*, p. 4.

126. "Entschliessung des Parteivorstands," *Berliner Lokal-Anzeiger*, 7 October 1932.

127. *Der Tag*, 29 September 1932; *Der Angriff*, 30 September 1932.

128. *Der Angriff*, 25 October 1932. Hugenberg took Goebbels to court on this issue and forced him to desist. See AH Rohbraken, P 23, Hugenberg to Brosius, 26 October 1932. *Der Tag*, 1 November 1932.

129. See the reply to Scherl's pamphlet, *Der Nationalsozialismus und wir*, in *Der Angriff*, 5 October 1932. In linking the DNVP with the forces of evil, the NSDAP circulated rumors that the Central Association of German Citizens of the Jewish Faith had encouraged its members to vote for the Hugenberg party. In a telegram to local party associations just before the elections, Hugenberg urged party leaders to work harder against Nazi lies and specifically mentioned this one. SA Düsseldorf, Lehr Papers, 7, DNVP, Circular of the East Düsseldorf party office, 28 November 1932. Also NSSA Osnabrück, 52, unlabeled brochure, "Bericht über Wahlarbeit."

130. *Der Angriff*, 5 October 1932. Earlier in September, the Nazis had ferreted out the facts of Duesterberg's ancestry and published them. *Der Angriff*, 3 September 1932.

131. BA Koblenz, ZSgI/44/2, "Vorwärts!"

132. NSSA Aurich 1, Rundschreiben Nr. 45 der Parteizentrale. See also Gemein, p. 84.

133. The party journal complained of a "Black-Red-Brown Front" and charged National Socialist "Untermenschentum" with shooting at DNVP speakers and wounding four of them. *Unsere Partei*, 15 October 1932, pp. 326–28. See also "Schluss mit der nationalsozialistischen Klassenkampfhetze" and "Jugendkriminalität und Nationalsozialismus." *Unsere Partei*, 8 October 1932, pp. 316–17 and 322–23. The Hugenberg syndicate followed the same anti-Nazi line with only slight modifications. The Berlin publications gave good coverage to the German National charges against the NSDAP, but the provincial publication at Detmold, the *Lippische Tages-Zeitung*, did not take such a hostile line as did the Hanoverian *Niederdeutsche Zeitung*.

134. Goebbels, pp. 178–79. See also Schmidt-Hannover, pp. 299–300; and "Sie lügen und fälschen," *Unsere Partei*, 24 October 1932, p. 353.

135. The speech is reprinted in Josef Goebbels, *Signale der neuen Zeit* (Munich, 1934), pp. 91–94. See the DNVP view in *Berliner Illustrierter Nachtausgabe*, 20 October 1932; and "Um Harzburg," *Der Tag*, 21 October 1932.

136. AH Rohbraken, P 17, Hugenberg to Vögler, 19 October 1932.

137. Dittmann, p. 4.

138. NSSA Osnabrück, 112, "Wahlstatistisches."

139. *Unsere Partei*, 11 November 1932, p. 389.

140. Hugenberg urged von Papen not to resign. International Military Tribunal, *Trial of the War Criminals before the International Military Tribunal* (1952), vol. 40, Document Papen 87, p. 575. The DNVP disliked the idea of a resignation because it weakened the idea of authoritarian government. NSSA Aurich 1, Mitteilung Nr. 10.

141. DZA Potsdam, Büro des Reichspräsidenten, 47, "Aufzeichnung über den Empfang des Führers der Deutschnationalen Volkspartei, Geheimrat Hugenberg, beim Reichspräsidenten am Freitag, dem 18. November 1932, 11:30 Uhr."

142. DZA Potsdam, Büro des Reichspräsidenten, 47, Vögler to Baron von Schröder, 21 November 1932.

143. See ibid., for various discussions and the exchange of notes with party leaders. Also Bracher, pp. 656–77.

144. Vogelsang, pp. 329–33.

145. Feldman, *Army, Labor, and Industry*, p. 532.

146. *Der Tag*, 19 November 1932; Alfred Hugenberg, "Das Präsidialkabinett," *Der Tag*, 13 December 1932; and *Berliner Illustrierter Nachtausgabe*, 30 November 1932.

147. This formulation was used in a petition sent by Vögler to various Ruhr industrialists. DZA Potsdam, Büro des Reichspräsidenten, 47, Vögler to Schröder, 21 November 1932. Stegmann ("Zum Verhältnis," pp. 434–35), emphasizes this as a means of stressing the importance of the Keppler *Kreis*; Turner ("Grossunternehmertum und Nationalsozialismus," pp. 58–63), repudiates this view.

148. HA, GHH, 400 101 290/37, Reusch to Vögler, 20 November 1932. The German National Industrial Committee, sensitive to the trend among industrialists, moderated the DNVP's strong opposition to a Hitler chancellorship with the claim that the party did not oppose the Nazi's becoming chancellor, but only the NSDAP's claim to total partisan control (*Parteiherrschaft*). BA Koblenz, Schmidt-Hannover Papers, 72, "Vertrauliche Bermerkungen zur Lage," 8 December 1932.

149. See Hallgarten and Radkau, pp. 209–10.

150. J. W. Reichert, "Krisenwende der Eisenwirtschaft im Jahre 1932," in BA Koblenz, R13I/1094; and Hugenberg, "Eine neue Präsidialregierung," *Der Tag*, 15 December 1932. Krupp von Bohlen also noted this in his speech to the main committee of the RDI on 14 December 1932. *Geschäftliche Mitteilungen des RDI*, no. 27 (23 December 1932), Appendix I.

151. Krupp speech, ibid.

152. See Springorum's comments at the "60. ordentliche Mitgliederversammlung des Vereins ... dem 23. November 1932," *Langnam Mitteilungen*, no. 21 (1932):5–6. Also note, Max Schlenker, "Vorwort: Gesunde Wirtschaft im starken Staat," ibid., p. 1.

153. WA Bayer, Leverkusen, 62/10. 4e, summary of the Minutes of the Board of Directors, 25 November 1932. The RDI distinctly opposed the plans of Schleicher's commissar for employment (*Arbeitsbeschaffung*), Günther Gereke. See Dieter Petzina, "Hauptprobleme der deutschen Wirtschaftspolitik," *Vierteljahrshefte für Zeitgeschichte* 15 (1967):27.

154. Bracher, p. 677. The RDI's agrarian expert, Dr. Pietrkowski, clearly indicated the divergent approaches of these two sectors of the economy. Industrialists thought that the best way to overcome the crisis was through an extension of the market. This obviously included an increase in exports. On the other hand, agriculture could produce only 90 percent of the nation's food and therefore sought not an increased market, but an increase in prices. Since inflation would hurt "finished products," Pietrkowski concluded that the best way for agriculture to improve its buying power would be to cut back on costs. Minutes of the RDI Board of Directors, 25 November 1932, WA Bayer, Leverkusen, 62/10. 4e. See also Petzina, p. 32.

155. Reichert, as the spokesman for the iron industry, was especially sensitive to the attacks of the *Reichslandbund* in two articles—"The Error of German Export Policy: an Instructive Example" and "Expensively Purchased Export"—

which both appeared in the *Grüne Wochenschau*. HA, GHH, 400 101 24/3, Reichert (VDESI) to Poensgen, Kastl, Klöckner, Klotzbach, Krupp, etc., 12 December 1932 and 17 December 1932. A week later, the same journal directly attacked Krupp and Dr. Pietrkowski. Ibid., Reichert to Poensgen, Kastl, etc., 23 December 1932. Count Kalkreuth indicated that this was done without his knowledge and expressed his regrets. Ibid. Nevertheless, Wilmowsky, Krupp's brother-in-law, wrote directly to him requesting that this press attack be called off. HA, GHH, 400 101 290/39, Wilmowsky to Kalkreuth, 24 December 1932. The personal note of frustration was again conveyed in the RDI circular of 12 January 1933. HA, GHH, 400 101 24/3. This bewailed the continued attacks of the *Reichslandbund*, which spoke of the "plundering of agriculture in favor of the almighty interests of the moneybags of the internationally oriented export industry and its satellites." The personal note of complaint was evident when the author of the circular complained, "In the interest of the entire nation, it is not tolerable that the factual work of responsible men is damned through highly deplorable incitement." On this theme of industrial-agrarian collaboration at the turn of the year, see Stegmann, "Kapitalismus und Fascismus," p. 57.

156. This was the "unanimous" view of the RDI's board of directors. The board was convinced that the improvement of the economy depended on the replacement of "current insecurity by a stable government basis," since nothing could injure the psychological factors of the economy more than "continual domestic unrest." WA Bayer, Leverkusen, 62/10e, Minutes of the RDI Board of Directors, 25 November 1932.

157. "Präsidialsitzung des Reichsverbandes am 19. Januar 1933," *Geschäftliche Mitteilungen*, no. 2 (31 January 1933), p. 11.

158. HA, GHH, 400 101 220/13b, Herle circular of 17 December 1932, and HA, GHH, 400 101 24/3, RDI circular of 12 January 1933.

159. In the Schmidt-Hannover/Hugenberg papers, there is an undated memo which reads: "The *Reichslandbund* is prepared fully and completely to support a government of von Papen which adopts its [the *Reichslandbund's*] program [Resolution of 29 November 1932]. It would view it as a complete guarantee, if Geheimrat Hugenberg had a seat and a vote in the cabinet." S 43 Hannover. From these papers it is not clear whether this was the position of the *Landbund* or the position that Hugenberg wished it to accept. There is no doubt, however, that the Hugenberg party remained strongly in favor of the agrarian legislation which would win the support of the *Landbund*. See S 49 Hannover Memorandum of the Agricultural Committee of the DNVP [von Winterfeld et al.] to Schleicher, 13 December 1932. See also Cerny, p. 537 and Weissbecker, p. 414. Hugenberg maintained steady contact with Vögler and other leaders of heavy industry throughout these months (e.g., see HA, GHH, 400 101 290/37, Reusch to Vögler, 10 January 1933).

160. Alfred Hugenberg, "Das Präsidial Kabinett," *Der Tag*, 13 December 1932; Alfred Hugenberg, "Kontingente," *Der Tag*, 14 December 1932; and Alfred Hugenberg, "Eine neue Präsidialregierung," *Der Tag*, 15 December 1932. This same paper also heralded the attention which foreign economists gave to Hugenberg's ideas. Ibid., 23 December 1932. Not even von Schleicher could afford to take Hugenberg lightly. The chancellor proposed that the Ger-

man National leader suggest a candidate for the powerful position of state secretary in the Prussian Ministry of Interior. Hugenberg nominated von Bismarck but insisted that this not be interpreted as support for parliamentary responsibility. AH Rohbraken, P 17, Hugenberg to Schliecher, 21 December 1932.

161. NSSA Osnabrück, 3, Hintzmann Report No. 4, 30 December 1932.

162. *Ibid.*; and Schmidt-Hannover, p. 316.

163. AH Rohbraken, U 3, "Betr. Personalien bei einer evt. Regierungsbildung." With the "Sofortmassnahmen" were eleven pages listing personnel in various ministries. Next to each name was a comment regarding the party affiliation of the man and indicating the German National reaction to him. For example, in the list dealing with the Ministry of Economics, State Secretary Trendlenburg's name was followed by the comment, "DVP inclined to the left, must be removed"; Ministerial Director Posse was listed as "DVP, questionable"; *Oberregierungsrat* Dr. Willuhn was regarded as "DNVP, confidant." Members of the bureaucracy of Jewish ancestry were clearly indicated as such. They and members of the SPD were universally categorized by the comment, "Must be removed immediately."

164. AH Rohbraken, P 17, Hugenberg to von Winterfeld, 15 January 1933.

165. The NSDAP refused to elect any member of the DNVP to the presidium of the Reichstag, and the Nazis mocked Hugenberg by electing him Reichstag secretary. NSSA Osnabrück, 30, Hintzmann Report No. 2, December 1932. *Der Angriff*, 8 December 1932, headlined their humiliation, "German National defeats, but consolation prize for Hugenberg."

166. AH Rohbraken, P 16, Hugenberg to Hitler, 28 December 1933. The letter begins with reference to a meeting of the two men which had apparently taken place beforehand; possibly this was the meeting which leaders of the *Reichslandbund* had arranged at the end of November. See Cerny, pp. 536–37. During the Hitler era, Hugenberg fought against the claim that the DNVP, at the end of 1932, remained passive and waited for Hitler's invitation to join in negotiations to establish a cabinet of national unity. The German National leader claimed that it was the DNVP and not the NSDAP which initiated the movement that ultimately led to collaboration. This claim was made in a debate over the historical validity of an article in *Meyers Lexicon* which asserted that the National Socialists forced the reactionary DNVP out of fruitless opposition in 1933. AH Rohbraken, GB 30, Bang to Hugenberg, 14 October 1937. In the following months, Hugenberg corresponded with Mann, the NSDAP party leadership, the *Bibliographisches Institut A.G.*, and Klitzsch, in order to have the article changed. See the correspondence in AH Rohbraken, GB 30.

167. Vogelsang, p. 351. Dr. Österreich, who apparently had good connections with the German National press chief, Brosius, wrote that it would be good if their meeting led to a revival of the Harzburg Front. *Niederdeutsche Zeitung*, 7 January 1933.

168. HA, GHH, 400 101 290/36b, Springorum to Reusch, 28 December 1932; Turner, "Ruhrlade," p. 224. The significance of these meetings for the ultimate formation of the Hitler cabinet remains a controversial topic. Cf. Axel Kuhn, "Die Unterredung zwischen Hitler und von Papen im Hause des Barons von

Schröder," *Geschichte in Wissenschaft und Unterricht* 24 (1973):709–22; and Turner, "Grossunternehmertum und Nationalsozialismus," pp. 3–22.

169. Vögler was a longtime member of the twelve-man *Wirtschaftsvereinigung*; Springorum was elected to replace Winkhaus, who died at the end of 1932. AH Rohbraken, P 17, Hugenberg's undated membership list.

170. HA, GHH, 400 101 2007/16, Reusch to Kötter, 8 January 1933. Reusch indicated that Hitler sought to control the Reichswehr ministry but that such a post was "out of the question" for the Nazis. Nevertheless, Reusch believed "the National Socialist movement should be brought into the state." Cf. Czichon, pp. 51–52. As late as 27 January, Goebbels (*Vom Kaiserhof zur Reichskanzlei*, p. 249) thought that von Papen would be named chancellor.

171. HA, GHH, 400 101 293/10, Reusch to Lehr, 10 January 1933, and 400 101 290/37, Reusch to Vögler, 10 January, 18 January, and 23 January 1933. Turner's "Ruhrlade" (pp. 224–26) is undoubtedly the best treatment of these developments. In his last study, Hallgarten moderated his earliest interpretation (*Hitler, Reichswehr und Industrie*, pp. 110–11) but insisted that the meeting of Papen and Schröder "is rightly considered the beginning of the development of the Third Reich." Hallgarten and Radkau, p. 213.

172. AH Rohbraken, P 17, the Thyssen threat of 20 December is cited in Hugenberg to Vögler, 9 January 1933. This threat did not cause Hugenberg to panic, but he was very concerned. See AH Rohbraken, P 16, Hugenberg to Klitzsch, 9 January 1933.

173. AH Rohbraken, P 16, Hugenberg to Klitzsch, 9 January 1933.

174. AH Rohbraken, P 16, Hugenberg to Flick, 12 January 1932. Hugenberg sought Flick's aid with his concern's creditors at the Danat Bank. (An industrial consortium had just prevented the collapse and state control of their bank.) HA, GHH, 400 101 290/12, Fickler to Reusch, 2 January 1932. Party coffers, of course, were in no better shape. DNVP treasurer, Scheibe, pleaded with local party organizations for assistance because "contributions were no longer available." NSSA Osnabrück, 10, Treasurer to the Chairman of the Local Party Associations, 12 January 1933. Two weeks later, Scheibe begged for contributions so that he could pay the rent of the party central office. Ibid., Treasurer to the Chairman of the Local Party Associations, 24 January 1933.

175. AH Rohbraken, Hugenberg to Wegener, 2 January 1933. The dangerous economic condition of the Scherl *Verlag* was graphically pointed out to Hugenberg by Klitzsch, who anticipated that Scherl would run a deficit for five months in the coming year. AH Rohbraken, P 16, Klitzsch to Hugenberg, 30 January 1933. As far as industrial support was concerned, Hugenberg's basis for independence was circumscribed. As he wrote to Class, when the ADV's *Deutsche Zeitung* ran into financial difficulties: "You will not get any further with the West. I know just how it goes there. I still hope to get some funds, but do not believe that you will accomplish anything with a single conversation. My action results from von L's [presumably von Loewenstein's] agreement to still procure a certain retroactive electoral contribution for me and his willingness to take further action together with V. [presumablly Vögler] for press matters." AH Rohbraken, P 16, Hugenberg to Class, 4 January 1933. In this letter, Hugenberg confirmed an arrangement whereby the Pan-German paper

would provide one full page for the use of the DNVP in return for subsidies from the party. See AH Rohbraken, P 16, "Vertrags-Entwurf vom 15.1.1933." Thus while the Hugenberg concern had grave problems, it was still not bankrupt. (Indeed, while Hugenberg believed that "it was hopeless to count on the West in forming any detailed plan," the financial subsidies for the *Deutsche Zeitung* could be found only "if Klitzsch would undertake a certain limited risk.") AH Rohbraken, P 16, Hugenberg to Class, 4 January 1933.

176. DZA Potsdam, Büro des Reichspräsidenten, 47, "Aufzeichnung über die Besprechung mit den Vertretern des Reichslandbundes am Mittwoch, den 11. Januar ..." One of the representatives was Hugenberg's supporter Hans-Joachim von Rohr. See also, Horst Gies, "NSDAP und landwirtschaftliche Organisationen in der Endphase der Weimarer Republik," *Vierteljahrshefte für Zeitgeschichte*, 15 (1967):359; and Petzina, pp. 37–38.

177. Vogelsang, p. 364.

178. See Goebbels, *Vom Kaiserhof zur Reichskanzlei*, 234ff. Not only had the NSDAP lost in the federal elections, but its popularity declined markedly in provincial campaigns. Orlow, pp. 288–91, 297.

179. AH Rohbraken, GB 26. In this series of documents, the normal sequence is thus: a handwritten copy, a typed copy, and a printed copy. The absence of a printed copy in this file does not absolutely disprove the printing and circulation of the manuscript, but there is no indication that this pamphlet was ever published. Such a document could certainly have been used in Hugenberg's denazification proceedings when such material was widely employed by his defenders. It was not; this, coupled with the tone of the campaign as manifested in the *Lippische Tages-Zeitung*, makes it virtually certain that Hugenberg dropped the idea of publishing his manuscript.

180. Ibid., and *Lippische Tages-Zeitung*, 12 January 1933.

181. In contrast to previous coverage of Hugenberg's campaigns, the newspaper buried its report of this talk in page 5. The editors took great pains to point out that in contrast to Hitler's mass rallies, Hugenberg developed his ideas "in tranquillity." Despite the tactics of the Nazis, the paper indicated that collaboration was possible; the country needed more than unbridled idealism— it needed the experience of Hugenberg. *Lippische Tages-Zeitung*, 7 January 1933.

182. NSSA Osnabrück, 105 Mitteilung Nr. 1, 19 January 1933. In view of his wide-reaching authority over the total party organization, a moratorium for such an important election could not have been initiated without Hugenberg's permission.

183. Even Hugenberg's *Niederdeutsche Zeitung*, in the neighboring province of Hannover, indicated that the Nazis gained at the expense of the DNVP. *Niederdeutsche Zeitung*, 17 January 1933.

184. *Lippische Tages-Zeitung*, 16 January 1933.

185. Vogelsang, p. 363; and Dorpalen, p. 417.

186. NSSA Osnabrück, 10, Mitteilung Nr. 1, 19 January 1933.

187. Goebbels, *Vom Kaiserhof zur Reichskanzlei*, p. 243; and von Papen, *Wahrheit*, p. 263. The official German National statement refusing to support the Schleicher regime emphasized the need for a unified economic approach which would bridge the gap between "the city and the country." AH Rohbraken, P

17, statement of 21 January 1933. See also *Der Tag*, 25 January 1933.

188. BA Koblenz, Schmidt-Hannover Papers, 30, "Aufzeichnungen von Otto Schmidt-Hannover betreffend Regierungsbildung."

189. As Reusch wrote to Kötter on 8 January 1933: "In my view the year 1933 will seal our fate and render major foreign policy decisions. If we have a large, united, national front, then with the present attitude of the French we will also resolve the question of the corridor. If we remain internally divided, the resolution of such tasks is unthinkable—also our influence on the World Economic Conference will be totally different if we have a strong national government which bases itself on a majority of the people...." HA, GHH, 400 101 2007/16.

190. BA Koblenz, Schmidt-Hannover Papers, 30, "Aufzeichnungen."

191. Papen believed that "it would be a disaster of the Hitler movement collapsed or were crushed," because the Nazis were the "last remaining bulwark against communism in Germany...." See *Documents BFP*, vol. 4, Rumbold to Simon, 25 January 1933, p. 390.

192. HSA Düsseldorf, Hugenberg's Denazification, Lemgo Protokoll.

193. For example, the "old Januschauer" thought the traditional nationalists could readily manipulate the Nazis. See Meissner, p. 265; and note Schmidt-Hannover, pp. 319–20. The revelations of the budget committee of the Reichstag under the Communist Ernst Torgler exposed grave scandals in the *Osthilfe*, the agrarian assistance program for the East. Reportedly, Oldenburg-Januschau himself had already received M 454,000 of a M 621,000 loan. Publications of such information would not deter agrarian leaders from seeking a cabinet more friendly to agriculture. *Berliner Börsen Courier*, 19 January 1933. Anxious to eliminate socialist influence, industrialists like Vögler found hope in the tractability of Hitler and the Nazis.

194. BA Koblenz, Schmidt-Hannover Papers, 30, "Aufzeichnungen"; and see Hans Brosius, "Die Gründe der deutschnationalen Absage," *Niederdeutsche Zeitung*, 27 January 1933.

195. See the editorial of Dr. Österreich in *Niederdeutsche Zeitung*, 29 Janaury 1933; and "Zur Lage (Nr. 21)," 24 December 1932, in S 2 Hannover. Both falsely claim that Hugenberg had never opposed the appointment of Hitler as chancellor.

196. BA Koblenz, Schmidt-Hannover Papers, 30, "Aufzeichnung;" Schmidt-Hannover, pp. 332–33; Picker, p. 429. It is quite possible that Hugenberg had already discussed his desire to preside over a "crisis ministry", controlling all areas of the economy. In a memorandum dated 7 July 1933, Hugenberg referred to "prenegotiations" (*Vorverhandlungen*) at the home of County Kalkreuth during which Hitler accepted the idea of a joint economic ministry under the leadership of the German National—provided that Shacht would replace Luther as president of the Reichsbank. BA Koblenz, Wegener Papers, 74.

197. BA Koblenz, Schmidt-Hannover Papers, 30, "Aufzeichnung." See also Lutz Schwerin von Krosigk, *Es Geschah in Deutschland*, 3d rev. ed. (Tübingen and Stuttgart, 1952), p. 173; and Schmidt-Hannover, p. 334.

198. On this agreement with Seldte, see BA Koblenz, R53/99, Hugenberg to Seldte, 17 April 1933. Precisely when Hugenberg persuaded Seldte to accept the Ministry of Labor is unclear. I have followed Schmidt-Hannover's timetable on

the final negotiations for the cabinet. It is quite possible, however, that this polemical defense of Hugenberg was totally deceptive in this regard. Hugenberg might have played a more active role throughout the last weeks of January in assisting von Papen to form the new cabinet.

199. Hitler's willingness to grant Hugenberg control over the agrarian sector of the economy, despite the strength of Walter Darré's Nazi agricultural movement, provided the DNVP with an opportunity to reestablish its prestige among the farmers. See Horst Gies, "Die Nationalsozialistische Machtergreifung auf dem agrarpolitischen Sektor," *Zeitschrift für Agrargeschichte und Agrarsoziologie*, 16 (1968):210.

200. Meissner, pp. 269–70. See also, von Papen, *Wahrheit*, pp. 275–76.

201. Picker, p. 368.

202. AH Rohbraken, E 5, Vogelsang to Hugenberg, 17 January 1948.

203. *Lippische Tages-Zeitung*, 31 January 1933.

204. *Berliner Lokal-Anzeiger*, 30 January 1933.

205. France, Ministère des Affaires Étrangeres, *Documents Diplomatique Français*, 1st series, 3 (1967):18, de Jouvenal [French Ambassador at Rome] to Paul-Boncour, 18 March 1933.

206. Ibid., 2: 549, François-Ponçet (French Ambassador at Berlin) to Paul-Boncour, 1 February 1933.

207. Ibid., 2: 586, Laroche (French Ambassador at Warsaw) to Paul-Boncour, 8 February 1933.

208. Joseph Becker, "Zentrum und Ermächtigungsgesetz 1933," *Vierteljahrshefte für Zeitgeschichte* 9 (1961): 198, n 23.

209. BA Koblenz, R43I/1459, Minutes of the Reich Cabinet, 30 January 1933; and see Meissner, pp. 286–87. Hitler's conciliatory tactics went beyond promises on the structure of the cabinet. The new chancellor also rejected a change in the electoral law "because the German National party might suffer by it." U. S., *Documents on German Foreign Policy*, series C, 1 (1957): 16, "Extract from the Minutes of the Conference of Ministers ... February 1, 1933." (hereafter referred to as *German Documents.*)

210. Ibid., pp. 5–7, "Minutes of the Conference of Ministers ... January 31, 1933."

211. Gerhard Ritter, *The German Reisitance*, trans. R. T. Clark (London, 1958), p. 28.

Chapter 6

1. BA Koblenz, R43I/1459, Minutes of the Reich Cabinet, 1 February 1933.

2. "Warum ist jetzt eine starke Deutschnationale Partei notwendiger denn je?" *Nationaler Wille*, 11 February 1933, pp. 69–70. *Nationaler Wille* was the new name for the party journal, *Unsere Partei*.

3. NSSA Aurich, 1, Mitteilung Nr. 3, 15 February 1933.

4. Ibid.

5. NSSA Osnabrück, 11, Hagen to Nagel, 2 February 1933. Vagts, the chairman of the local party association in Bremen, agreed with Hagen. NSSA Osnabrück, 28, Note of 7 February 1933.

6. NSSA Osnabrück, 12, Hagen to von Winterfeld, 6 February 1933. Hagen

complained that the policy of the central office made electoral work extremely difficult. See ibid., Hagen to the Local Associations, 3 March 1933; and NSSA Osnabrück, 10, Hagen's comments on the electoral procedure, 6 February 1933.

7. From Reusch's correspondence it would seem that his whole support for von Papen's negotiations with Hitler centered on this development. Von Papen, as the leader of the DNVP, would establish an antisocialist party transcending confessional ties. With the prospects of calling upon such a vast electorate, the new bourgeois party would divide the Nazis and truly "frame" Hitler. How much von Papen manipulated Reusch and the other industrialists instead of Hitler is not clear. See HA, GHH, 400 101 290/37, Reusch to Vögler, 10 January, 18 January, and 23 January 1933. Note also Schmidt-Hannover, pp. 326–27.

8. Hugenberg possibly judged the small-mindedness of his party correctly. The local party association in Westphalia apparently circulated a statement sharply condemning Hugenberg for giving Rademacher, an industrialist candidate who had seceded from the party in 1930, a secure place in their constituency. BA Koblenz, Wegener Papers, 14, undated circular from "Several severely deceived members of the Westphalian Regional Association of the DNVP." A copy of the same, along with a similar undated memo signed by "Several friends of Prof. Müller-Lenhartz," is in S 29 Hannover. Possibly, these circulars can be associated with the anti-Hugenberg propaganda later attributed to Oberfohren.

9. Von Papen, *Wahrheit*, p. 299; and AH Rohbraken, P 25, von Papen to Hugenberg, (copy), n.d. The vice-chancellor was most anxious to win the Catholic vote for the nationalist cause, and the Hugenberg press realized that it could exploit von Papen's Catholicism. See *Niederdeutsche Zeitung*, 12 February 1933. In explaining the role of the new front, party officials emphasized that it was not to be a permanent organization, since neither the DNVP nor the Stahlhelm intended to surrender their "thoroughly different tasks that lie in different fields." Just as the Reich Committee against the Young Plan had been geared for a specific purpose, so, the party central office argued, after the elections the work of the Battle Front was completed. Once the balloting was over, the DNVP would be involved with its "task of political and parliamentary leadership and responsibility in the state" and the Stahlhelm with its "establishment of a military footing and physical training of youths." The party thus admitted that the Battle Front was a political fiction and, at the same time, produced a second fiction. NSSA Osnabrück, 25, Mitteilung Nr. 6, 16 February 1933. The neat separation of the DNVP and the Stahlhelm into distinct wings working on different levels for the same goal was more a desideratum of the German Nationals than a reality. The Stahlhelm, while not a party, was very active in political affairs, and the DNVP, while not a military group, was more than ever organizing its own youth force. The German National youth leader, Herbert von Bismarck, demanded that his protégés wear distinctive green shirts and put all nonparty insignia aside. Ibid., Rundschreiben 10 der Reichsjugendführer, 22 February 1933. The DNVP and the Stahlhelm were, however, able to agree that all young men should have

one year of paramilitary training and that the German Nationals would provide this for those right-wing youths who were not members of the Young Stahlhelm. DZA Potsdam, Stahlhelm, 281, Rundschreiben Nr. 9, 3 February 1933.

10. *Der Tag*, 12 February 1933; and *Nationaler Wille*, 18 February 1933, p. 82.

11. "Hugenberg Rede," *Der Tag*, 4 March 1933.

12. Geschäftliche Mitteilung des RDI, 15 (1933):27; and HA, GHH, 400 101 220/14, circular to Herle, Kastl, and Krupp, 18 February 1933. Concerned industrialists were skeptical about enthusiastic support for the cabinet and urged a cautious but benevolent approach. See HA, GHH, 400 101 2007/16, Reusch to Kötter, 3 February and 9 February 1933.

13. Czichon, p. 53.

14. HA, GHH, 400 101 2024/11, Blank to Reusch, 21 February 1933, which includes detailed notes on the meeting—reprinted in Stegmann, "Zum Verhaltnis," pp. 477–80.

15. AH, Rohbraken, P 17, Hugenberg to Schacht, 2 March 1933.

16. AH, Rohbraken, P 17, Scheibe to Hugenberg, 1 March 1933, and Schacht to Hugenberg, 3 March 1933. See also, HA, GHH, 400 101 290/36b, Springorum to Reusch, 21 February 1933—reprinted in Stegmann, "Zum Verhaltnis," pp. 480–81.

17. AH Rohbraken, P 17, Hugenberg to Scheibe, 19 March 1933. This correspondence, dating after the election, dealt with the final settlement of accounts.

18. AH Rohbraken, P 17, Schacht to Scheibe, 15 March 1933, and Scheibe to Hugenberg, 15 March 1933. According to the latter, the Papen fund was to receive M 100,000 from I. G. Farben, M 35,000 from "western industry," and M 27,500 from western lignite corporations.

19. See AH Rohbraken, P 17, Schacht to Scheibe, 15 March 1933, and Scheibe to Hugenberg, 15 March 1933. The DNVP treasurer confided that central German lignite industries had contributed more than their share to the party—a fact of which Schacht was presumably uninformed.

20. See BA Koblenz, Wegener Papers, 14, undated circular from "Several severely deceived members of the Westphalian Regional Association of the DNVP." Possibly, this is one of the anti-Hugenberg circulars later attributed to Oberfohren.

21. It is not clear whether this and all the money raised by the coaling interests in the last years of the republic were derived from a special levy on the *Kohlenseite* of heavy industry or from investments and funds administered by the *Wirtschaftsvereinigung*. The amount discussed is very close to the quarter of a million marks supposedly contributed by western industry to the Hugenberg group as its share of the three-million-mark levy. This sum was to go directly to Hugenberg and not pass through the fund, "Nationale Treuhand, Dr. Hjalmar Schacht." AH Rohbraken, P 17, Schacht to Scheibe, 15 March 1933. In his accounting, however, Hugenberg noted that the sum was contributed to him by various "Parties" (*Seiten*), "partially as campaign assistance and partially as monies at his disposal for political purposes." AH Rohbraken, P 16, memorandum of 20 April 1933. Expenditures reveal the close relationship among the DNVP, the Hugenberg syndicate, and the Pan-German League:

DNVP—Outstanding printing costs and electoral
   publications (Scherl)
   (Remainder from the party treasury)   M 165,671.68
Regional Association Westphalia-East   6,000.00
National Club   1,000.00
For maintenance of the *Südeutsche Zeitung*   48,755.82
Reimbursement to the Telegraphen-Union   30,000.00
ADV Defense Fund (*Wehrschatz*)   20,000.00
For maintenance of the *Niederdeutsche Zeitung*   10,000.00
Petty Cash (*Verschiedenes*)   2,800.00
                                                          ─────────────
                                                          M 284,227.50

22. NSSA Osnabrück, 52, Rundschreiben Nr. 2 der Deutschnationalen
Schriftenvertriebsstelle, 8 February 1933. Hugenberg's papers widely circulated
the fact that cabinet members attended the premiere performance of the Ufa's
production, *Morgenrot*. The picture, circulated by Scherl, shows Hitler seated
between Hugenberg and von Papen; the Nazi leader was literally "framed in"
(*eingerahmt*) by the conservatives. *Berliner Lokal-Anzeiger*, 3 February 1933.
Morgenrot was not a Nazi film, but it was a very nationalistic one. Its theme
emphasized the common goals but slightly divisive approach of the exuberant
younger generation and the cautious older one. The film is preserved in the
Friedrich-Wilhelm-Murnau Stiftung in Wiesbaden. Cf. Hull (p. 17), who arbitrarily asserts that this film was made at the request of the NSDAP.
   23. BA Koblenz, Deulig Tonwoche No. 57/1933. The *Ufa* controlled three very
important newsreel shows (*Wochenschauen*) presented in German theaters: the
Ufa-Tonwoche, the *Deulig Tonwoche*, and the *Ufa Woche*. See Traub, *Ufa*, p. 87. Note
also the coverage of the DNVP rally in BA Koblenz, Deulig Tonwoche No.
59/1933.
   24. These theaters had approximately 106,302 seats. Truab, *Ufa*, p. 156.
   25. NSSA Osnabrück, 10, Blurb and Rundschreiben Nr. 1, 3 February 1933.
Propaganda pamphlets included titles such as *Die Nationalsozialisten, Nationalsozialismus und Zentrum, DNVP und NSDAP*, and *Vom Kinderkreuz zum
Hakenkreuz*. These had been produced for the last electoral campaign and consequently expressed an ambivalent or hostile attitude toward the different
wings of the NSDAP.
   26. *Der Tag*, 2 March 1933. Hugenberg used the state-controlled radio partially because he was ill with a respiratory infection from the end of February
through the middle of March. BA Koblenz, Wegener Papers, 66, Wegener to
Gertrude Hugenberg, 23 February and 12 March 1933. See also the *Niederdeutsche Zeitung*, 23 February 1933.
   27. *Der Tag*, 28 February 1933; and *Niederdeutsche Zeitung*, 22 March 1933.
   28. Hugenberg's speech on the radio, 1 March 1933, in *Nationaler Wille*, 4
March 1933, p. 126.
   29. NSSA Osnabrück, 25, Mitteilung Nr. 5 der Parteizentrale, 10 March 1933.
   30. Dittmann, p. 4.
   31. Ibid.; and *Nationaler Wille*, 11 March 1933, p. 137.
   32. Karl Dietrich Bracher, "Stufen der Machtergreifung," in Karl Dietrich

Bracher, Wolfgang Sauer and Gerhard Schulz, *Die Nationalsozialistische Machtergreifung* (Cologne and Opladen, 1962), p. 146.

33. NSSA Osnabrück, 11, Hagen to the Central Office, 22 March 1933.

34. André François-Ponçet, *The Fateful Years*, trans. Jacques LeClerq (New York, 1949), p. 66.

35. *German Documents*, "Minutes of the Conference of Ministers on 28 February 1933," p. 90.

36. *Hugenbergs Ringen*, 1:30.

37. *Nuremberg Trials*, "Reich Cabinet Conference, 15 March 1933," 31:407.

38. Ibid.

39. Ibid., "Ministers' Conference with Hitler," 31:412; see also Meissner, p. 291.

40. Brüning, *Memoiren*, pp. 654–55; *Hugenbergs Ringen*, 1:31.

41. Schmidt-Hannover, p. 351.

42. "Fraktionssitzung am 11. April 193," *Nationaler Wille*, 15 April 1933, p. 201. Hugenberg said that he had not given up the chairmanship of the party because he needed it as the "organized supporter of the concepts" that he represented in the cabinet. At the very beginning of the electoral campaign, Hugenberg pleaded wih his followers to understand that "it is now better for me to work than to talk and campaign." *Nationaler Wille*, 18 February 1933, p. 83. The party emphasized Hugenberg's decision by stressing his ministerial activities. See "Minister Hugenberg arbeitet," ibid., 25 March 1933, p. 161. Hugenberg himself argued that Frederick the Great was not only a great warrior, but also an economic leader. Alfred Hugenberg, "Der Geist von Potsdam," *Lippische Tages-Zeitung*, 14 April 1933. Note also Heinrich Class, "Deutsche Ostern," *Alldeutsche Blätter*, 22 April 1933.

43. Interview with Herr Hansjoachim von Rohr on 19 May 1967. BA Koblenz, Wegener Papers, 66, von Buchholz to Wegener, 23 February 1933.

44. The non-Nazi ministers in no way formed a bloc of opposition in the cabinet. Each man, except Seldte, was more or less an administrative expert in his own field. Hitler rapidly assumed the role of coordinator. See Meissner, p. 313. Not only did Hugenberg not oppose Hitler strongly, but he pointedly thanked him for the "splendid success that he achieved at the meeting of the Reichstag." BA Koblenz, R43I/1460, Minutes of the Reich Cabinet, 24 March 1933. Hugenberg thought the DNVP Reichstag delegation had been too reserved in expressing their gratitude. NSSA Osnabrück, 25, Hintzmann Report No. 8, 24 March 1933. The scanty records of the vice-chancellor's office which have been preserved indicate some attempt on the part of the minister and his subordinates to use von Papen as an arbitrator in differences with the Nazis, but these detail no coordinated attempt to keep Hitler "framed in" (e.g., see BA Koblenz, R53/23, von Rohr to von Papen, 6 May 1933 and Hugenberg to Hitler, 24 May 1933).

45. Bang was intimately connected with the *Bund für nationale Wirtschaft und Werksgemeinschaft*, which had organized many smaller industries against the RDI in 1924. Thieme, pp. 387–88.

46. Large steel corporations soon objected to Bang's partisanship for smaller, less efficient firms. BA Koblenz, R13I/1078, "Entwurf, 10 April 1933."

47. Bracher. "Stufen der Machtergreifung," pp. 279–80. Hugenberg used anti-Semitic prejudice and his own hostility against the Socialists as guide-lines in purging civil service personnel from the ministries under his control. See AH Rohbraken, U 3, DNVP party office [Nagel] to Hugenberg, 7 April 1933, and "Minister Hugenberg an der Arbeit," *Nationaler Wille*, 18 April 1933, 190–91.

48. Hermann Rauschning, *The Conservative Revolution* (New York, 1941), p. 3.

49. Interview with Herr Hansjoachim von Rohr on 19 May 1967.

50. *Der Tag*, 20 May 1933.

51. To protect native produce, Hugenberg and his state secretary secured approval for raising tariffs on such essential items as grains, milk, and eggs. Similarly, they revised trade treaties to favor the interests of the German farmer. Legislation promoting the availability of insecticides and regulating the slaughtering of animals was also introduced. In addition, the Ministry of Agriculture sponsored direct aid for the maintenance of agricultural buildings and for the prevention of foreclosure. BA Koblenz, R431/1459 and 1460. And see "Minister Hugenberg arbeitet," *Nationaler Wille*, 25 March 1933, p. 161; and *Der Tag*, 3 May 1933.

52. Since this would mean a rise in the cost of margarine or the purchase of the more expensive butter, poor people—an estimated 12 million—would receive special rebates in the form of government certificates enabling them to pay the increase. Revenue would largely come from the tariffs introduced. See discussions in BA Koblenz, R 431/1460, Minutes of the Reich Cabinet, 2 March, 7 March, 11 March, and 20 March 1933. Also "Wende in der deutschen Agrarpolitik," *Nationaler Wille*, 1 April 1933, p. 174.

53. "Die Rettung des Deutschen Bauern" (Hugenberg speech at the Agricultural Exhibition on 20 May 1933), *Nationaler Wille*, 27 May 1933, pp. 285–86. Hugenberg argued that a third of the nation was involved in agriculture and yet it received only a sixth of the national income. *Der Tag*, 20 May 1933.

54. *Der Tag*, 2 June and 7 June 1933; see also "Bauernbefreiung von den Schuldenfesseln," *Nationaler Wille*, 3 June 1933, p. 303.

55. "Landwirtschaft und Zinsproblem," *Nationaler Wille*, 13 May 1933, p. 258, and Gies, "Die Nationalsozialistische Machtergreifung," pp. 214–23.

56. NSSA Osnabrück, 110 [University professor] Hoffmann to Hagen, 13 April 1933.

57. NSSA Osnabrück, 28, Hagen to the Central Office, 8 April 1933.

58. NSSA Osnabrück, 12, Scheibe to Hagen, 21 April 1933. The leader of the German National Industrialists informed his associates that the situation was "worse than 1918." See ibid., Scheibe to German National Industrialists, 12 June 1933.

59. DZA Potsdam, DNVP, 19 Regional Association Frankfurt/Main to Hergt, 3 March 1933; Regional Association Hannover-South to Local Association Hannover of the DNVP, 7 April 1933; and Report from the Regional Association Kiel, 10 April 1933. Winterfeld implored Göring to guarantee equal rights to the DNVP in local government; his plea for a public agreement remained fruitless. BA Koblenz, Schmidt-Hannover Papers, 30, von Winterfeld to Gör-

ing, 27 March 1933.

60. BA Koblenz, R43I/1460, Minutes of the Reich Cabinet, 4 April 1933.

61. NSSA Osnabrück, 11, Party Central Office to Hagen, 24 April 1933; Bracher, "Stufen der Machtergreifung," pp. 210–11; and Friedrich Freiherr Hiller von Gaertringen, "Das Ende der Deutschnationalen Volkspartei im Frühjahr 1933," in Jasper, pp. 251–52.

62. LA Schleswig, DNVP, Statement of Dr. Rasmuss, Regional Leader of the DNVP in Kiel, 9 May 1933. See also Stoltenberg, pp. 151, 186. Oberfohren's distrust of the Nazis had led him, during discussions of the Enabling Act, to contact Brüning. Brüning, Brief, p. 17; cf. *Memoiren*, pp. 653–57.

63. LA Schleswig, DNVP, Records of the Police President in Kiel, 27 March 1933.

64. AH Rohbraken, P 25, undated notes of party caucus [ca. 7 April 1933]. Oberfohren wrote directly to the deputy party chairman, von Winterfeld, on 8 April 1933, explicitly stating that the anti-Hugenberg circulars attributed to him were totally false and that he had never been given a fair hearing. *Niederdeutsche Zeitung*, 12 April 1933. See also LA Schleswig, DNVP, Statement of Dr. Rasmuss, 9 May 1933; and Fritz Tobias, *The Reichstag Fire*, trans. Arnold J. Pomerans (New York, 1964), pp. 107, 110, 293–312.

65. NSSA Osnabrück, 25, Rundschreiben Nr. 23 der Parteizentrale, 27 March 1933.

66. NSSA Osnabrück, 25, Hintzmann Report No. 9, 12 April 1933. Here Hintzmann summarized the previous day's discussion in the meeting of the Reichstag delegates. Hugenberg had demanded "absolute unity" and an end to grumbling. Apparently, he also informed his followers of his isolation in the cabinet and convinced them that his task thus depended solely on "his personal relation to the Reich Chancellor."

67. "Minister Hugenberg vor.der Fraktion," *Eiserne Blätter*, 23 April 1833, pp. 219–20.

68. AH Rohbraken, P 17, von Wahlert to Nagel, 23 March 1933.

69. Hugenberg himself had written to Goebbels objecting to this policy, but in the revolutionary atmosphere of March 1933 such objections hardly affected developments. AH Rohbraken, P 25, Hugenberg to Goebbels, 11 March 1933. The film industry was even more frightened than the newspapers. Losses over one film could run into the millions. In line with the new governmental approach, the *Ufa*, by the end of April 1933, had purged most of its Jewish personnel. Not only actors and directors were affected, but also "nationalist Jews" in the administration. On 25 April, the board of directors sanctioned the purchase of rights to the film, *Hitlerjunge Quex*, and by 16 May the firm had rented *SA Mann Brand* to show in its theaters. BA Koblenz, R109/1028, 1029, Minutes of the *Ufa* Board of Directors, 11 April, 25 April, 28 April, and 16 May 1933.

70. Klitzsch was "very affected" (*sehr gepackt*) by the approach of the editorial staff, and Hugenberg was angered at Kriegk's position. AH Rohbraken, P 16, Klitzsch to Hugenberg, 25 April 1933 (with an enclosure detailing Kriegk's complaints).

71. Picker, p. 278.

72. NSSA Aurich 1, Rundschreiben Nr. 43, 22 May 1933. NSSA Osnabrück,

21, Politische Mitteilung Nr. 2, 27 May 1933; and NSSA Osnabrück, 26, Führerbrief 2, 6 June 1933. There is an excellent collection of Nazi anti-Hugenberg attacks in AH Rohbraken, P 27.

73. AH Rohbraken, P 16, Hugenberg to Göring, 6 May 1933. See also BA Koblenz, R 53/99, Hugenberg to Seldte, 3 April 1933, in Hugenberg to von Papen, 4 April 1933. The Nazis were not the only ones to cause trouble for the "economic dictator." Despite Hugenberg's demands that Seldte transfer the departments dealing with social policy from the Ministry of Labor to the Ministry of Economics, as had apparently been agreed, the Stahlhelm leader refused to honor his commitment. AH Rohbraken, P 16, Hugenberg to Seldte, 17 April 1933.

74. Gies, "Die Nationalsozialistische Machtergreifung," p. 229.

75. Hitler declared that Schmidt was hostile to him and his movement and demanded that Schmidt make a binding statement renouncing his anti-Nazi approach before he could be accepted for such a position. Schmidt apparently refused to do this. S 40 Hannover, Hugenberg to Hitler, 11 May 1933. Schmidt was so affected by the dire political situation that he suffered a physical and/or nervous collapse in the middle of May and was unable to play a role in the last weeks of the party's existence. BA Koblenz, Schmidt-Hannover Papers, 37, Schmidt to German National Reichstag delegates, 10 May 1933, and the enclosed doctor's certificate.

76. NSSA Osnabrück, 11, Hagen to the Party Central Office, 21 April 1933.

77. One German National Reichstag delegate argued, "Of course, I agree with the basic thought that it is not a matter of preserving a party, but of carrying out the political views and goals that it represents." To go from this point of view to the decision to carry out these goals through the NSDAP was only a small step. See NSSA Osnabrück, 28, Hintzmann to Local Association Osnabrück, 22 April 1933; and ibid., 11, Hagen to Hugenberg, 13 April 1933.

78. NSSA Aurich 1, Rundschreiben Nr. 36 [ca. 26 April 1933]. And see Roloff, pp. 147–60.

79. LA Schleswig, DNVP, Records of the Police Presidium.

80. AH, Rohbraken, P 17, "Aufzeichnung über die Besprechung des Herrn Reichspräsidenten mit dem Reichswirtschafts und Ernährungsminister Hugenberg und den stellvertretenden Führer der Deutschnationalen Front von Winterfeld am 17. Mai 1933 11 Uhr 45." After this meeting, von Winterfeld again sought to influence the president through Meissner. See NSSA Osnabrück, 12, von Winterfeld to Meissner, 23 May 1933.

81. Anton Ritthaler, "Eine Etappe auf Hitlers Weg zur Ungeteilten Macht: Hugenbergs Rücktritt als Reichsminister," *Vierteljahrshefte für Zeitgeschichte*, 8 (1960): 196–97. Hugenberg's ministry also sought to convince the vice-chancellor that his agricultural policies had already produced results and were establishing the basis for sound development in the entire economy. BA Koblenz, R52/23, von Rohr to von Papen, 6 May 1933. Rohr specifically requested that the vice-chancellor make sure that Hitler "be instructed" of these developments.

82. BA Koblenz, Wegener Papers, 74, Hugenberg's Memorandum, 7 July 1933.

83. "Hugenbergs Appell an Amerika," *Eiserne Blätter*, 5 March 1933. The Foreign Office under von Neurath had been preparing for the same conference. See John L. Heinemann, "Constantin von Neurath and German Policy at the London Economic Conference of 1933. Backgrounds to the Resignation of Alfred Hugenberg," *Journal of Modern History*, 41 (1969): 164–67.

84. *German Documents*, 1:293–97, Hugenberg to Hitler, 16 April 1933. A copy of this memo was sent to von Papen, BA Koblenz, R53/99, Hugenberg to von Papen, 16 April 1933.

85. *German Documents*, 1:335–42, "Minutes of the Economic Policy Committee, April 24, 1933." These minutes list Bang and not Hugenberg as the participant from the Ministry of Economics, but the text indicates that the minister himself presented and defended his own ideas. In the eyes of officials in the chancellery, the conclusions of the meeting amounted to a rejection of Hugenberg's proposals "on all sides, although without a formal vote." Ibid., p. 414, n 4.

86. The cabinet accepted von Neurath's position yet sent an evasive reply to the United States. *German Documents*, 1:380–81, "Session of May 5, 1933."

87. *German Documents*, 1:406–09, "Extract from the Minutes, May 12, 1933."

88. Ibid.; and p. 408, "Minute by Ministerial Director Ritter." Despite this tepid treatment of his views, Hugenberg later claimed that his ideas "were basically accepted by the entire cabinet" except for the Foreign Office, which was still "burdened" with Stresemann's approach. BA Koblenz, Wegener Papers, 74, Hugenberg's Memorandum, 7 July 1933.

89. Note also von Neurath's earlier objections to Hugenberg's tariff policy in BA Koblenz, R43I/1459, Minutes of the Reich Cabinet, 16 February and 27 February 1933.

90. On 22 April, the Hungarian Minister President Gömbös wrote to Hitler complaining about the exclusion of his country's agricultural produce from Germany. *German Documents*, 1:327: Hitler replied, on 28 April, that in the interests of developing "into political harmony the spiritual harmony already existing" he would seek an improvement. Ibid., 1:358. Later, when Hungarians initiated retaliatory measures against Germany, von Neurath informed Hugenberg that the "dilatory treatment" given to the Hungarian requests created a situation "very undesirable from the viewpoint of foreign policy." Ibid., 1:355. In addition, Hugenberg had informed the Italian ambassador of his plans for economic development, and the ambassador rejected these ideas. Ibid., 1:413–14, "Memorandum by the State Secretary."

91. Politisches Archiv des Auswärtigen Amtes, Bonn (henceforth AA Bonn), Büro Reichsminister, 119/4 Weltwirtschaftskonferenz, vol. 1, von Bülow to von Neurath, 9 June 1933. Wilmowsky, accompanied by Dr. Hahn, visited State Secretary Bülow to express his concern.

92. BA Koblenz, R43I/1462, Minutes of the Reich Cabinet, 31 May 1933.

93. *German Documents*, 1:506, von Neurath to Hugenberg, 1 June 1933.

94. BA Koblenz, Wegener Papers, 74, Hugenberg's Memorandum, 7 July 1933.

95. *German Documents*, 1:545, "Extract from the Minutes of the Cabinet Sessions of June 8, 1933."

96. Ibid., 1:562–67, "Unsigned Memorandum."

97. AA Bonn, Büro Reichsminister, 175/1, Hugenberg Memorandum, Neurath's statement of 19 June 1933. Hugenberg's provincial papers prefaced their front-page coverage of this memorandum with a text implying that the minister's memorandum was, indeed, an official statement of the German delegation. *Neiderdeutsche Zeitung*, 17/18 June 1933; *Lippische Tages-Zeitung*, 17 June 1933. In Berlin, however, the *Berliner Local-Anzeiger*, 17 June 1933, seemed to stress the personal aspect of the memorandum, emphasizing that "the basis of the views (*Anschauungen*) of the German economic leader lay in this [memorandum] clear and open before the entire world." While the *Lokal-Anzeiger* gave this news front-page coverage, *Der Tag*, on 16 June 1933, buried its report of the memorandum deep inside the paper.

98. *Lippische Tages-Zeitung*, 18 June 1933.

99. AA Bonn, Büro Reichsminister, 175/1, Hugenberg Memorandum, Neurath statement of 19 June 1933. The Foreign Office did everything possible to block publication of the interview in the German press, and Hugenberg's *Lokal-Anzeiger* cooperated. The Ministry of Propaganda believed that because of the time factor, several papers would probably still print it. Ibid., 119/4, Weltwirtschaftskonferenz, Brauweiler to Aschmann, 18 June 1933.

100. S 33 Hannover, Schacht's "Zum Briefe des Herrn Minister Hugenberg an Hernn v. Neurath vom 21. Juni 1933." Hugenberg rejected this rebuttal in his deposition, "Zu der Erklärung des Herrn Reichsbankpräsidenten Dr. Schacht vom 23. Juni 1933." AA Bonn, Büro Reichsminister, 175/1, Hugenberg Memorandum. See copies of many of these documents in BA Koblenz, Wegener Papers, 74.

101. AA Bonn, Büro Reichsminister, 175/1, von Neurath's statement of 19 June 1933. The foreign minister claimed that he knew in general of Hugenberg's planned interview with the reporter from the *Telegraphen-Union* but only learned its contents later.

102. Ibid. See the six-page rebuttal, Hugenberg to Neurath, 21 June 1933. Hugenberg's state secretary, Bang, supported his chief but, in doing so, substantiated Neurath's charges. The refusal of the Foreign Office publicly to accept the memorandum as an official position was, in his view, "the old drama," i.e., a refusal to permit "public expression of fundamental differences in opinion." S 33 Hannover, Bang to Hugenberg, 20 June 1933.

103. AA Bonn, Büro Reichsminister, 175/1, von Neurath's statement of 19 June 1933.

104. HSA Düsseldorf, Hugenberg's Denazification Process, Lemgo Protokoll. The same thought, in milder form, was expressed in his memorandum of 7 July 1933. BA Koblenz, Wegener Papers, 74.

105. NSSA Aurich 1, Anlage zum Rundschreiben Nr. 10, 10 June 1933. See also *Völkischer Beobachter*, Berliner Ausgabe, 10 June 1933.

106. He wrote this after the Nazi, Erich Koch, had been placed in charge of East Prussia (as *Oberregierungspräsident*) against the wishes of the DNVP. Hugenberg noted that the collaboration of Göring in the Prussian cabinet and Hitler in the Reich cabinet made it impossible for him to do anything. AH Rohbraken, P 17, Hugenberg to von Restorff, 7 June 1933.

107. In response to the pressure of the NSDAP against Hugenberg, the DNF

commented: "There can arise no doubt as to the seriousness of the situation in foreign policy. Just because of this reason, the departure of Hugenberg from the cabinet would be intolerable. He has the benefit of great respect in foreign lands." NSSA Osnabrück, 53, von Winterfeld to the Local Leaders, 15 May 1933. Bracher has insightfully analyzed Hugenberg's tactics in his "Stufen der Machtergreifung," p. 212.

108. See BA Koblenz, Schmidt-Hannover Papers, 57, undated memorandum.

109. *German Documents*, 1:603, "Extract from the Minutes of the Conference of Ministers, June 23 1933." In his memoirs, Meissner indicated that the conflict was primarily one between Hugenberg and Neurath. Meissner, p. 316.

110. NSSA Aurich 1, Rundschreiben Nr. 37, 28 April 1933, and Rundschreiben Nr. 43, 22 May 1933. The DNVP in Danzig clearly opposed the desires of the local NSDAP to win an absolute majority and fought a hard campaign. The Nazis directed their propaganda "mainly against the DNVP" with such vehemence that Hugenberg's followers charged that the League of Nations might let Poland occupy the city. *German Documents*, 1:287–88, Hugenberg to Hitler, 12 April 1933.

111. *Germania*, 20 June 1933. The Hugenberg press argued that the terms for a coalition presented by the NSDAP amounted to a demand for the dissolution of the DNVP and that the acceptance of such an agreement was not consonant with the "honor and dignity of a party." *Der Tag*, 20 June 1933. The Nazis argued that the "intrigues" of the German Nationalists had made cooperation impossible. *Völkischer Beobachter*, Berliner Ausgabe, 20 June 1933.

112. Otto Schmidt-Hannover, "Zum 19. Juni," *Nationaler Wille*, 17 June 1933, p. 530. This issue of the party magazine was filled with tributes to Hugenberg, whose birthday was 19 June.

113. NSSA Aurich 1, Rundschreiben 43, 22 May 1933. One issue of the party journal, *Nationaler Wille*, 13 May 1933, was confiscated because it reported a clash between the SA and Hugenberg supporters in Berlin. The party offices eliminated the story and put out a new edition of the same number in twenty-four hours. The following issue was also confiscated because of a report on a similar clash in Holstein—the chairman of the German National workers' organization had been dragged out of a local meeting by the Nazis and thrown down a flight of stairs. This issue of the journal was not replaced.

114. The central party office advised that "the most practical form of membership meeting is with invited guests." NSSA Osnabrück, 17 III, Rundschreiben Nr. 50, 15 June 1933.

115. BA Koblenz, R53/23, agreement of von Bismarck and Sander, 19 May 1933. Hugenberg's papers contain a list of incidents perpetrated by the SA against members of the *Kampfringe* and correspondence from local members on the relationship of the two associations. AH Rohbraken, P 26.

116. AH Rohbraken, P 16, Hugenberg to Hitler, 24 May 1933. See also BA Koblenz, R53/23.

117. The Bavarian minister of the interior banned the *Kampfringe* in that state on 24 March 1933. NSSA Aurich 1, Rundschreiben Nr. 29, 7 April 1933. The police in Hamburg did the same on 31 May 1933. BA Koblenz, R43I/2655.

118. *Der Tag*, 20 June 1933. Hugenberg sought to have the charges investig-

ated, but his repeated requests apparently remained unanswered. The official foundation for this action charged that in the check of 200 *Kampfringe* members, 140 had—until 5 March 1933—been active in the SPD, KPD, *Reichsbanner, Rote Hilfe,* etc. *Völkischer Beobachter,* Berliner Ausgabe, 24 June 1933.

119. AH Rohbraken, P 16, Kalkreuth to Hitler, 24 April 1933. Note also Gies, "Die Nationalsozialistische Machtergreifung," p. 216.

120. See the Hugenberg-Vögler correspondence of February-March 1933 in AH Rohbraken, P 17.

121. BA Koblenz, R13I/1078, "Aufzeichnung vom 3. Mai 1933." In this, as in Herle's circular of 31 March, it appeared that industry favored Hitler's expressed position on world trade as opposed to Hugenberg's. See HA, GHH, 400 101 220/14 Industrialists feared that some of Hugenberg's measures to protect agriculture indicated a vain attempt to favor one branch of the economy. See, "Präsidialsitzung am 23. März 1933," *Geschäftliche Mitteilungen des RDI*, 5 April 1933, p. 45.

122. The appointment of Alfred Möllers, chairman of the *Bund für nationale Wirtschaft und Werksgemeinschaft,* as one of the two commissars (the other was the National Socialist, Otto Wagener) to deal with the RDI and the Reich economy in general did not inspire confidence in industrial circles. In the reorganization of the RDI, the president of that association, Krupp, dealt directly with Hitler. There is no indication that he ever met with Hugenberg to discuss these developments, in which Wagener played a greater role than Möllers. WA Bayer, 62/10. 7a, Herle circular of 7 April 1933 and *Geschäftliche Mitteilungen des RDI*, 29 April 1933, pp. 51–52, and 17 May 1933, pp. 61–63. Also see Petzina, p. 51, and Gerhard Schulz, "Die Anfäge des totalitären Massnahmenstaates," in Bracher, Sauer, and Schulz, pp. 630–32.

123. *Der Angriff*, 1 May 1933.

124. The creation of the *Adolf-Hitler Spende* was an outgrowth of this mentality, which sought to curb violence and corruption with legal bribery. Schulz, p. 649.

125. HA, GHH, 400 101 290/Bosch correspondence, Hans Walz to Reusch, 27 May 1933. Stegmann's emphasis on the role of the Keppler *Kreis* in Hugenberg's downfall is an oversimplification. See his "Kapitalismus und Fascismus," pp. 62–63.

126. HA, GHH, 400 101 290, Reusch to Walz, n.d., and in AH, Rohbraken, GB 28, note the birthday telegram to Hugenberg, 19 June 1933. "After close and long-standing collaboration, we know and esteem the breadth of your vision, the soundness of your judgment, the purity of your love for the Fatherland, and the warmth of your sentiment for all the productive classes (*schaffende Stände*) of our nation.... It is our firm conviction that the German people in the terrible situation in which it now finds itself, could place no better man in the office which you have undertaken in the framework of the national government...." This message, which obviously was meant to counter the anti-Hugenberg sentiment in industry, presumably originated with Hugenberg's friends—especially von Loewenstein of the coaling industry. Over eighty leaders including such magnates as Kirdorf, Vögler, Reusch, E. Poensgen, Springorum, etc., signed it. The names of Thyssen and Krupp von Bohlen were conspicuous by their absence.

127. Instances of this are too abundant to cite. Not only did Hugenberg and Winterfeld appeal to the Reich president to mitigate this anticonservative pressure, but even local party officials sought to influence von Hindenburg. See AH Rohbraken, GB 28, Regional Leader of the DNVP in Pommerania to Colonel von Hindenburg, n.d. The Pommeranian wrote: "The forces of the Battle Front Black-White-Red are not only excluded from every form of cooperation just as are the Marxist forces, but they are fought with the sharpest terror and made alegal (*rechtlos*).... Members of the Battle Front ... who are involved in economic life are deprived of any source of livelihood through a sharply pronounced boycott...."

128. *Lippische Tages-Zeitung*, 28 and 30 May 1933. The key issue was clearly delineated by Bodelschwing himself when he stated, "before the German public in all earnestness, I repudiate the reproaches continually raised against me, that the reaction hides behind me...." Cited in ibid., 18 June 1933.

129. *Lippische Tages-Zeitung*, 25 June 1933. See also Bracher, "Stufen der Machtergreifung," pp. 332–33.

130. *Der Tag*, 20 June 1933. Seldte had already removed Duesterberg from his position as second leader of the veterans' organization. See Berghahn, pp. 255–62, and Mahlke, pp. 664–65.

131. Ritthaler, "Niederschrift Hugenbergs über seinen Rücktritt und das Ende der DNVP," p. 211; AH Rohbraken, P 26, "Bericht."

132. BA Koblenz, Schmidt-Hannover Papers, 30, "Sitzung des Reichsführerstabs ... den 26. VI. 1933 nachmittags." Hugenberg later claimed that a meeting on 25 June had supported him, that he had specifically forbade any official discussion of dissolution with Nazi leaders, and that in view of his preparations for resignation and the "sudden nervous breakdown" of some party leaders there was little that he could do to change the course of the meeting, which was summoned "against my wishes, i.e., without my knowledge." Besides, he added scornfully, "with such troops no battle at all could be fought." Ibid., 9, Hugenberg to Schmidt-Hannover, 7 September 1933.

133. Ritthaler, "Niederschrift Hugenbergs," pp. 208, 212. Ritthaler presumes that the messenger was the former chairman of the DNVP, Hergt. A letter from the party office to Oldenburg-Januschau, thanking him for the help given "at the conversations with Neudeck at this time," speaks of Hergt in the third person. The author of this letter had himself gone to see Hindenburg; his interpretation of events portrayed Hugenberg as being betrayed by the party leaders, especially von Winterfeld and von Freytagh-Loringhoven. BA Koblenz, Kleine Erwerbung 426, Brosius to Oldenburg-Januschau, 3 July 1933. Now in BA Koblenz, Traub Papers, 9.

134. *Hugenbergs Ringen*, Hugenberg to von Hindenburg, 26 June 1933, 1:82–84; reprinted in Ritthaler, pp. 204–07.

135. Frick, who had spoken with von Freytagh-Loringhoven before Hugenberg's conversation with the chancellor, had informed his leader of the negotiations for the dissolution of the DNF. Ritthaler, p. 205.

136. Ibid., "Niederschrift Hugenbergs," pp. 209–11.

137. Ritthaler, Hugenberg to von Hindenburg, 27 June 1933, p. 215, and "Niederschrift Hugenbergs," p. 214.

138. BA Koblenz, Kleine Erwerbung 426, "Sitzung der Landesführer, 27. Juni 1933, Nachmittag." And see BA Koblenz, Schmidt-Hannover Papers, 30, "Sitzung des Reichsführerstabs, 27.6. 1933," and Wegener Papers, 14, Freytagh-Loringhoven to Schmidt-Hannover, 6 August 1933. Helmuth Poensgen was a member of a powerful family in the Ruhr. Since 1931 he had been active in party work and, according to Gemein (pp. 97–98), Hugenberg had delegated him as deputy party leader in the West.

139. BA Koblenz, Traub Papers, 21, DNF to all Local Associations, 28 June 1933. Hugenberg reportedly said of the agreement, "that is really surprisingly much." BA Koblenz, Wegener Papers, 14, Freytagh-Loringhoven to Schmidt-Hannover, 6 August 1933.

140. BA Koblenz, Kleine Erwerbung 426, "Wiederzusammentritt des Versammlung am Dienstag, den 27. Juni 1933, ca 10:30 abends." Here Hugenberg's comments are partially added in pen to the typed minutes. They are presented in full in Ritthaler, 216, "Niederschrift Hugenbergs." Essentially the same comments are preserved in BA Koblenz, Schmidt-Hannover, 30, "Wiederzusammentritt der Versammlung den 27. Juni 1933."

Postscript

1. See for example, AH Rohbraken, M 27, "Mitwirkende politische Gesichtspunkte"; and Otto Kriegk, *Der deutsche Film in Spiegel der Ufa: 25 Jahre Kampf und Vollendung* (Berlin, 1943), pp. 118–24, 127, 150–51, 183–84, and 213–14.

2. The most obvious example is *Hugenbergs Ringen*, 1:1–54.

3. According to Klitzsch, Nazi pressure in 1933 caused approximately 50,000 customers to terminate their subscriptions to Scherl publications. AH Rohbraken, E 4, "Denkschrift von D. Klitzsch," n.d. See also, AH Rohbraken, P 16, Klitzsch to Hugenberg, 28 August 1933. Hugenberg thought that the regime possibly wanted "to starve us out." Ibid., P 17, Hugenberg to Vögler, 5 September 1933. Later in September, after Hugenberg had written to Hitler, Klitzsch was more optimistic about the future of Scherl. Also, the *Ufa*, film, *Hitlerjunge Quex*, was released in September 1933. Kriegk, *Der deutsche Film*, pp. 213–14. Whether these factors incluenced the change is not clear. AH Rohbraken, P 17, Mann to Hugenberg, 19 September 1933; and DZA Potsdam, ADV, 180, Hugenberg to Hitler, 13 September 1933.

4. Writing to his friend Class, who had offered him a special honorary post (presumably in the ADV) Hugenberg surmised, "In the course of recent events, I have gained the impression that great difficulties are in store for me..." AH Rohbraken, P 16, Hugenberg to Class, 28 August 1933.

5. Scherl's annual report noted that the firm received a good price for its shares in the *Ala*. BA Koblenz, Hugenberg Papers, 276. See also Oron J. Hale, *The Captive Press in the Third Reich* (Princeton, 1964), pp. 137–38.

6. See HSA Düsseldorf, Hugenberg's Denazification Process, Local Court of Alverdessen to the Detmold Denazification Committee, 8 July 1949.

7. See the pertinent correspondence in AH Rohbraken, A 28 and 29; also BA Koblenz, Wegener Papers, 66. Of all the members of the Hugenberg family, apparently only one became a member of the NSDAP (in 1942)—presumably to secure National Socialist support for continued family control of Scherl after the

eventual retirement of Hugenberg. See A. Groll to Gauschatzmeister des Gaues Berlin der NSDAP, 14 May 1942, in the appropriate folder of the Berlin Document Center. The NSDAP did not trust former German National and Pan-German leaders; many, including Hugenberg and Class, were specially listed as potential counterrevolutionaries. See the pertinent documents in Berlin, U.S. Document Center. Reportedly, Hugenberg's son was forced to join the SA in Uhsmannsdorf, where he owned an estate, but was thrown out of the organization when he refused to carry a sign reading, "Dogs and Jews are forbidden to enter Uhsmannsdorf." HA Rohbraken, E 4, Erich Held to Meesmann, 25 October 1949.

8. *Hugenbergs Ringen*, 1:38. The editor of this defensive publication stressed that "Hugenberg was placed on the electoral list without his cooperation." In response to a "friendly" letter from Hitler, Hugenberg had, however, indicated that it was his "life's wish that the task commonly undertaken on 30 January would lead to a happy conclusion." The general tone of the letter indicates the author's ambivalence toward political developments. DZA, ADV, 180, Hugenberg to Hitler, 13 September 1933. See also Hugenberg's testimony in HSA Düsseldorf, Hugenberg's Denazification Process, before the Denazification Committee of Lemgo on 24 September 1947.

9. See BA Koblenz, Wegener Papers, 66, Hugenberg to Wegener, 14 November and 21 December 1933. Acceptance of the status quo could make life easier for German Nationals—e.g., on 21 October 1933, Rudolf Hess, Hitler's deputy, sent a circular to all Nazi leaders reminding them of Hitler's agreement of 27 June with the DNF. S 49 Hannover.

10. AH Rohbraken, P 16, Hitler to Hugenberg, 24 December 1933, and reply; also Hugenberg to Hitler, 26 January 1934. Hugenberg used the last opportunity not only to reiterate seasons greetings and decline an opportunity to join in publicly celebrating the first anniversary of the regime, but also to remind Hitler of his contribution to the formation of the national cabinet and to point out that the government's demand for more than a half million marks in back taxes threatened his "economic existence." Hugenberg wrote to Hitler for the interview on 4 January 1935; two weeks later, Lammers made the appointment for 7 February 1935. S 35 Hannover.

11. Alfred Hugenberg, *Die neue Stadt: Gesichtspunkte, Organisationformen und Gesetzesvorschläge für die Umgestaltung deutscher Grosstädte* (Berlin, 1935).

12. Ibid., pp. 10–23.

13. Hale, pp 139–40, 188–89; Kozyk, pp. 237, 395; and Fritz Schmidt, *Presse in Fesseln: Eine Schilderung des NS Pressetrusts* (Berlin, 1947), pp. 154–55.

14. See the pertinent correspondence in AH Rohbraken, M 6. In dealing with these events, Hugenberg later confided to Meesmann, "The *Zechenverband* got back everything which it had originally given for the acquisition and development of the Scherl *Verlag*." AH Rohbraken, E 4, "Äusserungen Geheimrat Hugenbergs über Pressewesen."

15. Hugenberg boasted that he could have undertaken the operation of the corporation alone but preferred to establish a broad base. Ibid. For the actual business transactions, see the Scherl files in BA Koblenz, Hugenberg Papers, 215–228, 255, 468.

16. Hitler's criticism of German Nationals and Pan-Germans, especially

Hugenberg and Bang, is clearly voiced in Hermann Rauschning, *Hitler Speaks: A Series of Political Conversations with Adolf Hitler on his Real Aims* (London, 1939), p. 86; and Picker, *Hitlers Tischgespräche*, p. 278.

17. HSA Düsseldorf, Hugenberg's Denazification Process, Questionairre, 27 March 1946.

18. BA Koblenz, Hugenberg Papers, 296; Hale, pp. 245, 310; Schmidt, *Presse in Fesseln*, p. 158.

19. Ibid., the picture between pp. 160 and 161.

20. There is abundant information on this in BA Koblenz, Hugenberg Papers (e.g., 476).

21. BA Koblenz, Schmidt-Hannover Papers, 9, Hugenberg to Schmidt, 27 November 1944.

22. BA Koblenz, Hugenberg Papers, 476, 532; Schmidt, *Presse in Fesseln*, pp. 156–57; Hale, pp. 311–12; and especially Kozyk, pp. 237–38.

23. Schmidt-Hannover, p. 368.

24. See HSA Düsseldorf, Hugenberg's Denazification Process; and S 27 Hannover, Hugenberg's memorandum, "Wiederaufbau unsere Städte. Teil I: Die Aufgabe," and "Teil II: Hindernisse."

25. Schmidt-Hannover, p. 360; and AH Rohbraken, 0 8, "Betriebsprüferberbericht" and 0 9, "Informationsbericht: 25.4.1947."

26. Schmidt-Hannover, pp. 361–66.

27. *Hugenbergs Ringen*, Hugenberg to Borchmeyer, 14 May 1948, 2: 5–6. See also AH Rohbraken, E 4, [Meesmann's] "Der Herr über Presse und Film: Sinn und Entstehung des 'Hugenberg-Konzerns' und seine Zerschlagung durch den Nationalsozialismus."

28. AH Rohbraken, E 5, "Niederschrift über die 5. ordentliche Stizung des Kreistages Lemgo am 17. Juli 1947"; also HSA Düsseldorf, Hugenberg's Denazification Process, "Protokoll über die Vernehmung des Geheimrats Alfred Hugenberg, 24.9. 1947."

29. *Hugenbergs Ringen*, 3:1–9.

30. Ibid., 3:9–11.

31. In 1948, Hugenberg confided to Meesmann: "We had a German Reich, but no Reich which possessed a secure foundation in the consciousness of our people. The spiritual foundation of the Bismarckian spirit was lacking. To develop this foundation was the task of the 'Hugenberg press.' But it was already too late. The necessity of the Pan-German League has just now been fully demonstrated. Material on this can be found in Rohbraken...." AH Rohbraken, E 4, "Äusserungen Geheimrat Hugenbergs über das Pressewesen."

32. AH Rohbraken, E 5, von Dommes to Meesmann, 6 April 1951.

33. BA Koblenz, Traub Papers, 68, Wider to Traub, 28 March 1951.

34. Interview with Herr Werner von Kann, executive manager of the Baustoffwerke Rohbraken, Hugenberg und Co., 5 April 1972.

Conclusion

1. Even Hugenberg's closest friends privately admitted the significance of their radicalism. Wegner noted that "Hitler is only the fortunate heir of Hugenberg." BA Koblenz, Wegener Papers, 6, Wegener to Meydenbauer, 8 January 1932. Later, when the Nazis refused to admit their indebtedness to radical nationalism, Klitzsch wrote, "... no history writing in the world will be able to deny that *Herr* Hugenberg belongs to the pioneers of the national movement." Ibid., 14, Klitzsch to Wegener, 13 September 1933.

Bibliographical Essay

Virtually every book dealing with the Weimar era mentions Alfred Hugenberg. In examining sources, this bibliography will deal solely with archival data which might help researchers to develop Hugenberg's career more fully and reexamine it from different perspectives.

I. THE HUGENBERG *NACHLASS*

Leo Wegener once wrote that Alfred Hugenberg could accomplish much because of the clear and logical order that characterized his files. In 1972, the relatively few folios preserved at Hugenberg's estate, Rohbraken, could no longer bear witness to this praise. After the war, these originally extensive files were divided by occupation authorities charging him with political crimes, by legal consultants defending his financial interests, and by political friends desiring to explain the past. Of the order which once rationalized myriad volumes, only the barest outline remained. There was merely a fragment of the extensive correspondence, reports, and memoranda which had crossed the desk of Hugenberg as the general director of Krupp's, the organizer of the Scherl concern, or the chairman of the DNVP.

Once Hitler had forced him out of the cabinet in June 1933, Hugenberg, who was then sixty-eight years old, spent increasingly more time on his estate in Lippe. In his home were two offices as well as a library, and it is logical to assume that many of his personal files were there. Presumably, other records from his office on the *Viktoriastrasse* were brought to Rohbraken either during this period to avoid confiscation by the *Gestapo* or during the war years to avoid the danger of bombing. Precisely what files were at Rohbraken in 1945 remains a mystery. Older business files from the Wilhelminian era may have been lost earlier in the move from Essen to Lippe, or they may have been considered the possession of the firm or association for which Hugenberg had worked and thus were left in the Ruhr; at

Rohbraken in 1972 there was little from this period. Similarly, minutes from meetings of the various newspaper and banking firms that Hugenberg organized were not to be found at his estate. The same must unfortunately be said of DNVP meetings and correspondence. Apparently, however, there were many more documents in the Rohbraken archives in 1945 than there were in 1972. The exact history of these important papers is shrouded in the veil of secrecy, distortion, and misunderstanding which characterized the approach to a study of the German right in the immediate postwar period.

The most important lacuna in the Hugenberg Papers is the correspondence with Hitler. There are no original letters from Hitler and only a few carbons of Hugenberg's letters to the Nazi leader. That important exchanges between the two men took place is obvious. Despite the fact that Hugenberg did not like to deal with certain political problems in writing,* his legal and precise mind would not have left all important contacts to merely verbal record. Hugenberg was well aware of the problems of denazification after the war. Arrested more than sixteen months after the end of hostilities, he had adequate time to eliminate damaging documentation from his files. Once he was in custody, the office with his papers was sealed by the authorities. The Hugenberg family was arbitrarily forced to leave the estate. In the confusion, furniture as well as other belongings were haphazardly loaded on three trucks.† It is possible that the events of these traumatic days blurred the enforced departure from Rohbraken with the disposition of Hugenberg's personal papers. Reportedly, British soldiers confiscated the archives and removed them in an open van. According to some accounts, papers flew off the truck and were later found on the side of the road; others were found at a local dump and saved from in-cineration by an old friend. Nine months later, when Hugenberg had been remanded to German authorities for denazification, he argued that he could not adequately prepare his defense unless he had access to his files. Correspondence between Hugenberg and his defense counsel does not resolve the problem. The

* BA Koblenz, Wegener Papers, 66, von Buchholz to Wegener, 26 February 1932.
† BA Koblenz, Schmidt-Hannover Papers, 55, Jürg Hartmann, "Die Ausweisung der Familie Hugenberg aus Rohbraken."

denazification board at Lemgo indicated that it would speak with
the authorities, but the disposition of the case is unknown.‡

In any event, some time during this period an old and faithful
employee of Hugenberg, Heinrich Sandmann, received permission to enter the estate, which was under the control of the occupation forces, and to bring some of the papers from files to
him at Bad Meinberg. Obviously the British either had not
confiscated everything or had returned some documents. The
latter is improbable. The occupation forces did not use the house
but placed it under the administration of a German, Herr
Kreuzburg. When Sandmann arrived, Kreuzburg went with him
to the files and reportedly refused to allow the messenger to take
certain folios because they dealt with Hitler. According to the uncertain account of Sandmann, he then took about thirty volumes
of correspondence and memos to Hugenberg, and Kreuzburg
kept about ten aside.* Presumably there were other volumes also
left at Rohbraken. What Kreuzburg did with the folios, which he
supposedly refused to surrender, is unknown. In 1971 there were
over two hundred volumes preserved in the estate's archives, but
at least thirty-four originated in the postwar era and dealt with
Hugenberg's denazification. Many concerned the administration
of the estate itself and were of no significant political interest.
Since the original Hugenberg house at Rohbraken had just been
demolished, it was possible that in the process of moving all
documents had not yet been organized.

The man most directly involved with the files still preserved at
Rohbraken was Otto Meesmann, an executive secretary at the
Opriba in the postwar era. Meesmann was concerned with two
problems: the legal difficulties in defending Hugenberg's assets
and the political justification of Hugenberg. The two issues were
not unrelated. For legal purposes some documents were
removed to develop defense briefs. Others were used for the
book *Hugenbergs Ringen in deutschen Schicksalsstunden*. This study
dealt primarily with Hugenberg's denazification and was not
deemed an adequate historic explanation of his political role in

‡ See the pertinent correspondence in HSA Düsseldorf, Hugenberg's Denazification
Process. British authorities have no record of the Hugenberg Papers. Imperial War
Museum to the Author, 10 July 1972; Office of the Judge Advocate General to the Author,
19 July 1972; Foreign and Commonwealth Office to the Author, 29 August 1972.

* Interview with Heinrich Sandmann, 5 April 1972.

the Weimar era. Consequently, his family and associates projected a more detailed analysis. Both Meesman and Otto Schmidt-Hannover worked on this project separately. Tensions developed between the two men. Not Meesmann, but Schmidt presented the historic defense of Hugenberg in the semibiographical polemic, *Umdenken oder Anarchie*. Reportedly, Schmidt arrived at Rohbraken and took whatever folios he thought necessary for his research.† These included correspondence with Hitler. After Schmidt's death, some of these papers were brought by the Hugenberg family to Hanover.

After I had studied the documentation so graciously made available to me by Hugenberg's descendants, I informed Dr. Wolfgang Mommsen, at that time president of the Federal Archives, of the wealth of material which was still existent. The importance of such documentation for a fuller understanding of a complex period of German history is incalculable. In freely allowing me the opportunity to use these records, the Hugenberg family imposed no conditions whatsoever. It seemed to me that all historians should have the same opportunity. Through the expeditious work of Dr. Mommsen and the courageous understanding of the Hugenbergs, these valuable papers have been deposited in the Federal Archives at Koblenz.* Dr. Reiser and Frau Marschall have produced a very detailed *Findbuch*, which includes a concordance to the original guide that I composed for this book and for the use of the Hugenberg family. The Federal Archives have also received a wealth of material from the last successor of the *Opriba*. Most of this details the technical administration of the August Scherl G.m.b.H.; Frau Ludwig has produced an excellent guide to this material. Because the contents of the folios that I examined at Rohbraken more accurately reflected the manner in which Hugenberg systemized his correspondence and because certain folios were not available in the *Bundesarchiv*, I have used the citations explained below for the material preserved on the Hugenberg estate.

† Interview with Dankwart von Knobloch, 28 February 1972.

* Frau Hugenberg strongly opposed the deposition of any of the Hugenberg papers in a public archive. See BA Koblenz, Wegener Papers, 77, Gertrude Hugenberg to Erika Wegener, 12 February 1960. As long as he had any influence with the family, Dr. Meesmann frustrated the attempts of scholars to gain direct access to these documents. See AH Rohbraken, 0 17, for Meesmann's correspondence with historians. Dr. Dankwart Guratzsch was the first to use these papers for scholarly research; he used his own system for citing the archival volumes.

A.   The Hugenberg Papers at Rohbraken

The documentation preserved on Hugenberg's estate fell into two categories—that preserved in the library and that in the archival room. In the rebuilding of the house, the first group was carefully crated and indexed. Most of the volumes were light reading published by Scherl. It was impossible to derive any certain knowledge of Hugenberg's reading habits or of the authors which most influenced his ideals. From the myriad volumes that composed the estate's library, I have merely noted those which are traditional primary sources. The folio volumes preserved in the archives were less fully organized. A friend of the family had divided the bulk of the folders into five categories: politics, economic politics, concerns, denazification, and general. Since she had not arranged the folios within these general themes, I have organized them chronologically according to topics, when this was possible, and I have given each volume a number. Other folios were apparently found after this friend had completed her work. I have given these arbitrary designations based upon either the color of their bindings, the theme, or the place of storage. After the letter and the number follows the exact title written on the binding or the cover of the folio. Since the titles were at times misleading, I have, in most cases, added a very brief indication of the contents in each volume.

1.   THE LIBRARY

XXIV, 13   Alfred Hugenberg, "Stahleck," a drama in three acts

XXIV, 21   Alfred Hugenberg, "Gedichte, Notizen zu Gedichten, poetischen Aufzeichnungen"

XXIV, 26   Hugenberg, correspondence, including Hugenberg to Hartleben, 10 September 1881

XXIV, 27   Alfred Hugenberg, "Graf Otto von Enklenburg oder Osnabrücks Befreiung im Jahre 1236," a drama

XXIV, 28   Hugenberg's school and lecture notes on the study of Latin, Greek, and Italian

XXIV, 29   Hugenberg-Hartleben correspondence, 1885–1891

XXIV, 30   Hugenberg-Hartleben correspondence, 1881–1883

XXIV, 31   Hugenberg-Hartleben correspondence, 1884

XXIV, 32 Poems by Hugenberg and Hartleben in the same notebook

XXIV, 33 Hugenberg's lecture notes from the universities of Berlin, Heidelberg, and Strassburg

2. THE ARCHIVES

(a) Politics (P)

P 1. "Briefe 1904–1912"—correspondence with Bernhard, Merton, etc.

P 2. "Zeitungs-Ausschnitte 1907—30. Juni 1915"

P 3. "———" (kein Titel)—correspondence 1911–1913 with Hirsch, Hasslacher, Kirdorf, Lowenstein

P 4. "Briefwechsel: Jan. 1912–Jan. 1914"—correspondence with Klaasen on the Krupp workers' quarters at Clausheide

P 5. "Unterlagen ... von Februar 1912 bis 1914"

P 6. "Zeitungs-Ausschnitte 1. Juli 1915–30. Juni 1916"

P 7. "Zeitungs-Ausschnitte 1. Juli 1916–30. Juli 1917"

P 8. "Zeitungs-Ausschnitte 1917–1936"

P 9. "Hugenberg: Presse-Angriffe 1928 – April 1930"—newspaper clippings

P 10. "Z.A. 1928/31"—newspaper clippings

P 11. "Büro Hugenberg 1929–1931"—party circulars, correspondence with Brosius, Bang, Mejer, etc.

P 12. "Doppel von: Kassel 1929; Stettin 1931; Harzburg 1931"—mostly printed material

P 13. "Hugenberg: Allgemein 1929/32"—newspaper clippings

P 14. "Hugenberg: Allgemein—Über Hugenberg 1929/32"—newspaper clippings

P 15. "Glückwünschen—65. Geburtstag, 19.6.1930"

P 16. "Verschiedene Korrespondenz A–K vom Ende 1930"—includes correspondence with Class, Flick, Goerdeler, Göring, Hitler, Klitzsch, etc., from 1930 to 1934

P 17. "Verschiedene Korrespondenz L–Z vom Ende 1930"—includes correspondence with Loewenstein, Mann, Thyssen, Vögler, Wegener from 1930 to 1934

P 18. "Hugenberg: Reden 1930"—newspaper clippings

P 19. "Hugenberg: Allgemeines"—newspaper clippings from the fall of 1930

P 20.   "Hugenberg: Reden 27.1.1931–11.4.1931"—newspaper clippings

P 21.   "Hugenberg: Reden 25.4.1931–4.1.1932"—newspaper clippings

P 22.   "Hugenberg: Reden 2.3.1932–6.1.1933"—newspaper clippings

P 23.   "Hugenberg 1931"—1 April 1931 to 31 December 1932, includes correspondence with Brosius

P 24.   "Hugenberg: Allgemeines: Zeitungs-Ausschnitte 1933"

P 25.   "Hugenberg 1933: Presseangriffe"—mostly printed speeches and newspaper clippings

P 26.   "8(08a)"—reports on the relationship of the DNVP and NSDAP from March to May 1933

P 27.   (Mappe) "Spartakuslage"—attacks on Hugenberg and the DNF

P 28.   (Mappe) "Reden and Zitate von Geheimrat Hugenberg"—eulogies at Hugenberg's funeral in 1951

P 29.   "Aus dem Aktenschrank ... von Dr. Meesmann"—newspaper clippings

P 30.   (Mappe) "Herr Dr. Meesmann ...."—newspaper clippings, stenographic notes, postwar correspondence with Schmidt-Hannover

P 31.   (Mappe) "Stenographische Aufzeichnungen v. Dr. Meesmann"—printed constitutions of the Reich and Prussia; Hugenberg's letter to Duisberg, 24 June 1928

(b)   Economic Policy (*Wirtschaftspolitik*, WP)

WP 1.   "Genossenschäftliche Tätigkeit bei der Ansiedlungkommission (1896–1899)"

WP 2.   "Polenpolitik: Enteignung November 1897–December 1908"—legislative proposals, Pan-German announcements, correspondence with Otto Böse

WP 3.   "1–(1928)–01–47"—printed speeches and essays, 1899–1929

WP 4.   "2–(29/31)–48–187"—printed speeches and essays, 1929–1931

WP 5.   "3–(31–36)–188–337"—printed speeches and essays, mostly from 1931–1933

WP 6.   "Ostdeutsche Hauskreditanstalt"—printed material and correspondence, 1902–1909

WP 7. "Ostpreussische Landgesellschaft G.m.b.H. vom Ende 1904 bis 1. Juli 1907"

WP 8. "Ostpreussische Landgesellschaft G.m.b.H. 1. Juli 1907–31. Dezember 1908"

WP 9. "Ostpreussische Landgesellschaft January 1909"

WP 10. "Ostpreussische Landgesellschaft January 1910–1916"

WP 11. "———(illegible title)———"—deals with settlement in Posen, minutes and correspondence, 1905–1907

WP 12. "Deutsche Mittelstandskasse zu Posen 1905–1910"

WP 13. "Entschuldung (und Verschuldungsgrenze)"—legislative rationales, 1906–1907

WP 14. "Ev. Verein fur Waisenfürsorge Neuzedlitz: Oktober 1906–December 1909"

WP 15. "Ev. Verein fur Waisen Neuzedlitz—1906–1909"

WP 16. "Ev. Heim für Waisenpflege ... 1909–1914"

WP 17. "Krupp: Essen 1910–1918"—newspaper clippings

WP 18. "Weltkrieg 1914–1918"—correspondence A–Z

WP 19. "Wirtschaftliche Gesellschaften"—material dealing with Delbrück, Schickler and Co., Essener Creditanstalt, Zechenverband account

WP 20. "Denkschriften"—1919–1935—legislative proposals; correspondence of Quaatz–Bang–Lilienthal in May 1931; Meesmann's "Hugenbergs Tributabgabe—der Weg aus deutscher Tributnot"

(c) Organizations (O)

O 1. "Anzeignwesen: Haasenstein und Vogler: Neue Geschäftliche Korrespondenz: September 1910–December 1917"

O 2. "Scherlkauf: Konsortium"—Swart, Neumann, etc., from May 1916 to August 1920, two volumes

O 3. (Päckchen) "Rundschreiben von Scherl und Deutschem Gewerbehaus"—1937–1943

O 4. "Briefwechsel: Dr. Tetens 12.10.37–27.6.46"—Tetens was a legal consultant in the Hugenberg concern

O 5. ("Umschlag") "Tornado Fabrik elektrische Maschine u. Apparate"—correspondence 1939–1942

O 6. "Dr. Klitzsch—1. Juli 1940–29 August 1946"—correspondence, among other things, about his denazification in Kiel

O 7.   "Vorbereitendes Schriftwechsel ... 3.10.40 ..."
O 8.   (Mappe) "Bertriebsprüfer Bericht"—1946
O 9.   (Mappe) "Informationsbericht: 25.4.1947"—on Hugen-
         berg's assets
O 10.   "1949–1953: Plannungen und Aktenvermerke"—on the
         sale of *Ufa* and Scherl
O 11.   "Dr. Meesmann: Gesellschaftsausschuss 2.2.1950"—
         minutes of the *Opriba*, 28 October 1951 and 10 January
         1952
O 12.   "Gesellschaft—... Dr. Meesmann"—stenographic notes
         on the *Opriba*, 1952–1953
O 13.   "Dr.   Meesmann: Gesellschaftsvertag   und
         Gesellschaftsrundschr. / Opriba vom 14.1.1953"—ac-
         tually from 11 February 1952
O 14.   "Beck u. Henkel, Schöninger Tonwerke, Osterwalde
         Kalkwerke"—*Opriba* correspondence, 1954–1955
O 15.   "Ausarbeitungen Dr. Meesmann betr. Scherl ..."—
         notes on the *Ufa*, Hugenberg and NSDAP, Hugen-
         berg's role in the Hitler cabinet, etc.
O 16.   "Handakte: Dr. Meesmann"—stenographic note on the
         Opriba, Tornado, etc.
O 17.   "Dr. Meesmann: Dissertationen"—correspondence with
         historians seeking to use the Hugenberg papers

(d) Denazification (*Entnazifizierung*, E)

E 1.   "Entnazifizierung I"—including copies of "Dr. Hugen-
         berg und die Hitler Diktatur" and Klitzsch's
         denazification proceedings
E 2.   "Entnazifizierung II"—various articles, including "Der
         Herr über Presse und Film," "Der ADV," "Ver-
         folgung und Entnazifizierung Hbg"
E 3.   "Entnazifizierung III"—on Scherl, Lemgo process, etc.
E 4.   "Entnazifizierung IV"—Scherl, *Ufa*, Lemgo process
E 5.   "Entnazifizierung: Bereitschaftsunterlagen"—includes
         Hugenberg, "Soziale Frage," Lemgo Process, letter to
         Alexander, Brüning, etc.
E 6.   "Entnazifizierung: Versch. Material"—includes corres-
         pondence with Borchmeyer
E 7.   "Entnazifizierung"—varied, e.g., Schmidt-Hannover's
         view of Thyssen; Hugenberg to Ritthaler; "Was war
         eigentlich die Harzburger Front?"

E 8.   "Geheimrat"—Tetens-Klitzsch correspondence on the Vereinigte Stahlwerke, Klitzsch Korrespondenz on the *Opriba* (1948); varied letters, e.g., Tetens to Springorum, 23 December 1949

E 9.   (Mappe) "Geschäftsführung Opriba"—1948–1952

E 10.   "Entnazifizierung: Schriftwechsel"—Dr. Messmann's correspondence from 1949

E 11.   (Gebundene blaue Mappe) "Bücherschrank Dr. Meesmanns—Äusserungen Hugenbergs über Nationalsozialismus usw"

E 12.   (Mappe) "Entnazifizierung in Berlin 1951"—correspondence Fried. Rath-Tetens, 1950

E 13.   (Mappe) "Entnazifizierungsverfahren—Detmold 1951" —correspondence Schmidt-Hannover and Papen in 1953, essays by Schmidt-Hannover, ca. 1950–1953

E 14.   "Entnazifizierung: Presse"—newspaper clippings and correspondence with newspapers

E 15.   "Presse Stimmmen über Hugenberg 1946–1951"— newspaper clippings

E 16.   "Hugenberg ..."—newspaper clippings on the death of Hugenberg

E 17.   "Verteidigungsausshuss'—correspondence, 1951

E 18.   (Blaue Mappe) "v. H. Dr. Meesmann sortiert"—"Hugenberg und die Hitler Diktatur"

E 19.   (Mappe) "Buch Unterlagen"—preparation of *Hugenbergs Ringen*

E 20.   "Nachtrag: Verteidigungsschrift"—correspondence with various publishers and L. Steuer

E 21.   (Päckchen) "Neue Deutsche Biographie"—correspondence, 1953

E 22.   "Hugenberg Pressestimmung"—correspondence: Schmidt-Hannover to von Papen, 25 September 1953; newspaper clippings

E 23.   "Nachtrag: Verteidigungsschrift"—correspondence with Maximilianverlag, Ritthaler, Steuer, Meesmann

E 24.   "Verteidigungsschrift A–J"—correspondence dealing with Volume 3 of *Hugenbergs Ringen*

E 25.   "Verteidigungsschrift K–Z"—correspondence dealing with Volume 3 of *Hugenbergs Ringen*

E 26.   "Hugenbergs Ringen: Versand"—list of people to whom the books were sent

E 27.　　" Hugenbergs R. i.d. Sch'st Besprechungen"—reviews of
　　　　　the book

(e)　General *(Allgemeines,* A)

A 1.　　"Persönlicher Briefwechsel A–Z 1899–1909"
A 2.　　"Persönlicher Briefwechsel A–Z 1910–1911"
A 3.　　"Persönlicher Briefwechsel 1912"
A 4.　　"Persönlicher Briefwechsel A–Z 1912–1914"
A 5.　　"Persönlicher Briefwechsel A–Z 1915–1916"
A 6.　　"Allgemeiner Briefwechsel A"
A 7.　　"Allgemeiner Briefwechsel Ba–Boz"
A 8.　　"Allgemeiner Briefwechsel Br–Cz"
A 9.　　"Allgemeiner Briefwechsel D–Ez"
A 10.　 "Allgemeiner Briefwechsel Fa–Fy"
A 11.　 "Allgemeiner Briefwechsel Ga–Gy"
A 12.　 "Allgemeiner Briefwechsel Ha"
A 13.　 "Allgemeiner Briefwechsel He–Hoz"
A 14.　 "Allgemeiner Briefwechsel Hu–J"
A 15.　 "Allgemeiner Briefwechsel Ka–Ke"
A 16.　 "Allgemeiner Briefwechsel Ki–Ky"
A 17.　 "Allgemeiner Briefwechsel L"
A 18.　 "Allgemeiner Briefwechsel M"
A 19.　 "Allgemeiner Briefwechsel N–O"
A 20.　 "Allgemeiner Briefwechsel Pa–Ri"
A 21.　 "Allgemeiner Briefwechsel Ro–Rz"
A 22.　 "Allgemeiner Briefwechsel S"
A 23.　 "Allgemeiner Briefwechsel Sch"
A 24.　 "Allgemeiner Briefwechsel Ta–Vy"
A 25.　 "Allgemeiner Briefwechsel W–Z"
A 26.　 "Persönlich: Nov. 1937: L"—correspondence 1937–1945,
　　　　　includes exchange with Loewenstein, Lehmann
A 27.　 "Frl. Arendt: 1. August 1942"—correspondence to 1946
A 28.　 "Allgemeines ... 1949 ... 1950"—includes correspon-
　　　　　dence with Henning von Boehmer 1932–1943
A 29.　 "Allgemeines 1949–1950—includes correspondence with
　　　　　Henning von Boehmer 1933–1943
A 30.　 "Schriftwechsel　　Dr.　　Meesmann"—correspondence
　　　　　1950–1953
A 31.　 "Schriftwechsel　　Dr.　　Meesmann"—correspondence
　　　　　1950–1953

A 32. "Dr. Meesmann: H–Qu"

(f) Golden Folios (*Goldene Bände*, GB)—a collection of speeches and essays by Hugenberg. The first volume contains a table of contents. The last two folios in this series were apparently misfiled.

GB 1. "Reden und Aufsätze 1912–1919"
GB 2. "Reden und Aufsätze August 1919–Dezember 1924"
GB 3. "Reden und Aufsätze 1924–1926"
GB 4. "Reden und Aufsätze 1926–1927—including notes on Hugenberg's *Streiflichter*
GB 5. "Reden und Aufsätze 1927–1928"
GB 6. "Reden und Aufsätze 1928–1929"—including Hugenberg's letter to Duisburg, 13 July 1928
GB 7. "Reden und Aufsätze Närz 1929–Mai/Juni 1929"—including the resolution of the DNVP executive committee on constitutional questions, March 1929
GB 8. "Reden und Aufsätze Juni 1929–Oktober 1929"
GB 9. "Reden und Aufsätze Oktober–Dezember 1929"
GB 10. "Reden und Aufsätze Januar–März 1930"
GB 11. "Reden und Aufsätze März–Mai 1930"
GB 12. "Reden und Aufsätze Juni–September 1930"
GB 13. "Reden und Aufsätze September–Oktober 1930"
GB 14. "Reden und Aufsätze Oktober 1930–Februar 1931"
GB 15. "Reden und Aufsätze Februar–März 1931"
GB 16. "Reden und Aufsätze März–April 1931"
GB 17. "Reden und Aufsätze April–Juli 1931"
GB 18. "Reden und Aufsätze Juli–September 1930"
GB 19. "Reden und Aufsätze September 1931–Januar 1932"
GB 20. "Reden und Aufsätze März 1932–April 1932"
GB 21. "Reden und Aufsätze April–Juli 1932"
GB 22. "Reden und Aufsätze Juli 1932"
GB 23. "Reden und Aufsätze Juli 1932"
GB 24. "Reden und Aufsätze Juli–Oktober 1932"
GB 25. "Reden und Aufsätze Oktober–November 1932"
GB 26. "Reden und Aufsätze November 1932–Februar 1933'—including Hugenberg's handwritten *Nationalsozialistische Hetze gegen Dr. Hugenberg*
GB 27. "Reden und Aufsätze Februar–April 1933"
GB 28. "Reden und Aufsätze April–November 1936"—includ-

ing the birthday telegram of leading Ruhr industrialists, June 1933

GB 29. "Unterlagen betr. Rede-Einladungen und Reisen
1929–1932"

GB 30. "Politische Angelegenheiten: I Unterlagen betr.
Entnazifizierung"—including correspondence with
Schmidt, Hannover, Traub, and Vogelsang

GB 31. "Politische Angelegenheiten: II Unterlagen betr.
Entnazifizierung"

(g) Old Court Actions

Schmalfuss 1912
Janke 1920
Klasing 1924–1927
Kügge 1924–1927
Meyer 1925–1927
Weber 1925
Buthe 1927
Elektrizitätswerk Wesertal 1927–1930
Kuhlmann 1927–1930
Meyer 1928
Rügge 1928–1929
Meyer 1929–1931
Scherl/Bruhn 1930
Kraft und Wacquant 1934–1935
Bünte 1939–1941
Sprick 1944

(h) Files in Large Chest (*Mappen*, M)

M 1.   "Briefwechsel mit Dr. Kirdorf vom 29. Oktober 1910 bis
5. April 1918"—includes a letter from 1923

M 2.   "Briefwechsel mit Professor Bernhard vom 27. März
1914 bis 28. September 1922'

M 3.   "Verein für die bergbaulichen Interessen im Ober-
bergamtsbezirk Dortmund: Sal. Oppenheim jr. u. Co.,
Cöln—1916–1919"—on war loans, *Deutscher
Verlagsverein, Zechenverbandkonto* etc.

M 4.   "Briefwechsel mit Professor Hoffmann Münster vom 7.
Juli 1915 bis 21. January 1917"—on propaganda for
war aims

M 5.   "Briefwechsel mit Dr. Georg Wilhelm Schiele-Naumburg von 1918–1921"—on southeast Europe, *Deutsche Volkswirtschaftliche Korrespondenz*, DNVP

M 6.   "Briefwechsel mit Bergsassessor von und zu Loewenstein 1919—1920 (mit Briefwechsel Scherl / BbV März–April 1937)"—Wiedfeldt, Stinnes, etc.

M 7.   "Briefwechsel mit Dr. A. Vögler v. 1919–1921 (auch betr. Gründung Nationaler Club)"

M 8.   "Briefwechsel mit D. Gottfried Traub von 1920–1923"

M. 9   "Briefwechsel mit Dr. Leo Wegener und Frau Erika Wegener geb. Sehnsdorf von 27.5.1930–5.8.1941"—mostly Hugenberg to Wegener

M 10. "Bürische Zeitung"

M 11. "Verein für die bergbaulichen Interessen im Oberbergamtsbezirk Dortmund: Post und Berliner Neueste Nachrichten"

M 12. "Post: Gründung und Allgemeines"—1913–1917

M 13. "Post: Notarielle Verhandlungen"

M 14. "Post: Abschlüsse, Verträge usw."—1915–1917

M 15. "Post: Allgemeines 1916–1918"—Schriftwechsel Albrecht, Loewenstein, Reismann-Grone

M 16. "Post: Sitzungen der Gesellschafter und Aufsichtsräte"

M 17. "Post: Pfändung Spinzig"

M 18. "Patria"—on ownership; Zimmermann, as editor of the *Neuen gesellschaftlichen Korrespondenz*

M 19. "Handelskammer Essen I: 1912–1913"

M 20. "Handelskammer Essen II: 1914–30.6.1915"—including Hirsch correspondence

M 21. "Handelskammer Essen III: 1.7.15–30.6.17"

M 22. "Handelskammer Essen IV: 1.7.17–31.12.18"

M 23. "Handelskammer Essen: Stützung der Presse"

M 24. "Handelskammer Essen: Schriftwechsel mit A. von Schwerin I"

M 25. "Handelskammer Essen: Schriftwechsel mit A. Schwerin II'

M 26. "Geheimrat: Alter Steuerakten"—Lemgo 1925

M 27. "Geheimrat Hugenberg: alt 1935"—on the *Opriba* 1934, correspondence with Vögler

B.   The Schmidt-Hannover/Hugenberg Papers

After the death of Otto Schmidt-Hannover in 1970, the papers
at his home in Westerland/Sylt were in great disarray. Reportedly some documents had been destroyed; others were turned
over to the Federal Archives. One of the members of the Hugenberg family removed those folios which supposedly belonged to
the original Rohbraken collection; in 1971 these papers were
preserved in Hanover. An industrial archivist was commissioned
to examine the material and prepare a general inventory. With
the limited time available to him, this man listed all the material
collected from Sylt and prefixed the individual items, whether
boxed, bound, or printed, with the letter *S*. The following outline is a copy (and translation in abridged version) of his inventory. Only those published items which are readily available have
been omitted. This collection has been recently incorporated
into the Hugenberg and Schmidt-Hannover Papers preserved at
Koblenz.

S 1.   DNVP—Press Archives—includes press reports concern-
        ing the DNVP, especially Hugenberg, 1926–1934

S 2.   DNVP—Dr. Hugenberg—includes circulars from the
        National Club and the German National Committee
        of Industrialists

S 3.   DNVP—Correspondence—includes varied correspon-
        dence 1929–1933, e.g., Wegener to Schmidt-Han-
        nover, 25 December 1930; Hugenberg to his children,
        25 June 1932

S 4.   DNVP—Press Archives—clippings and seven printed
        speeches of Hugenberg 1919–1933

S 5.   DNVP—Printed Party Material 1928–1930—includes a
        list of Reichstag delegates

S 14.   Lebenserinnerungen von Dr. Erich Weinbeck 1876–1947
        (typewritten)

S 22.   DNVP—Schmidt-Hannover, Diary from 28 January to 4
        August 1932

S 23.   Nazis—includes correspondence of DNVP concerning
        the Nazis and copies of Hugenberg-Hitler correspon-
        dence 1930–1935

S 25.   DNVP—articles and manuscripts by Schmidt-Hannover—includes some from the postwar period

S 26. Dr. Hugenberg—includes manuscripts for speeches and articles, 1929–1933

S 27. DNVP—Dr. Hugenberg—includes notes on Hugenberg's life

S 28. DNVP—Dr. Hugenberg—Hugenberg's essay (written in 1949), "Als ich 1928 den Vorsitz der DNVP antrat ..."

S 29. DNVP—Dr. Hugenberg—party correspondence on the case of Dr. Oberfohren, 1933

S 30. DNVP—Dr. Hugenberg—correspondence with Msgr. Kaas on the Young Plan, 20 November 1929 and 7 January 1930

S 31. DNVP—Schmidt-Hannover—correspondence with Rudolf Hess, 1931

S 32. DNVP—Dr. Hugenberg—correspondence with the chancellor on the possibility of cooperation in February 1931

S 33. DNVP—Dr. Hugenberg—correspondence with Schacht, Neurath, and Bang on the World Economic Conference in 1933 and correspondence on his resignation as minister.

S 34. DNVP—Dr. Hugenberg—correspondence with Wilhelm von Ahlefeld concerning Treviranus, November 1929

S 35. DNVP—Dr. Hugenberg—correspondence with Count Westarp on the party crisis May–July 1930

S 36. DNVP—Dr. Wegener—material on the Pan-German "putsch" of 1927

S 37. DNVP—Press Archives—press views on the entrance of Germany into the League of Nations in 1926

S 38. DNVP—Dr. Hugenberg—letters from friends, e.g., Count Kalkreuth, 22 December 1925, and varied memos and interviews

S 39. DNVP—Schmidt-Hannover—includes printed articles

S 40. Schmidt-Hannover's Notes—on the formation of the cabinet in 1933 and varied correspondence, e.g., with Brüning in 1952.

S 41. DNVP—Dr. Hugenberg—minutes of the party executive committee on 25 April 1930

S 42. Hugenberg—Schmidt-Hannover correspondence, 1933–1950

S 43.   Varied Correspondence—including Fritz Thyssen's de-
         mands for cooperation with the NSDAP at the end of
         1930
S 44.   List of DNVP Reichstag Delegates, 1920–1930
S 45.   Photo Collection—concerns Field Marshal von Blem-
         berg, 1938
S 46.   Photo   Collection—concerns   politics,   Reichstag,
         1930–1933
S 47.   DNVP—Dr. Hugenberg/Schmidt—unordered papers on
         the election of the Reich president and correspon-
         dence with Vögler, 28 May 1926
S 48.   DNVP—Schmidt-Hannover—varied printed material on
         the Reichstag
S 49.   DNVP—Press Archives—varied
S 50.   DNVP—Press Archives—varied
S 51.   DNVP—Schmidt-Hannover—on the German Red Cross

II.   INDUSTRIAL ARCHIVES

As recent research has demonstrated, material preserved in
the cellars of some of the large corporations of the Ruhr is much
more extensive than had been imagined. Permission to use this
documentation, however, remains an elusive privilege dependent on several factors. General directors and boards of overseers
are understandably more interested in a good public image than
in historical research. Totally free access to the wealth of material
stored in corporate vaults could be an expensive undertaking for
entreprenuers. Not only would archivists have to be hired to
organize the material, but research rooms and copy machines
would be needed to assist researchers to work effectively. Corporate leaders are very concerned that the documentation they
have preserved be used carefully; their expression is possibly
deliberately ambiguous. "Careful usage" could apply to the
physical handling of old papers, which sometimes are on the
verge of physical disintegration, or to the select usage and proper
interpretation of content. Concerned as they are with their
public image and dutifully bound by tradition to protect the
reputations of former leaders of their corporations, some firms
prohibit all but a select few from examining their documentation. Such a policy hardly seems enlightened. In vew of the terri-

bly inaccurate and frequently prejudicial treatment accorded German industry during the Weimar era, logic might well conclude that the truth could hardly be more damaging. The interests of industry and society at large might well be best served if large corporations would turn over their files from the period before 1945 to an organization such as the *Deutsches Industrie-Institut in Cologne*. An expanded complex on the shores of the Rhine would guarantee not only professional organization of documentation, but free access to serious researchers. An even more desirable alternative for scholars would see the deposition of this material in the Federal Archives at Koblenz. To facilitate research under present conditions, Dr. Thomas Trumpp of the Federal Archives has edited a guide to business archives.

A.   The *Deutsches Industrie-Institut* in Cologne

This facility, under the aegis of Dr. M. Hanke and his very helpful research librarians, has an excellent library specializing in industrial history and a relatively limited selection of archival sources helpful to students of industrial and economic history of Weimar Germany. The ravages of war and the present day emphasis of this institute, which is the offspring of the Federal Association of German Industry, have not facilitated the collection of sources. Understandably there are large lacunae which the researcher must fill by utilizing other facilities. Nevertheless, a significant collection of publications, such as various volumes of the *Langnam Mitteilungen, Stahl und Eisen, Ruhr und Rhein,* and *Der Arbeitgeber,* are available. The *Sammlung* Funcke, a partial *Nachlass* of Otto Funcke, a member of the presidium of the *Reichsverband der Deutschen Industrie,* is valuable as is the collection of papers from the *Verein der Deutschen Eisen und Stahlindustrieller.* (The latter, however, is largely limited to newspaper clippings; the bulk of documentation from this association is preserved in the Federal Archives at Koblenz.)

B.   The *Bergbau-Bucherei* in Essen-Krey

This very specialized library dealing with the coaling industry is again a center which emphasizes contemporary industrial problems. Copies of *Glückauf,* annual reports of the coaling associations, and other printed materials of value to economic and industrial historians are available. In the cellars of the library are preserved the von Loewenstein Papers which will undoubtedly shed great light on the total activities of the coaling interests during the Weimar era.

C.   The *Rheinisch-Westfälisches Wirtschaftsarchiv* at Cologne

The regional specialization of this archive delimits the extent of its holdings. Dr. Klara von Eyll is extremely helpful and knowledgeable. Through her kindness, early issues of the *Deutsche Industriezeitung*, varied issues of reports from coaling associations, and documents dealing with the centenary celebration at Krupp's were made available.

D.   The Historical Archive of the *Gutehoffnungshütte A.G.* in Oberhausen

The sage policy of the board of overseers of this firm has apparently given the director of the archives, Herr Bodo Herzog, wide-ranging authority to permit scholars full access to the extensive collection preserved by the corporation. Intensely interested in historical research, Her Herzog is not merely a curator of records, but a scholar aware of the contents of his collection and fully abreast of modern scholarship in economic and political history. These very well organized files of the GHH contain not merely corporate correspondence, but the *Nachlass* of the powerful general director of the firm during the Weimar era, Paul Reusch. The intense correspondence carried on by Reusch with individual industrialists and the various associations with which he was connected (e.g., 400 101 290/Vols. 1–97) is extremely important. Of no less interest are his dealings with the Reich Association of German Industry (400 101 220/Vols. 1–14) and the Langnam *Verein* and the Northwest Group of the Association of German Iron and Steel Industrialists (400 101 221/ Vols. 1–11b). Most revealing for political historians are his letters exchanged with Dr. Martin Blank, who served as his political factotum in Berlin (400 101 2024/Vols. 1–11). Scattered throughout other provenances are important documents dealing with the press controlled by the Haniels and the GHH (400 101 2007/Vols. 1–16) and the conflict with Hugenberg over the control of these newspapers (e.g., 400 101 200/0). Since Reusch was a bitter opponent of Hugenberg, these documents are most important for an understanding of the latter's relationship with heavy industry.

E. *Werksarchiv, Farbenfabriken Bayer A.G.* in Leverkusen

Carl Duisberg was the chairman of the Reich Association of German Industry from 1925 through 1931. Herr Peter Gob, the archivist at Leverkusen, where Duisberg's *Nachlass* is preserved, recognized the importance of the papers stored there for a study of Hugenberg and granted me permission to use them. Before his death, Duisberg had begun the select organization of the *Autographen-Sammlung* Dr. Carl Duisberg. In this, letters of prominent personages to and from this industrial leader were separated from their normal provenance, placed on special placards, and arranged alphabetically. More important for this study, however, were the records of the Reich Association of German Industry (62/10. Vols. 9a–11) and the private correspondence of Duisberg (Du VIIIa/Vols. 15–21 and Vols. 31–46).

F. *Werksarchiv, August-Thyssen Hütte A.G.* in Duisburg-Hamborn

The very capable archivist, Frau Dr. Milkereit, was extremely helpful, but the holdings of the archives are meager. The three volumes which comprise the remains of the "Sekretatiat Fritz Thyssen: Allgemeines Schriftwechsel 1904–1922" were of little use. There is, however, a large packet of material reportedly dealing with the activities of the Poensgens and others, but this is presently *gesperrt*, and not even the archivist has any idea of the specific contents. The personal papers of Alfred Vögler, which would be extremely important for the fullest possible understanding of Hugenberg's relations with industrialists, were reportedly destroyed after the tragic death of Vögler.

III. PRIVATE ARCHIVES

Aside from the family archives of the Hugenbergs, the most important collection of papers dealing with the political life of Hugenberg as chairman of the DNVP is the Westarp *Nachlass*. As a historian as well as an active political leader, Count Kuno Westarp maintained an intensive correspondence which he carefully organized. His two devoted daughters helped preserve this impressive collection, which is now in Gaertringen. The count's grandson, Dr. Friedrich Freiherr Hiller von Gaertringen, has carefully catalogued this material and has made copies of much of the correspondence to facilitate its use by scholars. For the most part, researchers use these copies and not the original documents. Baron Hiller's own outstanding work on the history of the DNVP and his extensive research into other areas of recent German history made my visit to Gaertringen a most pleasant and rewarding research experience. Other documentation—for example, printed party brochures and the extensive correspondence of former German National leaders with the count's grandson—are also very valuable. Baron Hiller is currently editing some of the documents from the Westarp *Nachlass* for publication.

IV.   PUBLIC ARCHIVES

Because of the wide-ranging influence of Hugenberg, the records of individuals and organisations with which he had contact are spread throughout Germany. Sometimes the documentation is scant and merely peripheral, but on occasion very important pieces of the puzzle are found in tangential collections. The following archives are listed in alphabetical order.

A.   *Auswärtiges Amt, Politisches Archiv* in Bad Godesberg

Important documents detail the role of Hugenberg in the World Economic Conference of June 1933. The material preserved here, (e.g., *Büro Reichsminister* 119/4 and 175/1,) complements the documentation preserved in the Hugenberg Papers on his dispute with Baron von Neurath.

B.   Berlin Document Center

Most important is the fact that virtually nothing on Hugenberg, his family, or his most intimate colleagues, is preserved here. Almost none of them were members of the NSDAP. In fact, many of the leaders in the later years of the DNVP and many champions of the Pan-German League were officially categorized as conservative reactionaries and potential rebels against the Nazi system.

C.   *Bundes-Archiv* in Koblenz

The wealth of material preserved here and the expert guidance rendered the researcher by various archivists, especially the most helpful Dr. Trumpp, make this collection of material one of the most valuable in Germany. The expertise of Dr.

Wolfgang Mommsen has enabled the archives to preserve the personal papers of numerous men connected in one way or another with Hugenberg. The most important *Nachlässe* for this study are those of Leo Wegener and Gottfried Traub. In addition, the papers of Colonel Bauer, Eduard Dingeldey, Wilhelm von Gayl, Ludwig Kastl, Hans-Erdmann Lindeiner Wildau, and Paul Silverberg also reveal something of Hugenberg's activities.

The extensive collection of documents produced by the *Reichskanzlei* (R43I) sheds light not only on the political activities of the Weimar era, but on numerous other aspects of social and economic policy which help the researcher to understand Hugenberg. The incomplete documentation preserved from the period of von Papen's vice-chancellorship (R53, *Stellvertreter des Reichskanzlers*) provides limited insight into the workings of the Hitler cabinet during the first months of 1933. Important for an examination of domestic social and economic policy from the viewpoint of heavy industry are the extensive files (R13I) of the *Verein der deutschen Eisen und Stahlindustrieller*, which overlapped with the *Wirtschaftsgruppe: Eisenschaffende Industrie* of the Reich Association of German Industry. The pamphlet collection (ZSgI) is also very useful. Direct light on the organization of the *Universum Film A.G.* (the *Ufa*) and its control by Hugenberg and Klitzsch until the forced sale of the firm in 1937 is available in the extensive files of that corporation (R109); most interesting are minutes of the board of directors. A smattering of the films produced by that concern for its weekly news shows and for party propaganda are preserved in the fortress at Ehrenbreitstein. Dr. Barkhausen and his assistants were most helpful in providing me with an opportunity to see these.

D. *Bundes-Archiv (Militärarchiv)* in Freiburg

For the student of the DNVP, the most important collections housed here include the papers of Admiral von Tirpitz. As a German National Reichstag delegate from 1924–1928, Tirpitz preserved much of his correspondence and many party circulars. Because of his age, the admiral frequently remained on his estate at Sankt-Blasien and permitted Walther von Keudell to represent him in party caucuses; the letters exchanged between the two men rank with the Westarp Papers among the most important documents dealing with the history of the party. The Widenmann *Nachlass* reveals very little of the financial position of the party, despite the fact that he was the party treasurer throughout the middle years of the republic. The papers of Generals von Bredow, von Schleicher, von Lettow-Vorbeck, and Groener were less important for this work but provide interesting insight into contemporary reactions to Hugenberg and his policy.

E.   *Deutsches Zentral-Archiv* in Potsdam

Extremely important for an understanding of Hugenberg are the various collections preserved by the very helpful archivists of the German Democratic Republic. Were it not for the extensive files of the Pan-German League, the historian would not have known of the close collaboration of Hugenberg and Class. Aside from the *Akten des Alldeutschen Verbandes*, Potsdam also houses the *Akten des Stahlhelms* and the fragmentary *Akten der Deutschnationalen Volkspartei*. Although some of this material is now available in the Hugenberg Papers, any study of the "national opposition" which does not use these sources must remain incomplete.

F.   *Geheimes Staatsarchiv–Preussischer Kulturbesitz* in Berlin-Dahlem

Unfortunately, this depository contains little of value for a study of Hugenberg. Aside from some correspondence dealing with the Hartz book, *Irrwege der Sozialpolitik*, in the papers of Robert Wahlert (Repositorium 92) and some minimal correspondence in the von Dommes *Hausarchiv* (Repositorium 192) dealing with the possibility of a Hohenzollern presidential candidate in 1932, there is virtually nothing relevant to Hugenberg's career.

G.   *Hauptstaats-Archiv* in Düsseldorf

This is the central depository for the preservation of denazification proceedings held in the state of Rheinland-Westphalia. The slim volume of proceedings concerning the Hugenberg trial and the various appeals is valuable but leaves much to be desired. There is little documentation to substantiate either the prejudiced charges of the prosecution or the simplistic rebuttle of the defense.

H.   The International Institute for Social History in Amsterdam

The papers of Otto Braun and Albert Grzesinski preserved here shed important light on the abortive Pan-German putsch planned for the spring of 1926 and reveal growing governmental understanding of the ramifications of the Hugenberg concern.

I. *Landes-Archiv Schleswig Holstein* in Schleswig

The papers of the local association (Landesverband) of the DNVP preserved here provide insight into the policy of the party during the years that Hugenberg was chairman. Some documentation on the death of Ernst Oberfohren is also available.

J. *Niedersächsische Staatsarchive* in Aurich and Osnabrück

Again, the local party associations in these regions preserved circulars and correspondence with the central office in Berlin which shed light on the changing tactics and the financial problems of the DNVP. The collection in Osnäbruck is the most important of these regional holdings.

K. *Stadtarchiv* in Düsseldorf

The incomplete papers of Robert Lehr, German National mayor of Düsseldorf at the end of the Weimar era, contain virtually nothing of significance for an understanding of Hugenberg's activities.

V. Specialized Libraries

Aside from the excellent facilities of the New York Public Library at Forty-second Street, the Library of Congress, the Sterling Library at Yale University, and the university libraries at Bonn, Tübingen, and Berlin, the following institutions were extremely important, especially in the area of newspaper research. The *Institut für Zeitungsforschung* in Dortmund, under the very capable direction of Dr. Kurt Kozyk, was most helpful and cooperative in assisting me to locate some of the papers published by the Hugenberg concern. The files of the *Gesamtkatalog der deutschen Presse* at the University of Bremen are, however, seemingly more complete. The University of Bonn has complete copies of *Der Tag*. The newspaper division of the *Bibliotheque Nationale* at Versailles houses full copies of the *Berliner Lokal-Anzeiger*. Regional publications, such as the *München Augsburger Abendzeitung*, the *Lippische Tages-Zeitung*, and the *Niederdeutsche Zeitung*, are preserved in the central libraries of Augsburg, Detmold, and Hanover, respectively. Librarians in each of these centers were most helpful in securing photographic reproductions of these publications.

Index